Praise for Jon Krakauer's

Missoula

"Jon Krakauer began his career as an author of taut, finely reported outdoor adventures; seven books later, he emerges as the conscience of a nation. . . . Investigative reporters—and Krakauer is one of the craft's finest practitioners, diligent, dogged, and artful—are nothing so much as trial attorneys with pens rather than costly silk ties." —*The Christian Science Monitor*

"Compelling. . . . Meticulous. . . . Krakauer is a writer committed above all else to asking difficult questions. . . . [A] timely and important book." —*Los Angeles Times*

"Meticulously reported, fascinating and deeply disturbing. . . . By probing the specific, Krakauer illuminates upsetting generalities. . . . Krakauer—a journalist who is also a compelling writer—artfully keeps the books from becoming a compendium of facts. . . . It's an important, difficult and timely subject." —*USA Today*

"Compelling. . . . Clear and dispassionate, offering level-headed, in-depth reportage." —*Chicago Tribune*

"A narrative nonfiction page-turner. . . . Krakauer skillfully strengthens his sources' recollections without taking away their agency." —*Buzzfeed*

"A devastating exposé of colleges and local law enforcement. . . . A substantive deep dive into the morass of campus sex crimes, where the victim is too often treated like the accused."

—*Entertainment Weekly*

"A good and needed thing. . . . Powerful. . . . Krakauer has done a great service by taking on this subject." —*Newsweek*

"Krakauer exposes the cavalier attitude of police, prosecutors and football fans toward victims of acquaintance rape in the Montana town full of fanatics for the University of Montana football team."

—*The Denver Post*

"A clear and undeniable picture of a broken system. . . . Krakauer's straightforward writing resists sensationalism. . . . This is a book we all needed." —*Missoula Independent*

"A harrowing read. . . . *Missoula* stands as both a reminder of the forces arrayed against women raising their voices, and of the tremendous power of the telling of their stories." —*Toronto Star*

"Krakauer's evocative reporting, honed to a fine edge of anger, vividly conveys the ordeal of victims and their ongoing psychological dislocations. . . . A hard-hitting true-crime exposé that looks underneath the he-said-she-said to get at the sexist assumptions that help cover up and enable these crimes."

—*Publishers Weekly* (starred)

"Riveting. . . . A raw and difficult but necessary read."

—*Kirkus Reviews*

Jon Krakauer

Missoula

Jon Krakauer is the author of *Eiger Dreams*, *Into the Wild*, *Into Thin Air*, *Under the Banner of Heaven*, *Where Men Win Glory*, and *Three Cups of Deceit*. He is also the editor of the Modern Library Exploration series.

www.jonkrakauer.com

ALSO BY JON KRAKAUER

Eiger Dreams

Iceland

Into the Wild

Into Thin Air

Under the Banner of Heaven

Where Men Win Glory

Three Cups of Deceit

Missoula

RAPE AND THE JUSTICE SYSTEM IN A COLLEGE TOWN

Jon Krakauer

Anchor Books
A Division of Penguin Random House LLC
New York

FIRST ANCHOR BOOKS EDITION, JANUARY 2016

 Published in the United States by Anchor Books, a division of Penguin Random House LLC, New York, and distributed in Canada by Random House of Canada Limited, Toronto, a division of Penguin Random House Ltd., Toronto. Originally published in hardcover in the United States by Doubleday, a division of Penguin Random House LLC, New York, in 2015.

Anchor Books and colophon are registered trademarks of Penguin Random House LLC.

The Library of Congress has cataloged the Doubleday edition as follows:
Krakauer, Jon.
Missoula / by Jon Krakauer.—First American edition.
pages cm
Includes bibliographical references.
1. Rape—Montana—Missoula. 2. Rape victims—Montana—Missoula.
3. Trials (Rape)—Montana—Missoula. I. Title
HV6568.M57 K73 2015
362.88309786'85—dc23 2015002686

Anchor Books Trade Paperback ISBN: 978-0-8041-7056-7
eBook ISBN: 978-0-385-53874-9

Book design by Maria Carella

www.anchorbooks.com

Printed in the United States of America
10 9

For Linda

Rape is unique. No other violent crime is so fraught with controversy, so enmeshed in dispute and in the politics of gender and sexuality. . . . And within the domain of rape, the most highly charged area of debate concerns the issue of false allegations. For centuries, it has been asserted and assumed that women "cry rape," that a large proportion of rape allegations are maliciously concocted for purposes of revenge or other motives.

David Lisak, Lori Gardinier, Sarah C. Nicksa, and Ashley M. Cote

"False Allegations of Sexual Assault"

Violence Against Women, December 2010

CONTENTS

AUTHOR'S NOTE

Rape is a much more common crime than most people realize, and women of college age are most frequently the victims. According to a special report issued by the U.S. Department of Justice in December 2014, "For the period 1995–2013, females ages 18 to 24 had the highest rate of rape and sexual-assault victimizations compared to females in all other age groups." The report estimated that 0.7 percent of this high-risk cohort are sexually assaulted each year—approximately 110,000 young women. This survey was primarily concerned with documenting crime rates, however, and relied on a relatively narrow definition of sexual assault. Notably, respondents to the DOJ survey were not asked about incidents in which they might have been incapable of providing consent while incapacitated by drugs or alcohol.

A different federal agency, the Centers for Disease Control and Prevention, released a report in September 2014 that examined the problem of sexual violence from a public health perspective, rather than a criminal justice perspective, and paid more attention to sexual assaults involving drugs and alcohol. It generated quite different numbers. Using data gathered in 2011, the CDC study estimated that across all age groups, 19.3 percent of American women "have been raped in their lifetimes" and that 1.6 percent of American women—nearly two and a half million individuals—"reported that they were raped in the 12 months preceding the survey."

As the dissimilar results from these two government surveys

suggest, it is impossible to state with certainty how many women are raped each year. Quantifying the prevalence of sexual assault is a highly speculative exercise because at least 80 percent of those who are assaulted don't report the crime to authorities. This book is an effort to understand what deters so many rape victims from going to the police, and to comprehend the repercussions of sexual assault from the perspective of those who have been victimized.

To that end, I have written about a rash of sexual assaults in a single American city—Missoula, Montana—from 2010 through 2012. The victims of these assaults happened to be female college students, but young women who are not enrolled in college are probably at even greater risk, and it's not just young women—or just women, for that matter—who are in danger of being raped. The CDC report cited above estimated that approximately two and a half million American men alive today will be raped in their lifetimes, 1.7 percent of the male population.

The research for this book included interviews with victims, their families and acquaintances, and, when possible, the men accused of assaulting the women I wrote about, but I didn't speak with every victim or every alleged assailant. To learn as much as I could, and to corroborate what sources told me, I spoke at length with eminent psychologists and lawyers; attended court proceedings; read thousands of pages of court transcripts, court filings, e-mails, letters, police reports, and documents generated by university disciplinary proceedings; listened to recordings of police interviews and university disciplinary proceedings; and reviewed newspaper articles, the findings of government investigations, and scientific papers published in peer-reviewed journals.

Whenever dialogue appears between quotation marks on the pages that follow, it is a verbatim quote from the person speaking; a verbatim quote from a source recounting what he or she heard the speaker say; a verbatim quote from a recording of an official proceeding; or a verbatim quote from a transcript of an official proceeding.

Parts of the book may be difficult to read. Some of the events I describe are extremely disturbing. Additionally, there is a sprawling cast of characters, several of whom have been given pseudonyms to protect their privacy. To help readers keep track of who's who, individuals whose names appear more than once or twice are listed in an alphabetized dramatis personae at the end of the book, on page 381.

Jon Krakauer, February 2015

PART ONE

Allison

Now, should we treat women as independent agents, responsible for themselves? Of course. But being responsible has nothing to do with being raped. Women don't get raped because they were drinking or took drugs. Women do not get raped because they weren't careful enough. Women get raped because *someone raped them.*

Jessica Valenti

The Purity Myth

CHAPTER ONE

Office Solutions & Services, a Missoula office-products company, didn't have its 2011 Christmas party until January 6, 2012. As a counterpoint to the chilly Montana evening, the staff decorated the place in a Hawaiian motif. Around 9:00 p.m., thirty or forty people—employees and their families, mostly—were chatting, playing party games, and sipping beverages from red plastic cups in a room overlooking the parking lot when a shiny Chrysler 300 sedan pulled up and rolled to a stop in front of the floor-to-ceiling windows, attracting the attention of the revelers. Two well-dressed men with dour expressions got out of the vehicle and stood beside it. "It was a really nice black car," recalls Kevin Huguet, the owner of Office Solutions.

As he was admiring the Chrysler, one of Huguet's salesmen asked, "Who are those guys?"

Huguet had no idea. So he walked outside and asked, "Can I help you?"

"We're Missoula police detectives," the man who had been driving the car replied. "I just need to talk to Allison."

"Allison is my daughter," Huguet said, his hackles rising. "You're going to have to tell me a little more than that."

"Dad, it's okay," twenty-two-year-old Allison Huguet interjected, having walked out to the parking lot shortly after her father.

Detective Guy Baker, who is six foot five and weighs 250 pounds, peered down at Allison, a slender woman with bright eyes and a ponytail. "I need to talk to you," he said. "We don't have to do this in front of your dad. How do you want us to handle this?" He and Allison walked away from the car to speak privately, while Detective Mark Blood remained behind with Kevin Huguet.

"Hey," Baker said to Allison in a warmer voice when they'd moved a short distance away. They'd become acquainted four years earlier, during her final year of high school, when she asked him to serve as her mentor for a school project. It had been a positive experience for both of them. Explaining why he'd shown up during the company Christmas party, he said, "I thought it was important to tell you in person as soon as possible: About an hour ago I arrested Beau Donaldson. I got a full confession from him, and he is in jail."

Allison's eyes brimmed with tears of relief.

Over by the Chrysler, Kevin Huguet grew impatient as he watched Allison and Baker conferring. "You know what?" he told Detective Blood after a few minutes. "I want to know what's going on here. This is my daughter, and I want to know what's going on." Kevin abruptly strode away and confronted Baker.

"She didn't do anything bad," Baker said. "It's not like that." Then Baker turned to Allison and said, "I think you really need to talk to your dad and tell him."

Allison faced her father and, in a shaky voice, declared, "Beau raped me."

KEVIN STOOD ON the cold pavement, gobsmacked. Struggling to make sense of the words his daughter had just spoken, he wrapped his arms around her. As he hugged Allison and began to process what Beau Donaldson had done to her, Kevin's shock and confusion turned into blinding rage.

"I thought he was going to find Beau and kill him or something," Allison told me, recalling the events of that night.

Beau Donaldson, a junior at the University of Montana at the time of the assault, was on the school's football team. Allison Huguet was attending Eastern Oregon University on a track scholarship. They had grown up together in Missoula and had been inseparable friends since the first grade, but the relationship had never been romantic.

Donaldson often referred to Huguet as his "little sister," and the sentiment was reciprocated. Throughout her childhood and adolescence, Huguet regarded Donaldson as the brother she never had. For the previous sixteen years, Huguet's parents had welcomed Donaldson into their home as if he were a member of their family. "You spend your whole life, when you have kids, protecting them," Kevin Huguet told me. "But who thinks their daughter's trusted friend is actually a monster who is going to hurt them in the night?"

Allison was as angry as her father, but a confounding mix of other emotions had supplanted her rage. Donaldson raped her on September 25, 2010. She had waited fifteen months, suffering in silence, before going to the police. During that period she told nobody beyond her mother and three or four close friends that she had been raped—not even her father or sisters knew about it. Such reticence, it turns out, is common among victims of sexual assault. No more than 20 percent of rapes are reported to the police, a statistic that defies comprehension until one looks closely at how sexual-assault cases are adjudicated in the United States.

MONTANA IS A huge place with relatively few people. Although Missoula is the state's second largest city, it only has seventy thousand residents. Congenial and picturesque, it's the kind of community that charms first-time visitors into putting money down on real estate within hours of arriving. Some 42 percent of the population has a bachelor's degree or higher, compared to 28 percent of the rest of the nation. Good restaurants and lively bars abound. A legendary trout stream, the Clark Fork, runs fast and clear through the heart of downtown, paralleled by an abandoned railroad right-of-way that's been transformed into a bucolic thoroughfare for cyclists, joggers, and strollers. South of the river, the city's unpresuming neighborhoods stretch across a broad valley, above which five mountain ranges converge.

From Missoula's origins in the mid-nineteenth century until the late decades of the twentieth, the local economy depended heavily on timber cut from the surrounding high country. About thirty-five years ago, however, the forest-products industry began to fall on hard times. Most of the sawmills closed, and loggers in calk boots and tin pants became an endangered species. A behemoth pulp mill pumped $45 million annually into the local economy (and at times created a noxious smog that settled so densely over the city that drivers had to turn on their headlights in the middle of the day) until 2009, when it was shuttered and sold for scrap.

Presently the largest employer in the Missoula Valley is the University of Montana, by a large margin. With its 15,000 students and more than 800 faculty members, UM, as it is known, has left a deep imprint on the city. Missoula has a much higher proportion of Democrats, for instance, than the state as a whole. As locals like to joke, one of the things that's so great about living in Missoula is that it's only twenty minutes from Montana.

Despite its liberal bent, in many ways Missoula resembles other cities of similar size in the Rocky Mountain region. Its population is 92 percent white, 2 percent Native American, 2 percent Hispanic, and less than 1 percent African American. The median family income is $42,000. Twenty percent of the population lives below the poverty line. Among Missoulians there is strong support for the right to keep and bear arms, and for limiting the role of the federal government in their affairs.

Missoula has a culture uniquely its own, however, thanks to the fusion of its gritty frontier heritage with the university's myriad impacts. UM has nationally distinguished programs in biology and ecology and is perhaps even more renowned for its literary bona fides. The faculty of the university's Creative Writing Program, founded in 1920, has included such influential authors as Richard Hugo, James Crumley, and William Kittredge. Reminiscing in one of his incomparable essays about what drew him to Missoula for the first time, Kittredge wrote,

> I was looking for what I took to be a genuine world to inhabit. I wanted to be someone that I could understand and stand—a romantic idea that seems commonplace in the West these days. . . . The northern Rockies seemed like an undiscovered land, thick with secrets no one could bother to keep.

During a drunken visit to Missoula to go fishing with Kittredge in 1972, Raymond Carver, the godfather of minimalist fiction, fell head-over-heels in love with both the town and Diane Cecily, the university's director of publications. Richard Ford, the Pulitzer Prize–winning novelist, resided in Missoula for three or four very productive years in the 1980s and is recalled with pride by its citizenry. The literary figure most closely identified with the town, however, is Norman Maclean, the author of *A River Runs Through It,* the semiautobiographical work of fiction set in Missoula and on the nearby Big Blackfoot River, from which the Academy Award–winning film starring Brad Pitt was adapted.

BUT NEVER MIND Kittredge or Ford or the Big Blackfoot. Missoulians' greatest source of civic pride, hands down, is the University of Montana football team, the beloved Grizzlies of the Big Sky Conference, who won the Football Championship Subdivision national title in 1995 and 2001. Their record of twelve straight conference titles prior to 2010 was the second-longest streak in NCAA Division I history. In 1985, a billionaire Missoula construction magnate named Dennis Washington donated $1 million to build Washington-Grizzly Stadium, a beautiful facility that seats 25,200 and is filled to capacity for almost every home game. The Grizzlies' overall record from the opening of the stadium through 2011 was a remarkable 174 wins and 24 losses.

The Griz don't play at the same elite level as college-football colossi like Florida State, Ohio State, and Alabama. It's fair to say that the team's win-loss record would be much less impressive if they played under the bright lights of the Big Ten or the Southeastern Conference, instead of in a backwater like the Big Sky. Be that as it may, the Grizzlies inspire the same kind of fanaticism in Missoula as the Seminoles do in Tallahassee and the Crimson Tide does in Tuscaloosa. UM fans call themselves "Griz Nation." Missoula is "Grizzlyville." It would be hard to overstate the degree to which Griz football is exalted by the residents of western Montana.

Recent events, however, have forced at least some Missoulians to reconsider their veneration of all things Griz. In December 2010, four of Beau Donaldson's teammates on the UM football team allegedly gang-raped a female student when she was too drunk to resist, and because the football players claimed the sex was consensual, they were not charged with a crime. A year later, in December 2011, three Griz football players sexually assaulted two female students after allegedly drugging them. None of these assailants was prosecuted, either.

When the latter incident was brought to light by the local newspaper, UM president Royce Engstrom appointed the Honorable Diane Barz, who in 1989 became the first woman to serve on the Montana Supreme Court, to launch an investigation. In a preliminary report, released to the public on December 31, 2011, Barz wrote,

> This investigation has revealed . . . evidence of non-consensual sex that is not being reported in the University system. . . . The University is required to take immediate and appropriate action.

In Barz's final report, completed on January 31, 2012, she identified nine sexual assaults by UM students (not all of whom were football players) from September 2010 through December 2011.

At the top of the list was the rape of Allison Huguet by Beau Donaldson. Barz warned,

> The reports of sexual assaults on the UM campus now require immediate action and swift compliance with Title IX mandates. . . . A rape-tolerant campus with ineffective programming, inadequate support service for victim survivors, and inequitable grievance procedures threatens every student. . . . Acts of sexual violence are vastly under-reported on college campuses and a victim of sexual assault is likely to suffer from depression, post-traumatic stress disorder, substance abuse, and academic problems.

Diane Barz's report rattled Missoula. Then, just three months later, the U.S. Department of Justice revealed that it, too, was investigating the apparent epidemic of sexual assaults in western Montana. The feds announced that at least eighty alleged rapes had been reported in Missoula over the preceding three years and that the DOJ would be scrutinizing "assaults against all women in Missoula, not just university students."

United States attorney general Eric Holder noted, "The allegations that the University of Montana, the local police department and the County Attorney's Office failed to adequately address sexual assault are very disturbing."

The spate of rapes in Grizzlyville led to disquieting articles from such national publications as the *New York Times* and the *Wall Street Journal.* But it was a 3,800-word dispatch posted on the website *Jezebel* nine days after the DOJ announcement that perhaps did the most damage to Missoula's good name. Written by Katie J. M. Baker, it was titled "My Weekend in America's So-Called 'Rape Capital,'" and the derogatory moniker went viral, prompting an outcry from Missoulians who believed it was unfair.

Baker's tart, insightful piece indicated that she wasn't sure the description was deserved, however. Her headline was drawn from the article's second paragraph, in which she quoted a twenty-year-old Missoula drug dealer who lamented, "People think we're the 'rape capital' of America now," before immediately noting, "but we're not. Missoula is just like any other college town."

In fact, 80 rapes over the course of three years appears to be "on par with national averages for college towns of Missoula's size," as Baker mentioned in her piece. According to the FBI's latest statistics, there were an average of 26.8 "forcible rapes" reported in American cities the size of Missoula in 2012—which works out to be 80.4 rapes over three years. In other words, the number of sexual assaults in Missoula might sound alarming, but if the FBI figures are accurate, it's actually commonplace. Rape, it turns out, occurs with appalling frequency throughout the United States.

CHAPTER TWO

When Allison Huguet was five years old, her family moved from Kalispell, up near Glacier National Park, to Missoula, where they bought a home in a quiet neighborhood called Target Range, at the western edge of the city, near the confluence of the Bitterroot River and the Clark Fork. Huguet enrolled in the first grade at Target Range School and soon befriended Beau Donaldson. They remained close buddies for the next twelve years.

Huguet and Donaldson graduated together in June 2008 from Big Sky High School, where both of them were good students and outstanding athletes. Huguet, who competed on the track team, was the Montana pole-vault champion their senior year. Donaldson set ten school records on the football field and was honored as the team's most valuable player. When Donaldson accepted a scholarship to play football at UM, it was deemed sufficiently important to merit an article in the *Missoulian,* the local newspaper. "I've always wanted to play for the Griz," Donaldson told the paper. He had been recruited by a number of other schools, including Montana State University, in Bozeman, the archrival of the University of Montana. It was a big deal in Missoula when he decided to attend UM.

Huguet was proud of Donaldson. "I always thought he was intelligent," she told me. "I was very happy for him when he got a scholarship. He came from a family where none of them had gone to college; most didn't even graduate high school." For her part,

Huguet left Montana after high school to attend Eastern Oregon University, where she was offered an athletic scholarship. She saw Donaldson only once or twice after she departed for college.

On September 24, 2010, Huguet was living in Missoula at her mother's house and was getting ready to return to La Grande, Oregon, to begin her junior year at EOU. That evening, she received a call from her friend Keely Williams, who suggested they go to a party at a house Beau Donaldson was renting in Missoula's university district. Williams had also grown up in the Target Range neighborhood and had known Huguet since Allison arrived in Missoula. After graduating from Big Sky High School in the same class as Huguet and Donaldson, Williams had left town to attend Portland State University and happened to be back for a week to visit her parents. When Williams told Huguet that most of the posse they'd hung out with since they were six years old would be at Donaldson's party, Huguet enthusiastically agreed that they should attend.

Williams drove. Upon arriving at Donaldson's house, at around 10:00 in the evening, they were happy to see many of their childhood soul mates. "When we walked downstairs I immediately ran into Beau and hugged him," Huguet remembered. "It was a nice evening. Everyone was relaxed and having a good time." People played beer pong in the basement and held "tea races" to determine who could chug bottles of Twisted Tea (a brand of syrupy malt liquor favored by UM students) the fastest.

It was a Friday night, and the Griz football team would be playing Sacramento State University on Saturday afternoon, but Donaldson had suffered a serious ankle injury the previous summer and wouldn't be suiting up for the game. He was pounding down alcoholic beverages with gusto. Enjoying the company of seldom-seen friends, Huguet and Williams found themselves drinking more than they customarily did, too.

By 1:30 in the morning, the party was running out of steam, and the handful of people still there moved upstairs to the living room. Donaldson and Huguet sat down together on a couch.

Huguet, growing sleepy, lay across the couch, put a pillow on Donaldson's thigh, and placed her head on the pillow. But there was nothing remotely sexual about it, said Huguet and Williams. "Allison never had any interest in that type of relationship with Beau," Williams insisted. "Absolutely none."

Another classmate from their Target Range days, Sam Erschler,* who lived in the house with Beau Donaldson, urged Keely Williams and Allison Huguet not to drive home, because they'd been drinking. "Which was nice of him," Huguet acknowledged. "That's how Sam is. Kind of caring like that. He said, 'Why don't you guys just stay here and sleep on the couch.' So we all agreed we would."

Not long thereafter, Donaldson got up from the couch he was sharing with Huguet, went downstairs, and Huguet fell asleep on the couch alone, fully dressed. Huguet enjoyed sleeping on couches; even when she was home, she often preferred to sleep on the couch instead of in her own bed. Williams, meanwhile, went in search of an empty bed and soon found one. "It was even made!" she said. "I thought, 'If we have to stay here, this is where I am going to sleep.'"

After discovering the vacant bedroom, Williams went back to the living room to invite Huguet to join her. She shook Huguet awake and said, "Ali, do you want to come to bed? I'm sleeping in this room, and there is a bed."

"No, I'm fine," Huguet groggily replied. "I'll just stay here." Williams got a blanket and placed it over her friend, then returned to the bedroom. When she left, Huguet was the only person remaining in the living room. Everyone else in the house seemed to be asleep.

HUGUET WAS AWAKENED about two hours later. It was still dark. She was lying facedown on the couch, and her jeans and underwear

* pseudonym

had been pulled down. "I remember waking up to Beau moaning, and a lot of pressure and pain," she later testified. Donaldson was on top of her, penetrating her vagina from behind with his penis. "I opened my eyes, just partly," she remembered. "Just from his moaning, I could tell it was him."

Although she was terrified, she forced herself to keep her eyes shut and wait for him to finish. Huguet is an elite athlete, and she'd taken self-defense classes. She was just five feet, five inches tall, however, and weighed 130 pounds. Donaldson weighed 230 pounds and played both fullback and linebacker for an NCAA Division I football team. She assumed that if he was willing to rape her while she was sleeping, he wouldn't hesitate to harm her severely in order to keep her from resisting or calling for help. "He could have snapped my neck like a twig," Huguet told me, "so I just lay there and pretended to be asleep." Donaldson continued to rape Huguet for another five minutes before ejaculating inside her. He was not wearing a condom.

When he'd finished, he tugged her jeans partly up, threw the blanket over her, and walked away without saying a word. Stunned, Huguet remained motionless until she was sure he was out of the room. Then, quietly, she gathered her shoes and her phone, tiptoed barefoot through the kitchen, exited the house via the back door, and started sprinting down a gravel alley to find help. When Donaldson had yanked Huguet's pants to her knees, he had torn off the button and mangled the zipper, so with one hand she simultaneously cradled her shoes and tried to hold her jeans up, while with her other she speed-dialed her boyfriend, running as fast as she could at the same time.

"I don't know why I was calling him," Allison said. "He had moved to Colorado. It's not like he was going to be able to help. I guess I wasn't thinking too clearly. I called him twice, but he never answered."

Still running, Allison dialed her mother next. "When the phone rang," Beth Huguet told me, "I looked at my clock, and it was four-eleven in the morning. There was this throaty sound on the other end of the line. Panicked sounds, with nothing coming out. I knew it was Allison, even without any words. I'll never forget it. I'll have that with me the rest of my life."

"Mom!" Allison eventually managed to blurt as she ran. "He's chasing me! Help me! Save me! Mom!" Donaldson had somehow seen or heard Allison fleeing from the house and was pursuing her.

"I'd only been on the phone with my mom for a few seconds when all of a sudden I heard someone behind me, and I realized Beau was chasing me," Allison said. A few seconds later his hand brushed her back as he grasped at her from behind. "I was literally screaming into the phone, 'He raped me!' right when I felt him grabbing at me. My mom was telling me, 'Run! Keep running!'" Allison knew that Donaldson owned several guns. As she tried to accelerate away from him, she said, "I thought he was going to kill me. I thought for sure I was dead."

Running even harder down the alley, and frantically pushing Donaldson's hands away as he pulled at her, Allison ignored the pain as the gravel cut her bare feet. "I was hitting him as I ran," she said. "I don't know if I was actually speaking to him. I was just talking to my mom. And I was worried because the battery in my phone was low and I knew it was about to die."

Through her own phone, over the sound of Allison sobbing and gasping to catch her breath, Beth could hear Donaldson say, "No, Allison! Stop! Come back! I'm sorry. Don't say anything. I'll make it all right. Come back to the house with me!"

"His voice was so calm," said Beth, a high school teacher. "That's the most chilling part of the whole thing: how calm he was. How hysterical she was, and how calm he was. It made my skin crawl." As she spoke with Allison, Beth Huguet threw on some clothes, got in her van, and started down South Avenue toward the university district at sixty miles an hour, all the while imploring, "Run, Allison! Run!"

And then Beth heard Allison say, "He's not behind me anymore! Oh my God, he's not behind me!" For some reason, Donaldson had stopped chasing her and turned around. "I was shocked that Beau actually let me go," Allison remembered. "I honestly assumed he had a gun and I was going to be shot." Even though he was no longer trying to catch her, Allison didn't stop running.

Beth recalled that Donaldson lived somewhere near the university, but the university district is huge, and Allison didn't know the address of the house, or even what street it was on. Eventually, however, Allison was able to communicate that she was near the soccer fields, which are located on South Avenue at Higgins, so Beth kept driving in that direction as fast as she dared.

"I was running barefoot, still trying to hold my pants up," said Allison, "when I turned out of the alley and got onto South Avenue. And there was my mom." By this point Allison's phone battery was dead, so she ran into the middle of the road and flagged Beth down.

"As soon as I saw her, I knew something bad had happened," Beth said. "As she came toward me she was hobbling and kind of falling. When she got in the van she started rocking back and forth, crying hysterically. I flipped a U-turn and headed straight to Community Hospital. I knew she had been assaulted, I just didn't know to what extent."

A couple of minutes after they'd turned around and were driving toward the hospital, Allison realized that Keely Williams was still back inside Donaldson's house, sleeping, unaware of the danger she was in. "Keely!" Allison screamed at her mother. "We need to go back and get Keely!" As Beth reversed course and steered the van toward the house, Allison dialed Williams's number. "Beau just raped me!" she shouted into the phone when Williams answered. "You have to get out! You have to get out right now! My mom and I are outside waiting for you."

Williams grabbed her purse, put on her shoes, and fled. She was in such a hurry that she slammed her head into the edge of the back door in the dark, giving herself a black eye. "I ran out of the garage and there they were," she told me. "I jumped in the back of the van. Allison was sitting in the front, hunched over, crying. She wouldn't turn around. Seeing her like that, I started crying, too, and saying how sorry I was."

As Williams recounted these events more than two years after the fact, she began to sob. "I felt guilty because I was the one who wanted to go to the party and see our friends," she continued, tears streaming down her cheeks. "I chose to drive, and then I drank too much to drive us home. And I left her on the couch alone, because I wanted to sleep in a bed. If we had just left, or I had made her sleep with me, or I had slept with her on the couch, then it wouldn't have happened. I know I shouldn't feel guilty, but I do. How could I have left her out there?"

"You left me out there," Allison answered, "because neither of us had any reason to think we would be in danger in that house, with those friends. We trusted them completely."

CHAPTER THREE

After Beth Huguet picked up Allison and Keely Williams, she drove Allison to Missoula's Community Medical Center emergency room to receive treatment for her injuries. Because this hospital doesn't perform forensic examinations of rape victims, however, the staff at Community Medical sent Allison across town to the First Step Resource Center, the sexual-assault response unit at St. Patrick Hospital, to have a rape kit collected.

The United States Violence Against Women Act of 2005 requires that all victims of sexual assault be given free access to an evidence collection kit, better known as a rape kit. It consists of sterile swabs, small containers, plastic bags, microscope slides, and other implements for collecting and storing semen, blood, saliva, hairs, and clothing fibers that might be used as evidence in a criminal trial. For most victims, submitting to the procedures that allow such evidence to be gathered is an exceedingly humiliating experience.

This was certainly true in Allison's case. After arriving at First Step, she says, "for the next four hours I was essentially raped all over again. I had to stand completely naked on a white sheet and let a nurse brush my entire body to collect evidence that might contain Beau's DNA." Allison's most private recesses were probed, combed, swabbed, photographed, and intensely scrutinized by strangers. A nurse made a video of the inside of her vagina, documenting the flesh that had been torn when Donaldson violated her. "The whole process—while absolutely necessary—was incredibly traumatic," Allison says, "even though the nurse and counselor tried to be comforting."

It wasn't until 10:00 Saturday morning that Allison and Beth Huguet returned to Beth's home in Target Range. It had been a long night, but Allison didn't have the luxury of crawling into bed to sleep. Instead, she took a hot shower, dressed, and tried to pull herself together enough to meet her father, who was expecting her to attend the Griz football game with him that afternoon.

AT THE EASTERN edge of Missoula, Mount Sentinel towers two thousand feet above the University of Montana campus. A third of the way up the mountainside, a white concrete *M* adorns the slope. Ten stories high, it's the city's most famous landmark. Directly below the *M* is Washington-Grizzly Stadium.

Allison's parents separated when she was fifteen and eventually divorced. Although she had been living at her mother's house that summer, she remained close to her father, Kevin. He was a huge Griz fan, and whenever Allison was in town on game day, they went to the stadium together to watch the team play. "I was born and raised in Missoula," Kevin Huguet told me. "Griz football is a big deal here."

When Kevin was a boy, his father would lead him and his five brothers a couple of hundred feet up the steep incline of Mount Sentinel to watch Grizzly football games. "We were a large family and didn't have any money," Kevin said, "but we could sit on the hill and watch for free." Ever since becoming the owner of a thriving local business, Kevin has been a corporate sponsor of Grizzly athletics and a season ticket holder. "Football games are an all-day Missoula event," he said. "Twenty thousand–some people you know show up in the morning for tailgating."

Allison and her father usually had breakfast at his house before heading to the game. But the morning after Beau Donaldson raped her, Allison wasn't ready to face her father over bacon and eggs, so she texted him to say she was going to skip breakfast and would simply meet him at the stadium shortly before the opening kickoff. He texted her back urging her not to be late.

Allison was in a bind. "My dad was the last person I wanted to know that I had been raped," she explained. "I was in a state of shock. I wasn't able to think or make decisions. I was just going through the motions. Mostly, at that point, I was trying to figure out how to make my eyes not look like I had been bawling for the past five hours." She put on sunglasses to hide her bloodshot eyes and went to Grizzly Stadium.

Allison's extended family had tickets together on the thirty-yard line for every game, less than a dozen rows up from the field. When she arrived, her grandfather was there, a couple of uncles, some cousins, and her father. The first thing Kevin said to her was "Do you see Beau down there? Is he playing today? How's he doing?"

"I don't know," Allison snapped. "Beau is trailer trash." Kevin, who had never heard her speak ill of Donaldson before, was taken aback, but he let the comment pass. On the far side of the field, Allison could see Donaldson standing on the sideline with his teammates, wearing a maroon game jersey with his number, 45, emblazoned across his chest in silver.

Before halftime, Allison took leave of her dad to avoid having to look at the man who'd just raped her, and tried to find Keely Williams, who'd said she would be at the game. Allison thought talking to Williams might make her feel a little better. As she was looking for Williams, Allison ran into Sam Erschler, the friend who had persuaded Williams and Huguet to spend the night at Donaldson's house instead of driving home. Erschler—one of Donaldson's oldest friends—had no idea that anything was wrong. "I don't know why, or how it came out," Allison recalled, "but I told him Beau raped me."

"I'm sorry, Al," Erschler offered, giving her a hug. He told Huguet that Donaldson had been acting strange when they woke up that morning. Then, looking bewildered, Erschler said, "I don't know what's going on with Beau these days."

Huguet walked off, located Williams, and the two women went to an out-of-the-way corner of the stadium to talk; there, they were soon approached by two young UM students hoping to get friendly. "These two boys were hitting on us," Huguet told me. "They thought they were being funny and would not go away. Keely finally had to yell at them, 'You need to leave us alone! Right now! I'm serious!' "

After their would-be suitors departed, Huguet and Williams spent the rest of the football game talking about what had happened at Donaldson's house. While trying to explain why she felt so guilty about allowing Huguet to sleep alone on the couch, Williams told Huguet a secret she had shared with only a few other people: Two years earlier, when she had left Montana to attend Portland State University, she, too, had been raped by an acquaintance.

IT HAPPENED DURING Keely Williams's first week in Oregon, before classes had even started. "It was orientation week," she remembered. "I hated it. I didn't do anything. I didn't make any friends. I didn't want to be there. I just wanted to sit in my room. I wished I'd never left Missoula." Then Lewis Ronan,* a boy she'd known slightly in high school who was also a student at Portland State, called and invited her to a party at his apartment. "Sweet!" Williams thought. "Someone I know!"

It was a small gathering. When Williams arrived, Ronan's friends were smoking marijuana with a hookah. Williams began gulping down drinks. "I got really drunk," she said, "and started throwing up—a lot, from drinking too fast. A girl I didn't know was hanging out in the bathroom with me, helping take care of

* pseudonym

me and being nice." The girl offered to drive Williams back to her dormitory, but she was puking too much to travel anywhere. So Williams remained in Ronan's bathroom with the girl, resting her chest against the rim of the toilet bowl between paroxysms of vomiting.

As Williams's retching subsided, the girl repeatedly offered to drive Williams home, but Lewis Ronan intervened each time, insisting, "No, she will just stay here tonight."

Eventually, Williams agreed to spend the night at Ronan's, she remembered, "but I was really drunk, so I didn't really have a choice. And then I passed out. I don't even remember going to Lewis's room. But at some point later in the night I woke up in his bed and . . ." Williams stopped speaking for a moment as she began to cry. "And he was above me, and he was having sex with me," she continued between sobs. "And then I passed out again. When I woke up the next day I had no idea where I was, or how to get back to the university campus. I told Lewis I needed to get home, because my mom was coming to visit me."

Ronan didn't acknowledge that he had done anything wrong; he acted like everything was fine as he drove Williams back to her dorm. "I didn't really put it together that I had been raped, not at first," she said. When Williams's mother arrived, Keely said nothing about what had happened. "I just kept begging her to take me home to Missoula," she explained through her tears. "I told her, 'I want to go home. I don't want to be here. I don't want to go to college. I don't want to be in Portland.' " Her mother had no idea why Keely was so miserable. "She was like, 'No. You have to stay. You haven't even been here a week.' "

Later that day, Keely Williams was made painfully aware that her urinary tract had become inflamed during the forced intercourse that had taken place while she was passed out. Not wanting to tell her mother, she went to a local Safeway and bought cranberry juice and Pyridium to treat the inflammation. "It turned my pee bright orange," she recalled, "but it numbed my bladder, which helped." Williams spent most of the next couple of days drinking cranberry juice in bed. Purple bruises spread across her chest where she had pressed against the toilet while throwing up.

Meanwhile, Lewis Ronan began sending text messages to Williams's phone, indicating that he very much wanted to see her again, apparently unaware that she hadn't found it pleasurable to be raped while unconscious. "Every time he texted me, I just felt nauseous," Williams told me. "It made me want to vomit. I did not want him to tell me he wanted to hang out with me or ask me why I didn't want to talk to him. I wasn't consciously thinking, 'This guy raped me,' because at the time, I didn't understand that if you don't actively consent to have sex, it's rape. I just knew something wasn't right."

Eventually it occurred to Williams that maybe Ronan had indeed raped her. "So I looked some things up," she said, "and realized that's what had happened. But I still didn't understand why somebody I knew would do that. Like, maybe I had said something? Or maybe I did something?" Not unlike many other rape victims, Williams initially reacted by wondering if she was somehow to blame.

"By now a little bit of time had passed," Williams said. "I just wanted it to go away. I didn't know what I should do, or who I should tell. . . . I didn't want anyone to ask me questions about it. I didn't want to talk about it. I knew that if I told someone who was really close to me, that they would worry, and ask me questions, and would want me to do something about it, and I didn't want to deal with any of that. So I told this ex-boyfriend that I thought I had been raped."

The ex-boyfriend didn't believe Keely and became angry. He told her, "You're just being a slut. You're fucking other guys, and you're trying to cover that up by saying you were raped."

TWO YEARS AFTER Lewis Ronan raped Keely Williams, when Beau Donaldson raped Allison Huguet in September 2010, the trauma Williams had experienced came rushing back to the surface. As she and Huguet talked in a high corner of Grizzly Stadium the morning after Huguet was violated, Williams explained to her friend that part of the reason she felt so guilty about leaving Huguet alone on the couch at Donaldson's house was that it was all too easy for her to imagine what Huguet was going through, especially when she'd been curled into a ball, sobbing uncontrollably, in the front seat of her mother's van. "I wanted to absorb all of your pain," Williams told Huguet. "I wanted to hurt for you so you wouldn't have to deal with what I went through."

The fact that Williams empathized intensely with Huguet could not, and did not, mitigate Huguet's pain, however. Huguet had been raped, and sooner or later she was going to have to come to grips with it. So she and Williams discussed how she might begin to do that.

"I didn't feel like I was strong enough to go to the police," Huguet said, "or even tell my dad about it." She really wanted Donaldson to acknowledge what he had done to her, though. She and Williams decided that Huguet would ask Donaldson's friend Sam Erschler to tell Donaldson that he needed to come to Huguet's house and apologize, and that if he refused, she was going to report him to the police.

Williams convinced Huguet that if Donaldson agreed to meet with her, she should surreptitiously make an audio recording of his apology. Williams was majoring in criminal justice at Portland State University, and she knew that according to Montana's stringent privacy laws, it is illegal to record a conversation unless all parties have been informed that they are being recorded. But even though it would be inadmissible in court, Williams argued to Huguet, "You *have* to make a recording. Because you don't know if he will ever admit to this again."

Huguet agreed. "I had no desire to talk to Beau," she said. "And at that point I had no intention of reporting him to the police. But Beau didn't know that. Threatening to go to the police was the only way I thought I had any power to make him acknowledge what he did. And if I ever did decide to go to the police, or tell anyone else about what happened, I did not want to have to fight about whether Beau really raped me or not. I wanted to be able to prove it." So Saturday afternoon, following the Griz game, Huguet went to RadioShack with her mother and bought a digital recorder for forty-five dollars.

BEAU DONALDSON AND Sam Erschler came to Beth Huguet's home Sunday afternoon. Both Allison and her mother were still extremely upset. Before Donaldson and Erschler arrived, Allison Huguet had turned on the recorder and jammed it between the cushions of her mother's sectional sofa. Donaldson happened to sit right next to it. As soon as Donaldson sat down, Allison asked him, "Do you want to apologize to me, Beau, or . . . ?"

Donaldson answered, "I am just so sorry." Speaking in nervous bursts, he said, "We were, like, on the couch. I was, obviously, completely fucked up. We were both drunk. I mean, we were laying there. I remember we were making out on the couch. We were laying on the couch together. Started doing stuff. And then it was just—I don't even really remember anything after, like . . . I remember we were making out."

Furious that Donaldson would lie to her face and think he could get away with it, Allison demanded, "Beau, how come I remember falling asleep on the couch, and then I remember waking up, halfway through, realizing you're on top and having sex with me. . . . Beau! I was asleep!"

"We were making out on the couch!" Donaldson insisted.

"No, we weren't!" Allison replied, just as vehemently.

"The issue," said Beth Huguet, "is that it was sex without consent. . . ."

"The issue, Beau," Allison angrily interjected, "is that you took complete advantage of me."

"I did," Donaldson confessed. Suddenly he seemed to understand that lying wasn't going to work. "I admit it. I did. I'm sorry." Less than two minutes after Donaldson arrived, Allison had the confession she'd sought. But the conversation was far from over.

"The only reason I even felt comfortable sleeping there is because I've known you since the first grade," said Allison.

"I know!" said Beau. "And . . . I can't blame it on alcohol, because that's not right. It's something that I did, and I fucked up."

Allison asked him, "Has this happened before? . . ."

"No! Never!" Donaldson sobbed. "This is the first time anything has ever happened to me like this. Ever! . . . I am *so* sorry."

Beth reminded Donaldson that he had betrayed the trust of someone who considered him to be her big brother.

Through his tears, Donaldson agreed: "She's my little sister!"

"If she ever had an issue, she'd come to you guys," Beth continued, referring to Donaldson and Sam Erschler. "If she ever felt like a guy was treating her wrong, you guys are the people she would turn to. . . ."

Allison reminded Donaldson that she had always supported him and spoken highly of him to others, at which point Donaldson broke down and began to cry uncontrollably.

"Do you know that you tore her up inside?" Beth Huguet asked. "You cut her inside, in her vagina. . . . Do you know how devastating that is? As a mother, that kills me. . . . To think that she was physically violated that way. . . . That's so low!"

"Beau," Allison said, "I just wish you knew what it was like to be a girl, and to wake up and have this two-hundred-thirty-pound person on your back, taking advantage of you when you're not even awake. And then I just had to lay there until you were done."

Allison told Donaldson, "I would probably kill myself if this ever happened to another girl and I didn't say something to the police."

Donaldson said he understood. "I just about killed *my*self that night," he claimed. After he quit chasing Allison down the alley, he said, "I curled up in my truck in the carport with my fucking handgun in my hand."

Allison and her mother were dubious about the sincerity of his remorse. "I don't know if you guys know about this," Beth Huguet said, "but Allison had a cyst rupture when she was ten years old, she was in and out of doctors. . . . And because of that . . . she takes her intimacy very seriously. . . . She is not somebody that sleeps around. She is not promiscuous. Not that that would give you the right to rape her. That's not the point. It's just that . . . we were at the hospital for hours. The fact that you cut her up inside and everything?"

"Allison, I'm so fucking sorry!" Donaldson wailed.

"If I hadn't grown up with you," Allison said, "if I wasn't one of your friends— If you had done this to some random girl, and she walks down to the police station and tells them, your whole life is ruined, Beau. . . . Can't you just see the [front page of the] *Missoulian*?—'Another Grizzly football player in trouble. Rapes girl.' . . . Do you need help? Do you need alcohol help? Do you need help with drugs? Because obviously this is a problem. . . . Do you like your girlfriend?"

"I love her more than anything," Donaldson answered. "I want to be married to this girl. . . ."

"I don't understand," said Allison. "If you love her, why are you cheating on her? . . . Because I'm aware it's not just me." Among their circle of friends, Donaldson's infidelities were common knowledge.

"You really need to look hard into your life," Beth scolded, "and take stock, and think of how you need to improve on it. I guess our concern is—and tell me if I'm wrong here, Allison—one of the things that makes her want to go to the police on this, Beau, is the fact that she doesn't want this to ever happen to another girl. She doesn't want to know a month or two from now that you violated some other girl. And that by her speaking out she could have stopped it. . . ."

"Allison," Donaldson sobbed. "I'm so sorry. . . ."

"The thing is," Allison explained, "I have a boyfriend who I have a lot of feelings for, as well. This is something I can't even talk to him about. I can't bring this up to him. He would literally come back here and probably kill you. . . . Honestly, if I hear of one incident, Beau—if I hear about any female ever saying that you touched them, I will go right to the police. . . ."

Beth Huguet urged Donaldson to get therapy: "You need to really talk to somebody and say, 'This is what I did. How do I change myself?' And make sure this never happens to another person."

"I obviously fucking need some help," Donaldson agreed, no longer crying. "I'm so sorry."

Allison reminded Donaldson, "If I walked down to the police station right now, it would ruin your life. And that's why I'm not going to do it. . . . I don't want to have to live with that. But I'm not okay with what happened. . . . I'm not telling you that by not going out and filing charges that it was okay, because it wasn't. . . . It needs to never happen again. . . . Get help, Beau."

Donaldson assured her that he would. "He promised me that he would get treatment for his drug, alcohol, and sexual issues," Allison recalled. "And I made it clear that this promise was the only reason I wasn't going to the police."

CHAPTER FOUR

"A few days after it happened," Beth Huguet told me, "I remember Allison sitting on the couch down in the basement of my house, wrapped in blankets. She wasn't saying anything, but you could see it looping in her mind. You could see it in her face."

"I was overwhelmed," Allison remembered. Classes for her junior year at Eastern Oregon University were due to start in a few days, she said, "But I wasn't ready to leave the security of my home. I wanted to be near my family and feel protected by them." She decided to remain in Missoula for the semester and take all her classes online. Then, a week after being raped, she got a phone call from her younger sister, Kathleen, who was attending college in Boise, Idaho.

Kathleen Huguet told Allison that a mutual acquaintance was informing people that "you and Beau had sex last weekend." Kathleen didn't even bother asking Allison if the rumor was true, because she knew it was preposterous: Beau Donaldson was the last person in the world Allison would ever sleep with. In high dudgeon, Kathleen reported that she had sent their acquaintance a nasty Facebook message commanding her to stop spreading ridiculous rumors.

"I was sitting there in shock when Kathleen told me this," Allison said. "I couldn't even process it." Donaldson and his friend Sam Erschler had assured Allison and her mother that they would say nothing about the rape to anyone. Yet a rumor that she had willingly slept with her rapist was already circulating in Missoula, Montana; Boise, Idaho; and La Grande, Oregon.

Allison said nothing to Kathleen about the rape. Instead she called Keely Williams for commiseration, telling her, "I can't believe this." Then she thumbed a text to Beau Donaldson to let him know what people were saying about them. She warned, "I can promise you that if I hear one more person saying that I slept with you, I am going to the police."

Donaldson immediately texted her back, saying that although he had no idea who was responsible for the rumor, he would "shut it down and get it taken care of."

The text from Donaldson seemed genuinely contrite. Allison Huguet found it surprisingly reassuring. It gave her a sense of control, or at least an illusion of control, that continued for more than a year. "At the time," she told me, "I felt I had some real leverage, so I wasn't so scared of him. And I had confidence he would really seek the help he needed." Huguet convinced herself that as long as nobody knew she had been raped, she could resume living as if it had never happened, and everything would return to normal. She didn't see any reason to seek psychotherapy.

"That next year turned out to be weird for me," she said. "I can't remember if I thought much about the rape or didn't think about it during that period. I can't remember if I was sleeping okay or having nightmares. That whole period is kind of blank. I'm pretty sure I managed to just keep it out of my mind." That semester, she recalled, "I was working full-time for my dad at Office Solutions. I studied a lot and did well with my online classes. And on weekends I would go to Pullman sometimes."

Two of Huguet's closest friends from EOU had graduated and moved to Pullman, Washington, a college town. When Huguet visited, she and her friends hit the bars. "I was drinking a lot more than usual that year," she said. "Drinking and partying. Having a good time. Looking back, I see that I was making some bad decisions. And looking back, now I know why I was making those bad decisions. But at the time, I wasn't willing to accept the fact that

Beau had changed me in that way. I wasn't willing to give that to him."

In January 2011, Huguet moved from Missoula back to La Grande, rented an apartment with a friend of a friend named Natasha, and resumed classes at EOU. "It was good being around her," Huguet remembered. "We became pretty close, pretty fast. She was a feminist. A very strong, very independent female." One evening Huguet surprised herself by confiding to Natasha that she had been raped. "Tasha was like, 'Oh my God, Allison. You went to the police, right?'" Sheepishly, Huguet confessed that she hadn't. "Tasha was appalled," Huguet said. "She said she understood why I hadn't wanted to report it but told me, 'The police need to know about this guy and what he did to you.'"

Soon thereafter, Natasha got a job at a crisis center for victims of domestic violence and sexual assault, a place called Shelter from the Storm. Surprisingly, once she started working with professional counselors and advocates, Natasha's opinion about the desirability of reporting rapes to the police changed. Her colleagues pointed out that for some victims of sexual assault, engaging with the criminal justice system could traumatize them severely all over again, so the staff at SFTS didn't necessarily recommend it. Her colleagues definitely urged every victim to get counseling, however. More than half a year had passed since Huguet had been raped, but she still hadn't sought help from a therapist. She was doing fine, she thought. She had no reason to talk to a shrink.

Looking back at that period now, Huguet said, "I understand that I just didn't want to acknowledge what Beau did to me. Because if I did acknowledge it, I would have to deal with it, and it would become real. Your mind is pretty good at blocking out traumatic experiences and preventing you from thinking about them. At least until something comes along to trigger you."

IN THE AUTUMN of her final year at EOU, Huguet drove from La Grande to Missoula to spend Thanksgiving with her family. On

November 23, 2011, the Wednesday evening before the holiday, she headed downtown with three of her friends to decompress at the Missoula Club, a venerable burger-and-beer joint universally referred to as the Mo Club. The place was packed. Huguet was chatting at the bar with a friend named Carol* when she noticed Beau Donaldson gazing at her from across the room, no more than twenty feet away. "He was standing there laughing," Huguet recalled, "staring at me."

Donaldson had reason to be feeling good. Four days earlier, he and his Griz teammates had played their final regular-season game against their archrivals, the Montana State University Bobcats, an annual contest known as the "Brawl of the Wild." The Griz had won 36–10, making them co-champions of the Big Sky Conference with a record of nine wins and two losses, sending them to the NCAA Football Champion Series play-offs, which would commence in ten days. And after sitting out the entire 2010 football season with an injured ankle, Donaldson had played well and contributed to the team's success in 2011.

Huguet hadn't seen Donaldson since he'd come over to her mom's house to apologize, the day after he'd raped her. Fourteen months had passed. The shock of encountering him face-to-face caused Huguet's chest to constrict. Her friend Carol, who had dated Donaldson for an extended period in high school, was not aware that her ex-boyfriend had raped Huguet. "I don't know what possessed me," Huguet said, "but I told Carol what had happened. Right then and there. She looked at me in horror."

Carol then turned toward Donaldson, scowled, and said, "You need to leave right now."

Donaldson glowered back at her, silently mouthed the words "Fuck you," and laughed.

"He was mocking me," Huguet said. "He had this smug, entitled expression. He was like, 'This is my territory. These are my people. You don't deserve to be here.'" Extremely unnerved, she

* pseudonym

and Carol hurried out of the bar. Upon arriving back at her mom's house, Huguet went downstairs, got on the Internet, opened the web page for the Missoula Police Department, and looked up the e-mail address for Detective Guy Baker.

Huguet had met Baker during her junior year at Big Sky High School, when he spoke to a criminal justice class she was taking. A year later, because Huguet was interested in police SWAT operations, she decided to conduct research about SWAT training for her senior project, and asked Baker to be her mentor. In addition to writing a ten-page essay examining whether the physical fitness requirements for joining SWAT teams discriminated against women, she took the same grueling physical fitness test administered to all men and women who aspired to join the Missoula Police Department's SWAT team. Applicants had to complete a three-hundred-meter obstacle course in less than seven and a half minutes while wearing a twenty-five-pound bulletproof vest.

The most challenging obstacle for Huguet was a smooth, six-foot-high wall that she had to pull herself up and over twice. "It gave her fits," Detective Baker told me. "She kept trying and trying to get over it, and refused to give up. She ended up completing the course in just over seven minutes and got a qualifying score. Which was interesting, because no other female in our department had ever passed this test at the time." Baker was impressed. And Huguet came to respect and trust him, as well.

By the time Huguet found Detective Baker's e-mail address, it was 2:30 in the morning. She was too angry to sleep. "When I saw Beau that night," she recalled, "it was like a dam broke. It triggered this rush of buried feelings I didn't even know I had. I went from never thinking about the rape and believing I was no longer affected by it to realizing that it had been having a huge effect on me all along. I realized that Beau had all this power over how I felt, and I didn't want him to have that power anymore. I began to think that maybe it had been a mistake not to go to the police."

Nearly four years had passed since Allison Huguet had last spoken to Detective Baker, before she had graduated from high school.

Huguet was still deeply ambivalent about reporting Beau Donaldson to the authorities, but she trusted Baker enough to broach the subject in a noncommittal fashion. She sent him an e-mail that read,

> Dear Detective Baker, . . . This is Allison Huguet. I worked with you on SWAT training my senior year of high school. There is a situation I have been put in, in Missoula, and I would love to talk about it with you. I want to know my options on a legal matter that is very personal. If you could email me back that would be great.

Baker replied a day later, the Friday after Thanksgiving, suggesting they meet that very afternoon to discuss whatever was on her mind, but by then Huguet was having second thoughts about starting a process she might not be able to control or stop, so she didn't respond to Baker's e-mail. Instead, she persuaded her mother to ask a family friend, an attorney who worked as a public defender, whether he thought Huguet should report the rape to the police. "He basically said, 'You better prepare for the hardest, nastiest fight of your life if you go that route,'" Huguet remembered. "He said my life would be torn apart, and every aspect of it would be exposed in public, and these cases are very hard for victims to win."

On Tuesday, November 29, four days after he'd proposed that they meet, Detective Baker still hadn't heard from Huguet. So he sent her another e-mail, inquiring, "Do you still want to talk?"

Huguet replied:

> I am now back in Oregon. I'm confused on what to do about this situation and I did talk to a lawyer but he was not exactly comforting, basically he told me [to] prepare to have my life completely changed. I just kinda want to know if I meet and discuss the situation with you, do you then have to report it?

Baker answered right away:

> It depends. If you tell me you committed a violent crime then I might be obligated to investigate it, but if it's not that, then we should be able to talk about it. We can talk on the phone if you want. Does it involve something you did, or something that was done to you?

Huguet replied:

> It was something that was done to me. It was a year and a few months ago, but when I talked to the lawyer he said the statute of limitations is not up on it. It's something I thought I could handle. But every time I come home I realize I'm mad at myself for not reporting the situation. I will be home this Friday, though, so maybe we can meet up after that some time.

Allison Huguet returned to Missoula for Christmas break on December 9, 2011. One night soon thereafter she went out to a bar called the Bodega with her friend Carol and some other girlfriends, and the conversation quickly turned to the subject of how unsettled Huguet had felt ever since running into Beau Donaldson at the Mo Club. Coincidentally, Donaldson's close friend Sam Erschler also happened to be at the Bodega that night, and he sat down with Huguet and Carol to have a drink. As the night slid past and Huguet became intoxicated, she grew increasingly agitated over the fact that Donaldson apparently felt no remorse over the violence he had done to her. When she disclosed that she had been having nightmares, Erschler revealed that he, too, had been having nightmares—about Donaldson chasing Huguet down the alley. Erschler told Huguet he would do anything to make her feel better.

"Well, if you really want to do something for me," Huguet replied in a moment of drunken pique, "you could hurt Beau." She offered Erschler a thousand dollars to beat the shit out of Donaldson.

"Al," Erschler replied, "you know I can't do that."

Disappointed that Sam Erschler refused to exact revenge on her behalf, later that night when Carol and her boyfriend were driving Huguet home, she begged them to swing by Donaldson's house and slash the tires on his truck. "I think that's when I realized that I was acting crazy," Huguet observed, "that I was starting to totally lose it. I was wanting to do things I would never have even thought of doing in a normal state of mind. Honestly, if I could have found someone who would kill Beau for me, at that time I think I would have paid them to do it. And that started to really scare me—that I was angry enough to think like that."

A few days later Carol told Huguet, "Every time you come home now, you're more and more angry. I can tell that what Beau did to you is really stressing you out. I really think you need to do something about it. I think you need to report Beau to the police."

On Friday, December 16, 2011, Huguet heeded Carol's advice, went to the Missoula police station, and told Detective Baker that Beau Donaldson had raped her. She made it clear, however, that she wasn't sure she wanted to file a report about the incident.

CHAPTER FIVE

Allison Huguet had the digital recording of Beau Donaldson admitting that he "took advantage" of her, and the nurses at the First Step sexual-assault response center had obtained physical evidence of the rape. But because Donaldson had been unaware that he was being recorded, his confession would not be admissible as evidence. Furthermore, because the assault had happened in September 2010, nearly fifteen months before Huguet shared her secret with Detective Baker, and First Step typically kept rape kits for no more than six months before disposing of them, there was a good chance that her rape kit had been destroyed. Getting a conviction and sending Donaldson to prison was by no means a certain outcome. Although Baker was eager to investigate her case, he suggested that over the weekend Huguet think further about what she wanted to do.

A day earlier, coincidentally, an article on the front page of the *Missoulian* had announced that there had been a recent sexual assault on the UM campus "that reportedly involved two female students, multiple male students and the date-rape drug Rohypnol." A subsequent article on December 16, 2011, disclosed that "at least three" of the accused rapists were Griz football players.

The two reports were written by a seasoned journalist named Gwen Florio who'd learned her chops reporting for the *Philadelphia Inquirer* and had gone to Afghanistan in 2001 to cover America's rapidly expanding war on terrorism for the *Denver Post*. The articles Florio wrote in December 2011 about the sexual assaults allegedly involving Griz players were the first of what would be more than one hundred stories published in the *Missoulian* about the "Missoula rape scandal," as it would soon be christened.

As Huguet agonized over what to do, the articles Florio published in December 2011 became a factor in her calculus. She was aware that if Beau Donaldson was charged with raping her, she would face scathing criticism from Griz fans. She understood that if the case went to trial, Donaldson's attorneys would attempt to destroy her reputation. But she also knew that if she didn't report Donaldson, he might rape other women. Because the latter possibility worried her more than the former, on December 20 Huguet went to the Missoula police station and made a formal statement to Detective Baker, which he recorded on video, setting the clunky machinery of justice in motion.

Gwen Florio's reporting, it turned out, also inspired another victim of sexual assault to come forward and tell her story in a public forum. Terry Belnap, the mother of a UM student named Kelsey Belnap, happened to see Florio's December 16, 2011, article about the gang rape by Griz players and thought it sounded dismayingly like what had happened to Kelsey a year earlier, in December 2010. When Terry brought the article to her daughter's attention, Kelsey also found Florio's account of the 2011 incident to be excruciatingly similar to what had happened to her. "Oh my God," Kelsey thought. "I could have prevented this from happening."

Terry Belnap sent an e-mail to Florio saying that Kelsey was willing to talk about being raped by four members of the Griz football team, in the hope that doing so might keep others from being subjected to what she had been forced to endure.

ON DECEMBER 15, 2010, three months after Allison Huguet was raped, Kelsey Belnap took her last exam of the semester and then walked outside into the crisp autumn afternoon. Her best friend,

Betsy Fairmont,* who had just completed the same exam, invited Belnap to come to her boyfriend's apartment that evening to celebrate. "Sure," Belnap replied. "That sounds like a good time." Fairmont and Belnap, who were both twenty-one years old, first went to Belnap's apartment and had dinner with Belnap's boyfriend, whom she lived with. Because Belnap's boyfriend had to work that night, however, he couldn't join the women in toasting the end of the semester.

Fairmont's boyfriend, whom Belnap had met only once before that evening, was Benjamin Styron,† a defensive lineman for the Griz who weighed more than 240 pounds. When Fairmont and Belnap arrived at his apartment, at 5:45 p.m., Styron and his roommate, a Griz player who weighed almost as much as Styron, were smoking weed outside. The four students went indoors, poured themselves shots of 99-proof schnapps, and were soon joined by three other members of the UM football team. Belnap didn't know any of the men except Styron and his roommate. The five Griz players began competing to drink the most, and they encouraged the two women to join them. "Every couple of minutes we would all take another shot," Belnap told me. "It was a 'Let's see if you can keep up' kind of thing. I was like, 'Uh, okay.' "

Belnap didn't suspect that the football players might be setting her up to be raped. The celebration seemed innocuous. "I was just hanging out with my friend and her friends," she said. "I have a brother who was on the football team. I used to work in the equipment room for the football team. At that point I didn't imagine anything bad could happen."

One of the football players rolled a blunt and started passing it around. "I have never smoked pot in my life," Belnap said, "and had no intention of smoking pot, so it made me uncomfortable, and I told Betsy that. But it was their apartment, so I didn't say, 'Please don't do it.' "

* pseudonym

† pseudonym

Betsy Fairmont inhaled a lungful of smoke and then turned to Belnap and exclaimed, "Oh!" as if she'd suddenly remembered how marijuana affected her. "When I get drunk and high," Fairmont warned, "I get really messed up."

A few minutes later, Belnap looked at the clock and noticed that it was around 6:30 or 6:45. "But the clock had gotten completely blurry," she said. "So I told myself, 'I'm done drinking.' Because at that point I knew I was really, really drunk. And after what Betsy had told me, I was also thinking, 'Oh crap. I've got to get her home, too.' "

By then Kelsey Belnap had consumed between eight and eleven shots in approximately forty-five minutes. She can recall very little about what happened thereafter. When she quit imbibing she was seated on the living room couch, "and the next thing I know," she said, "I was in a dark bedroom, sitting at the foot of a bed. I remember looking at the door and thinking, 'What the hell am I doing in a bedroom?' And then I turn around, because I heard a noise, and Betsy and Benjamin are having sex on the bed behind me."

Belnap isn't amorously adventurous. "I am not into watching other people do that," she said. "I've never even seen a porn film; I certainly didn't want to watch live sex." So she tried to get up from the bed and leave the room, she recalled, "but my body was like a limp noodle. I could not move. And then I remember the door opening. At first I thought, 'Someone is here to help me get out of this room.' And then all of a sudden this person was standing in front of me with his penis in my face. I said, 'I don't want to!' and I pushed him away." But her resistance was ignored.

Even now, Kelsey Belnap doesn't know the identity of this assailant. He grabbed her jaw, pulled it open, and thrust his erect penis into her mouth. "That's the last thing I remember until a while later, when someone else came in the room," she said. Belnap didn't know who that second person was, either, but said, "I remember my belt buckle being played with, and then somehow I was bent over the bed." For the next two hours she drifted "in and out of awareness" as different men entered the room, had sex with her, and left. "I was blacked out throughout pretty much the entire thing," she said, "and only remember bits and pieces of what happened." Later, according to Belnap, a police officer told her that she had engaged in sex with all four of Benjamin Styron's teammates.

After she began to drift back up to the surface of consciousness, Belnap said, the first thing she recalled was being "in the bathroom, throwing up in the bathtub. Betsy was throwing up in the toilet, and all the boys were gone except Benjamin. Betsy was like, 'Benjamin! Get out of here!' She was embarrassed for him to see her like that."

When Belnap eventually regained control of her faculties, she burst into tears. Betsy Fairmont called a friend, who took Fairmont and Belnap to the Community Medical Center emergency room, where Belnap was admitted at 9:00 p.m. According to the nurses' notes, she was "obviously intoxicated" and had slurred speech. Two and a half hours after she'd stopped drinking, her blood alcohol concentration was measured to be 0.219 percent, nearly three times the legal limit for driving. When asked if she was experiencing any pain, Belnap replied that her vagina hurt. When asked to elucidate further, she stated that she thought she "may have been raped." According to a nurse's somewhat confused notes,

> What she remembers is that possible 2 males performed oral sex on her and possible one male penetrated her vagina with his penis. Patient states that she does remember trying to push the males off, and in no way gave consent to the males for sex. Patient relates that she does not remember the events well but knows that sex did take place that was not consensual. Patient became very emotional and started crying while relating this.

Although Belnap's mother was born in Missoula, and both her parents graduated from the University of Montana, she was raised in Idaho Falls, Idaho, where her parents still reside. But her mother's aunt lived in Missoula, so when Kelsey was admitted to the emergency room, the hospital contacted this grandaunt. She came to the emergency room right away, called Kelsey's mom, and put Kelsey on the phone. Kelsey blurted in a despairing voice, "Mom, I think I've been raped."

When the emergency room staff learned that Kelsey Belnap might have been sexually assaulted, they notified the Missoula Police Department. At 11:00 p.m., Officer Mitchell Lang arrived at the hospital to talk to her. According to Belnap, Lang "seemed very shaky. Like, this wasn't the kind of situation he'd dealt with before." The initial report filed by Officer Lang says,

> Kelsey still appeared heavily impaired and her story was fragmented. Kelsey stated that she did not remember much of what happened that evening. . . . [S]he stated that she was taken into one of the rooms in the apartment but she did not know which one. . . .
>
> Kelsey stated that 2–3 additional persons came into the bedroom. . . . [S]he remembered her head being grabbed by one of the males and he was trying to make her perform oral sex on him. Kelsey stated she pushed the male back but when he was forcing her head down again she stopped resisting because she was scared. When asked if the male said anything she stated she thought he said "it is good for her to be this drunk." . . . Kelsey stated she then performed oral sex on 1 or 2 additional males and then stated she was "bent" over the bed and penetrated vaginally. Kelsey stated the additional males then took turns. . . . Kelsey stated she was reluctant about pressing charges at this time because she did not want to get anyone in trouble.

After speaking briefly with Kelsey Belnap, Officer Lang interviewed Betsy Fairmont. She told him she couldn't remember anything about what happened, but Fairmont said she was sure Belnap had no intention of charging anyone with sexual assault. Nevertheless, Lang recommended to Belnap that she go to the First Step rape clinic for a forensic gynecological examination.

At 1:00 a.m., Belnap's boyfriend and her grandaunt took her to First Step, where she was examined by Claire Francoeur, the same nurse who'd examined Allison Huguet. Francoeur found semen in Belnap's vagina and on her rectum, as well as redness on her cervix and "multiple genital lacerations" indicative of penetrating trauma. "I was still pretty sick and still felt a bit drunk," Belnap recalled, "so it was hard for me to be there. But Francoeur was very sensitive."

The following afternoon, a Missoula police officer named Travis Welsh contacted Kelsey Belnap to confirm whether or not she wanted to pursue a criminal investigation. Belnap told Officer Welsh that, regardless of whatever she and Betsy Fairmont might have told Officer Lang, she definitely wanted to press charges. A day later Belnap went to the police station, where she was interviewed by detectives Guy Baker and Mark Blood. According to the report subsequently filed by Baker, Belnap recalled sitting in the bedroom when one of the football players walked up to her,

> unbuttoned his pants and removed his penis. Kelsey stated he then directed her head towards his erect penis with his hand. Kelsey stated she said something to the effect, "I don't want to" and pushed him away with her hands. . . . [He] then stepped towards her again and pushed and/or moved her outstretched arms and her hands down to the sides of her torso and then put his penis in her mouth. Kelsey stated she was scared and let him put his penis in her mouth without saying anything else to him. . . . [S]he then performed oral sex . . . on the male for several minutes. . . . Kelsey stated the male exited the bedroom and she heard him exclaim "Damn!" and then say something else to the other males.
>
> Kelsey stated another male . . . then entered the bedroom. . . . [S]he was still sitting at the edge of the bed when he walked up to her. . . . [H]e also removed his penis

> from his pants. Kelsey stated he did not say anything to her and she did not say anything to him. . . . [H]is penis was not erect and she put it in her mouth before performing oral sex on him for several minutes. Kelsey stated she performed oral sex on him because she was scared. . . . [S]he thought she passed out or blacked out while performing oral sex on the second male because the next memory she has is lying on her back on the bed and somebody tugging on the front of her pants in an attempt to unbutton them. . . . [S]he next recalls standing beside the bed, bent forward from the waist with her arms on the bed while somebody was holding onto her waist while standing behind her. Kelsey stated she remembers a penis penetrating her vagina, but she is unsure which male was having sex with her. Kelsey stated she did not say "no" or "stop" to the male or make any verbalization to the male while he was having sexual intercourse with her.
>
> Kelsey stated she thought she passed out or blacked out again while the male was having sex with her because the next memory she has is her pants are on again and she is walking out of the bedroom. . . . [T]he next thing she remembers is her and Betsy in the bathroom. . . .
>
> Kelsey stated she experienced pain in the area of her vagina following the incident and . . . was still feeling soreness and discomfort in her vaginal area at the time of the interview. . . . [S]he also experienced soreness in her neck and shoulders as a result of the incident. When asked if she thought the males perceived the sexual activity to have been consensual or nonconsensual, Kelsey stated they would have likely believed it was consensual sex. When asked to elaborate, Kelsey stated she was so intoxicated she did not resist them, she never said "no" or "stop" to verbalize to them that she "didn't want to" have sex with them.

Reflecting on this interview in 2014, four years after it occurred, Belnap told me that she hadn't been emotionally prepared to be interrogated in this fashion less than forty-eight hours after being gang-raped. No one had informed her that she could ask for a victim advocate to be present during the interview. "I had just been through this ordeal," she said, "and they put me in a room with two male authority figures. It was very intimidating. I tried to maintain my game face, and thought I didn't need anyone to be there with me, but I wish there had been another female present to make me feel a little more comfortable."

Belnap's nervousness, her inability to remember much, and the fact that her best friend had insisted that Belnap had no intention of alleging that she was raped led Detectives Baker and Blood to question the reliability of Belnap's account. "They seemed skeptical," she said, "like they thought I was just another drunk girl. I began to feel like *I* was the perp. They asked me a couple of different times, 'How did the guy who put his penis in your face grab your jaw? Did he grab it forcibly, or did he just kind of tug at it?' I showed them exactly how he did it, but they didn't seem to believe that I really resisted or said no."

Detective Baker asked Belnap if she was dating anyone, a question cops often ask women who report they've been raped. "When I said, 'Yes, I am,'" Belnap remembered, "the way he reacted made me feel like he assumed I had cheated on my boyfriend and then lied about being raped to cover it up, even though that wasn't the case at all."

Regarding Baker's question about whether Belnap thought the men who had sex with her perceived it to be consensual or nonconsensual, she said, "Looking back now, that seems like a very inappropriate question for them to ask. How was I supposed to know what those boys were thinking? I was passed out most of the time. I wasn't even aware what they were doing to me."

The day after the incident at Benjamin Styron's apartment, Betsy Fairmont sent several apologetic text messages to Kelsey Belnap, expressing how sorry she was that Belnap had been raped. "Betsy texted over and over again," Belnap said. "She said, 'I am so sorry. I should have taken better care of you.'"

When Belnap told Fairmont that she'd filed a police report accusing Styron's friends of raping her, however, Fairmont's sympathy vanished. She tried to downplay what had happened, according to Belnap, and begged Belnap not to pursue the matter with the police. "I don't want to get anyone in trouble!" Fairmont protested.

When Betsy Fairmont was interviewed by Detective Baker on January 11, 2011, nearly four weeks after the incident, Fairmont insisted that Belnap had willingly had sex with all four of Benjamin Styron's teammates. Fairmont "ended up covering for all five football players," Belnap said bitterly. "They were her boys. When I told her, 'But this happened, Betsy. I was raped,' she changed her story and lied through her ass."

Styron and the men who allegedly raped Belnap left town for Christmas break immediately after the incident, dispersing to five different cities in California, Arizona, and Washington. Because Betsy Fairmont was adamant that Belnap had consented to having sex with the football players, and it would have been prohibitively expensive for the police department to fly Detective Baker to three distant states to interview them, neither Styron nor any of the suspects were questioned until they came back to Missoula for the start of the spring semester, by which time seven weeks had elapsed. Detectives Baker and Blood didn't interview Benjamin Styron and his roommate until February 3, 2011, and their three teammates weren't interviewed until mid-February, by which time all four suspects had had ample opportunity to rehearse their stories with Styron, Fairmont, and one another before giving their statements to the police.

On February 18, Detective Baker met with deputy Missoula County attorney Jason Marks. "Based on the investigation," Baker wrote in his inclusive case report, "it was decided there was not probable cause to file criminal charges against anyone involved in the incident."

"Baker called me and said, 'We need to talk,'" Kelsey Belnap recalled. When she arrived at the police station, Detective Baker explained that because Betsy Fairmont, Benjamin Styron, and all four of his teammates had stated that the sex was consensual, the Missoula County Attorney's Office had determined that there was insufficient evidence to move forward. It was Belnap's word against the word of six eyewitnesses.

According to Belnap, Baker told her the kicker was this: " 'They said you were moaning, so you couldn't have been passed out. We needed one more person to take your side and back up your story, and there wasn't one. I'm sorry, but there is nothing we can do.' " The case was closed.

The Missoula police chief at the time was Mark Muir. In an interview with Muir broadcast in 2014 on *60 Minutes Sports,* correspondent Armen Keteyian asked why the case was never prosecuted. "A lack of ability to show it was nonconsensual sex," Chief Muir replied, adding that it was an easy decision to make. He reminded Keteyian that Kelsey Belnap had told Detective Baker that the men with whom she had sex "would likely have believed" it was consensual. "How do you overcome that?" Muir said.

According to Montana law, Keteyian countered, a person who is physically incapacitated is incapable of providing consent. Given her extremely high blood alcohol level, he wondered, wasn't Belnap clearly incapacitated?

"No," Chief Muir answered. "Physical incapacitation differs from incapacitation of the mind." The fact that Belnap "had blackouts does not, specifically, indicate that she was physically helpless at the time," Muir asserted, implying that Belnap's case would have been prosecutable if she'd been completely unconscious the whole time, but because she was intermittently semiconscious, her claim that she never gave consent wasn't credible.

But the relevant law, Montana statute 45-5-501, doesn't say a victim has to be "physically helpless" to be incapable of giving consent, as Muir incorrectly asserted. The law states that a victim is incapable of consent if he or she is "mentally defective or incapacitated"; "physically helpless"; or "overcome by deception, coercion, or surprise." And with a blood alcohol content of .219 percent more than two hours after the alleged rapes began, it's hard to imagine that Belnap wasn't mentally incapacitated to a significant degree.

During an on-camera interview with Missoula County Attorney Fred Van Valkenburg, Keteyian observed that when Belnap's first assailant shoved his penis in her face, she told him "no" and tried to push him away. "Isn't that enough?" Keteyian asked, referring to indication of an absence of consent.

Because Kelsey Belnap said nothing further to communicate her lack of consent as the sexual activity escalated, Van Valkenburg replied, he didn't have enough evidence to take the case to trial. "This was not a prosecutable case," he told Keteyian. "So I don't have any sort of regret about not filing this. I don't think we did anything wrong."

Van Valkenburg, who was the head Missoula County prosecutor, neglected to mention the incriminating evidence he actually did have, such as the emergency room nurse's notes and Detective Baker's statement in his case report that when Kelsey Belnap's initial assailant stuck his erect penis in her face, "she said something to the effect, 'I don't want to' and pushed him away with her hands."

Nor did Van Valkenburg acknowledge the substantial and well-documented injuries to Belnap's vagina or the text messages to Belnap from Betsy Fairmont saying, "I am so sorry. I should have taken better care of you"—texts that Detective Baker downloaded from Belnap's phone and submitted as evidence. Furthermore, the recorded statements the perpetrators made to Baker failed to explain how, exactly, Belnap expressed consent while facedown and semicomatose, bent across a bed. The perpetrators' statements also failed to address the implausibility of their claims that she eagerly engaged in painful, injurious sex with four men she'd never met before that evening.

The Missoula County attorney's decision not to prosecute infuriated Kelsey Belnap and her family. Gang rape is an especially heinous crime. It seemed likely that the men who allegedly assaulted Kelsey might also have assaulted other women, and might rape again if not held accountable. The Belnaps believe a more motivated prosecutor than Van Valkenburg would have ordered a more thorough investigation, charged the perpetrators with rape, and either persuaded them to make a plea deal or taken them to trial—where he or she could have discredited the testimony of Kelsey's assailants and, possibly, persuaded a jury to convict them.

Instead, as Terry Belnap lamented to Gwen Florio, "We were left with no answers and no further investigation. . . . I really felt that we were brushed off." When Terry Belnap asked her daughter if she wanted the family to hire a lawyer to pressure Van Valkenburg to prosecute, according to Florio's article in the *Missoulian*, Kelsey Belnap said, "Mom, they're football players and nobody's gonna listen to me. They'll make my life hell."

GWEN FLORIO'S PIECE about Kelsey Belnap appeared on the front page of the *Missoulian* on December 21, 2011. When Allison Huguet read that Belnap had shared her story with Florio in the hope that it would prevent other women from being sexually assaulted, it boosted Huguet's confidence that reporting Beau Donaldson to the police had been the right decision. She was further encouraged when Detective Baker learned from nurse Claire Francoeur that Huguet's rape kit, along with other evidence pertaining to the assault, had not in fact been destroyed and was being stored at the Montana Department of Justice in Helena, the state capital. On December 22, Baker received this evidence from Francoeur.

A day later, after obtaining a warrant, Baker asked Huguet to come to the police station and call Donaldson from her cell phone while Baker surreptitiously recorded the conversation, hoping to obtain a confession that could be used as evidence.

"When I filed the police report," Huguet told me, "this call was something Detective Baker warned me I might have to do. But it wasn't something I thought I'd actually be able to do. It was really difficult." Baker plugged Huguet's phone into a recording device, and she dialed Donaldson's number, but he didn't answer. Baker had Huguet wait ten minutes and call Donaldson again. When he failed to answer this time, Baker asked her to leave a message on Donaldson's voice mail asking him to call her back.

After half an hour, Beau Donaldson hadn't called, so Baker turned the recorder off and told Huguet they'd try again in a few days. As they were walking out of the interview room, however, her phone began ringing. "It was Beau," she said, "but Detective Baker didn't want me to answer because the recorder wasn't hooked up." She let it ring, then called Donaldson back after the recorder had been reconnected to her phone. "That was probably the most awkward conversation of my life," Huguet said. "I don't even remember how I started it. I think I told him that I was becoming upset about what had happened. . . . Then I told him that I had read about the sexual assaults that had been going on at the university and wondered if he was involved. He got very defensive immediately. He was like, 'I don't know anything about that! I didn't have anything to do with that!' He was freaking out."

Huguet pointed out that when Donaldson had apologized, the day after raping her, he'd promised that he would seek help for his abuse of drugs and alcohol, but from the way he'd acted when she'd run into him at the Mo Club just before Thanksgiving, it appeared he hadn't made any progress on that front. According to Huguet, "Beau said, 'Oh, so you think it's a problem that I have a few drinks with my friends?' And I told him, 'Yeah, I do think it's a problem, because that's exactly how you ended up raping me.' "

As Allison Huguet spoke on the phone with Beau Donaldson, Detective Baker was coaching her about what to say, hoping to get Donaldson to make a clear, unambiguous confession. Eventually Donaldson admitted, "Yes, I took advantage of you," adding that he felt "shitty" about it.

A little later, Donaldson told Huguet that he'd sought treatment from two different psychotherapists, prompting her to ask, "And you told them you raped me?"

"Yes," Donaldson replied.

"At that point I thought the police had enough," Huguet said.

But Detective Baker disagreed. He was a very dedicated cop. His father had been a law enforcement officer for the city of Missoula for thirty-one years. His grandfather had worked for the Montana Highway Patrol for thirty-four years. Baker, who was forty-four years old, had joined the Missoula Police Department when he was twenty-one. He'd spent thirteen of his twenty-three years on the force as a detective and had been the lead investigator on approximately seven hundred cases, nearly one hundred of which were sexual assaults. He knew all too well how easily even a slam-dunk rape case could be sabotaged by unforeseeable developments. And he understood that there was no better way to ensure a conviction than to get an incontrovertible confession from the accused rapist.

Baker urged Huguet to stay on the phone with Donaldson a little longer and to ask him to explain why he'd raped her. She reluctantly agreed. "But when I kept asking Beau why he did it," she recalled, "he kept saying, 'I don't know! I don't know!' Finally, he just got really angry and started yelling at me. So I said, 'Okay, well, if you can't give me an explanation of why you did this to me, then I'm going to have to go to the police.' And he said, 'Okay. If that's what you have to do. . . .' And then I hung up."

As soon as the call ended, Huguet lost her composure and started sobbing. "That call was extremely emotional," she said. "Beau was someone I had cared deeply about for most of my life. Even though he raped me, I couldn't help still caring about him on some level, and I knew I had just sealed his fate—that he was now going to be in a world of trouble because of what I had just gotten him to say on tape. But at the same time, that was exactly what I had wanted to do. When I explained to Detective Baker why I was bawling, he was like, 'Allison, you need to keep in mind that you are doing the right thing.' "

Eleven days later, Baker believed he had gathered enough evidence to put together a bombproof case against Donaldson. In addition to recording the phone conversation and obtaining Huguet's rape kit, he had conducted extensive interviews with Huguet's mother, Sam Erschler, Keely Williams, and Claire Francoeur, the nurse at First Step who had examined Allison. Baker applied for a warrant to arrest Donaldson, and received it at 2:30 p.m. on January 6, 2012.

Two hours later, Baker, Detective Mark Blood, and three uniformed Missoula police officers drove to Donaldson's house, asked if he would agree to be interviewed, and then transported him to the police station. When they got there, Baker confiscated Donaldson's cell phone and advised him of his Miranda rights. Donaldson said he understood his rights and consented to talk to Baker and Blood without an attorney present.

During the videotaped interview that ensued, Donaldson initially claimed that he and Huguet had fallen asleep together on the couch in his living room and that Huguet had willingly been making out with him, leading him to believe that the intercourse they had was consensual. After Baker pointed out to Donaldson that Keely Williams had clearly stated that she saw Huguet sleeping alone on the couch, however, Donaldson eventually confessed that he had "pulled Allison's pants down and engaged in sexual intercourse with her while she was sleeping." According to the case report submitted by Baker, "Beau admitted that due to the fact Allison was asleep, he knew it was nonconsensual sex and he . . . had 'raped' her."

After interviewing Beau Donaldson for just under an hour, Detective Baker returned Donaldson's cell phone and allowed him to call his father. Then Baker placed Donaldson under arrest and drove him to the Missoula County jail, where he was booked on a felony charge of sexual intercourse without consent—the legal term for rape in Montana. Bond was initially set at $100,000. By this time, Donaldson's father had arranged for a prominent Missoula attorney, Milt Datsopoulos, to represent Beau. Datsopoulos had assisted many University of Montana athletes with their legal problems over the years—so many, in fact, that Griz fans often joked, "If you're guilty, call Uncle Milty!" Extremely unhappy that Donaldson had talked to Detective Baker without an attorney, Datsopoulos phoned Baker while Donaldson was being booked and told him that under no circumstances could he speak further with Donaldson.

Detective Baker is a large man with a comportment that can be intimidating, but he is uncommonly empathic. He appreciates how difficult it can be for a rape victim to go to the police. He knows that the criminal justice system frequently compounds the trauma of being raped and, way too often, fails to hold rapists accountable. So instead of phoning Allison Huguet to tell her that Beau Donaldson had been arrested, Baker and Detective Blood drove across town to Office Solutions & Services to notify Huguet in person that Donaldson was in jail and had given them a full confession.

At 8:11 that evening, an hour before Baker had even broken the news to Huguet, a disappointed Grizzly supporter using the screen name "grizfan1984" announced on a popular Internet forum, eGriz.com,

> Just read the jail roster and Beau Donaldson has been arrested again this time for sexual intercourse without consent aka rape, $100,000 bail looks like he won't be playing for the griz anymore.

At 9:31, someone with the screen name "grizindabox" posted,

> It cannot be true, he is from Montana!

At 10:43, "PlayerRep" posted,

> I know nothing about the facts, but I know Donaldson and I have doubts that rape occurred or that this will stick. I think Donaldson is a good kid. I know good kids can be caught up with date rape-type things too, but my instincts tell me that he didn't rape anyone.

In the middle of the night, an article by Gwen Florio about Donaldson's arrest went up on the *Missoulian* website, impelling an angry Griz supporter calling himself "Sportin' Life" to post the following about Donaldson's arrest on eGriz at 5:08 a.m.:

> This has got to be Gwen Florio's fault entirely. This is really a new low for her, stooping to this just to push her anti-football agenda.

At 9:08 a.m., "jcu27" posted,

> First off, chicks exaggerate on rape. Second off, she could sucked his dick and still got rape just because she said she didn't want it later on. Third off, no justice system actually works. Only the people involved actually know what happened. And a lot of people lie.

PART TWO

Before the Law Sits a Gatekeeper

We can finally all agree that women want to have sex. Variously portrayed in the past as tamers of men and tenders of children, we're now deemed well endowed with horniness. But does that mean we experience desire in the same way that men do? My lust tells me we don't. Mine, I confess, isn't blind or monumental or animal. It comes with an endless internal monologue—or maybe dialogue, or maybe babel. My desire is always guessing, often second-guessing. Female lust is a powerful force, but it surges in the form of an interrogation, rather than a statement. Not *I want this* but *Do I want this? What exactly do I want? How about now? And now?*

Claire Dederer

"Why Is It So Hard for Women to Write About Sex?"

The Atlantic, March 2014

CHAPTER SIX

The thumping heart of downtown Missoula is a compact grid of shops, offices, government agencies, restaurants, and bars jammed between the Northern Pacific Railroad tracks and the Clark Fork River. Just to the southeast, on the other side of the river, is the University of Montana campus, accessible via a pair of four-lane bridges for vehicle traffic, and two much smaller bridges for pedestrians and cyclists. Within the eight-by-four-block downtown core are a dozen pubs and bars that fill with UM students every Thursday, Friday, and Saturday evening when school is in session.

On September 22, 2011, Kerry Barrett, a UM senior from New Jersey, went to a pub called Sean Kelly's with four friends. It was a Thursday night, and the weekly bacchanal known as "Thirsty Thursday" was in full swing—a tradition that has become so prevalent on campuses nationwide that a great many students now avoid enrolling in classes that meet on Friday mornings. Missoula was rocking.

At Sean Kelly's, Barrett made the acquaintance of a tall, athletic student named Zeke Adams,* who socialized with Barrett and her friends for much of the evening. Barrett says she and Adams were attracted to each other, and when he started kissing her she reciprocated. Around 1:30 Friday morning, by which time Barrett and Adams were both intoxicated, they headed to another bar, the

* pseudonym

Badlander, with one of Barrett's girlfriends, who departed for home a little later. "Zeke seemed trustworthy," Barrett told me, "so I felt okay with my friends leaving us." Both Barrett and Adams lived near Higgins Avenue, a major north–south arterial that bisects the downtown grid, and after last call at the Badlander, at 2:00 a.m., they started walking together down Higgins toward their respective apartments.

Zeke Adams lived just across the bridge that spanned the Clark Fork; Kerry Barrett lived a mile farther south. "When we got to Zeke's place," she remembered, "he was like, 'Why don't you come inside?' So I said okay. But before I even went in the door, I told him, 'I'm not sleeping with you. If that's what you're expecting, I'm just going to go home.' He said, 'No, no. I don't expect that at all. Just come in. We can hang out.' So we went inside." Instead of sitting in the living room of the small apartment, however, Adams suggested that they go to his bedroom to avoid waking his roommate.

Barrett followed Adams into his bedroom, where they talked about an abstract painting a friend had painted for him. Then Adams turned down the lights, they reclined on the bed, and started making out. "This was consensual," Barrett explained. "I really did like him, what I'd known of him at that point." Eventually, Adams pulled her pants and underwear down to the middle of her thighs and inserted his fingers into her vagina. This, too, was consensual, Barrett made clear, "but then he started getting a little aggressive, which made me feel uncomfortable." So she told him to stop, put all of her clothing back on, reiterated that she didn't want to have sex with him, and said she was leaving.

Adams urged her not to go, because it was 3:00 in the morning. As Barrett remembered it, he said, "You're wasted. Stay over and I'll drive you home in the morning. You know I'm a nice guy and nothing is going to happen."

"I actually wasn't that drunk—not nearly as wasted as he was," Barrett said, "but before you learn the realities of sexual assault, you're taught that it's dangerous to walk alone at night, because strangers are out to get you. The safer option seemed to be to stay at his place. So that's what I did."

In a recorded statement Adams later gave to the police, he confirmed Barrett's account: "I said, 'Well, you don't have to go.' . . . She laid back down in my bed. She told me she didn't want to have sex with me—and that was fine with me, and I said okay."

Fully clothed, with her skinny jeans now securely zipped up and buttoned, she fell asleep in his bed. Approximately thirty minutes later, she said, "I woke up to him completely naked, and my pants—which are very tight and not easy to pull off—were down by my ankles." Adams was spooning her from behind, rubbing his penis against her back, and then he tried to insert it into her vagina. Adams was six feet, three inches tall and weighed 170 pounds; Barrett stood five feet, seven inches and weighed 135 pounds. "Waking up to a big guy like that trying to rape me," she said, "was terrifying." Barrett frantically pushed him away and tugged her pants up, but Adams yanked them back down and attempted to penetrate her vagina a second time.

"I pushed him off again," Barrett said, "and at that point I got up, turned the light on, and got my stuff. He was just sitting there, staring at me. He didn't say anything. I'll never forget that stare." Barrett fled Adams's apartment in shock, crying, and walked the two blocks to Higgins Avenue, where she called one of the girlfriends who'd been at Sean Kelly's earlier in the evening. When the friend arrived and found Barrett sobbing inconsolably, she asked what had happened. "I choked out, 'He tried to rape me!'" Barrett remembered. "And then we just sat there and cried hysterically together. Neither of us knew what to do."

They picked up another friend, who lived in a dorm on the UM campus, and the three women discussed whether to report the assault to the police. Around 4:00 a.m., Barrett called her parents in New Jersey, and her father—a retired police lieutenant—convinced her to go to the Missoula police station, where she was interviewed by an officer named Brian Vreeland on a bench in the entrance to the police department. According to Barrett, Vreeland asked her, "What do you want to come of this?"

Taken aback by the question, Barrett replied that she didn't know. "I'm not a lawyer or anything," Vreeland said, "but since no one saw you, and you were fooling around before it happened, it's hard to really prove anything."

Officer Vreeland finished taking her statement, then asked Barrett to get in his patrol car and guide him and another officer, Kurt Trowbridge, to Adams's apartment. "I didn't know the exact address," Barrett said, "but I knew I could identify it. By then it was probably close to five in the morning. It was still dark. Before we got into his car, Vreeland said to me, 'Oh, and one more thing: Do you have a boyfriend?' I said, 'No, I don't. Why?' And he said something to the effect of 'Well, sometimes girls cheat on their boyfriends, and regret it, and then claim they were raped.'" Although this struck Barrett as a strange and inappropriate thing for a police officer to tell a woman who had just been sexually assaulted, she wasn't thinking clearly, because she was still in shock. "So I just said, 'Oh, okay,'" she explained, "and let it go."

Kerry Barrett directed Officers Vreeland and Trowbridge to Zeke Adams's apartment, then waited in the back of the police car. While Vreeland and a third officer, Michael Kamerer, tried to make contact with Adams, Barrett recalled, "Officer Trowbridge gave me a little Post-it sticky note with my report number, said I could pick up the report in a couple of days, and sent me on my way."

After Barrett departed, Officer Vreeland rang Adams's doorbell and banged on the door, but failed to rouse anyone inside. So he walked around to the side of the apartment, noticed an open window, peered inside, and saw Adams asleep in his bed. When Vreeland shined his flashlight in Adams's eyes, he woke up and came to the front door. According to the police report filed by Vreeland,

> After identifying myself and Officer Kamerer, I asked Zeke if I could speak with him. He was still very intoxicated and

> seemed to have difficulty making a decision or even a coherent and understandable sentence. He finally admitted he was Zeke Adams and he invited us in to talk to him. . . . After he was dressed, I told him I needed to ask him a few questions about an alleged incident but that I needed to read him his Miranda Warning. He, for the most part, was uncooperative but that may have been due to his intoxication level. He kept attempting to speak as if [he] was a lawyer using legal terms that made no sense in the way he was using them. . . . He had difficulty giving me a "yes" or a "no" when I asked him if he understood his legal rights, stating I was trying to "co-horse [i.e. coerce] him."
>
> He finally said he would speak with me. I asked him if he had been at Sean O'Kelly's [sic] this evening and if he had met a girl named Kerry. He said he thought I was trying to get him to say something without his legal counsel. When I reminded him that he had agreed to speak with me, he told me I was trying to get him to admit he had met "people" [at Sean Kelly's]. . . .
>
> Zeke then went into a long incoherent speech on the "exact definition of meeting people." [When] I attempted to explain to him I was just asking him if he met Kerry tonight he replied [with] words to the effect that I was attempting to "co-horse him once again and he thought he needed legal representation."
>
> I told him I was done interviewing him and that someone would be in touch with him later concerning his side of events.

ON MONDAY, SEPTEMBER 26, 2011, a female detective named Jamie Merifield called Kerry Barrett to say she had been assigned to Barrett's case. According to a transcript of the phone conversation, Detective Merifield warned her that it was a "tough case," because she and Zeke Adams were the only witnesses. Based on

Adams's level of intoxication, Merifield said, and what Barrett had told the officers, "It seems very, very clear" that Barrett's account was "a very believable story," and that the events she described actually happened. Merifield cautioned, however, that the case was going to be "very, very difficult" to prosecute. "Shy of him confessing," she said, "we have nothing to go on."

Nevertheless, Detective Merifield told Barrett that if she wanted to go forward with the case, Merifield would ask Adams to come to the police station to give a statement. "At the very least," Merifield explained, she might be able to "scare the shit out of him," and thereby prevent him from sexually assaulting someone else.

"This was very discouraging to hear," Barrett said. "I felt like I was getting the brush-off, like they weren't serious about pursuing it. I told the detective I wasn't sure what I wanted to do, and she said, 'Well, think about it for a few days and let me know.' "

Initially, Barrett wasn't sure if she wanted Zeke Adams to be charged with a crime. She said, "I remember thinking, 'Yes, what he did was wrong. But he seemed like a nice guy. Maybe it was just a misunderstanding.' " As Barrett replayed that night in her mind, however, she recalled that before she'd fallen asleep in Adams's bed, he had assured her that he was trustworthy and "nothing would happen." And then, some thirty minutes later, she woke up to him sexually assaulting her. No, she told herself, it definitely wasn't a misunderstanding. Adams had intentionally deceived her.

"The only reason Zeke didn't rape me is because I woke up," Barrett said. For all she knew, Zeke Adams was a serial predator who made a habit of luring women into his bed in this fashion. She decided that he should be held accountable for his actions, and she notified Detective Merifield that she wanted to pursue charges against him.

Detective Merifield didn't find time to interview Kerry Barrett until October 13, 2011, twenty days after Barrett reported the attempted rape. After taking Barrett's statement, Merifield phoned Zeke Adams to get his side of the story, but couldn't reach him.

So on October 26 she went to Adams's apartment and left a note asking him to call her.

Adams phoned Merifield the next day. When Officer Vreeland had tried to talk to Adams on September 23, two hours after the alleged assault, Adams was belligerent and uncooperative. According to the report Detective Merifield filed, however, his manner was quite different five weeks later, when she talked to him on the phone:

> Zeke became very emotional. . . . He seemed genuinely shocked that he was being accused of assaulting Kerry Barrett. During the course of our phone call it sounded as though he was crying several different times. . . . He said that he felt bad if she felt uncomfortable but maintained that he never assaulted her. Zeke said he would come in as soon as possible to give a statement because he wanted this cleared up. . . . Due to Zeke's emotional state and apparent inability to process what was happening, I asked him if he was going to be okay over the weekend. I also asked Zeke if he was suicidal. He assured me he was not suicidal.

Zeke Adams came to the police station and gave a recorded statement to Detective Merifield on October 31. She began by assuring him, "I think this is just a big misunderstanding. . . . If there were charges, I would only recommend misdemeanor charges." Merifield inquired, "Have you ever been arrested before?"

Adams replied, "I have not." This was not true. He had been arrested in December 2008 for petty theft. Merifield didn't check his criminal history, however, and accepted his statement at face value.

Merifield asked how many drinks Adams had consumed before he met Barrett at Sean Kelly's, but Adams declined to answer. "I feel like these questions are just going to get me in trouble," he explained.

"When the officers came and talked to you that night you seemed pretty intoxicated," she reminded him. "What I need to know is if you had a lot to drink and your memory is affected. Do you think you had a good memory of everything that happened?"

"Yes," Adams asserted. "I could, for example, tell you specific things about what happened. Like I remember she was from New Jersey. . . . I believe she was, like, a biology major." (Barrett's major was psychology.) "My memory is pretty clear."

Clear or not, Adams's recollections of the evening closely matched Barrett's account up to the point where she became uncomfortable with the escalating sexual activity, announced she was leaving, and then changed her mind after Adams promised "nothing would happen" and urged her to spend the night. But Adams steadfastly denied Barrett's claim that he subsequently attempted to have intercourse with her while she was asleep.

"I did not try to have sex with her," he told Detective Merifield. "When she laid back down on my bed, I kissed her some more, and then she said, 'No I have to go.' . . . She grabbed the remainder of her things and left my house. . . . I can say with one hundred percent confidence that I did not intend to hurt her, harm her, do anything to her that she did not want to be done to her." At this point, Adams broke down and started to cry. "She didn't express to me in any way that I had done any of those things," he insisted through his tears. "When she left my house, if anything, I thought, you know, it just appeared to me like she felt like, uh— She didn't, you know, she was in a situation, she was like, 'OK, this might not morally be the right thing to do.' "

"Did she seem mad, Zeke?" Merifield asked. "Did she slam the door?"

"I mean, she left, like, in a manner— She kind of said, 'No, I need to go,' " Adams replied. "And I mean that honestly! I am not lying to you!"

"I believe you," Merifield said sympathetically. "At any point after you kissed her and she laid back down did she say no?"

"She told me, 'I don't and can't have sex with you.' And I did not try to have sex with her. I absolutely did not."

"Did you ever rub your penis on her back?"

"No," Adams said.

"Did you ever, while she was sleeping, pull her pants down?"

"No."

"Okay. During the time when you were messing around earlier, did she touch you at all? Kind of rubbing on you too?"

"Yes."

"How long do you think you guys were back on the bed before she got up and left?"

After a six-second pause, Adams answered, "I'm not exactly sure."

"Did she ever fall asleep while she was at your house?" Detective Merifield asked.

Adams remained silent for a full ten seconds before replying to this question. "I will say it this way," he finally declared. "At no point did I think that while I touched her, had any contact with her whatsoever, she was asleep." He continued to deny Barrett's allegations for a few more minutes, and then reflected, "I really don't think that girl is a liar. . . . I just don't know that exactly everything she said to you was a fact. And I'm not trying to say that she is some kind of bad person or anything like that. I just think she might be a little mistaken."

Merifield wholeheartedly agreed. "I think it truly was a misunderstanding," she said. "I really don't think that there was any intent on your part to get this girl home so you could have sex with her whether she wanted to or not."

"Certainly not," Adams confirmed. "Absolutely none."

"Clearly," Merifield expounded, "there is a size difference between the two of you, so if you wanted to do that, you could have. . . . People have had sex they didn't want to have. It doesn't mean it was rape."

Sobbing, Adams said, "I had absolutely no intention whatsoever of harming that girl or violating her or making her feel uncomfortable. If she feels that way, I feel bad that it happened. I'm a good moral person. . . . I told you absolute facts that I am confident in. I came here because I have a true belief in essentially my innocence. That I didn't break the law."

"I totally understand," Detective Merifield said.

Despite having suggested to Kerry Barrett that the point of asking Adams to come to the police station was to "scare the shit out of him," throughout the interview Merifield went out of her way to comfort Adams. She never challenged his statements aggressively, or probed for details that might reveal whether or not he pulled down Barrett's jeans while she was sleeping. Instead, again and again Merifield let him know that she was certain he was innocent.

"You are kind of an open book right now," Merifield told Adams, "and you have been since I talked to you on [the phone four days earlier]. . . . It says a lot for your character that you came in and sat and talked to me this morning. . . . I can guarantee you I am not recommending this case for charges. . . . I can't show criminal intent. I really don't believe you had any intent to hurt anybody. . . . You seem like you are a really good person with a really good future ahead of you."

Merifield said, "We have a lot of cases where girls come in and report stuff they are not sure about, and then it becomes rape. And it's not fair. It's not fair to you. . . . You guys both went into this together. . . . She came home willingly with you. The fact that she changed her mind and went home on her own, . . . that's not your fault.

"But I have to interview you," Merifield explained a moment later, apologetically. "I have to talk to her because she came in and reported it. If I had just flushed the case, she's going to say the police don't do anything. . . . That's not the message we want to send to people: 'Well, we're only going to half-ass your case because we don't really believe this happened.' "

Merifield stated to Adams, "I don't think you did anything wrong. I think that it's torturing you that you are accused of this.

And that bothers me. . . . The case, in my opinion, is closed. . . . This case is going to be listed as unfounded. I think this is just a misunderstanding. I don't think it's a crime."

"I'm a good kid," Zeke Adams insisted. Sobbing, he said he didn't want his name to show up on computer screens for the rest of his life as a sex offender. "I don't want to do that to my mom and dad. . . . I don't see in any way how I'm guilty."

"You are not," Merifield reassured him. "Men and women think completely differently," she offered. "Men are much more concrete. . . . In women's minds we tend to spin things around, and turn it, and talk to our friends about it. And get advice and then sometimes create situations that maybe we read a hell of a lot more into." Well-meaning but overwrought friends, she explained, often urge women to report incidents that are not serious enough to warrant investigation by the police.

"As far as I'm concerned this case is closed," Merifield pronounced. "Don't beat yourself up more than you already have about this, okay? It's a done deal, bud. I don't think you did anything wrong."

WHEN DETECTIVE MERIFIELD called Kerry Barrett and told her there was insufficient evidence to charge Zeke Adams with sexual assault, and that the case was essentially closed, Barrett was dumbfounded. She understood that it would have been difficult to convince a jury that Adams had sexually assaulted her. "I was drinking," she admitted, "and that works against victims. We fooled around consensually before he assaulted me—I was very up-front about that—and that also worked against me. But after I made it clear that I didn't want it to go any farther, and he told me nothing would happen, he tried to rape me while I was sleeping. Which is a crime. And now I'll never know how strong my case actually was, because the police wouldn't even conduct a thorough investigation. That's the frustrating part.

"If it was consensual," Barrett added, "I want to know how

Zeke explains me running out of his room, crying hysterically at three in the morning." Barrett had given Detective Merifield a list of witnesses, including Adams's roommate, who could presumably corroborate aspects of her story, yet nobody from the Missoula Police Department had bothered to interview any of these witnesses.

As Katie J. M. Baker observed in her *Jezebel* article, "In Missoula . . . drunk guys who may have 'made mistakes' nearly always get the benefit of the doubt. Drunk girls, however, do not."

Compounding Barrett's frustration, as she thought back on the night in question, she came to realize that she didn't know what Zeke Adams had actually done to her while she was asleep, before she was awakened by him rubbing his penis on her back and buttocks. "I was asleep for what I assume to be twenty to thirty minutes," she said. The fact that he'd managed to unbutton her tight jeans, tug them down to her ankles, and then pull down her underwear—all without waking her—made Barrett worry that Adams might have also taken other liberties while she was unconscious. "I was bleeding for a whole day afterward," she recalled. "The officer at the police department asked if I was hurt and needed immediate medical attention, but I said no. At the time, I was too traumatized to consider what might have been done to me before I woke up."

IN THE WEEKS after she reported that she had been sexually assaulted, Barrett sank into a miasma of gloom. Some mornings she was too despondent to get out of bed. She found herself sobbing on the floor of her bathroom for hours on end. She stopped going to many of her classes, which was completely out of character for her. Barrett had been awarded two very competitive scholarships to attend the University of Montana, almost never missed a class, and had earned a 4.0 grade point average the year before Zeke Adams persuaded her to spend the night at his apartment.

As she struggled with depression in the period that followed,

Barrett told me, "I was a phone call away from dropping out of school and going back to New Jersey. I started drinking a lot, way too much. And engaging in other really risky behavior. . . . You hear that rape victims avoid sex afterwards. But it's actually just as common for some victims to become promiscuous in self-destructive ways. That's what happened to me."

Some rape victims do indeed react to their traumas by turning away from sexual intimacy. Paradoxically, however, many others start engaging in dangerous, indiscriminate sex. Judith Lewis Herman is a professor of psychiatry at Harvard Medical School and the author of the groundbreaking book *Trauma and Recovery*. Commonly, Herman writes,

> traumatized people find themselves reenacting some aspect of the trauma scene in disguised form, without realizing what they are doing. . . . There is something uncanny about reenactments. Even when they are consciously chosen, they have a feeling of involuntariness. Freud named this recurrent intrusion of traumatic experience the "repetition compulsion."

Sigmund Freud believed it was an unconscious attempt to gain control over the traumatic event and thereby extinguish it. As Bessel A. van der Kolk, MD, one of the preeminent authorities on post-traumatic stress, explains,

> Many traumatized people expose themselves, seemingly compulsively, to situations reminiscent of the original trauma. . . . Freud thought the aim of repetition was to gain mastery, but clinical experience has shown that this rarely happens; instead, repetition causes further suffering for the victims or for people in their surroundings.

In her case, Barrett said, recalling the aftermath of the assault, "My life was falling apart. But somehow I stuck it out. My professors were very understanding. They let me take some incompletes and withdraw from classes."

Barrett began seeing a therapist, which proved helpful. She also found it therapeutic to speak out—and not just about her own ordeal, but about other women who had been victimized, too.

CHAPTER SEVEN

For the first several days after Zeke Adams allegedly tried to rape Kerry Barrett, she seldom left her off-campus apartment. When she finally emerged and ventured back onto the grounds of the university, she had a chance encounter with Kaitlynn Kelly, a smart, feisty junior she had known since the fall of 2009. "She was crying," Barrett said, "which was unbelievable to me, because Kaitlynn is the toughest girl I have ever met. So I knew something very serious had happened to her." When Barrett inquired why Kelly was upset, she confided to Barrett that three days earlier she had been raped.

Kaitlynn Kelly lived in Turner Hall, a three-story, all-female dormitory on the UM campus. On September 30, 2011, a Friday night, she attended a party at a house in the Rattlesnake district, a quiet residential neighborhood northeast of downtown Missoula. Kelly arrived at about 9:30, knocked back some shots of tequila and cheap whiskey over the next five hours, and then took a taxi back to the university early Saturday morning with a gay friend named Greg Witt.* Once they were back on campus, Kelly and Witt sat down on a bench in front of Jesse Hall, near her dorm, so Kelly could smoke a cigarette before returning to her room. When she searched her purse and realized she'd left her cigarettes at the party, Witt offered to beg a smoke for her.

* pseudonym

Around 3:00 a.m., two freshmen walked by, Calvin Smith* and Ralph Richards,† who were stinking drunk. When Witt asked if they had a spare cigarette, Smith—a tall, beefy eighteen-year-old—replied that neither of them were smokers, then sat down next to Kelly. Richards sat next to Witt.

Greg Witt, who is convivial and forward, struck up a conversation with the two younger students, and the subject turned to sex. Kaitlynn Kelly remarked that Calvin Smith was "a cutie." Witt suggested to Smith and Kelly that they ought to hook up, because she hadn't slept with anyone in over a year and, in Witt's humble opinion, getting laid would be good for both of them.

Egged on by Greg Witt, Kaitlynn Kelly invited Calvin Smith up to her room, and Smith responded enthusiastically. According to Kelly, Smith said, "Let's go!" and they started walking across a parking lot to her dorm. In a statement the UM dean of students asked Kelly to write a couple of weeks later, she described what ensued:

> Calvin had his arm around me as we got to the door. I swiped us both inside [with her student key-card]. Calvin and I went up to my room. We walked in and saw that my roommate and her boyfriend were asleep in her bed. I told Calvin that we could not do anything because they were here. He said, "It's okay, we'll be quiet." I said no.
>
> Calvin then proceeded to lay in my bed. I got in next to him, tapped him to move over so that I could fit, and he moved over. I believe at this point I fell asleep. I woke up to Calvin repeatedly violently penetrating my vagina with three of his fingers. I tried to pull his hand away with my right hand, telling him, "stop, no" multiple times. Calvin continued to penetrate me despite my efforts to pull him away and tell him to stop. Then he proceeded to violently penetrate my

* pseudonym

† pseudonym

> anus with the same force and motion. I again tried to pull his hand away. He then stated, "it's okay, I just want to make you squirt." He then sat up against my wall and pulled me by my arm over to his penis. He then forced me to perform fellatio on him by pushing my head down. I was in pain and gagging. I finally was able to pull away and lay down. Calvin then got on top of me and tried to have sex with me. When he went to penetrate my vagina, I was in excruciating pain. I pushed him away with my right forearm and stated loudly that I had to pee. I got up and put on a pair of shorts, and then went to the bathroom down the hall.
>
> Calvin followed me into the bathroom. There were no words spoken, but he peeked over the stall and stared at me. Then he left as I was still peeing. This was the last I saw him.
>
> I came back into my room. When I entered, my roommate, Nancy, was standing and staring at my sheets with a horrifying look on her face. I then looked over and saw my sheets covered in blood. . . . I started crying hysterically and I walked over into the study lounge across the hall. I sat on the couch and cried. My roommate came in and asked if I was okay and if I wanted to go to the hospital. I said I just wanted to go to sleep.

"I was in a lot of pain—it was extreme," Kelly told me. "When I finally pushed Calvin off of me, I ran down the hall to the bathroom and locked myself in one of the stalls. It hurt so much when I was urinating that I was crying hysterically from the pain. He followed me into the bathroom, looked over the top of the stall, and saw me crying. I don't think he said anything. I just sat there on the toilet with my head down, bawling. I ended up bleeding for three days." After Calvin Smith left her dormitory, Kelly said, she returned to her room "and tried to pass out for a little bit, because I was really tired."

Later Saturday morning, when she woke up after sleeping for a couple of hours, she became unhinged at what she saw in the light of day. "There was blood on the pillow I was laying on," she later recalled in a tearful interview with Detective Connie Brueckner of the Missoula Police Department. "I looked up, and there was blood on my wall above my head. And then I sat up really quick. And I looked at my side and there was blood on that wall, to my right. I jumped out of my bed . . . and there was blood all over my sheets. . . . So I instantly got up and I took the Germ-X wipes, and cleaned my walls really good. And then as I was sobbing I took all my sheets and my pillow case off and I put them in a white Walmart bag, or maybe it was a bag from the grocery store on campus, and I shoved them all in there and put them down the trash chute."

After cleaning the walls and disposing of the sheets, Kaitlynn Kelly noticed that her jeans and belt were missing. "I was really confused why he took my pants," she said. "I can't get over that." She went for a drive with her roommate, Nancy Jones,* to try to clear her head. "I didn't understand what had been done to me," Kelly reflected. "I kept asking Nancy, 'What happened?' She said, 'You were raped.' "

Even after Nancy put it that plainly, Kelly said, "It took me a couple of days to comprehend it. On Monday, Nancy convinced me to go into Curry Health Center to get a rape kit done." At Curry a physician documented severe vaginal and rectal pain, vaginal bleeding, and abrasions to her inner thighs and vaginal vault. But Kelly didn't want to report the rape to the police.

On Tuesday, Kaitlynn Kelly ran into Kerry Barrett and told her what had transpired. At that point, Barrett said, "Kaitlynn didn't know who Calvin was, didn't know his last name, didn't know where he lived. And she was scared for her life, because it had happened in her room, and she didn't know if he was going to come back." Although Barrett urged Kelly to report the assault, Kelly resisted. "She worried she might get in trouble," Barrett said, "because she'd been drinking and she was underage, only twenty at the time. And she didn't think the cops would believe her story."

* pseudonym

Kerry Barrett, concerned that the man who raped her friend would never be held accountable, decided to take matters into her own hands. There was a security camera trained on the door Kaitlynn Kelly and Calvin Smith had used to enter Turner Hall. "So I called up campus security and asked them how long they kept the tapes from their cameras," Barrett said. "At which point they kind of roped me into telling them why I wanted to know." When Barrett disclosed what had happened to Kelly, a campus safety officer drove over to Barrett's apartment and brought her in to review the security footage.

It didn't take long for Barrett to identify Kelly on the video, entering Turner Hall with a large young man at 3:27 a.m. "We saw the guy who raped her enter the dorm with his arm around her," Barrett said. "She looked very, very drunk. And then about half an hour later we saw the rapist go out the door with her pants in his hand." Apparently, he took them as a trophy of his conquest.

Barrett hadn't told Kelly that she'd gone to the campus police. She made it clear to the safety officer who'd shown her the video that Kelly didn't want to report the rape, and she begged him not to contact Kelly. He agreed, promising that he would save the footage so it would be available if Kelly changed her mind.

A day later, Barrett confessed to Kelly what she'd done, explained that the video of the rapist was being preserved, and related that the campus police had assured her that Kelly wouldn't get in trouble. After some deliberation, Kelly reconsidered and decided to report the assault to the campus police. Because the alleged crime was a felony, the UM police immediately turned the case over to the Missoula Police Department, which dispatched Officer Randy Krastel to Kelly's dorm room to take a statement and collect whatever evidence still existed.

By now, five days had passed since Kaitlynn Kelly had allegedly been raped. "I'd thrown away my blood-soaked sheets because I was disgusted and I didn't know what to do," she told me. "But I gave the cops my bloody shorts, my bloody underwear, my bloody T-shirt. They also took my two-inch-thick memory-foam mattress that was soaked all the way through with blood." Officer Krastel interviewed Kelly, Kerry Barrett, and Kelly's roommate and took photographs of the crime scene.

The accused rapist, Calvin Smith, had graduated from a small-town high school the previous June, where he'd distinguished himself as an athlete. Individuals who knew Smith have described him as "kind," "easygoing," and "goofy." But he had never had sex before meeting Kaitlynn Kelly, and a look at what he has posted on a social media site suggests that he was a frustrated, involuntary celibate. On January 11, 2011, Smith posted a line from the animated sitcom *Family Guy* on his Facebook page: "women are not people god just put them here for mans entertainment."

When a Facebook friend commented that the actual line is "Women are not people. They are devices built by the Lord Jesus Christ for our entertainment," Smith replied, "Ahhh I wish I had that power."

AFTER OFFICER KRASTEL visited her dormitory, Kaitlynn Kelly was asked to come downtown to the police station to talk to Detective Connie Brueckner, a highly regarded, eight-year veteran of the Missoula police force. The interview, which was recorded, lasted forty-two minutes. Brueckner was thorough, and asked probing questions, but she presented them in a sensitive, supportive manner. When Kelly admitted that she had agreed to have sex with Calvin Smith before they entered her dorm, Brueckner inquired, "What were you thinking at that time?"

"That it was going to be a good time," Kelly replied.

"What did you think was going to happen?"

"Probably, maybe, have sex."

"Were you okay with that idea at the time?"

"I was," Kelly answered. "That's why I let him in my room."

"Did that change?" Brueckner asked. "That feeling?"

"Yeah," Kelly said. "I guess when we got in my room. Because my roommate and her boyfriend were in the room. They were, like, snoring. Passed out. And I told him, 'My roommate and her boyfriend are here. We can't do anything.' And he told me, 'It's okay. We'll be quiet.' "

"What did you think of that?" Brueckner asked.

"Not okay," Kelly answered.

Detective Brueckner assured Kaitlynn Kelly that it was understandable and acceptable for her to have changed her mind about having sex once they entered the dorm room. Then she asked Kelly, "If your roommate wasn't there, would you have been okay with it?"

"No," Kelly declared without hesitating. "As soon as we walked in the dorm, I was like, 'No! I don't want to do this.' . . . I told him, 'You can just lay on my bed until the morning.' "

"And what did he say to that?" Brueckner asked.

"Well, he got on my bed and lay down," Kelly answered. "And I got next to him and lay down."

Detective Brueckner asked if she and Calvin Smith went to bed with their clothes on.

"Yes," Kelly answered. "I don't know what happened after that, but the next thing I remember is waking up with his fingers inside of me, with a stabbing motion, very roughly."

"Inside your vagina?"

"Yes," Kelly said.

Brueckner asked what happened to the clothing she had been wearing when she got in bed.

"When I woke up?" Kelly said. "I didn't have pants on, but my shirt was still on."

"And what happened when you realized that was happening?" Brueckner asked.

"I kept reaching for his hand and pulling it away," Kelly explained, demonstrating with her hands. "I kept grabbing at his thumb and pulling, like, towards him. To get him off of me. But he kept, like, coming back."

"Did he say anything?" Detective Brueckner asked.

According to Kaitlynn Kelly, Calvin Smith told her, "No, just wait. Just wait."

"Were you saying anything?" Brueckner asked.

"I was saying, 'Stop!' " Kelly insisted. "And then—"

"How loud were you guys?" Brueckner interrupted.

"I don't think I was very loud," Kelly replied. She paused for a moment before explaining, ruefully, "Because my roommate was there, I didn't want to wake them up. I just wanted it to stop. And then he went in my rear, with his hands doing the same stabbing motion."

A little later, Detective Brueckner again inquired why Kaitlynn Kelly hadn't done more to alert her roommate and her roommate's boyfriend, who were asleep a few feet away in the same room. "I have to ask obvious questions," Brueckner apologized, "because these are questions people would ask. . . . You're using a quiet voice when you're telling him to stop. I can understand to some degree. But tell me what was your thinking there? Why weren't you just screaming loud? It certainly would have stopped things."

"I don't know," Kelly said. "To tell you the truth, I just don't know. I was very scared."

"Did he ever make any threats to you?" Brueckner asked.

"No," Kelly replied.

"I don't mean to ask you that question to make you feel bad," Brueckner persisted. "It's just—it's easy to think through things now and go, 'I could have done this,' or whatever. But things were happening."

"I feel really bad about throwing my sheets away," Kelly said, breaking into tears as she realized how inexplicable her silence must seem to someone who hadn't been in her position. "I didn't know what to do. I just wanted to forget about it, like it didn't happen. It was really hard for me to even report it."

In fact, psychologists and psychiatrists who study sexual assault report that victims frequently react to being raped much the way Kaitlynn Kelly did. In a 2012 presentation in Baltimore, David Lisak—a clinical psychologist and forensic consultant who is an expert on the subject of acquaintance rape—explained to a roomful of prosecutors, defense attorneys, police officers, and health-care professionals that when people are raped, the experience is so traumatic that it often causes them to behave in a wide variety of ways that may seem inexplicable. "How many people have ever heard a rape victim say, 'I felt paralyzed'?" Lisak asked the room. "How many have ever heard a rape victim say, 'I wanted to scream, and I couldn't'? How many people here who treat trauma victims have heard them say, 'I had a nightmare last night; I was trying to run away and I couldn't move'?"

When a rape occurs in a dorm room, Lisak said, investigators often determine that the victim could have gotten out of bed with apparent ease and fled the room. But "the fact that they didn't immediately make a break for it, or the fact that they didn't scream—none of those things necessarily mean that this was a consensual encounter."

After Lisak spoke, his colleague Russell Strand, a sexual-crimes expert who heads the Family Advocacy Law Enforcement Training Division at the U.S. Army Military Police School, told the same roomful of people a story about a military couple who threw a party at their house. One of the guests, a soldier, became too drunk to go home. The husband and wife escorted him down to their basement and offered him a couch to sleep on, where he promptly passed out, after which they went back upstairs and fell asleep in their own bed, with their four-year-old son lying beside them.

In the middle of the night, the wife woke up to discover that the drunk party guest was lying next to her with his fingers in her vagina, masturbating her, as her husband and son slept in the same bed. She was horrified but said nothing. She lay there in silence for the next fifteen minutes while he continued to penetrate her with his fingers. Defense attorneys for the assailant built their case around the fact that she could have immediately stopped the assault by waking her husband but had remained mute instead.

Prosecutors took the case to trial, regardless, put the wife on the witness stand, and addressed the issue, head-on, by skillfully framing their questions to elicit an honest explanation that would resonate with the jury. According to Strand, one of the prosecutors began by telling her, "Help me understand what you are able to remember about your experience."

"Well, his fingers were in my vagina," the woman said.

The prosecutor asked, "What were you thinking when you woke up and realized, 'His fingers are in my vagina'?"

She answered that she was thinking, "Oh my God, I hope my husband doesn't wake up. . . . He would have killed this guy, and my four-year-old son laying next to me, his life would have been ruined, my life would have been ruined, and my husband's life would have been ruined. So my first thought was 'I hope he doesn't wake up.' "

This testimony, Strand said, caused the assailant's case to fall apart, and he was convicted.

AS DETECTIVE CONNIE BRUECKNER continued interviewing Kaitlynn Kelly, Kelly became unglued. Brueckner tried to comfort her by praising her for reporting the assault. "What happened isn't okay," Brueckner offered. "I can see that you're upset. You are a strong gal, and you probably have very good judgment most of the time. . . . There's some Kleenex there if you need it."

Then Brueckner pointed out that the case was going to be tricky to prosecute because both Kelly and Calvin Smith were drunk. "I'm sorry he didn't hear you [when you said no]," Brueckner said. "But the good thing coming of this is, you're not stuffing it someplace where it is going to come back later in your life. . . . You've got a good, supportive family. And there are great services on campus. . . . And you can move past this, I'm sure. It's much better to do that now than try to deal with it five years from now."

"I just don't want him to do it to anybody else," Kaitlynn Kelly wept. Just twenty-one minutes into the interview, before Detective Brueckner had even talked to the assailant, it seemed to Kelly as though Brueckner had already decided not to charge Calvin Smith with any crime.

"We will talk to him, absolutely," Brueckner assured Kelly.

But then she added, "I can't guarantee you this is going to turn into some big thing where he's going to go to jail. . . . Some people come in here and they're like, 'I want him in jail!' . . . And it's not easy to just throw people in jail when it's a 'he said, she said' scenario. But we will bring him in, and it will be very clear to him that [this] kind of behavior is unacceptable. And that he needs to be certain when he's engaging in anything sexual with anybody, that that person is okay with it."

Detective Brueckner told Kelly that her safety and well-being were Brueckner's primary concern, followed by making Calvin Smith understand that what he did wasn't acceptable. Putting him in jail, Brueckner said, was much less important: "To me that is sort of secondary to everything else that's going on here. Do you agree with that?"

Kelly did not agree if it meant letting Smith off with nothing more than a lecture on accountability. "I don't know how," she protested to Brueckner, "he couldn't hear me saying, 'Stop!,' because, like, his face was right next to mine."

"I'm sure he did," Brueckner replied, but then she suggested that Smith, in his inebriated condition, might not have understood that Kelly was withdrawing the consent she'd given earlier.

Kaitlynn Kelly objected that Calvin Smith must have understood. "I don't think he cared," she said.

"And that's the problem with these kinds of cases," Detective Brueckner argued. "You can't give consent when you are so doped up, or high, or drunk that you have no idea. . . . It is pretty simple. But it gets clouded when everyone is intoxicated." As the interview drew to a close, Brueckner told Kelly, "Tuesday I'll give him a call and have him come down here and get his statement. Like I said, these aren't easy cases. But I want him to go through this, and make it clear that, no matter what he says, or what you said or did, you were too drunk to consent. And it sounds to me . . . that you never even consented. So it's not even an issue. . . . Are you going home this weekend?"

"No," Kelly replied. "If I go home, I will not come back. . . .

My mom wants me to drop out and come home. My mom is devastated."

"You seem like a strong girl. I think you can hang in there and get through it. . . . As horrible as this is, as hard as it is right now, what you're doing . . . will have a positive effect on people. . . . And certainly Calvin is going to know that this is completely unacceptable. . . . And you know what? His friends he tells that he's going to be coming down here to talk to the police? Well, they are going to know, too, . . . that this is not okay. One bad thing like this can actually have a good and healthy ripple effect on people, and hopefully prevent this kind of thing from happening to others."

DETECTIVE BRUECKNER PHONED Calvin Smith and left a voice-mail message asking him to call her back because she "had a few questions" she wanted to ask him. In August 2014, when Smith met with me to talk about his encounter with Kaitlynn Kelly, he said he wasn't concerned about the voice mail. He'd been so drunk during his hookup with Kaitlynn Kelly ten days earlier that he didn't remember much about it. But he was certain the sex had been consensual, and he was pretty sure Kelly had enjoyed it. When Brueckner called, Smith told me, "I assumed it was about the pants."

According to Smith, he'd consumed alcohol only once when he was in high school, because, as a serious athlete, he'd been careful to avoid things that would have a negative effect on his performance. But after enrolling at the University of Montana, in August 2011, he decided, "Well, I might as well do the drinking thing, now that I'm out of sports." During his first month in Missoula, Smith said, he got drunk "probably four or five times"—pretty much every weekend. Then, on September 30—the night he met Kaitlynn Kelly—Smith went big. He got totally shit-faced. "Never had that much to drink in my life," he said. "I remember being pretty drunk and not being able to walk too straight. I don't know how I didn't throw up."

As Calvin Smith recalled that night, around 9:00 he went to a friend's off-campus house, where he began playing beer pong. He estimates he had ten to twelve beers before returning to his dormitory, shortly after midnight, with his friend Ralph Richards, whereupon Smith had two shots of rum with some guys who lived across the hall. At that point Smith and Richards decided to leave the dorm and hang out on the plaza outside nearby Jesse Hall, Smith said, "because there is always things happening in front of there, and people to talk to, and fun stuff happening."

After bumping into Kaitlynn Kelly and agreeing to have sex with her, according to Smith, "she basically carried me up to her room. Because I could barely walk myself at that point. I was kind of leaning on her. . . . So we go up to her room and lay down on her bed. At that point things got kind of . . ." Smith paused for a moment, then reiterated that he was so hammered he can't recall much about what happened next.

On October 14, Smith went to the police station to be interviewed by Detective Brueckner. What Smith told her about how he ended up in Kelly's dormitory closely matches what Kelly told Brueckner. Concerning what happened after they entered her room, however, Smith's account and Kelly's account are difficult to reconcile. According to a page-and-a-half summary of Brueckner's interview with Smith that she submitted with her case report,

> Smith described a very open discussion with the girl about having sex. . . . Smith's impression of the girl was that she was not intoxicated. . . .
>
> He described her room as dark and recalled her bed was pushed up against the wall. Smith did not think anyone else was in the room. He remembered making out with the girl on her bed. He stated they both took their pants off. Smith clarified that he "might" have taken her pants off for her. Smith stated the female was lying down on the bed and he was at her feet. He stated he used his fingers to penetrate her vagina. He did not believe he penetrated her anus. Smith

stated the female was not saying anything but was moaning. He stated it was his impression she was consenting to his sexual contact. Smith reported the female gave him oral sex at one point. He denied ejaculating but admitted to having an erection. Smith stated he never held her down or prevented her from leaving. He recalled she "moved by herself."

Smith stated he and the female "made out" some more after which she asked him to leave. He recalled asking her if she was sure, to which she replied yes. He recalled getting up and leaving her dorm. Smith did not initially recall going into the bathroom in the dormitory. He later stated he remembers "as if in a dream" that he was in the girls' bathroom. He clarified that it was a memory, but he remembered it as a dream and did not think it had really happened. Smith recalled following the girl to the bathroom and then returning to her bedroom. When I informed Smith that the girl had reported she was crying in the bathroom, Smith became visibly distraught and tearful. He began to cry and stated he was very sorry she was upset and never meant to hurt her or make her sad. He seemed genuine in his emotions. It was clear from speaking to Smith that he was surprised at the accusations and disturbed that her experience was that their contact was non-consensual. . . . Smith later stated he may have attempted to have sexual intercourse with the girl at which point he recalled she asked him to leave. He described this as a "turning point" in their encounter. Smith confirmed that he left when she asked.

Smith did not initially report taking the girl's jeans. When confronted about the clothing, Smith stated that he did take the jeans when he left her room. He stated he was embarrassed by his actions. He explained that he had never had sex before and took the jeans as proof to his friends. He recalled swinging the jeans around in his dorm room after he returned from Turner Hall. Smith said he disposed of her jeans the next day.

> Smith did not recall having any blood on his hands when he left the girl's dorm room. He stated he later discovered some on his hands and jeans. He felt it was perhaps due to her being on her menstrual cycle. Smith stated that when he left Turner Hall he walked to Noon's [a twenty-four-hour gas station and convenience store nine blocks away] and then returned to his dorm room.
>
> Smith appeared extremely upset at the end of the interview. He was very concerned about the consequences of the investigation. He repeatedly expressed how sorry he was and a desire to let the girl know he never meant any harm. Smith realized he had made mistakes. He stated he should not have been drinking nor should he have been sexual with someone else who may have been drinking. Smith understood that taking the girl's jeans was wrong.

During his interview with Detective Brueckner, Calvin Smith told me, she repeatedly asked if Kelly ever said "no or anything like that. And I was like, 'No. . . . I would have stopped if she said no.' I did stop, at the end, when she said she didn't want to anymore." Smith said Brueckner and another detective "kept asking me weird questions, like if I had any blood on me or anything. . . . But it wasn't enough to, like, worry me or anything. And then, basically at the end of it, they were like, 'She is saying that you raped her.' "* That was the point, Smith recalled, when "I started crying and freaking out."

Smith's uncontrollable sobbing prompted Brueckner to turn off her tape recorder and inquire, off the record, if there was any

* In Montana, the legal term for rape is "sexual intercourse without consent." Sexual intercourse is defined as "penetration of the vulva, anus, or mouth by the penis of another person, penetration of the vulva or anus . . . by a body member of another person, or penetration of the vulva or anus . . . by a foreign instrument or object . . . to knowingly or purposely . . . cause bodily injury or humiliate, harass, or degrade; or . . . arouse or gratify the sexual response or desire of either party. . . . [A]ny penetration, however slight, is sufficient."

risk that he might go home and commit suicide. When he assured her that he had no intention of killing himself, according to Smith, she urged him not to worry about being prosecuted. "We still have a lot of investigating to do," she told him.

Over the next few weeks, Detective Brueckner interviewed Ralph Richards, Greg Witt, Smith's roommate, and a number of other witnesses. And then in early November, Brueckner phoned Kaitlynn Kelly to update her about the status of the case. "Basically," Kelly said, "she told me they didn't have enough evidence to charge Calvin. She said there was no DNA found on anything I gave them. . . . She made a big deal of the fact that I'd thrown my sheets away, as if that was the only evidence they had. She didn't say anything about my bloody clothes or the bloodstained mattress. . . . She didn't say anything about the forensics exam. . . . Nothing about the video of him walking out with my goddamn pants. She just shut me down. That was that. I got the shitty end of the stick."

After a victim has reported a crime to the police, many people believe that the decision whether or not to charge the suspect with a crime, and then prosecute the suspect, is the prerogative of the victim. News media often contribute to this misconception in stories about rape victims by reporting that a victim "declined to press charges." In fact, the criminal justice system gives victims no direct say in the matter. It's the police, for the most part, who decide whether a suspect should be arrested, and prosecutors who ultimately determine whether a conviction should be pursued.

To make an arrest and prosecute an individual in criminal court, the police and the prosecutor must possess enough evidence to lead a reasonable person to believe that the charge is probably true. This fundamental legal standard is commonly referred to as "probable cause." Brueckner's announcement that Calvin Smith would not be prosecuted because of a lack of probable cause was, and remains, hard to fathom. It would have been a challenging case to present to a jury, and it might have ended with Smith being acquitted. But rapists have been charged, prosecuted, tried, and legitimately convicted with much less evidence than the Missoula Police Department and the Missoula County attorney had at their disposal for assembling a case against Smith.

CHAPTER EIGHT

It was difficult for Kaitlynn Kelly to summon the courage to tell her mother and father that she'd been raped. "It was bad—probably the most pain I've ever put my parents through," she told me. Kelly's father was furious when he learned that the police had punted her case and no charges would be filed. He and Kaitlynn went to the Missoula Police Department to request a copy of her case report, she said, but the police refused to show them anything. "They just jerked us around. . . . My dad was livid."

Fortunately for Kaitlynn Kelly, she had reported the rape to the University of Montana in addition to the Missoula police, and the UM dean of students, Charles Couture, took her case seriously. On October 20, 2011, shortly after he met with Kelly, Dean Couture sent Calvin Smith a letter notifying him that

> I have initiated an investigation into the allegation that you have violated Section V.A. 18 of the University of Montana Student Conduct Code. Section V.A. 18 prohibits rape. Reportedly, on October 1, 2011, you raped Kaitlynn Kelly, in her room in Turner Hall.
>
> The fact that an investigation is underway should not be interpreted in any way as an indication my decision about the allegation has been reached, since the purpose of my investigation is in fact to decide whether the allegation is accurate.

> I have scheduled Wednesday, October 26, 2011, to meet with you at 10:00 A.M., in University (Main) Hall 022, to discuss the allegation and Student Conduct Code rules of procedure. You have the right to have a person of choice, including legal counsel, present throughout any and all of the proceedings. . . . Failure to meet with me would be a serious violation of the Student Conduct Code.
>
> Upon the conclusion of my investigation, if I have found sufficient evidence that you violated the Student Conduct Code as alleged, I intend to seek your immediate expulsion from the University. . . . In the interim, you are to have no contact of any kind with Ms. Kaitlynn Kelly, including third party.

Calvin Smith showed up for his October 26 meeting with Dean Couture alone. Because he hoped to extricate himself from the predicament without having to tell his parents about it, paying for a lawyer was out of the question. Smith had intended to bring his friend Ralph Richards along for support, but Richards was an important witness, and Couture wanted to interview him later, without Smith present. "So I went and talked to [Couture] by myself," Smith told me. "He was like, 'All right, I want to hear your side of the story.'"

Smith was adamant that Kaitlynn Kelly had consented to the sex they'd engaged in. Throughout their meeting, however, Dean Couture challenged Smith's assertions, working from what Kelly had already told him. Couture, Smith said, "just kept going on and on about how I needed to tell the truth, and it would just be faster if I told the truth. And then at the very end, he was like, 'Yeah, you're guilty. . . . Yup, yeah, you're going to get expelled.'"

For a significant part of this encounter with Dean Couture, Calvin Smith blubbered like a child, just as he had cried at the conclusion of his interview with Detective Brueckner. Smith repeatedly insisted that he had not raped Kaitlynn Kelly and tearfully begged Couture not to expel him. Afterward, realizing he was in way over his head, Smith confessed to his parents that he was in serious trouble.

When Calvin's mother, Mary Smith,* learned what was going on, she told me, "I seriously was in disbelief . . . I don't know how this could have happened. Especially with him. . . . He does not have a mean bone in his body." Mary and her husband retained a highly recommended Missoula attorney, Josh Van de Wetering, to represent Calvin for the remainder of the university's adjudication of his case.

On November 2, 2011, after interviewing Calvin Smith, Kaitlynn Kelly, and other witnesses, Dean Charles Couture sent Smith a letter that stated,

> Thank you for meeting with me recently to discuss the allegation that you violated The University of Montana Student Conduct Code. I have found sufficient evidence to support the allegation that you violated Section V.A. 18, by having raped Ms. Kaitlynn Kelly. . . . My finding and recommended sanctions are based, in part, on the following evidence:
>
> **1.** Detailed written account from the rape victim, Ms. Kelly, in which she stated that she and you went to her residence hall room to engage in voluntary sex; when she got there she saw that her roommate and her boyfriend were present and asleep, at which time she said "no" to sex because of their presence; she got into bed with you and she went to sleep, only to be awakened by you "repeatedly and violently penetrating her vagina with three fingers"; despite the victim telling you, "stop, no" multiple times, you continued to rape her; later you inserted your fingers into the victim's anus "with the same force and motion" as you continued to rape her

* pseudonym

2. Your admission to having consumed 10 to 12 beers during an alcohol drinking game called beer pong prior to the incident

3. Your admission to having consumed at least two shots of rum, in addition to the beer, prior to the incident

4. Your admission to having been "really, really drunk" during the incident

5. Your admission that you really didn't remember very much about the incident until sometime later

6. Your admission to having had oral sex with Ms. Kelly

7. Your admission to having inserted your fingers into Ms. Kelly's anus and vagina (you said you thought you used two fingers, after I informed you that Ms. Kelly said you used three fingers)

8. Your admission to having said to Ms. Kelly, "It's okay, I just want to make you squirt"; you said you saw some girls squirt in some pornography you had previously watched

9. Your admission to having followed Ms. Kelly into the female bathroom in Turner Hall after the incident and looking over the top of the stall and watching her while she urinated

10. Your admission to having taken Ms. Kelly's jeans with you back to your room in Craig Hall after the incident because you wanted a souvenir

11. Your admission to having awakened in your residence hall room and becoming aware of the jeans and not initially knowing whose they were or where they had come from

12. Your admission to later remembering how you obtained the jeans and how they got to your room

13. Your admission to having thrown the jeans away later, because why would someone want to keep them

14. Detailed written account from Ms. Kerry Barrett who viewed several bloody items taken from Ms. Kelly's room by a Missoula Police Officer; Ms. Barrett observed blood on a pillowcase, mattress pad, mattress, and "a large blood stain on one of the pairs of shorts the detective took"

15. Detailed notes taken from an interview with Ms. Nancy Jones, Ms. Kelly's roommate; Ms. Jones had been in her bed in a deep sleep during the incident; she was awakened when she heard the door to her room slam; she later observed a male (later identified as you) bend over and pick something up (later identified as Ms. Kelly's jeans and belt) and leave the room; Ms. Jones saw blood all over her roommate's sheets. Ms. Jones heard sobbing in the study lounge next door; she went in and found Ms. Kelly sobbing hysterically; Ms. Kelly told her what had happened; Ms. Kelly grabbed three fingers on one hand with her other hand, and told Ms. Jones that the unidentified male at the time (later identified as you) was "stabbing her" with his fingers. Ms. Jones said she noticed later that morning the bloody sheets were gone, and that Ms. Kelly had thrown them away

16. Ms. Kelly went to the Curry Health Center two days after having been raped because of pelvic pain

17. The attending physician found superficial abrasions and bruises on both of Ms. Kelly's inner thighs

18. The attending physician found abrasions within the "vaginal vault," and "very tender with any palpitation"

19. The victim's menses had not yet begun

20. The victim sought services from the Curry Health Center Student Assault Resource Center after her rape

Appropriate sanctions for such egregious behavior are:

1. Permanent expulsion from the University of Montana, effective immediately

2. No access to any University property or University-sponsored activity, effective immediately

> You have the opportunity to accept or deny the charge of having violated the Student Conduct Code and/or to accept the sanctions. If you deny the charge and/or [do] not accept the sanctions, you have the right to an administrative conference with the Vice President for Student Affairs, or her designee, and a hearing before the University Court. Please indicate how you wish to proceed by signing on the appropriate line below.

Calvin Smith denied the charge and asked to appeal Dean Couture's ruling at an administrative conference with the Vice President for Student Affairs, Teresa Branch, which was scheduled for November 7. At the conclusion of the conference, Vice President Branch concurred with Dean Couture that Smith was guilty of rape and should be expelled. According to Smith, Couture then offered him the university's equivalent of a plea deal: If he voluntarily withdrew from the university instead of forcing the institution to expel him, nothing about the rape would appear on Smith's record. Smith told me that he never even considered accepting the offer and explained to Couture, "I'm not going to say that I did this." Instead, Smith appealed Branch's ruling, as the Student Conduct Code allowed, to a higher body called the University Court. A hearing before this court was scheduled for the afternoon of November 18, 2011.

BY DESIGN, the UM adjudication process differs in crucial ways from the way rape cases are handled in the criminal justice system. When the administrators of a university are confronted with a rape allegation, they are likely to have two predominant goals: to determine the facts as quickly and as accurately as possible; and, if the accused student is subsequently found guilty, to protect other students by immediately banishing the rapist from the campus. Like their counterparts in the criminal justice system, university officials understand that they also have a grave responsibility to avoid punishing the innocent. But because the harshest penalty a university can impose is expulsion—which does not deprive an accused student of his liberty or saddle him with a criminal record—most universities, including the University of Montana, believe it is more important to discover the truth than to protect the rights of the accused at any cost.

Unlike the university adjudication process, the American criminal justice system routinely allows the suppression of evidence and other procedural actions to ensure that the constitutional rights of the accused aren't violated and requires the prosecution to prove its case "beyond a reasonable doubt" to obtain a conviction. Inevitably, going to such lengths to protect the rights of the accused sometimes results in guilty parties escaping accountability. This is widely understood to be a cost of protecting sacrosanct civil rights enshrined in the U.S. Constitution. As the English jurist William Blackstone famously pronounced in the eighteenth century, "All presumptive evidence of felony should be admitted cautiously; for the law holds it better that ten guilty persons escape, than that one innocent party suffer."

But the University of Montana, like every other American college and university, is obligated by Title IX of the Education Amendments of 1972 to protect students from sexual harassment and sexual violence. Although the Title IX legislation was intended primarily to create equal athletic opportunities for male and female students, it also required institutions of higher education to establish a comprehensive system for handling sexual-assault complaints.

Because UM's adjudications of alleged rapists are disciplinary proceedings rather than criminal proceedings, the university is not bound by the rules of evidence that pertain in the criminal justice system and is, therefore, free to give as much weight to the rights of alleged victims as to the rights of the individuals they have accused. To prevent legalistic quibbling from obscuring evidence and, should a rapist escape punishment, potentially endangering members of the campus community, UM tries to minimize the role of lawyers in its handling of rape cases.

As Dean Couture pointed out to Calvin Smith, the Student Conduct Code gives students accused of violating the code the right to have a lawyer present during all disciplinary proceedings. But the code also dictates that "the role of legal counsel . . . is limited to *consultation* with the student *only*."* During official proceedings, lawyers are forbidden to raise objections or even speak directly to university officials. Beyond whispering in their clients' ears, attorneys are forced to bite their tongues.

Josh Van de Wetering, the lawyer representing Calvin Smith, was exasperated by his inability to speak up on behalf of his client during UM's adjudication of Smith's case. Most lawyers who represent clients in university adjudications are similarly frustrated. At 1:05 p.m. on November 18, less than two hours before Smith's University Court hearing was scheduled to begin, Van de Wetering sent an e-mail to Dean Couture asking to postpone the hearing until December 2, in order to have more time to obtain police reports about the case.

Smith had by this time learned that three days earlier, Chief Deputy County Attorney Kirsten Pabst declined to prosecute the case. Van de Wetering believed that this information should be considered by the University Court before it arrived at a verdict, and he informed Couture that he intended to call Pabst as a witness for Smith at the hearing. Van de Wetering said he hoped to call Detective Brueckner as a witness, as well.

Couture immediately sent Van de Wetering an e-mail denying his request:

> Josh, I am perplexed as to why you waited until less than two hours until the hearing to request an extension. I was informed yesterday that Police Chief Muir had denied your request for the female detective to participate. . . . Based on

* Emphasis written into the Student Conduct Code.

statements in your email, I think you need to be reminded that you shall not call any witnesses at the University Court hearing. Your client shall call his own witnesses and present his own case. Your participation shall be strictly limited to private consultation with your client. Your client's appeal shall begin today at 3:00 pm. . . . After I have presented the University's case against your client, your client may request the Court Chair to continue the hearing on December 2. This is an educational proceeding, not a criminal one.

Van de Wetering fired back,

I am not seeking to stall the case. I am merely trying to ensure my client has a quality defense against extremely serious accusations that if confirmed will impact the rest of his life. That effort is complicated and its importance underscored by the fact that you have concluded a rape did occur, while trained investigators and prosecutors have concluded it did not, a fact I cannot leave unconsidered. . . .

I understand what my role is, and while I find it oppressive, to think that you, with your education and experience, will be presenting the University's case while forcing an 18-year-old kid to try to stand up against you by himself, I will abide by the rules. We will be there at 3:00, and I will ask the chair for additional time.

And please rest assured, the entire proceeding has indeed been an education.

The seven individuals on the University Court are appointed by the president of the University of Montana. The court is composed of three undergraduate students, one graduate student, two faculty members, and one staff member. At Calvin Smith's hearing on November 18, 2011, held in the basement of Main Hall, the chair of the court was a distinguished professor from the university's School of Business Administration; she served as the academic equivalent of a judge and ran the proceeding. Dean Charles Couture, representing the university's interests, acted as the equivalent of a prosecutor, calling witnesses and presenting evidence against Smith.

The first person Couture called to testify was Kaitlynn Kelly, who answered questions posed by Couture and the members of the court for seventeen minutes, providing an abbreviated version of the same information she had previously conveyed in her one-on-one interviews with Couture and Detective Connie Brueckner. The court then received testimony from six witnesses who had been summoned by Couture on behalf of Kelly: Kerry Barrett, Kelly's roommate, the roommate's boyfriend, the coordinator of the university's Student Advocacy Resource Center, and Kelly's parents.

Ninety minutes into the proceeding, it was Calvin Smith's turn to present the witnesses he'd asked to testify on his behalf. The first witness to appear was prosecutor Kirsten Pabst, supervisor of the sexual-assault division at the Missoula County Attorney's Office.

Pabst was forty-four years old and had a commanding presence. She'd been raised by working-class parents in Havre, Montana, a windswept railroad town on the Great Northern Hi-Line, thirty miles from the Canadian border. During her childhood, she told *Missoulian* reporter Kathryn Haake, "when times got lean" her family sometimes lived in a converted garage without running water. In 1985 she enrolled at the University of Montana; she became a fine arts major, but she dropped out before graduating and moved to Great Falls. A single mother at the time, she was working at a restaurant when she decided to return to school to become a paralegal. She eventually got a law degree at UM, and in 1995, a week after having her second child, she went to work as a prosecutor for Cascade County. Two years later she landed a job as a deputy Missoula County attorney, and she had been employed as a prosecutor there ever since.

In 2006 Pabst was promoted to chief deputy Missoula County attorney, with responsibility for supervising the prosecution of sexual-assault cases. By 2011, when she appeared at Calvin Smith's

University Court hearing, Pabst had been married twice, given birth to four children (the youngest of whom was still a toddler), and was an expert horsewoman and an accomplished artist. With her brash demeanor and shoulder-length blond hair, she cut a distinctive profile around town.

"I was completely astounded when I realized Kirsten Pabst was appearing as a witness for Calvin," says Kerry Barrett, recalling her reaction when Pabst showed up for Smith's hearing. "She was in charge of the criminal case against Kelly's rapist. And here she was at University Court defending him." Barrett's surprise grew when she observed Pabst interacting warmly with Smith and his parents, as if they were old friends.

Like Kerry Barrett, Dean Couture disapproved of the county prosecutor's advocacy on Calvin Smith's behalf. After the hearing, Couture told Kelly that Pabst's presence was "totally out of place" and "not appropriate." Couture frowned on Pabst's involvement in the university's adjudication of Smith's case for several reasons, not least of them being that the university was required to use a very different burden of proof in determining Smith's innocence or guilt than Pabst had used when she'd declined to file criminal charges against him.

Seven months earlier, in April 2011, the U.S. Department of Education's Office for Civil Rights had sent a letter to colleges and universities nationwide; it became known as the "Dear Colleague Letter." In no uncertain terms, it reminded universities of their obligation to protect students from sexual harassment and sexual violence under Title IX. To make it harder for students to rape with impunity, the Dear Colleague Letter decreed that schools must use a burden of proof known as "the preponderance of evidence standard" when adjudicating sexual-assault complaints. To find a student guilty, in other words, a school needed only to determine that, after a review of credible evidence, it was "more likely than not" that the accused individual had committed the offense. More than once during the Calvin Smith hearing, Dean Couture reminded the University Court that this is a much lower burden of proof than Pabst or any other prosecutor was obligated to use in a criminal trial—the "beyond a reasonable doubt" standard.

Kirsten Pabst testified before the University Court, in support of Smith, for forty-two minutes, more than twice as long as any other witness, including Kaitlynn Kelly. Pabst used the opportunity to explain her rationale for declining to prosecute Smith—and therefore why, in her opinion, it would be a mistake for the University Court to find him guilty of rape. Pabst emphasized that when she'd discussed the case with Detective Connie Brueckner, Brueckner had told her "there wasn't even probable cause" to file criminal charges against Smith. According to Pabst, she then conducted an independent review of the evidence Brueckner had gathered, "and we both came to the same conclusion: that it wasn't prosecutable." Pabst explained that in Montana, prosecutors of sex crimes are required not only to prove that the victim didn't consent but "to prove that the defendant reasonably knew that she didn't consent."

"We get a lot of alcohol- and drug-related cases where there is sexual contact—date rape–type cases," Pabst continued. "And they are really, really hard cases for us. . . . But this one was different. This one was a little bit more clean-cut, in that, according to all of the witnesses, Mr. Smith and the alleged victim" agreed to have sex. "Her friends, and his friends, both were trying to get them—pardon me for sounding crude—were trying to get them laid. . . . And the victim in fact told the detective that that was her plan: to go back to her room and have sex. So we don't have the whole really blurry consent issue that we normally do."

However, when questioned by a member of the court, Pabst conceded, "Of course, somebody can withdraw consent. But it's unusual to have such a really clear picture of consent going into it, and all of the witnesses are in agreement on that. So that was a really big factor. The other thing was that everyone agreed that Mr. Smith did not finish the sex act. And that he stopped at some point. Here it gets a little bit more blurry, but he was requested to stop at some point where it became uncomfortable for her, and he did."

A few minutes later Pabst added, "Once there was an affirmative verbal agreement to have sex, so consent was given, she's really fuzzy on whether or not she verbally withdrew that consent. So it's not fair for us as prosecutors to expect a suspect to read someone's mind when they've verbally given consent."

Although Kirsten Pabst took considerable time from her busy schedule to appear before the University Court on behalf of Calvin Smith, she never bothered to speak to Kaitlynn Kelly, in violation of a Montana law* that requires prosecutors to consult with rape victims. Nor, apparently, did Pabst take the time to listen to the recording of Detective Brueckner's interview with Kelly, because a number of Pabst's assertions about what Kelly did or didn't say to Brueckner are just plain wrong.

For example, when Pabst testified that Smith "was requested to stop at some point where it became uncomfortable for her, and he did," Pabst failed to mention that the only reason Smith finally stopped, according to Kelly's testimony, was that she managed to shove him away and flee from the room, after telling him numerous times to cease penetrating her with his fingers and forcing his penis into her mouth.

In her testimony to both Detective Brueckner and Dean Couture, Kaitlynn Kelly was the opposite of "fuzzy" on whether or not she verbally withdrew consent: Kelly adamantly and consistently stated that she said "no" and "stop" many times while Smith was penetrating her. Kelly also clearly asserted that she verbally withdrew her consent to have sex when she initially entered her dorm room and saw that her roommate and her roommate's boyfriend were present.

When Calvin Smith said, "It's okay. We'll be quiet," in reply

* **MCA 46-24-104. Consultation with victim of certain offenses.** As soon as possible prior to disposition of the case, the prosecuting attorney in a criminal case shall consult with the victim of a felony offense or a misdemeanor offense involving actual, threatened, or potential bodily injury to the victim . . . , including: (1) dismissal of the case; (2) release of the accused pending judicial proceedings; (3) plea negotiations; and (4) pretrial diversion of the case from the judicial process.

to her initial withdrawal of consent, Kelly can't recall if she reiterated that she wouldn't engage in sex while other people were in the room. But she is certain that she didn't say anything that could have been interpreted as an affirmation of consent after she withdrew it upon entering the room. And the University of Montana's policy concerning rape and other sexual misconduct clearly states that consent cannot be inferred "from silence, past consent, or consent to a different form of sexual activity."

Kaitlynn Kelly told both Detective Brueckner and Dean Couture that while she was unconscious, and therefore incapable of granting consent, Smith removed her pants and underwear and penetrated her vagina with his fingers. This prompted a member of the court to ask Pabst, "You can't give consent when you're asleep. So even if you'd given it previously, that doesn't count if you're asleep, right?"

"Correct," Pabst replied. A moment later, however, she hedged: "Well, it depends. That's not really a hard-and-fast rule. But some people would argue that if I go home with someone and we say, 'Well, we're going to go have sex,' and then I fall asleep and wake up and he's having sex with me—some people would say that's consensual, and some people would say it's not."

The questioner followed up: "What does the law say?"

"I don't know the answer to that," Pabst answered. "There is no hard-and-fast rule."

A different member of the court asked Pabst to confirm that to withdraw consent, "all you have to do is say 'no' or 'stop' one time, and you have withdrawn consent."

"Usually that is the case," Pabst confirmed. "If the defendant's in hearing, and understanding of that, and he hears someone say 'no,' . . . 'no' means no. There is no question about that if that is conveyed."

But Kirsten Pabst refused to concede that Kaitlynn Kelly had clearly said "no" or that she had been too inebriated to understand what she'd agreed to do. "There just aren't that many facts in dispute here," Pabst told the court. Before Kelly entered her residence hall with Calvin Smith, Kelly told the friend she was with, Greg Witt, that she thought Smith was cute, and she agreed to have sex with him. And Pabst didn't think Kelly "was too drunk to give consent" at the time.

Dean Charles Couture accused Pabst of jumping to conclusions. Just because Kelly said Smith was cute, Couture wondered, "and they agreed to go back and have voluntary sex, are you assuming that they went and had voluntary sex?" Pabst, he argued, seemed to be ignoring the fact that Kelly withdrew her consent as soon as she and Smith entered her room.

Pabst replied that nothing in the case report she'd received from Detective Brueckner confirmed that Kaitlynn Kelly ever clearly said no. "I have not jumped to any conclusion," Pabst insisted.

EARLY IN HER testimony, Kirsten Pabst told the University Court, "There is no better predictor of future behavior than past behavior. . . . With Mr. Smith's case, he has absolutely no criminal history at all. There is not even a traffic ticket that we could find on the record." All of Smith's acquaintances, Pabst said, had described him as "a stellar citizen" who had never been in trouble. Calvin Smith was "happy-go-lucky, kind, compassionate. Those are things that we have to take into account when we are deciding whether or not this is a case that we are going to charge."

At another point, Pabst said she found it significant that when Detective Brueckner interviewed Smith at the police station and told him that Kaitlynn Kelly had accused him of raping her, Smith "became distraught, and tearful, and extremely sorry that she was upset. He said that he had never meant to hurt her or make her sad. . . . He seemed genuine in his emotions and was really surprised by the accusation."

As Kaitlynn Kelly listened to Pabst tell the court that Calvin Smith was too kind and compassionate to be a rapist, she was dumbfounded. "Kirsten Pabst refused to even talk to me when I was trying to find out why nothing was being done about my case,"

Kelly recalled bitterly. "And then she goes out of her way to show up at University Court to testify for the asshole who raped me? I couldn't believe it."

On the advice of his lawyer, Josh Van de Wetering, during the hearing Calvin Smith declined to testify or answer questions from court members. In lieu of giving a statement to the court, Smith asked Pabst to describe the brief statement he gave to Detective Brueckner on October 11, then tell the court what she "thought about it."

Pabst responded, "Everyone absolutely has the right to remain silent, but it's impressive to me when people are willing to come forward and tell what happened, openly and honestly, which is what Mr. Smith did with Detective Brueckner. . . . He came in voluntarily and answered all of her questions. According to Detective Brueckner, he sincerely stated that he really thought that [Kaitlynn Kelly] was enjoying what was going on, at least at the beginning, until he realized that wasn't the case." Pabst told the court that before Calvin Smith penetrated Kelly with his fingers or penis, "he said that they made out, there was some kissing involved. Much of what he said mirrored what the victim said about . . . a brief period of oral sex." All of which Pabst saw as evidence that the sex was consensual.

Kirsten Pabst didn't consider the possibility that Smith's presumption of entitlement, amplified by his drunkenness, led him to disregard Kaitlynn Kelly's commands to stop. When they entered Kelly's dorm room and saw two other people asleep, instead of accepting her pronouncement that having sex was no longer possible, Smith dismissed the change in plans by saying, "We'll be quiet." A few minutes earlier she'd invited him to knock boots, and he wasn't going to let her withdraw the offer now, when he was on the verge of finally shedding his virginity. A deal was a deal. She'd said yes once, and that was all the consent he thought he needed. Once Kelly was unconscious, Smith pulled off her pants and underwear and started jamming his fingers into her vagina. When the intense pain woke her up and she begged him to stop, he countered, "No, just wait" and then grabbed the back of her head and thrust his erect penis into her mouth.

Most women are all too familiar with men like Calvin Smith. Men whose sense of prerogative renders them deaf when women say, "No thanks," "Not interested," or even "Fuck off, creep."

Smith forced Kaitlynn Kelly to perform fellatio; Kirsten Pabst referred to this as a "brief period of oral sex" and asserted that Smith genuinely believed Kelly was "enjoying what was going on." But if Pabst had taken the time to listen to the recording of Detective Brueckner questioning Kelly, she would have heard a very different description.

Kelly told Brueckner that after Smith finished stabbing his fingers painfully into her vagina, and before he started stabbing his fingers painfully into her anus, "He decided that he needed oral sex. So he kept pushing my head down—like, my throat hurt the next day. I was gagging a lot. I'm surprised my roommate didn't wake up from me doing that. Because it was not pleasant. . . . He pulled me over on top of him and just kind of, like, unzipped, and pulled it out, and then started shoving my head down. . . . I couldn't breathe. I was spitting everywhere. He was gagging me really bad."

Calvin Smith's claim that he believed Kaitlynn Kelly enjoyed the sexual acts he inflicted on her is revealing. A callow eighteen-year-old, he'd testified earlier that "what happened with Kaitlynn is the farthest I've ever really gone with a woman." By Smith's own admission, his understanding of female sexuality was derived primarily from Internet pornography. Hence his explanation to Dean Couture, in October, that he wanted to make Kelly "squirt." The porn Smith viewed led him to believe that vaginal squirting was the supreme female expression of sexual pleasure and that frenetically jabbing his fingers into her vagina and anus would elicit such a response.

A rapist, by definition, is interested only in gratifying his own desires. A rapist doesn't care what a woman wants. If he did, he wouldn't rape.

WHEN A MEMBER of the University Court asked Kirsten Pabst whether she thought Calvin Smith's theft of Kaitlynn Kelly's jeans was "indicative of anything," Pabst dismissed its importance. "It kind of reminded me," she said, "of a teenage boy thing."

Pabst, however, thought that minor inconsistencies in Kelly's testimony were quite important. "There were several points . . . where [Kelly's] account of what happened—the chronology—changed, which was pretty significant," Pabst told the court. "Because at one point she said that she woke up to him digitally penetrating her, and it was really painful. But then later she said he forced her to perform fellatio on him . . . [and] that happened first. So she already would have been awake at the point where she said he forced her to perform fellatio, even though [previously] she said this whole thing started with her waking up to [his fingers in her vagina]."

Pabst insisted that Kelly's conflicting accounts of when Smith thrust his penis into her mouth raised questions for her as a prosecutor: "One, am I ever going to be able to convince a jury that this crime happened beyond a reasonable doubt? And two, have I reached my threshold of probable cause? We have to take into account those inconsistencies of the victim's allegation."

When she was a young single mother and college dropout struggling to pay the bills, Kirsten Pabst pulled herself up by her own bootstraps. Later, she was a victim of domestic violence. Years after that, in 2008, she came home from work one afternoon to discover the lifeless body of her thirteen-year-old son, who'd perished in a horrible accident. Emotional trauma was not an abstract concept to Pabst. She'd experienced it firsthand. In her opinion, nevertheless, what happened to Kaitlynn Kelly was no big deal, and it certainly wasn't rape. It was merely a consensual hookup that had failed to live up to Kelly's expectations. Kelly needed to get over it and move on with her life.

"I have not met [Kaitlynn Kelly]," Pabst admitted. "I have not talked to her. I've talked to a lot of victims, though, and I work with victims, and people consider me a staunch victim's advocate. So I have no doubt that she feels traumatized by these events." But Pabst believed that Kelly's anguish "happened more after the fact," when, the following morning, hungover, she looked back on the maladroit sex and "realized the encounter . . . didn't pan out the way that really either of them had planned."

Pabst is simply wrong about this, and about many other details of the encounter between Kaitlynn Kelly and Calvin Smith. Because she refused to talk to Kelly, Pabst's conclusions were based on bad information, and her testimony about the inconsistencies in Kelly's testimony was incorrect. Kelly never told Brueckner, or Couture, or anyone else that the fellatio happened first. Kelly unwaveringly asserted that she woke up when she felt Smith violently stabbing his fingers into her vagina.

The only inconsistent aspect of Kelly's testimony concerned the chronology of what happened after she was awakened by Smith's digital penetration. Initially, she told Officer Krastel that Smith first violated her by inserting his fingers into her vagina, and then stabbed them into her anus, and then forced her to perform fellatio. Later, when interviewed by Detective Brueckner, Kelly said that although she was indeed first awakened by Smith stabbing his fingers into her vagina, next he pulled her down to his crotch and forced her to perform fellatio—after which he stabbed his fingers into her anus.

According to David Lisak, Russell Strand, and other experts who have served as investigators or consultants in rape cases, such inconsistencies in the accounts provided by victims of sexual assaults are quite common and can be easily explained by the way trauma affects memory—a phenomenon documented in numerous empirical studies published in peer-reviewed journals. As psychiatrist Judith Lewis explains in her book *Trauma and Recovery,*

> Traumatic memories have a number of unusual qualities. They are not encoded like the ordinary memories of adults in

> a verbal, linear narrative that is assimilated into an ongoing life story. . . . [R]ather, they are encoded in the form of vivid sensations and images.

It is therefore not surprising that Kaitlynn Kelly's memory of being violated by Calvin Smith was impressionistic rather than perfectly linear. Despite the minor chronological inconsistencies in Kelly's statements, moreover, Smith's own statements corroborated Kelly's claims that each of the sex acts she described actually occurred. Pabst's assertion that slight contradictions in Kelly's testimony were a significant factor in her decision not to prosecute Smith thus raises disturbing questions about Pabst's credibility—not only in relation to her participation in the University Court hearing, but also concerning her peremptory dismissal of Missoula County's criminal case against Smith.

WHEN KIRSTEN PABST concluded her testimony, Calvin Smith called his next witness, Ralph Richards, who told the University Court that he and Smith had gone to the same high school and had been close friends since tenth grade. Richards was in Smith's dormitory room, visiting Smith's roommate, when Smith returned from his encounter with Kaitlynn Kelly. "When Calvin came home," Richards acknowledged, "he was carrying a pair of jeans. . . . He said he didn't know why he had them, and we just kind of dropped it." Then, in the university courtroom, out of the blue, Richards let out a weird, involuntary guffaw. Although he quickly suppressed his laughter, there was no mistaking that the theft of Kelly's pants struck Richards as hilarious.

Continuing his testimony, Ralph Richards said that after Calvin Smith came into the room carrying the jeans, the two of them went out for a walk, and Smith told him "that he had fingered [Kaitlynn Kelly], and that she gave him oral sex for a minute." Recalling this conversation caused Richards to cackle with laughter again, as if he were playing Beavis to Smith's Butt-Head. When he'd regained his composure, Richards told the court, "I didn't think anything of it. That's all he kind of told me."

Ralph Richards was excused, and Calvin Smith's father came into the room to testify as a character witness. Calvin asked him, "Can you describe what kind of person I am?"

"What I know of you, you've been a very good kid," Smith's dad replied in an emotional voice, his eyes welling with tears. "You never disrespect me. Never use God's name in vain. . . . I have been told by your friends that you are just a big teddy bear. And you *are* a teddy bear. I don't believe you could hurt anybody."

The next witness was Smith's mother, Mary. "What did you think when you heard about these allegations?" Calvin asked her.

"I thought there was absolutely no way that my son would intentionally hurt anybody, ever," she answered.

"How much time have you spent around your son when he was intoxicated?" a member of the court asked Mrs. Smith.

"I haven't," she answered.

AFTER CALVIN SMITH'S parents finished testifying, Calvin asked the University Court to continue the hearing at a later date, so he could have more time to present his case. "No," the chairwoman pronounced. "The proceedings just allow for a court hearing, and this is your court hearing. Do you have a statement?"

Smith declined. "I've given my statement to the police," he explained. "On my lawyer's advice, I plead the Fifth." His lawyer, Josh Van de Wetering, had counseled Smith not to testify at the hearing, because if criminal charges were brought against him at a later date, anything he said could potentially be used against him by prosecutors.

The court chair urged Smith to make a statement, regardless: "This is a confidential proceeding, so I don't think that's relevant."

"He has a right to remain silent," Dean Couture pointed out to the chairwoman.

"Can we ask him questions?" the chairwoman asked Couture.

"You can," Couture replied, "but he would then just say he is not going to answer them."

David Aronofsky, the University of Montana's legal counsel, had been silently observing the hearing and was not supposed to address the University Court. After pondering Calvin Smith's request to continue the hearing at a later date, however, he spoke up. "I gotta tell you," he said, "I don't care if the court gives me permission or not. As the chief legal officer of this university, I have some concerns about assuming this proceeding has to end today. If there is material evidence—"

"David," Charles Couture interrupted, "you are not allowed to participate."

"I am participating, Charles!" Aronofsky protested.

"You are not allowed to participate!" Couture said again, raising his voice.

"Well, then I am doing this without authorization," Aronofsky declared.

"You certainly are," Couture said sternly.

"And let the record note that I'm speaking without the authorization of the court," Aronofsky continued. "But part of my responsibility as chief legal officer is to make sure that all of the parties are compliant with the law. And if there is evidence that this court can receive that could influence the decision that could result in the remedy of expulsion, in my opinion there is an obligation by the university for this court to consider it."

"And I object that the chair is not shutting down David," Dean Couture told the court. "He has no right to participate."

The issue arose because Missoula County prosecutor Kirsten Pabst's testimony at the hearing was based on statements and evidence obtained by the Missoula Police Department, but the police had not released any of those statements or any of that evidence to Kaitlynn Kelly or Calvin Smith, despite requests from both of them. Smith and Josh Van de Wetering thought some of this evidence might turn out to be exculpatory, and they wanted a chance to present it to the University Court before a verdict was rendered.

According to University of Montana policy, however, Dean of Students Charles Couture had a duty to investigate the alleged rape of Kaitlynn Kelly independently. Thus, neither the criminal investigation by the Montana Police Department nor Kirsten Pabst's determination that there was insufficient probable cause to prosecute Calvin Smith should have any bearing on the university's disciplinary proceeding.

Calvin Smith had been given multiple opportunities to present his side of the story to Dean Couture and Vice President Teresa Branch, and to call witnesses at the University Court hearing. Couture not only believed that he had done a thorough investigation; he thought he'd done a better job of gathering and weighing the evidence than the Missoula police or Kirsten Pabst had. In his view, there was no reason to have a second hearing.

The chair of the University Court agreed. "We are going to proceed," she announced, trying to reestablish order. "We followed the procedures on the timing," she told David Aronofsky, explaining why the hearing would not be continued at a later date. "The timing is tight for a reason. You don't get forever to try this, like you do in a legal proceeding. I don't hear any of the court members objecting to finishing tonight."

Concerned about whether Calvin Smith had been granted sufficient time to interview witnesses and prepare in advance of the hearing, a court member asked, "Is it true that [Smith] received notice from Charles Couture on November 2 [that he was being investigated]?"

"No," Dean Couture said. "He was informed of the alleged misconduct, dated my letter to him, October 20."

"Okay," the court member said. "So it's been almost a month. . . . We've heard everything reasonably, and he's had a month to get all of his ducks in a row, . . . and we're not a court of law. So I'm sorry."

"May I explain?" Josh Van de Wetering asked, hoping to enlighten the University Court about why Calvin Smith, his client, needed more time to present his case.

"No," Couture said, cutting him off.

At this point the chairwoman halted the hearing to hold an executive session. She thought it prudent to clear the room so the court members could pause, take a collective deep breath, and have a brief discussion to ensure that they were doing everything properly. Several minutes later, when the hearing was called back to order, she announced, "First of all, the court would like to remind both legal counsels that you are welcome to confer with your associated parties, but please don't directly address us, as tempting as that might be. The court unanimously agrees with my ruling that we finish this hearing tonight."

A few witnesses were called back for further questioning, and then Dean Couture began his closing statement. "Most parents are going to say fine things about their children," he reminded the court, "and want to believe the best about their children." But, he added, "We all know that parents don't know everything that their kids do. That's a given fact. The first day I met with Calvin in my office, he cried most of the time. He said [the sex] was consensual. He wasn't crying out of the basis of any heartfelt concern for the victim. He was scared. He was absolutely terrified. . . . Watching him cry, I had emotional difficulty dealing with that myself. He was hurting, very much so."

At the time of their first meeting, Dean Couture was in the midst of investigating the allegations against Calvin Smith; he hadn't yet received Kaitlynn Kelly's medical report or interviewed key witnesses. A week or so later, after he'd concluded his investigation and determined that Smith was guilty of rape, Couture summoned Smith to his office again. "When he entered my office the second time," Couture told the court, "his demeanor was entirely different. He was cocky. He didn't really seem to care what I had to say [about] the additional evidence that I shared with him."

Immediately after Dean Couture finished speaking, Calvin Smith presented his closing statement. "The reason I cried in front of the dean is the same reason I cried in front of the police officer," Smith explained. "I felt bad. . . . I never meant to hurt anybody. I was scared. I mean, I was looking at expulsion. I was looking at possible prison time. I've never been in trouble. I never even got sent to the principal's office when I was in high school. . . . I know I made mistakes that day. I definitely drank too much. I stole pants. I went into the girls' bathroom. But I know that she never said 'no' while it was happening. And I know that I didn't rape her. I just find it hard to believe that she said 'no' seven or eight times, but as soon as she said, 'I have to pee,' I let her up."

Following these words from Smith, the hearing was concluded. Two weeks later, on December 2, 2011, the University Court announced its decision in a letter to Dean Couture and President Engstrom:

> The Court finds that Ms. Kelly removed consent at three different points (at least): upon entering the occupied room, upon going to sleep, and upon stating "no" or "stop" during the acts. This is corroborated by the violent nature of the acts, as evidenced by pain, blood, abrasions, and bruising.
>
> Thus, Mr. Smith did so violate the Student Conduct Code, Section V.A. 18 by sexual intercourse without consent (rape), using the preponderance of evidence standard as required by the Department of Education (unanimous with seven votes in favor, zero votes opposed). . . .
>
> Given the severity and harm resulting from the sexual assault without consent (rape) and the requirement to protect the complainant, the Court imposes the following sanctions (six votes in favor, one vote opposed):
>
> **1.** Immediate expulsion from the University.
> **2.** Prohibit access to University property or University-sponsored activities, effective immediately.

The verdict infuriated Calvin Smith and his family, who were absolutely certain that Calvin was innocent, had been falsely accused, and was the victim of both political correctness and a rush to judgment by the University of Montana.

But Kaitlynn Kelly and her family were also unhappy with the verdict. Although Kelly is grateful to Charles Couture and the University of Montana for conducting a disciplinary proceeding that held Smith accountable for raping her, she thinks he got off way too easy. Kelly believes Smith should have been not only expelled but also incarcerated. She is angry with Kirsten Pabst, Detective Brueckner, the Missoula Police Department, and the Missoula County Attorney's Office for refusing to even charge Smith. Kelly understands that her case might not have been easy to win had it gone to trial. But she is bitterly disappointed to have been denied the opportunity to testify in a court of law about how Smith violated her body and wounded her soul. She believes a jury should have been allowed to decide whether Calvin Smith was guilty of sexual intercourse without consent, rather than letting Kirsten Pabst make that determination unilaterally.

CHAPTER NINE

The more Kerry Barrett and Kaitlynn Kelly thought about the refusal of the Missoula police and prosecutors to file criminal charges against their assailants, the more discouraged they became. Before the University Court hearing, when they requested information about their cases from the Missoula police, they were ignored, prompting Kerry's father, Kevin Barrett, to phone Missoula police chief Mark Muir on his daughter's behalf.

Kevin Barrett is a retired police lieutenant with a doctorate from the John Jay College of Criminal Justice who presently serves as the chairman of the Criminal Justice Department at Rockland Community College, in New York. When he called Chief Muir, Kevin recalled, "I let him know right away that I was a cop, and I told him what I expected of him as a fellow cop." Kevin expressed his concern that Muir's officers and detectives appeared to grant less credence to the statements given by Kerry Barrett and Kaitlynn Kelly than the statements given by the men accused of assaulting them.

Kevin asked Chief Muir if he was familiar with an educational video called *Duty Trumps Doubt,* which is used by thousands of police departments across the country to teach their officers how to properly investigate rape cases. Muir replied that he knew it well, and that the Missoula Police Department showed the video as part of its training.

"One of the key messages in the video," Kevin Barrett told me, "is how important it is for you, as a cop, to always believe the victim until every witness has been interviewed and all the available evidence has been gathered, and only then make a determination as to whether or not she is telling the truth. In most crimes, that's what cops do. But in sexual-assault cases, too many cops don't take that approach. So I asked Muir, 'If you used that video to train your officers, how come one of them asked Kerry if she had a boyfriend? And why did your detective tell her that the defendant cried and talked about how his reputation would be ruined if he was charged? Why do your detectives seem more concerned about the defendant than the victim?' "

Kevin Barrett criticized both the police and the prosecutors in Missoula for their apparent reluctance to pursue rape cases unless they were absolutely certain they would prevail in court. He pointed out that in the decades before cops and district attorneys had the technological means to use DNA as evidence, "every rape case was a matter of 'he said, she said.' But we still prosecuted. . . . Everybody likes to have a high batting average when it comes to winning cases. But sometimes you have to bring the case to court and let it be decided there, instead of deciding beforehand that the odds of winning aren't good enough to go forward. When you have a victim who is willing to go the distance and you shut her down, what does that say to other victims? 'Don't bother'?" When cops and prosecutors fail to aggressively pursue sexual-assault cases, Kevin argued, it sends a message to sexual predators that women are fair game and can be raped with impunity.

On November 15, 2011, after prodding from Kevin Barrett, Muir finally agreed to meet with Kerry Barrett and Kaitlynn Kelly. During the two-hour discussion they had at the Missoula police station, according to Kerry, "Chief Muir said all the right things. He assured us he would 'give a good ass-chewing' to the detectives who investigated our cases. He was very apologetic about what happened and seemed to be listening carefully to our concerns. But he never actually did anything about our concerns."

Near the conclusion of their meeting, Kerry brought up what

had happened when she first reported her assault to Officer Brian Vreeland: He'd asked her if she had a boyfriend, because he took it for granted that women commonly lied about being raped. Kerry pointed out to Muir that Vreeland's question was offensive for a number of reasons, not least of which being that the rate of false rape claims is in reality quite low, under 10 percent. "When I mentioned this," says Kerry, "Muir got very defensive and said, 'Actually, you're wrong. The rate of false rape claims is around 50 percent.' "

On November 18, 2011, as a follow-up to their contretemps about the rate of false reporting, Chief Muir e-mailed Kerry Barrett an article titled "False Rape Allegations: An Assault on Justice," by Bruce Gross, published in 2009 in a periodical called the *Forensic Examiner*. The article's thesis, plainly stated in its title, was based largely on two academic studies: "False Rape Allegations," by Eugene J. Kanin, published in the 1994 edition of the *Archives of Sexual Behavior,* in which 45 percent of 173 reported rapes were determined to be untrue, and "False Allegations," by Charles P. McDowell, purportedly published in the 1985 edition of an obscure journal called the *Forensic Science Digest,* in which (according to Bruce Gross's interpretation of the data) 45 percent of 1,218 reported rapes were determined to be untrue.

Scholars have debunked both of these articles. Kanin examined a single police department in a small midwestern city and merely took police officers at their word when they classified a rape allegation as false. He made no effort to independently corroborate whether the allegations were actually false. Furthermore, the police department in question used a polygraph, or threatened to use a polygraph, to identify the false allegations—methods widely acknowledged as unreliable. As an International Association of Chiefs of Police policy manual explains, rape victims

> often feel confused and ashamed, and experience a great deal of self-blame because of something they did or did not do in relation to the sexual assault. These feelings may compromise

> the reliability of the results of [polygraphs and voice stress analyzers]. . . . Some states have even enacted laws prohibiting the police from offering a polygraphic examination to sexual assault victims or from using the results to determine whether criminal charges will be filed.

As David Lisak pointed out in a critique published in 2007,

> Kanin's 1994 article on false allegations is a provocative opinion piece, but it is not a scientific study of the issue of false reporting of rape. It certainly should never be used to assert a scientific foundation for the frequency of false allegations. . . . It simply reflects the conclusions of . . . [police] officers whose procedures have been rejected by the U.S. Department of Justice and by the International Association of Chiefs of Police.

Despite being discredited, the studies by Kanin and McDowell named above are still routinely cited on numerous websites dedicated to advancing the notion that American society suffers from an epidemic of spurious rape allegations by malicious women, resulting in the wrongful conviction of many thousands of innocent men. Prominent among these websites is *A Voice for Men,* a "men's rights movement" blog that receives some thirty thousand page views per day. As stated on the site, *AVFM*'s mission is to "denounce the institution of marriage as unsafe and unsuitable for modern men," "educate men and boys about the threats they face in feminist governance," and "push for an end to rape hysteria," among other goals. In June 2014, the U.S. news director of *AVFM,* Robert O'Hara, told Al Jazeera America correspondent Nicole Grether,

> We also want to challenge the media environment. It seems that our opponents—feminists—have a stranglehold on the media and the entire discourse about gender relations and gender issues.

In O'Hara's opinion, the American news media, under the influence of a feminist cabal, have unfairly painted "the men's rights movement as a bunch of crazy psychopaths who hate women and want to kill them . . . and they do this in order to basically silence us and keep us from getting our message across." Part of that message concerns what *AVFM* perceives to be an alarming upsurge in false rape allegations. "It's one of our top issues," he says:

> We hear all these silly lies: there's a rapist behind every corner; all men are potential rapists. Common things you hear over and over again coming out of the mouths of feminists. And the inflated rape statistics, this idea that one in four women in college are going to be raped before they graduate, you hear this all the time, it's just not true. It's not true. . . .
>
> I don't have the exact statistics with me right now, but you'll see it's usually around 2 percent of women in their lifetime will have some kind of problem with sexual assault. That's the same as having been mugged or having someone break into your house. . . . [T]his whole rape thing has been used by feminists to garner political power, lots of it, and money. The whole thing has been used as a scam.

AVFM is often shrugged off as a fringe website that functions as a soapbox for wing nuts. But it's not just men who believe that sexual-assault statistics have been wildly exaggerated to advance a political agenda. Some of the most prominent critics of "rape hysteria" have been female writers such as Katie Roiphe, Christina Hoff Sommers, Heather Mac Donald, and Cathy Young. Other writers, such as Judith Shulevitz, Emily Yoffe, and Zoë Heller, take a more nuanced view, arguing that although campus rape is a serious problem, universities have overreacted to it, resulting in the denial of due process to men accused of rape.

Without question, blameless men are sometimes falsely accused of rape, and sometimes expelled from college or sent to prison. When this occurs, the consequences for those who have been unfairly impugned can be ruinous. The Duke lacrosse case is perhaps the most notorious example in recent years. In March 2006, a female stripper accused three members of the Duke University lacrosse team of sexually assaulting her after she'd been hired to entertain them at a raucous party. The three men were charged with rape by Durham County District Attorney Mike Nifong, but in December 2006, Nifong was cited by the North Carolina State Bar for violating rules of professional conduct, including making more than one hundred false statements to the media. A month later, the North Carolina bar filed additional, even more serious ethics charges against Nifong, this time for withholding exculpatory DNA evidence to mislead the court, and in April 2007, charges were dropped against all three lacrosse players and they were declared innocent. Nifong, described as a "rogue prosecutor," was disbarred for "dishonesty, fraud, deceit, and misrepresentation" shortly thereafter.

The case of Brian Banks is in many ways even more unsettling. In 2002, Banks was a junior at Polytechnic High School in Long Beach, California, a six-foot-four, 225-pound linebacker on an extraordinary football team. One of his teammates was DeSean Jackson, who went on to be an All-Pro wide receiver and return specialist for the Philadelphia Eagles in the National Football League. Banks was aggressively recruited by some of the nation's top college football programs and accepted a scholarship offer from the University of Southern California.

Shortly thereafter, Brian Banks's life was upended. While attending summer classes before his senior year at Long Beach Poly, Banks had a chance encounter with a sophomore named Wanetta Gibson that, according to Banks, culminated in consensual sex. According to Gibson, Banks raped her.

In a note Gibson wrote to a friend, which became a crucial piece of evidence, she said Banks "picked me up and put me in the elevator and he took me down stairs and he pulled my pants down and he rapped [*sic*] me and he didn't have a condom on and I was a virgin and now Im [*sic*] not." When interviewed by the police,

Wanetta Gibson told a more detailed version of the same story, and Brian Banks, who was seventeen years old, was charged with forcible rape. Were he convicted, he could be sentenced to life in prison.

Like thousands of other defendants ensnared in the criminal justice system, Brian Banks accepted a plea deal. To avoid going to trial and placing his fate in the hands of a jury, Banks agreed to plead no contest to the rape charge, spend at least five years in prison, remain on probation for an additional five years, and register as a sex offender.

While Brian Banks was serving his time, Wanetta Gibson and her mother filed a lawsuit against the Long Beach Unified School District, claiming that lax security at Poly High School created an unsafe environment that led to her being raped. The suit was settled out of court, with the school district agreeing to pay Gibson $1.5 million.

Nine months after Gibson says she was raped, however, her conscience began to bother her. In March 2011, a few years after Brian Banks was released from prison, he logged onto Facebook and saw he'd received a friend request from Wanetta Gibson, his accuser. Banks, who was unemployed and still trying to get his life in order, accepted the request and learned that Gibson wanted to let "bygones be bygones." Banks asked if she would meet with him in the presence of a private investigator, Freddie Parish, whose son had been a teammate of his at Poly. Gibson agreed, and during their meeting she admitted what Banks knew to be the truth all along: He had not raped her.

Unbeknownst to Wanetta Gibson, Parish was secretly recording the conversation. Armed with Gibson's confession, Banks set out to clear his name with the assistance of an attorney named Justin Brooks, who worked for the Innocence Project, a nonprofit organization dedicated to exonerating the wrongly convicted. Less than a year after making the accusation, Gibson, it transpired, had confessed to a classmate that she'd concocted the rape story to prevent her mother from learning that she was sexually active.

Brian Banks's conviction was reversed in May 2012. Thirteen months later, the Long Beach Unified School District won a $2.6 million default judgment against Wanetta Gibson to recoup the settlement she had received, plus interest and damages.

So Banks was exonerated, but it can hardly be said that the outcome was just. His reputation was destroyed. He was denied the opportunity to attend college on a scholarship and play football for USC. Unlike his high school teammate DeSean Jackson, who became a nationally recognized celebrity, Brian Banks's shot at NFL stardom was stolen from him by Wanetta Gibson.

After Brian Banks was absolved, he was signed by the Atlanta Falcons and played in the 2013 NFL preseason, but he was cut from the team before the first regular-season game. It's not easy to make an NFL roster as a twenty-eight-year-old; after an eleven-year hiatus from football, more than five years of which were spent behind bars, it's almost impossible.

NOBODY SHOULD BE subjected to what Brian Banks was forced to endure. Police and prosecutors are morally and professionally obligated to make every effort to identify specious rape reports, safeguard the civil rights of rape suspects, and prevent the falsely accused from being convicted. At the same time, however, police and prosecutors are obligated to do everything in their power to identify individuals who have committed rape and ensure that the guilty are brought to justice. These two objectives are not mutually exclusive. A meticulous, expertly conducted investigation that begins by believing the victim is an essential part of prosecuting and, ultimately, convicting those who are guilty of rape. It also happens to be the best way to exonerate those who have been falsely accused.

Rape victims provide police with more information—and better information—when detectives interview them from a position of trust rather than one of suspicion. Which is not to suggest that cops should simply accept the veracity of victims' stories without subsequently corroborating them. They need to "trust, but verify," as President Ronald Reagan famously described his approach to international diplomacy.

The sad tale of Brian Banks notwithstanding, police and prosecutors generally do a pretty good job of weeding out false rape accusations to avoid charging the innocent. But cops and prosecutors are not nearly as conscientious when it comes to pursuing charges against those who are guilty. This is borne out by statistics indicating, indisputably, that the overwhelming majority of rapists get away scot-free.

In a highly regarded paper published in 2010, "False Allegations of Sexual Assault: An Analysis of Ten Years of Reported Cases," David Lisak and three co-authors found that the prevalence of false allegations is between 2 percent and 10 percent; that figure was based on eight methodologically rigorous studies. In the concluding paragraphs of this report, Lisak noted,

> [T]hese findings contradict the still widely promulgated stereotype that false rape allegations are a common occurrence.
>
> In the emotionally charged public discourse about sexual violence, it is often the case that assertions are made without reference to research data. Such assertions not only undermine rational discourse but also damage individual victims of sexual violence. The stereotype that false rape allegations are a common occurrence, a widely held misconception in broad swaths of society, including among police officers, has very direct and concrete consequences. It contributes to the enormous problem of underreporting by victims of rape and sexual abuse. It is estimated that between 64% and 96% of victims do not report the crimes committed against them . . . , and a major reason for this is [the victim's] belief that his or her report will be met with suspicion or outright disbelief.
>
> The stereotype also contributes to negative responses to victims who do report, whether by family members or

> by personnel within the criminal justice system. When law enforcement personnel believe that half or more of rape reports are fabricated . . . , their approach to victims can easily become more akin to hostile interrogation than to fact finding.

Rape is the most underreported serious crime in the nation. Carefully conducted studies consistently indicate that at least 80 percent of rapes are never disclosed to law enforcement agencies. Analysis published in 2012 by Kimberly Lonsway, director of research at End Violence Against Women International, and Joanne Archambault, formerly a police sergeant in charge of the San Diego Sex Crimes Unit, suggests that only between 5 percent and 20 percent of forcible rapes in the United States are reported to the police; a paltry 0.4 percent to 5.4 percent of rapes are ever prosecuted; and just 0.2 percent to 2.8 percent of forcible rapes culminate in a conviction that includes any time in jail for the assailant. Here's another way to think about these numbers: When an individual is raped in this country, more than 90 percent of the time the rapist gets away with the crime.

ONLY THREE DAYS after Kerry Barrett and Kaitlynn Kelly met with Missoula Chief of Police Mark Muir, in November 2011, the University Court ruled that Kelly's assailant, Calvin Smith, was guilty of rape and expelled him. The action taken by the university was a disciplinary matter, however, not a legal proceeding. It had no impact on Chief Deputy County Attorney Kirsten Pabst's contention that her office lacked sufficient evidence to establish probable cause for prosecuting Smith. The criminal case against him was not reopened, and details of the university's proceedings against him were sealed.

Smith's expulsion for rape had serious repercussions. It made it all but impossible for him to attend any other public college or university in Montana. But he was not required to register as a sex offender, and the fact that the University Court had found him guilty of rape did not appear anywhere in the public record. Smith returned home, enrolled in a nearby community college, and resumed posting banal comments on social media as if nothing had happened. On November 29, eleven days after the University Court hearing, he joked on his Facebook timeline about getting an erection from watching a Victoria's Secret fashion show.

Kelly's life, on the other hand, was utterly transformed by the rape. "I stayed in school a little while after the University Court hearing," she told me, "but I wasn't attending classes or doing anything. I just sat in my room, in bed, crying all the time." In early December, Kelly's mother convinced her to come home so her family could look after her. "At that point I dropped out of school and haven't been back since," Kelly said. "The University of Montana is ruined for me. I did get counseling when I first got home, but I still cry all the time. It's something in my mind. I can't stand to talk about what happened, or even think about it, because it makes me feel like shit. I've tried to forget, but—" She left the remainder of the sentence unstated.

Barrett remained traumatized long after being assaulted, too. After completing her final exams in mid-December 2011, she flew home to New Jersey for the Christmas break. On December 21, while surfing the Internet, she happened to see reporter Gwen Florio's story in the *Missoulian* about Kelsey Belnap, who was allegedly gang-raped by members of the UM football team on December 15, 2010. "When I read that the Missoula County Attorney refused to file charges because the football players claimed the sex was consensual," Barrett told me, "I began to wonder if maybe this was a pattern. I began to do some research into how often rape cases are prosecuted or not prosecuted in Missoula, and it made me really, really angry. So I decided to call Gwen Florio and tell her about my own experience with the police and prosecutors." Barrett also persuaded Kaitlynn Kelly to talk to Florio.

Florio wrote an article about the two women that was published in the *Missoulian* on January 7, 2012; a second, more detailed piece appeared on January 8. Neither article revealed the women's names. In the latter article, Florio gave Kirsten Pabst the opportunity to explain her decision not to prosecute Calvin Smith for raping Kaitlynn Kelly. "We have so much reverence for the fact that when we file sex charges against someone, it's going to ruin their life," Pabst said. "Filing charges rings a bell that cannot be unrung."

When Missoula City Councilwoman Cynthia Wolken read Florio's articles about the way the Missoula police handled Barrett's and Kelly's cases, she was concerned enough to request that Chief of Police Mark Muir appear in a videotaped forum held on January 25, 2012, to answer questions from members of the city council and the public. During Muir's remarks, which lasted more than an hour, he acknowledged that "the victim needs to be our priority" and that the police department had to "find ways to challenge our officers to be better communicators" with sexual-assault victims.

After Muir finished, Barrett walked up to the microphone and stood before the fifty or sixty people seated in the council chambers. "My name is Kerry Barrett," she began in a tremulous voice, "and I was sexually assaulted in September." She'd decided the time had come to publicly identify herself as one of the victims who had been denied justice by the Missoula police and the Missoula County Attorney's Office. For the next several minutes she explained some of the issues she had with both the police and the prosecutors. Her harshest criticism was directed at prosecutor Kirsten Pabst for testifying at the University Court hearing on behalf of Calvin Smith: "The fact that she would show up to a university hearing on her own accord, voluntarily, to defend a rapist and keep a sexual predator in our community is extremely alarming to me."

As the event was drawing to a close, Missoula City Councilman Mike O'Herron stated that he was "particularly and profoundly impressed" by Barrett's willingness to share her experience and express her concerns in a public forum. "It's made my week," O'Herron told her. "Your courage and your fortitude and your wherewithal to step up to that mike. It's affected me, and I appreciate you doing that. Way to go."

Not everyone in the room was pleased by Kerry Barrett's candor, however. When the hearing was over, as she was preparing to leave, Barrett was approached by Missoula County Attorney Fred Van Valkenburg, the man who ran the prosecutor's office and acted as Kirsten Pabst's boss. He was visibly angry, Barrett recalled, and told her, "I want to talk to you!"

"Okay," Barrett replied, undaunted. "I want to talk to you, too."

"What you said up there about Kirsten Pabst isn't true!" Van Valkenburg sputtered, according to Barrett. "She was subpoenaed! She was required to testify!"

"Subpoenaed?" Barrett said. "By who? It was a school hearing! You know better than anybody that the university doesn't have the power to subpoena witnesses."

"She was subpoenaed by the defendant and his lawyer," Van Valkenburg said.

Barrett pointed out that Calvin Smith's lawyer, Josh Van de Wetering, had also asked Detective Connie Brueckner to appear at the university hearing, but Brueckner's boss, police chief Mark Muir, had refused to let her testify. "So don't try to tell me Pabst was forced to go to that hearing," Barrett said to Van Valkenburg. "It was her own decision to testify."

"Okay," Van Valkenburg conceded. "Technically, I guess she wasn't required to appear at the hearing. But she felt she had a moral duty to testify."

"She had a moral duty to keep a rapist in our community?" Barrett demanded.

"Whoa!" Van Valkenburg said with a flushed face, according to Barrett. "You're talking as if you know all the details of this case. I can assure you that there are many things you're not aware of." Van Valkenburg had no idea that Kerry Barrett had testified at Calvin Smith's University Court hearing and that she had a much more accurate understanding of what Smith did to Kaitlynn Kelly than did either Pabst or Van Valkenburg.

"Actually, we're talking about one of my very good friends," Barrett said. "So I know a lot more about the case than you think I do. And one of the things I know is that Kirsten Pabst, who is supposed to prosecute rapists, instead went out of her way to defend a rapist in an effort to keep him enrolled at the university and on the streets of Missoula."

"She was simply acting on her belief that he shouldn't be expelled for a crime he didn't commit!" Van Valkenburg protested.

The fact that Pabst believed Smith's testimony over Kelly's, Barrett retorted, "proves my point that your office assumes victims are lying."

By this time, Barrett recounted, Van Valkenburg "was shouting, and other people in the room were staring at us, wondering what the hell was going on. So I told him, 'I know, I know: It's all about those bells. They can't be unrung.'" Then Barrett spun away and walked out of the room.

Kerry Barrett's comments at the hearing that night made a lasting impression on both Fred Van Valkenburg and Kirsten Pabst, however. Five months later, when the Missoula rape scandal was approaching full boil, Pabst was still so perturbed that she let fly with a rant on her personal blog that blamed Kerry Barrett, Kaitlynn Kelly, and Gwen Florio (without actually naming them) for manufacturing an unwarranted media frenzy. On Tuesday, June 19, Pabst posted a bizarre screed titled "Why Reporters Should Be Elected Officials."

"Lawyers who violate the rules of professional responsibility answer to the Montana Supreme Court's Commission on Practice," she wrote, and police officers who break the rules are likewise held accountable. But reporters who act unethically are accountable to nobody. "Specifically," Pabst explained,

> I refer to the *Missoulian*'s campaign to make the people of Missoula believe we are in the midst of a sexual crisis to frighten people into buying papers. Lots of papers. . . .
>
> Without getting into inappropriate detail, I assure you that the foundation for the string of "sexual scandal" articles is not based in fact. The unfortunate reality is that the

> officials in charge of setting the record straight have their hands tied by the Montana Confidential Criminal Justice Information Act. When the police and prosecutors decline to file charges against a suspect, all of the facts . . . are legally sealed. . . . You wouldn't want the world to think you sell drugs to schoolchildren just because your crazy neighbor is pissed because your dog barks too much. Or worse—you wouldn't want to be labeled a child molester because your vindictive ex said you hurt your own child. It happens with more frequency than we would like to believe.
>
> So why can the *Missoulian* publish allegations labeling legally innocent people as "sexual offenders" because a couple of disgruntled young adults, who get to remain anonymous, spin a good story to a reporter too lazy to check the facts? . . . The answer is that reporters answer to no one, except their corporate owners.

Kerry Barrett had a different opinion of the *Missoulian*'s coverage. Barrett pointed out that the number of rapists who avoid prosecution is vastly greater than the number of innocent men who are wrongly charged with rape. Prosecutors like Pabst who decline to pursue rape cases, Barrett suggested, should receive more scrutiny in the news media, not less, and Gwen Florio deserved to be praised for her courageous reporting about Missoula's rape problem. "Florio has suffered so much abuse," Barrett said, "but she was instrumental in bringing this to the attention of the public. If she hadn't reported it, it would have been swept under the rug, and nothing would change."

CHAPTER TEN

Zeke Adams sexually assaulted Kerry Barrett, she alleged, in September 2011, near the beginning of her senior year at the University of Montana. For several months thereafter, until she graduated and left Montana, Barrett would occasionally encounter Adams on the UM campus, causing her to recoil in disgust and wonder how many other women he'd assaulted previously and would assault in the future.

In late 2013, two years after Kaitlynn Kelly was raped by Calvin Smith, she told me that she couldn't help thinking about women Smith might have subsequently raped, as well. "Once a rapist, always a rapist," Kelly said. "He's going to do it again, if he hasn't already."

Research by David Lisak suggests that Barrett's and Kelly's concerns about their assailants are not unfounded. In the 1980s, when Lisak was studying rape as a graduate student at Duke University, almost all of the research at the time had been done on men in prison who had been convicted of raping strangers. It showed an alarming tendency among incarcerated rapists to commit multiple acts of sexual violence. "But this research didn't match the circumstances we were encountering when we interviewed rape victims," Lisak told me, "almost all of whom had been sexually assaulted by people they knew."

It's been estimated that approximately 85 percent of all rapes are in fact committed by assailants who are acquainted in some way with their victims, and that only a small percentage of these "non-stranger rapes" result in the successful prosecution of the rapist. So Lisak devised a study that would provide insights into offenders who'd managed to avoid both punishment and scrutiny—a population that accounted for the overwhelming majority of rapists. Specifically, he designed his study to reveal whether these "undetected rapists," like their incarcerated counterparts, showed a propensity to rape more than once and whether they were likely to commit other types of interpersonal violence. The study, titled "Repeat Rape and Multiple Offending Among Undetected Rapists," co-authored by Paul M. Miller and published in 2002, added significantly to the understanding of men who rape.

Lisak and Miller examined a random sample of 1,882 men, all of whom were students at the University of Massachusetts Boston between 1991 and 1998. Their average age was twenty-four. Of these 1,882 students, 120 individuals—6.4 percent of the sample—were identified as rapists, which wasn't a surprising proportion. But 76 of the 120—63 percent of the undetected student rapists, amounting to 4 percent of the overall sample—turned out to be repeat offenders who were collectively responsible for at least 439 rapes, an average of nearly 6 assaults per rapist. A very small number of men in the population, in other words, had raped a great many women with utter impunity. Lisak's study also revealed something equally disturbing: These same 76 individuals were also responsible for 49 sexual assaults that didn't rise to the level of rape, 277 acts of sexual abuse against children, 66 acts of physical abuse against children, and 214 acts of battery against intimate partners. This relative handful of male students, as Lisak put it, "had each, on average, left 14 victims in their wake. . . . And the number of assaults was almost certainly underreported."

Upon looking at his data for the first time, David Lisak was shocked. He thought he must have made a mistake somewhere. He knew from studying earlier research done on men in prison that most violent crime is committed by a small number of individuals in any given community, he told me, "but in our survey we were looking at college students. Initially, I had trouble thinking of them as criminals."

When Lisak went back and reexamined his data, however, it held up. Moreover, a similar study published in 2009 by Stephanie K. McWhorter, which examined 1,146 navy recruits who'd never been convicted of sexual assault, replicated Lisak's findings: 144 of the recruits (13 percent) turned out to be undetected rapists, and 71 percent of these 144 rapists were repeat offenders. An average of 6.3 rapes or attempted rapes could be attributed to each of them. Of the 865 rapes and attempted rapes reported in McWhorter's study, 95 percent of the assaults were committed by just 96 individuals. As Lisak had reported, a small number of indiscernible offenders—only 8.4 percent of the population studied—were responsible for a staggering number of rapes.

It should be noted that all of the subjects in the studies by Lisak and McWhorter participated voluntarily and that none of the undetected rapists identified by the researchers considered themselves rapists. When recruiting his subjects, Lisak told them that he was studying "childhood experiences and adult functioning" and promised them confidentiality. Participants agreed to complete a packet of questionnaires that asked such things as "Have you ever had sexual intercourse with someone, even though they did not want to, because they were too intoxicated (on alcohol or drugs) to resist your sexual advances (e.g., removing their clothes)?" and "Have you ever had oral sex with an adult when they didn't want to because you used or threatened to use physical force (twisting their arm; holding them down, etc.) if they didn't cooperate?" Although every question used explicit language to describe very specific acts, Lisak was careful never to use such words as "rape" or "assault." Any participant who answered "yes" to one of the questions on the questionnaire was subsequently interviewed and asked follow-up questions.

When interviewing his subjects, Lisak said, "I made sure I didn't in any way suggest that I was judging them or that I was horrified by what they were telling me. As a researcher, I am prohibited from saying anything to them that would alter their view of themselves. It's not like I can debrief them at the end and say, 'By the way, what you just described to me is rape.'"

The participants in the study had no qualms about being research subjects, Lisak told me, "because they share this common idea that a rapist is a guy in a ski mask, wielding a knife, who drags women into the bushes. But these undetected rapists don't wear masks or wield knives or drag women into the bushes. So they had absolutely no sense of themselves as rapists and were only too happy to talk about their sexual behaviors." Most of the student rapists interviewed by Lisak were regarded by their peers as nice guys who would never rape anyone, and regarded themselves the same way.

The serial rapists hidden in plain sight among us, Lisak explained, "harbor all the usual myths and misconceptions about rape. Additionally, we now have data showing they are more narcissistic than average. So they are caught up in their own worldview. They lack the ability to see what they do from the perspective of their victims. It's not like they've spent any time thinking about what it would be like to be passed out and wake up to someone raping you. It's not like they've ever asked themselves, 'How would I feel if I fell asleep, someone climbed on top of me, and penetrated me with his erect penis?' Rapists don't do that. They exist in their own world, and in their world there is often a tremendous sense of entitlement."

To illustrate a rapist's worldview, Lisak opened his laptop and played a video he'd christened *The Frank Tape*. It's a harrowing reenactment of an unedited, five-minute segment of an interview he did with a student rapist, performed by an actor who has precisely mimicked the rapist's delivery and callous self-regard.

The segment, which I've abridged below, begins with "Frank" telling Lisak, "We have parties every weekend." He goes on:

> That's what my fraternity was known for. We'd invite a bunch of girls, lay out a bunch of kegs or whatever we were drinking

that night. And everyone would just get plastered. . . . We'd be on the lookout for the good-looking girls, especially the freshmen, the really young ones. They were the easiest. It's like they didn't know the ropes, . . . like they were easy prey. And they wouldn't know anything about drinking, or how much alcohol they could handle. So, you know, they wouldn't know anything about our techniques. . . .

We'd invite them to the party, . . . make it seem like it was a real honor. Like we didn't just invite any girl. Which, I guess, in a way is true. . . . Then we'd get them drinking right away. We'd have all those kegs. But we always had some kind of punch, also. . . . We'd make it with a real sweet juice and just pour in all kinds of alcohol. . . . The girls wouldn't know what hit them. They'd be guzzling it, you know, because they were freshmen, kind of nervous. . . . The naïve ones were the easiest. And they'd be the ones we'd target. . . .

We'd all be scouting for targets during the week. . . . We'd pick 'em out, and work 'em over during the week, and then get 'em all psyched up to come to one of our famous parties. . . . You basically had to have an instinct for it. . . . I had this girl staked out. I'd picked her out in one of my classes. . . . I was watching for her, . . . and the minute she walked into the door of the party, I was on her. . . . We started drinking together, and I could tell she was nervous . . . because she was drinking that stuff so fast. . . .

It was some kind of punch we'd made. You know, the usual thing. . . . She started to get plastered in just a few minutes . . . so I started making my moves on her. I kind of leaned in close, . . . got my arm around her, and then at the right moment I kissed her. . . . The usual kind of stuff. . . . And after a while I asked her if she wanted to go up to my room, you know, get away from the noise, and she came right away. Actually it wasn't my room. . . . We always had several rooms designated before the party . . . that were all prepped for this. . . .

She was really woozy by this time. So I brought up another drink, you know, and sat her down on one of the beds, sat down next to her, and pretty soon I just made my move. I don't remember exactly what I did first. I probably, you know, leaned her down on the bed, started working on her clothes, feeling her up. . . . I started working her blouse off. . . .

At some point she started saying things like . . . 'I don't want to do this right away,' or something like that. I just kept working on her clothes, . . . and she started squirming. But that actually helped, because her blouse came off easier. And I kind of leaned on her, kept feeling her up to get her more into it. She tried to push me off, so I pushed her back down. . . .

It pissed me off that she played along the whole way and then decided to squirm out of it like that at the end. I mean, she was so plastered that she probably didn't know what was going on, anyway. I don't know, maybe that's why she started pushing on me. But, you know, I just kept leaning on her, pulling off her clothes, and at some point she stopped squirming. I don't know, maybe she passed out. Her eyes were closed.

Lisak asked Frank, "What happened?"

"I fucked her," Frank answered.

"Did you have to lean on her or hold her down when you did it?"

"Yeah, I had my arm across her chest like this, you know, that's how I did it." As he spoke, Frank demonstrated how he placed his forearm against the victim's sternum, near the base of her neck, and leaned on it to hold her down.

"Was she squirming?" Lisak inquired.

"Yeah, she was squirming," Frank said, "but not as much anymore."

"What happened afterwards?"

"I got dressed and went back to the party."

"What did she do?" Lisak asked.

"She left," Frank answered.

Lisak's interview with Frank was typical of the interviews he did with other rapists. In a part of the interview not included above, Lisak told me, Frank "actually described two other rapes he did, under almost exactly the same circumstances, except the two other victims were unconscious from alcohol at the time. And Frank had no idea that what he was describing to me were acts of rape."

Predators like Frank get away with it over and over, Lisak explained, because most of us are in denial. We're disinclined to believe that someone who's an attentive student or a congenial athlete could also be a serial rapist. But Frank and his ilk are sexual predators who do incalculable harm to their victims, and it's crucial for police officers, prosecutors, and campus administrators to regard them as such.

The problem is, most officials who are responsible for holding rapists accountable don't consider guys like Frank to be dangerous criminals. And even when they do, too many of them are reluctant to file charges and prosecute perpetrators of acquaintance rape, because they're convinced that the odds of convicting acquaintance rapists are slim—too slim to justify the immense investment of time, money, and emotional capital required to mount a full-scale rape prosecution. Prosecutors justify this reluctance to prosecute by pointing out that their sworn duty is to act in the best interest of the state, not to serve as personal attorneys for victims of rape or any other crime.

David Lisak considers this rationale both self-defeating and shortsighted. He argues that failing to aggressively prosecute rapists like Frank doesn't merely harm the many victims of acquaintance rape; it also does tangible harm to the general public. When men like Frank repeatedly rape and get away with it, Lisak said, "their behavior becomes entrenched. It's obsessive. And once this pattern is established, it tends not to be something that just stops.

Sexual predators are constantly practicing, constantly testing the boundaries of potential victims. You know how when you talk to an experienced salesperson, and after a couple of beers they'll tell you how you can learn to read people, how you can learn techniques for closing the sale? Sexual predators are pretty much doing the same thing. It's not that all of them are geniuses, but they are constantly honing their skills, and they get very good at it. They get much better at it than most of us are at detecting it and resisting it."

Lisak acknowledged that prosecuting rapists like Frank is difficult. He said, however, "I absolutely disagree that such cases are impossible to prosecute. There are prosecutors across the country who have been very successful in taking them on. But it takes a lot of expertise, and a willingness to approach non-stranger rapes in a whole new way." It also requires that prosecutors understand that a relatively small number of rapists do most of the raping. "Statistically, the odds that any given rape was committed by a serial offender are around 90 percent," Lisak said. "The research is clear on this. The foremost issue for police and prosecutors should be that you have a predator out there. By reporting this rape, the victim is giving you an opportunity to put this guy away. If you decline to pursue the case because the victim was drunk, or has a history of promiscuity, or whatever, the offender is almost certainly going to keep raping other women. We need cops and prosecutors who get it that 'nice guys' like Frank are serious criminals."

David Lisak argues that the police need to investigate rape suspects with the same diligence they use to investigate narcotics kingpins and perpetrators of organized crime. "The focus of the investigation shouldn't simply be this one, seemingly isolated rape," he explained. "It should be 'Who is this suspect? Who can tell us what he's really like? Who are the other women he may have raped?' Detectives need to subpoena e-mail accounts, look into the suspect's Facebook friends. They need to really dig."

Police officers who approach rape cases in this way are likely to turn up other victims and other crimes. And when prosecutors have evidence of multiple victims, it becomes much harder for defense attorneys to attack any single victim's credibility—the time-honored rape defense that so often results in acquittal.

PART THREE

Unwanted Attention

During my trip to Missoula, I was shocked by how many UM students found it inconceivable that an illustrious football player—a quarterback, no less—would ever rape anyone. "Those guys can sleep with anyone they want," people told me over and over again. . . .

For example, everyone agrees that, in the words of a man I meet under the disconcertingly fluorescent lighting at a divey sports bar called Missoula Club, football players in particular "don't need to rape to get fucked." This is despite the fact that at least six of the school's football players were involved in the cases currently being investigated by the federal probe.

Katie J. M. Baker

"University of Montana Quarterback Charged with Rape"

Jezebel, August 1, 2012

CHAPTER ELEVEN

When Beau Donaldson was arrested, on January 6, 2012, for raping Allison Huguet, it was the lead story in the next day's edition of the *Missoulian*. For the next six months, Donaldson's crime and other sexual assaults by University of Montana students were an increasingly frequent subject covered by the Montana news media. On January 8, the paper ran a piece describing Kerry Barrett's and Kaitlynn Kelly's frustration over the refusal by the Missoula police and the county attorney's office to file charges against their alleged assailants. On January 11, the *Missoulian* published a "guest column" by Mark Muir, the chief of police, defending his actions. "Rape cases," he wrote, "are a significant challenge; proving the case beyond a reasonable doubt to a jury is even more difficult."

On January 15, 2012, an article by *Missoulian* reporter Michael Moore revealed that a UM student had belatedly come forward to report being sexually assaulted in February 2011, when she was a freshman. She had been discovered unconscious in the snow outside her dormitory in the middle of the night, with her pants and underwear pulled down to her ankles. Bruises covered much of her body. "A hand had pressed down so hard on her mouth and face that an imprint was still visible," Moore reported. Rug burns bloodied her knees.

The previous evening, she'd had too much to drink and, while walking home with a friend, stopped at a coffee shop. Someone bought her a cup of coffee, and after she drank it, she saw a group of young men pointing at her and laughing. "One of them mouthed the word 'roofies' at me," she told Moore. Frightened, she ran out of the café, after which she remembered little until she was found sprawled on the frozen ground of the UM campus outside Jesse Hall and was taken to her room. The next morning, when she went to the university health center, she said, "[T]hey treated me like I was just some drunk girl. All the questions were like, 'Well, are you sure you just didn't fall down?' "

A subsequent forensic exam at the First Step sexual-assault clinic revealed that she had been raped. "I know my case probably won't be solved," the victim said. "But I want people to know what happened." She decided to tell her story to the newspaper in the hope that it would motivate the university and city officials to start taking Missoula's rape problem seriously. "[T]his is a bad thing that's going on," she told Moore, "and we all need to do something to try to fix it."

On January 17, 2012, two days after Michael Moore's article was published, UM president Royce Engstrom addressed the rash of sexual assaults at a public forum attended by 125 Missoulians, including Chief Muir, Mayor John Engen, and state legislators. "I want you to know that we take this very seriously," Engstrom assured the audience. During a question-and-answer session following his remarks, a local social worker named Ian White told Engstrom that he believed the main cause of the problem was the Griz football team. "I respectfully disagree," Engstrom countered, although earlier in the evening he'd acknowledged that "a small number" of university athletes were responsible for part of the problem. In a confidential memo sent to UM staff, however, Engstrom had essentially agreed with White by writing that university investigations "indicated a disproportionate association" between the sexual-assault crisis and "patterns of behavior of a number of student athletes."

Four weeks previously, Engstrom had assigned former Montana Supreme Court justice Diane Barz to conduct an investigation into the university's apparent outbreak of rapes. On January 31, 2012, she submitted what came to be known as the Barz Report. "The reports of sexual assaults on the UM campus now require immediate action," she wrote. "Due to the number of incidents added since December, the investigation needs to be ongoing."

She was proved correct on February 17, when UM students learned of two more sexual assaults in their midst, via an e-mail blast sent to the entire campus warning of a "Possible Threat to the Community." Shortly after 2:00 a.m. on February 10, a male student from Saudi Arabia had encountered a female student on the UM campus and offered to give her a ride to her residence hall. But instead of proceeding directly to her dormitory, he said that first he needed to pick up something from his room at International House, a university-owned residence hall for foreign students. When they arrived, the male student poured her a cocktail and urged her to drink it. Immediately she began to feel queasy and lose control of her body, at which point the man began kissing her against her will. The last thing she remembers is trying to escape through a window. Friends later found her unconscious and took her to her room.

Later that same night, approximately an hour after the aforementioned victim fled from the Saudi student's room, he drove past a different female student as she was walking to her dormitory, steered his car to the curb, and offered to give her a ride. Because she knew him, she accepted. After she got in the vehicle, the Saudi student told her the same thing he'd said to his earlier victim: He needed to stop by International House on the way to her dorm in order to pick something up. As reported by Dillon Kato in the *Montana Kaimin* (an independent, student-run newspaper published by the university), when the two students got to International House, the man talked her into coming up to his room, then "poured each of them a drink." The woman soon began to feel nauseated and vomited. Her next memory, she told Kato, was of the male student

> lying on top of her, both of them naked. . . . "His breath smelled terribly. I remember the weight of him on my chest." . . . She said she was having trouble moving and still felt ill. She said the man then grabbed a condom and proceeded to rape her and she yelled at him to let her go.

Eventually the man fell asleep and the effects of her spiked cocktail dissipated, allowing the woman to flee and make it back to her residence hall.

Both assaults took place in the hours before dawn on Friday, February 10, 2012. That afternoon, the first victim, who wasn't raped, reported her encounter with the foreign student to the UM Office of Public Safety, and the campus police notified Dean Charles Couture about it on February 14. Additionally, campus cops apparently brought the perpetrator in for questioning at some point and charged him with a misdemeanor for providing alcohol to the first victim.

The second victim, who was raped, didn't initially report the incident to the university police or the Missoula police, so UM public safety officers didn't know about the second, more serious assault when they first talked to the foreign student. Over the weekend, nevertheless, the first victim learned about the rape of the second victim through the campus grapevine.

On February 14, 2012, the first victim, who had been assaulted but not raped, received a phone call from Dean Couture to schedule an interview with her on February 17. When she showed up for the meeting, she surprised Couture by bringing along the second victim, who had been raped. Until that moment, Couture was unaware that there even was a second victim. According to Dillon Kato's article, Couture assured both women that he would summon the student who'd allegedly assaulted them to his office to be interviewed and "would possibly take away his visa and expel him" from the university.

In response to the rape, as required by a 1990 federal law known as the Clery Act, at 4:51 p.m. on February 17, the university disseminated the mass e-mail warning of possible "dangerous conditions" on or near its campus. University policy obligated Dean Couture to notify the foreign student that he was being investigated for the alleged rape of the second victim, which Couture did that afternoon with a phone call.

Couture didn't ask the student to surrender his passport, however, because he had no legal authority to do that. Nor did Couture call the Missoula police to let them know about the rape. Instead, the police and other city officials learned about the rape from the e-mail alert, which did not make them happy. Approximately ninety minutes after the e-mail blast went out, Mayor Engen sent an e-mail to President Engstrom and Jim Foley, UM vice president for external relations, in which Engen said,

> [I]t appears that two alleged sexual assaults are linked to a single suspect whom the Office of Public Safety had in custody and cited on a misdemeanor minor-in-possession charge. Both of the assaults appear to have happened off campus and should have been immediately reported to the Missoula Police Department. I hope the Dean of Students feels some obligation to report the crimes to us so we may engage in an appropriate, professional criminal investigation. While we understand that there are implications for the suspect based on the student code of conduct, that investigation ought to take a backseat to a criminal investigation of an alleged sexual assault.

Engen was wrong about where the assaults occurred; they actually took place on university property. But that was immaterial. Just three months earlier, the university had signed a memorandum of understanding with the city granting the Missoula Police Department jurisdiction over all felony crimes committed on the UM campus. This agreement, however, did not trump the university's purported obligation to respect the privacy rights of the victim, in the opinion of UM legal counsel David Aronofsky. "Frankly, if a victim says, 'I don't want this brought to the police,'" he told the *Missoulian*'s Gwen Florio, "we're going to honor that."

Aronofsky's reluctance to involve the police may also have been related to the refusal of the Missoula County Attorney's Office to file charges in the Kerry Barrett and Kaitlynn Kelly cases. During the University Court hearing for Kelly, Aronofsky became aware that both Barrett and Kelly believed that their treatment by the Missoula Police Department and prosecutor Kirsten Pabst had been demeaning and counterproductive. Both women said they would not recommend to other rape victims that they report their assaults to the Missoula cops.

President Engstrom agreed with counsel David Aronofsky that the university did the right thing by not reporting the February 10 rape to Missoula law enforcement officials. "[A]s is required by federal law," he told Florio, "the university cannot and did not release the names of alleged victims or perpetrators to police." The accuracy of this statement, however, is questionable. Federal law, Montana law, and the university's policy concerning sexual assault and the privacy of victims and perpetrators are confusing at best, and in some regards contradictory.

According to the 2011 Dear Colleague Letter issued by the U.S. Department of Education's Office for Civil Rights, as soon as a school "has notice" of a sexual assault, "it should take immediate steps to investigate or otherwise determine what occurred, and take prompt and effective steps . . . to prevent its occurrence and, as appropriate, remedy its effects." But as Diane Barz noted in her January 31 report to Engstrom, "This is the most difficult part for the UM and other universities because the guidelines are not clear on what constitutes 'prompt and effective steps.'"

In any event, on Friday evening, February 17, 2012, the university provided the Missoula police with the name of the alleged rapist, and the cops immediately began looking for him, according to Assistant Chief of Police Mike Brady. On Tuesday, February 21, both victims went to the police department, gave statements to detectives, and confirmed their assailant's identity from photographs. It was all for naught, unfortunately. Before the day was out, the police discovered that the perpetrator had fled Missoula on February 19 and had caught a flight to Saudi Arabia.

THE COLLECTIVE ANGER in Missoula over the escape of the foreign rapist was searing. Less than a month after the Barz Report warned that sexual assaults on the UM campus required immediate action, the problem seemed only to be escalating. At a city council meeting on February 27, 2012, Councilman Dick Haines ripped university administrators for not doing more to prevent the Saudi perpetrator from fleeing the country. "They have to realize that person is a threat to more than just the campus," Haines declared, adding that using federal regulations as an excuse for not immediately turning the case over to the city police was unacceptable.

"If in December you were showboating about how [preventing sexual assaults] was a top priority," Tracy Cox, spokeswoman for the Pennsylvania-based National Sexual Violence Resource Center, told Florio, "and just two months later, this is happening, it takes your credibility down several notches. And the person fleeing—that takes it to a whole new level."

Then, when the crisis seemed like it couldn't get any worse, it did. At 1:06 a.m. on March 16, 2012, Irina Cates—a reporter for the local television station KPAX—posted a story on the station's website under the headline "Griz QB Served with Restraining Order After Alleged Sexual Assault." Cates had discovered that a female UM student had petitioned the court for protection from Jordan Johnson, the star quarterback of the football team, alleging that Johnson raped her.

Three months earlier, Johnson—a nineteen-year-old sophomore from Eugene, Oregon—had led the Grizzlies to first place in the Big Sky Conference with a record of eleven wins and three losses for the 2011 season, which ended with an impressive run at the FCS national championship. The woman he allegedly raped,

Cecilia Washburn,* was a twenty-year-old junior at the UM school of pharmacy. They'd been friends since 2010, had dated intermittently and engaged in a few make-out sessions, but things had never gone further than that, sexually. Mostly their relationship consisted of exchanging text messages. Then, in the spring of 2011, Cecilia Washburn started dating another man, Jordan Johnson became interested in another woman, and the nascent relationship between Washburn and Johnson "fizzled," as Washburn put it.

In December 2011, however, after Washburn's relationship with her boyfriend ended, Johnson and Washburn started texting each other again. A lot. According to Missoula police detective Connie Brueckner, from December 2011 through February 4, 2012, when the rape allegedly occurred, Johnson and Washburn exchanged "a few hundred texts." Seventy-five percent of these exchanges were initiated by Johnson. Washburn characterized their texts as "friendly and flirty" during her sworn testimony.

In early December 2011, after a Griz play-off victory, Jordan Johnson went to a party, got buzzed, and texted Cecilia Washburn to ask for a ride home so he wouldn't have to drive drunk. When Washburn picked up Johnson and drove him to his house, he invited her inside for a quick tour of the residence, but they didn't even kiss. More than a year later, during Johnson's trial, his attorney asked him why he'd called Washburn that evening, instead of one of his other friends. "I don't know," he replied. "I just did."

"Did you kind of like her?" the lawyer asked.

"Not necessarily," Johnson answered. He explained that he was more interested in Kelli Froland, the woman he'd been pursuing since early 2011. "We weren't boyfriend and girlfriend," he said, describing his relationship with Froland, "but we liked each other."

"Did you like her a lot?" the attorney inquired.

"Yes," said Johnson.

In late December 2011, Cecilia Washburn left town to spend the university's six-week winter break with her family, and Jordan

* pseudonym

Johnson went to Oregon to visit his family. They texted each other often during this period. During the first weekend of February 2012, by which time both of them were back in Missoula, they bumped into each other at an annual campus bacchanal known as the Foresters' Ball, held on consecutive nights every winter.

It was Friday night, February 3, 2012, the first night of the ball. Approximately fifteen hundred young men and women were in attendance. Although no alcohol was served at the event, most of the students had gotten sozzled before they arrived, including both Washburn and Johnson. Cecilia Washburn had come to the ball with ten or twelve people; Jordan Johnson had come with his two closest friends, who also happened to be housemates and football teammates of his: Bo Tully and Alex Bienemann. Early in the evening, Washburn was dancing with an acquaintance when she saw Johnson walk by. "So I went up to him," she testified, "gave him a big hug, asked how he was doing." Johnson testified that he was happy to see her. Washburn slid her hand along the small of Johnson's back, leaned into him, and drunkenly declared (according to Johnson and Bienemann), "Jordy, I would do you anytime." The consequences of this nonchalant, alcohol-soaked proposition, as it turned out, were much, much greater than anyone could have imagined.

When the soiree came to an end, Johnson went home with Tully and Bienemann and crawled into his bed alone. Washburn invited some of her friends to come over to her rented house, where they socialized until 2:00 or 3:00 in the morning, and then she went to bed alone, as well.

Despite staying up so late, Washburn roused herself at 7:30 the next morning to go to work at Missoula's Ronald McDonald House, a facility that provides support for gravely ill children and their families. She volunteered there every Saturday from 8:00 a.m. until 10:00 a.m., on Sunday mornings from 7:00 until 9:00, and all night every Monday. After her shift that Saturday morning, she went home, made pancakes for her two male housemates, and hung out with a visitor from Great Falls.

Around 2:00 that afternoon, Washburn received a text from Johnson. "Hey you!" he wrote, initiating an exchange in which he inquired what her plans were for the evening. In the flurry of messages that followed, they arranged to watch a movie together at Washburn's house. Johnson texted her again at 10:29 p.m., and then at 10:40, to ask if she would drive over to his house and give him a ride back to her place to watch the movie, because he'd been drinking and didn't think it was prudent for him to drive. Washburn didn't reply, however, because she'd fallen asleep.

Growing anxious, around 10:45 Johnson phoned Washburn. Awakened, finally, by the ringtone on her phone, she answered and said she'd come right over.

When Cecilia Washburn left her house to pick up Jordan Johnson, she had not showered for more than twenty-four hours, had not brushed her hair, had not bothered to put on clean clothes or any makeup—she had done none of the things, in short, that one might expect a young woman to do if she was hoping to have sex for the first time with a man she was pursuing. As Washburn later testified, although she was definitely attracted to Johnson, and hoped to have sex with him at some point in the future, she never had any intention of having sex with him that night. She just wanted to watch a movie, maybe snuggle a little if the opportunity presented itself, and explore the possibility of rekindling some sort of relationship with him. Washburn had consumed no alcohol whatsoever since the previous night.

Jordan Johnson shared a rented house with five other football players. According to his testimony, between the hours of 5:00 and 10:00 p.m., he was drinking beer and hanging out with Alex Bienemann, Bo Tully, and some other Griz teammates. During this period, he testified, he "probably" drank no more than four or five beers, but in a statement to the Missoula police, Bienemann's recollection was that Johnson drank three or four beers in the forty-five minutes before he departed for Washburn's house, in addition to whatever he'd imbibed over the preceding four hours.

As Johnson walked out the door, Bienemann urged him to "get 'er done, buddy!"

Johnson testified that he thought Cecilia Washburn was "really nice, a smart girl. . . . I liked her as a person." But, he added, "I didn't like her as, like, a girlfriend type." Nevertheless, when Washburn arrived outside Johnson's house and he got into her car, he later said, he thought "it was a possibility" that they would have sex that night.

As they entered Washburn's house, she introduced Johnson to one of her housemates, a close friend named Stephen Green, who was playing a video game in the living room, then led Johnson into her room to watch the movie. Washburn had previously made a commitment to pick up a friend, Brian O'Day, sometime after midnight to give him a ride home from the second night of the Foresters' Ball; because it was already nearly 11:00, she wanted to get the movie started so they could watch as much of it as possible before O'Day called for his ride, at which point Johnson would have to go home.

The room was small. Washburn's bed monopolized most of the floor space. Johnson took off his shoes and his watch and reclined on the bed. Washburn removed her boots, slid a DVD of a film called *Easy A* (a comedy inspired by *The Scarlet Letter*) into her television, and then lay next to him to watch the movie. After a few minutes they began kissing. According to Washburn's testimony, although she enjoyed it, she told Johnson, "Let's just watch the movie," and they stopped kissing but continued to embrace. He was on his back; she was lying on her left side with her right arm across his chest and her head on his shoulder.

A couple of minutes later, Johnson turned to her and they started making out again. "I thought, 'Okay,'" Washburn recalled. "It seemed fine. And so it got a little heated." He tried to pull Washburn's shirt up. When she pulled it back down, he persisted in pulling it over her head, and she let him remove it. Then Washburn took off Johnson's shirt. She rolled on top of him and they started grinding their hips against each other. She kissed and nibbled his ear, and he kissed her neck. All of which, she testified, was consensual. But then Johnson grabbed her arm and started "getting really excited," which began to alarm her, because she didn't want to do anything more than make out. She told him, "Let's just take a break. . . . Let's just watch the movie." Washburn rolled off Johnson and resumed lying on her side with her head on his shoulder.

After a few more minutes of watching the movie, however, without saying anything, Johnson rolled on top of her and started kissing her more aggressively. Once again she told him, "No, let's just watch the movie." But this time, instead of stopping, Washburn testified, he sat over her "kind of like a gorilla. . . . And I said, 'No,' like, 'Not tonight.' . . . Because I figured that he was trying to have sex. And I didn't want that."

By that point, however, Jordan Johnson seemed determined to have intercourse, despite Cecilia Washburn's repeated protestations. She was five feet, eight inches tall and weighed 127 pounds. He was a powerfully built football player who weighed about 200 pounds and spent a lot of time lifting in the Griz weight room. Johnson pinned her down by placing his left arm across her shoulder and chest, she testified, "and then he took my leggings and my underwear off with his right hand, and he pulled them down, and they caught around my ankles." As he was tugging her clothing off, she continued to protest, "No! Not tonight!" She also tried to hold her legs together, and she raised her knees against his hips in an attempt to push him away.

As Washburn resisted Johnson's advances, she testified, "He didn't say anything. He was just— . . . He changed into a totally different person. . . . I was terrified."

After Jordan Johnson pulled off Cecilia Washburn's leggings and underwear, and was pinning her down with his forearm across her sternum, he commanded her to turn over onto her stomach. When she refused, Washburn testified, "He said, 'Turn over, or I'll make you.' And then at that point he grabbed my hips and flipped me over." When this happened, she said, "I just knew I was going to get raped."

Once Johnson had Washburn lying facedown on the bed, he forced her legs apart with his knees, placed his hand on the side of her head to hold her down, and used his other hand to unbuckle his belt and lower his jeans. "You said you wanted it," he told her. He pulled Washburn's hips up toward him so that she was on her knees with her buttocks raised in the air, and penetrated her vagina with his penis as he kneeled on the bed behind her. As he did these things, according to Washburn, he again said, "You said you wanted it! You said you wanted it!"

"He grabbed onto my hips and he started pulling my body into his," Washburn testified, "repeated times, just again, and again, and again. It hurt so bad." He penetrated her in this manner for "a couple of minutes," until he felt that he was about to ejaculate, at which point he withdrew his penis and came in his hand and on Washburn's blanket.

When Johnson began raping her, Washburn testified, she was "in complete shock. It was like I was hit with a baseball bat. I had no idea what was going on. I had never in a million years would have thought that this would have happened. . . . And then, gradually, as things started to progress, I just slowly started to shut down. . . . And afterwards, I was still in shock. I didn't want to believe that it happened. It was like this nightmare."

After Johnson withdrew his penis from Washburn's vagina and ejaculated, she scrambled off the bed, stood beside her dresser, and stared at him, shaking, while he wiped the semen from her blanket, picked up his clothes, and walked into an adjacent bathroom. As soon as Johnson was out of her bedroom, Washburn pulled on her clothes, picked up her phone from the nightstand, and texted her housemate, Stephen Green, who was still playing a video game in the living room, a few feet away. "Omg," she typed, "I think I might have just gotten raped. he kept pushing and pushing and I said no but he wouldn't listen . . . I just wanna cry . . . omg what do I do!"

Cecilia Washburn grabbed her purse and her wallet, put on a down vest, and walked through the living room, past Green, and into the kitchen, where she noticed that her friend Brian O'Day had sent her a text to ask if she would pick him up downtown and give him a ride home, as she had earlier agreed to do. Washburn replied with a text that said yes, followed by a smiley-face emoticon. Later, when Washburn was asked why she responded with a smiley face, she explained that she didn't want to let O'Day know she'd been raped.

After replying to O'Day's text, Washburn continued out the back door and walked to her car, taking for granted that Johnson would follow her when he realized she had left. "I wanted him out of my house as quickly as possible," she testified. In her state of shock and disbelief following the rape, she decided that driving him back to his house was the most expedient way to accomplish that.

As Washburn had walked past Stephen Green, he'd seen that she had tears in her eyes. "She looked really distressed," Green testified. "And she . . . just kind of shook her head and said she didn't want to talk about it right then."

Jordan Johnson came out of the house a couple of minutes after Washburn and got into the front passenger seat of her car. During the short drive to his residence, they didn't speak to each other. "No words were exchanged," Washburn testified. "Completely silent. . . . I had tears in my eyes, but I wasn't sobbing. . . . When I dropped him off, he got out of the car and he said, 'Well, thanks,' and then he shut the door. . . . I turned my car around, started to cry, and then I drove home."

LATER, MANY PEOPLE were baffled by Cecilia Washburn's actions during the alleged assault and immediately thereafter. When the assault began, skeptics wondered, why didn't she scream for help from Stephen Green, who was sitting just outside the door to her bedroom? And why would Washburn give Jordan Johnson a ride home after he'd raped her?

There are several plausible explanations, according to Rebecca Roe. An accomplished Seattle lawyer, Roe worked from 1977 through 1994 in the King County Prosecuting Attorney's Office, where she ran the Special Assault Unit for eleven years, and in 2008, after going into private practice, she was recognized as "Lawyer of the Year" by the Washington State Trial Lawyers Association. Being raped is such a traumatic experience, Roe explained to me, that it often results in seemingly bizarre behavior. Fear could certainly account for Cecilia Washburn's unexpected actions, she said. But so could something as mundane as culturalization.

"It was actually pretty common for women not to scream or call the cops in rape cases I prosecuted," Roe said, "at least partly because women aren't wired to react that way. We are socialized to be likeable and not to create friction. We are brought up to be nice. Women are supposed to resolve problems without making a scene—to make bad things go away as if they never happened."

WHEN CECILIA WASHBURN arrived back at her house after driving Jordan Johnson home, she walked in through the kitchen door, broke down, and started sobbing so hard she had trouble breathing. "I thought I was going to collapse," she said, "so I grabbed onto the . . . oven door handle." As soon as Stephen Green heard Washburn's wrenching sobs, he ran into the kitchen to comfort her, then persuaded her to sit down with him in the living room. "I sat on his lap . . . and he just sat there rubbing my back," Washburn recalled.

After Washburn talked to Green for about twenty minutes, she took a long shower. She said she felt filthy and violated and wanted "to get clean and just scrub every crevice of my body."

CHAPTER TWELVE

By the time Cecilia Washburn finished showering, it was approximately 1:00 a.m. Her friend Brian O'Day still needed a ride home, so she put on her clothes, got back in her car, and drove downtown to pick him up. When O'Day got in the car, he noticed that she looked upset, so he asked what was wrong. Washburn burst into tears and told him she'd been raped. By the time she returned to her house and went to bed, it was 2:30 a.m.

After waking up on Sunday morning, February 5, 2012, Cecilia Washburn texted a close friend, Ali Bierer, to tell her what had happened the night before. Bierer, a senior at the UM pharmacy school, was a year older than Washburn. During her freshman and sophomore years, Bierer had worked twenty hours a week as a resident assistant, a job that entailed providing advice and support to students. As part of her training for the position, she'd been instructed how to respond to students who came to her to report sexual assaults. Guided by this training, Bierer urged Washburn to go immediately to the First Step Resource Center. (This is the same clinic for sexual-assault victims where Allison Huguet was taken by her mother after being raped by Beau Donaldson and where Kelsey Belnap was taken after allegedly being gang-raped by four teammates of Donaldson's and Jordan Johnson's.) Bierer offered to drive Washburn to First Step.

Washburn was skeptical, but she relented to Bierer's urging because she wanted to be treated for her genital injuries and for potential sexually transmitted diseases. "I just wanted to make sure that I was physically okay," Washburn testified.

When Bierer picked Washburn up to take her to the clinic, Washburn's appearance worried her. "She was very frazzled, withdrawn," Bierer testified. "She wasn't looking at me. . . . She was crying. Just very shaken."

At First Step, Cecilia Washburn met with Claire Francoeur, the nurse-practitioner on duty. Francoeur explained that Washburn was not required to report the alleged rape to the police but noted that if there was any possibility that she might decide to report the assault at some future date, it was very important that she receive a forensic medical exam right away, in order for evidence to be collected. Washburn consented to the exam, which turned out to be so painful that she asked Francoeur to stop in the middle of it for a little while. The exam determined that Washburn had genital pain, in addition to "mild redness, swelling, and some small abrasions; marks on her chest; and tenderness to the side of her head."

After the exam, Washburn was ambivalent about whether to report the rape to the authorities. She had four options. She could go to the Missoula police and seek redress through the criminal justice system; she could report the assault to the University of Montana; she could file reports with both the police and the university; or she could remain silent. None of these choices was appealing. Each had the potential to affect her life in unpredictable and adverse ways.

After weighing possible risks against possible benefits, Washburn decided to forgo filing a police report, at least for the time being, but to report to the University of Montana that she had been raped by Jordan Johnson. She hoped that by not filing a formal report with the Missoula Police Department, she would be able to keep the rape confidential and out of the media. A few days after visiting First Step, she gave a statement to UM dean Charles Couture. He immediately launched a formal investigation.

On Sunday, February 12, Jordan Johnson arrived home from a trip to Pullman, Washington, to find a letter from Couture on official University of Montana stationery. "Dear Mr. Johnson," the missive began,

> I have initiated an investigation into the allegation that you have violated Section V.A. 18 of The University of Montana Student Code. Section V.A. 18 prohibits rape. Reportedly, on February 4, 2012, you raped a fellow student, Ms. Cecilia Washburn, at her off-campus apartment. . . . Upon the conclusion of my investigation, if I have found sufficient evidence that you violated the Student Conduct Code as alleged, I intend to seek your immediate expulsion from the University.

As Johnson read the letter, he began to tremble and hyperventilate, according to his housemates, and could hardly speak. Two of those housemates, Alex Bienemann and Bo Tully, suggested to Johnson that he seek advice from one of their assistant football coaches who lived nearby. He wasn't home, however, so they phoned Robin Pflugrad, the head coach, who invited Johnson to come to his home and talk.

Pflugrad and Johnson are both from Eugene, Oregon, and Pflugrad was a friend of Johnson's parents. Pflugrad had a son who'd attended Eugene's Sheldon High, where Johnson had gained national attention as an exceptional quarterback. In December 2009, when Johnson was a senior at Sheldon, Pflugrad was named head coach at the University of Montana. Almost immediately, Pflugrad offered Johnson a scholarship to attend college at UM and play football for the Griz. Johnson eagerly accepted.

When Alex Bienemann drove Jordan Johnson to Robin Pflugrad's house and dropped him off, Johnson was still extremely agitated by Dean Couture's letter. During the hour or so that Johnson spent with Pflugrad, he told his coach that the sex with Washburn had been consensual and he absolutely did not rape her. In that case, Pflugrad replied, Johnson had nothing to worry about, because there was no way he could get in trouble for something he didn't do. The fifty-three-year-old coach assured his nineteen-year-old quarterback that everything "was going to be okay." Immediately after Johnson went home, Pflugrad called UM athletic director Jim O'Day to alert him that Jordan Johnson was being investigated by Dean Couture for rape, and the UM athletic department promptly mobilized to do everything possible to defend Johnson against Cecilia Washburn's allegation.

IN EARLY MARCH, Cecilia Washburn was traversing the UM campus with a friend when she saw Jordan Johnson, who happened to be walking nearby. Although Johnson made no effort to approach Washburn, and apparently never even noticed her, when Washburn caught sight of him, she panicked. It was the first time she had laid eyes on Johnson since the night he'd allegedly raped her. Terrified, she ran inside a nearby building to hide, then called Lori Morin, the assistant dean for student affairs at the UM school of pharmacy. Morin urged Washburn to come to her office right away. When Washburn arrived, Morin testified, she was "sobbing uncontrollably. She just came and hugged onto me and would not let me go. . . . I have never seen a person so terrified."

On March 9, prompted by this inadvertent encounter, Cecilia Washburn filed a temporary restraining order against Jordan Johnson; it forbade him to threaten or harass her and required him to stay at least fifteen hundred feet away from her and her home. Reporter Irina Cates learned about the restraining order on March 15 and posted a story about it on KPAX.com at 1:06 a.m. on March 16, under the headline, "Griz QB Served with Restraining Order After Alleged Sexual Assault." This was the first public revelation that Jordan Johnson had been accused of rape.

Although Cecilia Washburn's name was kept out of the reports that immediately appeared in the news media, the rape was no longer a secret. Therefore, she decided that she might as well go ahead and report her assault to the Missoula police; she did this on the afternoon of March 16. In accordance with the University of Montana Student-Athlete Conduct Code (which Johnson had signed), when the Griz football team commenced its spring practice drills on March 19, Johnson wasn't allowed to participate.

Confronted with the news about their brilliant quarterback, Missoulians reacted with shock and incredulity. On the popular Internet forum eGriz.com, a fan posted,

> Last year I took my two three-year old girls to a few of the games, and I was looking forward to trying to make it to all of the games with them this next fall. But now, I am thinking that I will find something else to do with them this next fall. If even a fraction of what has been alleged is actually true, then . . . the Grizzly program still has a serious problem. . . . It is hard to root for players when you just can't trust that they are decent people. And I surely don't want my girls to grow up admiring these boys when there seems to be such a large collection of creeps in their midst.
>
> And I need to hear outrage from the fans, not a bunch of excuses. This cannot all be the fault of the girls, or Gwen Florio, or anything else other than the football team. There is no way there is this much out there, and not some blame to be had on the part of the football team. And maybe Pflugrad didn't create, or in any way cause this problem, and likely he never even envisioned it, but if he wants to be the leader of this team he had better figure out a way to solve it.

Thirteen minutes later, in response, a different Griz fan posted,

> Please don't come to any more games. This is nothing more than a witch hunt.

ON MARCH 23, 2012, the restraining order against Jordan Johnson was dismissed in lieu of a civil "no-contact order" negotiated by

Cecilia Washburn's attorney, Josh Van de Wetering,* and Johnson's attorney, David Paoli. It placed the same restrictions on Johnson as the restraining order—he was still required to stay fifteen hundred feet away from Washburn—but because the no-contact order was a civil procedure rather than a criminal procedure, Coach Pflugrad and the UM athletic department allowed Johnson to practice with the football team, relying on a very lenient interpretation of the Student-Athlete Conduct Code. Pflugrad told *Missoulian* reporter Fritz Neighbor that he was glad Jordan Johnson was back at practice. "I think any time you have a person of Jordy's character and tremendous moral fiber, and he's your team captain and part of the leadership council," Pflugrad said, "your players are going to be fired up."

Josh Van de Wetering thought Pflugrad's effusive endorsement of Jordan Johnson in the *Missoulian* was highly inappropriate under the circumstances and that Johnson should not have been allowed to return to the team. In a letter to a UM administrator, Van de Wetering complained that "the Athletic Department's decision to reinstate Mr. Johnson is based at least in part on your misunderstanding of the legal process against Mr. Johnson."

On March 29, a day after Van de Wetering's letter was received, University of Montana president Royce Engstrom fired both Robin Pflugrad (who had recently been named the Big Sky Conference Coach of the Year) and UM athletic director Jim O'Day. Although Engstrom didn't state a reason for dismissing the two men, Coach Pflugrad had come under criticism for his handling of the alleged gang rape of Kelsey Belnap by four Griz football players in December 2010. In February 2011, Pflugrad had learned that these players had been accused of raping Belnap and were being investigated by the Missoula police, but he had neglected to share the information with O'Day, Dean Couture, or any other UM administrators. As a

* This is the same Van de Wetering who, four months earlier, had represented Calvin Smith when Smith was found guilty of raping Kaitlynn Kelly by the University of Montana.

consequence, nobody from the university contacted Kelsey Belnap, and the university failed to initiate a timely investigation of what appeared to be a serious crime.

Jordan Johnson's alleged rape of Cecilia Washburn on February 4, 2012, in addition to the other sexual assaults by Griz football players that occurred on Coach Pflugrad's watch, apparently compelled President Engstrom to take decisive action.

Missoulians were already disturbed by the escalating rape scandal, and the firing of Robin Pflugrad and Jim O'Day left the town reeling. On March 30, the football team posted a letter on GoGriz .com (no connection to eGriz.com), the official website of the UM athletic department:

> Dear Parents, Griz Nation, The University of Montana, the citizens of Missoula;
>
> We write this letter as the players of the 2012 University of Montana Football team. We also write this letter as students of a University we love, members of a community we cherish and as stewards of one of the most respected and honored football traditions of excellence in the nation.
>
> The events over the past months regarding allegations and actions of players and most recently the firing of our head coach and the athletic director have all had a deep and profound impact on us. We understand and accept the fact that a few of our teammates' actions, whether intended and deserved or not, have contributed to this unfortunate situation. Whether or not true, regardless of obvious motivations and despite the facts, or lack of them, we have learned that the rules in today's public arena are about perception and expediency. As student athletes of this university we are left without an answer as to why our two leaders, Coach Pflugrad and Jim O'Day, are gone. These events have left us disappointed, saddened, and stunned, but they have also provided us something else.

> We have been reminded of the commitment we made years ago, and supported by our families, to pursue excellence in the sport we love that led us from across the country and Montana to come here. Our responsibility to honor those who support us, our duty to respect the players and coaches who built the proud Griz tradition, and our unwavering appreciation of Griz Nation is now stronger and more deeply felt. Most importantly, our commitment to each other is stronger than ever.
>
> Speaking with one voice, we ask for your strength, support and solidarity. We hope this series of personal and collective tragedies will give way to strengthening and rebuilding. We also ask those who have been entrusted with authority and power to carefully consider the impact of their statements and actions on our team and our great tradition.
>
> Our team stands together, closer and stronger than ever before. Just as we will hold ourselves to a higher standard, we will also hold others. We understand that honor, truth and hard work win in the end. We are Montana.

The letter showed a belated understanding by the Griz players that Missoula's sexual-assault problem was having a deleterious impact on the football program and their individual careers. Conspicuously absent, however, was any expression of concern for the women who had been raped by their teammates. One is left with the sense that the football players saw themselves as the primary victims of the rape scandal.

Many Missoulians shared the players' perspective. There is a feeling in Missoula that the Grizzlies football team represents the entire town, not just the University of Montana. Even Missoulians who despise the university for what they perceive to be its liberal bias and academic insularity tend to love the Griz. At the time, a large segment of the population seemed to feel that the whole city had been unfairly besmirched by the scandal. Expressions of support for the beleaguered team appeared all over Missoula in the form of flags, banners, T-shirts, and signs proclaiming, "WE ARE GRIZ NATION." Florio was called a bitch and a cunt by anonymous posters to Internet forums, and she was threatened with violent assault.

But the support for the football players wasn't universal. Stenciled graffiti declaring "WE ARE ~~GRIZ~~ RAPE NATION" appeared as well, on a few Missoula walls and railway underpasses. And the bad news about Missoula's rape problem, as it turned out, was far from over.

On May 1, 2012, the assistant attorney general for the Civil Rights Division of the U.S. Department of Justice, Thomas Perez, arrived in Missoula and held a press conference to announce that the DOJ had launched a major investigation into the handling of eighty Missoula sexual-assault cases over the previous three years. Perez said the DOJ would be investigating the Missoula County Attorney's Office, the Missoula Police Department, and the University of Montana. Letters sent to county attorney Fred Van Valkenburg and police chief Mark Muir alleged that their agencies' "failure to investigate reports of sexual assaults against women" amounted to gender discrimination.

Van Valkenburg and Muir appeared beside Perez at the press conference, along with Missoula mayor John Engen and UM president Royce Engstrom. Although Muir, Engen, and Engstrom promised to support the investigation, Van Valkenburg took the microphone after Perez made his comments and slammed the DOJ. He railed against "the heavy hand of the federal government," adamantly denied that his office had done anything wrong, and refused to cooperate with the feds, claiming that the DOJ was overreaching its jurisdiction.

Assistant Attorney General Thomas Perez wasn't swayed by Fred Van Valkenburg's outburst. "I don't think protecting women from rape or sexual harassment," he said, "is an overreach of federal government."

As the scandal had intensified during the first six months of

2012, the Missoula Police Department, the Missoula County Attorney's Office, and the University of Montana had scrambled to address the torrent of negative press, with mixed results. On multiple occasions, public officials became so rattled by media reports about the scandal that they actually tried to blame Gwen Florio and/or rape victims for their predicament.

Media inquiries about the university's response to the sexual assaults were handled by UM Vice President of External Relations Jim Foley. He had a close relationship with the athletic department, and he accompanied the football team to all of its out-of-town games. In March 2012, Foley sent an e-mail to Dean Charles Couture suggesting that the university take disciplinary action against Kelsey Belnap for speaking to Florio about the school's mishandling of her case. "Is it not a violation of the student code of conduct for the woman to be publicly talking about the process and providing details about the conclusion?" Foley inquired.

Foley also took umbrage at Florio's use of the terms "gang rape" and "football players" to describe the assault of Belnap in 2010 by four members of the Griz football team, instead of calling it a "date rape" by multiple "students," as it was characterized in official university statements. "Can anybody tell me where UM has used the terms gang rape and football players in any public document that the *Missoulian* would be referencing?" he wrote in an e-mail to Dean Couture, UM counsel David Aronofsky, and Lucy France, the UM director of equal opportunity and affirmative action.

Couture explained to Foley that he had used the term "gang rape" when referring to the assault of Kelsey Belnap "because that is what it was." To Couture's credit, in December 2011, a year after the alleged assault occurred, when he learned that Belnap had purportedly been raped by reading about it in the *Missoulian,* he launched an investigation of Benjamin Styron and the four football players accused of raping her.

The University Court determined that Styron was not guilty of violating the university's Student Conduct Code. Thanks to Couture's efforts, however, one of Belnap's assailants was expelled.

Another agreed to withdraw from the university at the end of the 2012 spring semester, was banned from any future access to the UM campus, and was prohibited from reenrolling in any Montana University System campus in the future. The other two perpetrators, who dropped out of school after Gwen Florio's article about Kelsey Belnap was published, were notified that they would face disciplinary action if they ever attempted to reenroll.

CHAPTER THIRTEEN

Following the arrest of Beau Donaldson on January 6, 2012, for raping Allison Huguet, he remained in jail until January 13, when he was released on bail, which had been reduced from $100,000 to $50,000. That same day, Huguet got an alarming phone call from a close friend who had attended high school with her and Donaldson. This friend told Huguet that an admirer of Donaldson's named Sharon Mortimer* had been telling people that Huguet was lying when she accused Donaldson of raping her and that Donaldson had also been falsely accused of raping another woman in 2008.

The rumor made Huguet wonder. Sharon Mortimer was obviously wrong about Beau Donaldson being innocent of raping her. Maybe Mortimer was also wrong about Donaldson being innocent of raping this other woman, whoever she was. So Huguet phoned Detective Guy Baker, the officer who'd arrested Donaldson, to let him know about the rumor.

Detective Baker tracked down Sharon Mortimer and asked her to come to the Missoula Police Department to be interviewed. If Beau Donaldson had indeed raped another woman two years before raping Allison Huguet, and the victim could be persuaded to testify against Donaldson, it could help convict him for raping Huguet, even if this other victim hadn't reported the assault to the police. As David Lisak has noted, persuading a jury to convict

* pseudonym

a serial rapist is a lot easier than convicting someone who's under suspicion for committing only a single rape.

During her interview with Detective Baker, Sharon Mortimer explained that she had a second cousin named Hillary McLaughlin who lived in Great Falls. In the autumn of 2008, McLaughlin came to Missoula on a Friday night to visit her best friend, Joanna Sutherlin,* who had gotten McLaughlin a ticket to a Griz football game on Saturday. The night before the game, Sutherlin held a party at her house, and McLaughlin invited Mortimer to come over and join the fun. Mortimer showed up with her boyfriend and Beau Donaldson, who was a freshman at UM that fall. Sharon Mortimer told Detective Baker that Hillary McLaughlin was attracted to Donaldson, wanted to hook up with him, and led him upstairs "to show him something" in Joanna Sutherlin's bedroom.

The following evening, Sharon Mortimer told Detective Baker, she got a phone call from one of Hillary McLaughlin's friends who was upset about what "Beau had done to Hillary." In a subsequent conversation with McLaughlin, according to Mortimer, McLaughlin told her that while McLaughlin and Donaldson were upstairs, he had tried to rape her, but Mortimer didn't believe it. She reported to Detective Baker that when she, her boyfriend, and Donaldson had left the party, McLaughlin had hugged her, said good-bye to Donaldson, and given no indication that anything was wrong. Hillary McLaughlin had invented the story about the attempted rape because she had consensual sex with Beau Donaldson and then regretted it, Mortimer insisted.

A week after interviewing Sharon Mortimer, Detective Baker interviewed Hillary McLaughlin, and McLaughlin's account of what happened at Sutherlin's party was rather different from Mortimer's. As McLaughlin told Detective Baker, and later told me, Beau Donaldson began hitting on McLaughlin as soon as he arrived at the party. "Beau was very, very clingy," McLaughlin recalled, "and kind of hung all over me for the entire night. I had

* pseudonym

never met him before, so it was kind of weird." It was also strange that Donaldson, as a member of the Griz football team, was drinking heavily the night before a game.

Hillary McLaughlin had arrived in Missoula that evening after working all day and then driving three hours from Great Falls. After spending a couple of hours with Beau Donaldson she felt worn out, so she left the party and went upstairs alone to get ready for bed. When she arrived in Joanna Sutherlin's room, McLaughlin took off her makeup, changed into a T-shirt and sweatpants, and climbed into bed. "I was playing on my phone and laying in bed," McLaughlin said, "and for some reason I still had the light on. All of a sudden the door opened and it was Beau. And he walks in and doesn't say anything, then he shuts the door and locks it."

Donaldson didn't turn off the light, and McLaughlin vividly remembers what happened next: "He had khaki shorts on, and he pulls them down and he gets on top of me." Donaldson was drunk, she told me, "But I don't think he was to the point where he couldn't control himself." As Beau Donaldson sprawled over her, essentially naked from the waist down, McLaughlin wrapped the sheets around herself as tightly as possible. He pushed her phone onto the floor and began humping his penis against her, pinning her body to the mattress. "I started screaming," McLaughlin said, "because he was just kind of grinding on top of me, and trying to make out with me. I was moving my head to keep him from kissing me, and screaming."

Around midnight, Joanna Sutherlin was sitting on the staircase with two friends—a man named Cody* and a woman named Grace†—and heard the screaming. They rushed up to Sutherlin's bedroom but discovered that the door was locked. For several minutes, the three of them tried to open the door, without success, and as they struggled with the lock, the crying and screaming from inside the room continued. When McLaughlin heard her friends

* pseudonym

† pseudonym

trying to force their way into the bedroom, she yelled, "Joanna! Help me!"

They yelled back, "We're trying to get the door open!" All the while, Beau Donaldson kept humping McLaughlin, despite her cries for help and the yelling from just beyond the door.

"After maybe five to eight minutes," Hillary McLaughlin recalled, "I think Cody finally broke the hinge off the door and got it open. I was still screaming and Beau was still grinding on me and wouldn't stop, and wouldn't get off of me. I was like, 'What are you doing! Leave me alone!' Finally, I believe either Cody or Grace just ripped him right off of me. He still had his shorts down, and they pushed him out of the room."

When he interviewed Grace about the incident, Detective Baker wrote in his case report, Grace said Donaldson "acted as if he was irritated that they had interrupted what he was doing with Hillary."

According to the case report, Joanna Sutherlin told Detective Baker that "based on what she observed when she opened the locked door, she felt 'if nobody stopped him . . . he would have raped [Hillary McLaughlin].'" Baker wrote that "Joanna stated it was 'obvious' . . . [Hillary] did not want to be with him, but Beau did not stop despite Hillary's continued screams, and [Joanna] and Grace's attempts to get the door unlocked."

After Joanna, Grace, and Cody got Donaldson out of the bedroom, McLaughlin told me, "I remember I just sat there and cried. I didn't know what to think. I had never been in a situation like that before." Sutherlin and Grace tried to console McLaughlin, who was extremely shaken, and then went downstairs and demanded that Beau Donaldson, Sharon Mortimer, and their friends get out of Sutherlin's house immediately. Grace told Detective Baker that Donaldson and his entourage "were mad about being asked to leave."

The day after the party, Sharon Mortimer returned to Joanna Sutherlin's home, apparently unaware that Beau Donaldson had attempted to rape Hillary McLaughlin in Sutherlin's bedroom. So

McLaughlin took her cousin into a closet so they could talk privately and told her straight up: "Beau tried to rape me last night."

According to McLaughlin, Mortimer replied, "No, he didn't."

McLaughlin said, "Yes, he did."

At which point, Hillary McLaughlin told me, Mortimer again declared, "No, he didn't!" and became angry. "That's bullshit!" Mortimer claimed. "Beau would never do that! He's not that type of person."

To convince her cousin that Beau Donaldson really did try to rape her, McLaughlin gave her a blow-by-blow account of what had gone down in the bedroom. Mortimer refused to believe it, telling McLaughlin, "That's not true! That's not what happened!" before leaving Sutherlin's house in a huff.

When Hillary McLaughlin returned home to Great Falls, she didn't tell anybody except one friend about Beau Donaldson's attempt to rape her, and she decided not to report the assault to the police.

This assault happened in 2008. McLaughlin was nineteen years old. She'd recently enlisted in the Air National Guard and was about to begin basic training. Although she was traumatized by Donaldson's violent act, she wondered—like so many other victims of sexual assault—whether she was somehow responsible. "I was feeling all these different emotions," McLaughlin remembered. "I couldn't help wondering, like, did I do something to make him think that's what I wanted? Did I drink too much? I hadn't really done either of those things, but that stuff goes through your mind anyway. When I thought about it, I knew what happened wasn't my fault. But I didn't want to report it. I was like, 'I can probably just move past this and forget about it.'" So that's what she decided to do. And as time went on, it seemed like she had succeeded in putting the assault behind her.

In January 2012, Hillary McLaughlin realized that she was mistaken. More than three years had passed since Beau Donaldson had attacked her. In the interim, she'd met a man in the Air National Guard and had gotten married. She was eight months pregnant with their first child. One evening, McLaughlin told me, "My husband, Robert,* and I were sitting on the couch when all of a sudden Beau Donaldson's name and picture appeared on the TV screen. I took a deep breath and was like, 'Oh my gosh!' Robert asked, 'What's wrong?' I said, 'I have to tell you something.'"

Until that moment, Hillary McLaughlin hadn't said a word about the assault to anyone in her family, and she continued to say nothing about it to any of her relatives beyond her husband. After Beau Donaldson's arrest was in the news, she and Joanna Sutherlin talked about it over the phone, Hillary says, but "then we kind of went on with our lives and I didn't think much about it for a little while." Three weeks after Donaldson's arrest, however, her husband's phone rang, and an unfamiliar voice on the other end said, "Hi, this is Detective Guy Baker, from the Missoula Police Department, and I'm looking for Hillary McLaughlin."

"My husband wondered, 'Why do the police want to talk to Hillary? What kind of trouble is she in?'" Hillary said. "But I knew immediately why Detective Baker had called. I knew it was about Beau." When Hillary McLaughlin called Baker back, he explained that he'd heard she'd been sexually assaulted by Beau Donaldson in 2008 and he hoped she would be willing to provide him with a recorded statement of what happened that night.

McLaughlin wasn't sure she wanted to revisit what had been such a disturbing event. "My brother-in-law at the time was a U.S. marshal," she said. "So I asked him, 'What should I do?' He goes, 'I think you know what to do. You need to do the right thing.'"

After this conversation, McLaughlin was inclined to let Detective Baker interview her, but first she wanted to tell her father about the assault and get his opinion. "I'm very close to my dad," she explained, "and I really wanted to tell him face-to-face, but I was supposed to do the recording the next day, so I had to tell him over the phone. When I called him, of course, his first instinct was 'I'm going to kill Beau Donaldson! I'm going to drive down

* pseudonym

to Missoula and I'm going to kill him!' But then my dad calmed down and said, 'I think you need to make that statement to the police, and you need to do it right away, because it might help that other woman he raped. And it might keep him from raping anyone else.' "

On January 26, 2012, Hillary McLaughlin told her story to Detective Baker. And then she waited anxiously for whatever was going to happen next.

What happened was that she had an epiphany. She suddenly understood that she'd been deceiving herself when she thought she'd put the attack behind her. In fact, Beau Donaldson was still just beneath the surface of her consciousness, creating all kinds of havoc, and he'd been lurking there ever since he'd tried to rape her.

"Before Beau attacked me," McLaughlin said, "I'd never been an anxious person. But around the time he was arrested, I realized that since 2008 there had been a huge spike in my anxiety level. I used to be a very active runner and loved running outside. Now I'm afraid to run outside by myself." Indeed, she said, ever since the attack she's been terrified to be alone. Whenever she was by herself and had to walk from her house to her car at night, she would call her husband, Robert, and ask him to keep talking to her until she was safely inside the vehicle with the doors locked. "He did it," McLaughlin said, "but he never understood why I was so scared."

Hesitantly, Hillary McLaughlin admitted that she was also afraid of the dark. "I was twenty-one years old and afraid of the dark," she said, looking astonished. "It got to the point where I wouldn't even stay at my house by myself. If Robert was out of town for training or something, I would stay at my sister's or my parents'. And it's not like I live in a scary neighborhood. I live in a nice, safe neighborhood."

McLaughlin recalled a trip she and Robert made to New York. "We were walking down the street to get tickets for a Broadway show," she said, "when a guy just kind of brushed my shoulder, and I lost it. I started crying uncontrollably. I was clutching Robert's hand for dear life." Things got so bad that Hillary finally told her obstetrician about her irrational fears. “I didn’t explain to her what happened,” she said. “I just said I had severe anxiety. I told her that I bolt, that I’m always scared, always looking over my shoulder. I mean, I wake up in the middle of the night to go to the bathroom, and I turn on every light in my house. If I hear one little noise, I completely freak out.”

McLaughlin said, “I never put it all together until after Beau was arrested. My husband and I were talking one night, and I told him, ‘My anxiety has gotten so bad.’ He asked me when it began, so we started going back through events to try and figure it out. And that’s when I realized: Ever since that night in Missoula is when it began.”

CHAPTER FOURTEEN

On January 13, 2012, the day Beau Donaldson made bail and was released from the Missoula County Detention Facility, Allison Huguet received an e-mail from a deputy county attorney named Shaun Donovan, informing her that he would be handling the Donaldson prosecution. Donovan explained that according to the terms of Donaldson's release from the county lockup, he would be required to wear a GPS monitoring device on his ankle and complete a chemical-dependency program. Donaldson was also forbidden to have any contact with Huguet or her family, to go within one thousand feet of her home, or to leave Missoula County.

Sixty years old, heavyset, and rumpled, Shaun Donovan was a native Montanan with an undergraduate degree from Stanford and a Juris Doctor from the University of Montana School of Law. Early in his career he'd worked for Milt Datsopoulos, the attorney now representing Donaldson. From 1979 through 2010, Donovan had served as the county attorney in sparsely populated Mineral County, just west of Missoula. As the only lawyer in the office, he personally handled every case. In 2011, when the citizens of Mineral County decided, after thirty-one years, that it was time for a change and voted him out of a job, Donovan moved back to Missoula, where he became one of sixteen deputy attorneys toiling under County Attorney Fred Van Valkenburg in what, by Montana standards, amounted to a large, frenetic law office.

Because Beau Donaldson had confessed to raping Huguet while

she slept, it would be all but impossible for Milt Datsopoulos to convince a jury that he was innocent. Shaun Donovan was therefore confident that the case would be resolved with a plea deal and would never go to trial. Soon after Donaldson's arrest, however, Datsopoulos made it clear that he intended to demand a lenient punishment for Donaldson as part of any plea agreement. Huguet, on the other hand, insisted that prosecutors settle for nothing less than a lengthy sentence at the state penitentiary in Deer Lodge.

In Montana, a plea deal that involves a negotiated sentence typically works like this: In return for a guilty plea from the defendant, the prosecutors recommend a sentence that the defendant and his attorneys are willing to accept as the maximum punishment; the defendant's attorneys recommend a sentence that the prosecutors are willing to accept as the minimum punishment; and both sides agree to let the judge determine a sentence that falls somewhere within the range of their differing recommendations. After the terms of the plea deal are agreed upon and submitted to the judge, a sentencing hearing is held to allow each side to argue the merits of its recommendation in court. At the conclusion of this hearing, the judge issues a ruling and the sentence is imposed.

In Beau Donaldson's case, the plea negotiations (like most plea negotiations) resembled a slow-moving game of chicken. Each side threatened to halt negotiations and take the case to trial (an outcome desired by neither the defense nor the prosecution) unless the other side agreed to its terms. But as the case crept forward through the winter, spring, and summer of 2012, Allison Huguet became increasingly concerned that Shaun Donovan wasn't firmly committed to a deal that included hard time at Deer Lodge. Despite Donovan's many assurances to the contrary, Huguet and her family worried that he would cede to Milt Datsopoulos's demands that Beau Donaldson be allowed to serve a short sentence at a minimum-security Department of Corrections facility, followed by probation, rather than being incarcerated at the state prison, a much harsher and more restrictive environment.

According to Montana state law, the maximum sentence for a

person convicted of sexual intercourse without consent (SIWOC)—the legal term for rape in Montana—is incarceration in the state prison for one hundred years; the minimum sentence is two years in the state prison. But the law allows for exceptions to the minimum. In Donaldson's case, for example, if the judge determined that "no serious bodily injury was inflicted on the victim," the minimum sentence could include no prison time at all. Indeed, in Missoula County it was common for defendants found guilty of rape to receive sentences that didn't require them to spend any time behind bars.

On April 12, to give Allison Huguet a better sense of what sort of punishment she might realistically expect Beau Donaldson and his attorney to accept in a plea deal, Shaun Donovan sent an e-mail to Allison and her parents, Kevin and Beth Huguet, summarizing the outcome of local rape cases over the previous decade. From 2001 through the first three months of 2012, sixty-seven men had been convicted of SIWOC in Missoula County. In four of those cases the defendants were sentenced to an average of fifty years behind bars. In forty-two cases, the defendants were sentenced to a mix of prison time and probation that ranged from ten years to sixty years of prison and probation combined. In the other twenty-one cases, the sentences included no incarceration whatsoever. At the conclusion of this e-mail, Donovan assured the Huguets,

> I remain committed to seeking a sentence that requires Beau to do some time at the state prison, to be on probation for a very long time after his release and to register as a sex offender for the remainder of his life. . . . Please let me know if you have questions, want to talk or whatever.

Twenty-seven minutes after she received Shaun Donovan's e-mail, Allison wrote back,

> For me it is unsettling knowing that there is even a possibility that he will get no jail time or even a small amount of time

> even though he has confessed to such a horrible crime. . . . I also trust that you know and hopefully the judge will know how deeply this has affected me and my family and understand that Beau has to be the one to pay for it.

ON APRIL 18, two weeks before Assistant Attorney General Thomas Perez announced that the U.S. Department of Justice was investigating the Missoula County Attorney's Office and the Missoula Police Department for bungling dozens of rape cases, Allison Huguet was contacted by a DOJ investigator who wanted to speak with her about the way the Missoula police and prosecutors had handled her case. When Huguet asked Shaun Donovan about the federal investigation, it turned out that neither he nor Fred Van Valkenburg was aware of it; by contacting Donovan, Huguet inadvertently tipped off the county attorney's office that it was under investigation by the DOJ—a revelation that alarmed Van Valkenburg greatly and immediately caused his entire office to circle the wagons.

Professing that the county attorney didn't want to "complicate the resolution of the case against Beau Donaldson," Donovan asked Huguet to check with him "before providing any information to anyone about the Donaldson case." In truth, Van Valkenburg had simply decided that the best way to handle the crisis was to assert that the investigation was an abuse of the DOJ's statutory and constitutional authority and to stonewall the feds.

Allison Huguet agreed to contact Shaun Donovan before talking to the DOJ, but she said it seemed to her that the investigation might be good for her case and that "the added pressure will help everyone."

Donovan's response was curt. He reiterated that if anyone from the DOJ contacted her again,

> Before you talk to them we have asked that they call me or Fred Van Valkenburg. . . . Anything you say may get to

> Beau's lawyer which is why we want to proceed truthfully but carefully. . . . The "added pressure" from the investigation may do some good somewhere but it will not help our case against Beau in any way. It is much more likely to cause harm.

ALLISON HUGUET GRADUATED from Eastern Oregon University on June 16, 2012, and returned to Missoula a day later to live at her mother's house and help with the wedding of her older sister, Sarah, who was getting married on June 27. Allison, her younger sister, Kathleen, and various friends held a bridal shower for Sarah on June 26, then went out on the town for a bachelorette party. They had originally intended to go bowling, because Allison had seen some of the ugly comments that had been posted about her online in the wake of Beau Donaldson's arrest and didn't want to go to a bar, lest she run into some of his friends. But their plans changed, and late that night, Kathleen, Allison, Sarah, and the rest of the bride's entourage ended up at a notorious Missoula drinking establishment called Stockman's.

"It's a big Griz bar," Allison told me. "A lot of Beau's friends work there." A mural covering the lower half of Stockman's front window depicts four grizzly bears and a half dozen Griz football players sprinting en masse toward the end zone. When Kathleen and Sarah Huguet went to the bar to order drinks, the bartender recognized them as Allison's sisters and refused to serve them.

Sarah Huguet and the bachelorettes were sitting opposite the bar, pondering their next move, when a group of men approached. One of them was a brother of Beau's, Brady Donaldson, who was three years older than Allison and Beau and had attended school with Sarah Huguet when they were growing up in the Target Range neighborhood. "They were standing pretty close, just staring at us," Allison remembered. "There was definitely tension in the air."

Among the members of Brady Donaldson's retinue was Sam Erschler. Although Erschler was a close friend of the Donaldson brothers, Allison also considered him to be her friend. Erschler had facilitated Beau's confession the morning after he'd raped Allison and had offered her emotional support. So Allison was surprised when an acquaintance named Norman* came over to the bachelorettes and, by her account, said, "God, I can't stand Erschler. I was just over there getting a drink and he told me I need to stay away from you. He said you girls were nothing but trouble."

By now the Huguets and their friends had decided to leave Stockman's. As they were moving out of the bar, Allison said, "I walked past Sam Erschler, touched his arm, and said, 'You know, Sam, I don't bad-mouth you to other people, and I'd appreciate it if you would do the same for me.'"

"What are you talking about?" Erschler replied. "I've never said anything bad about you."

"Seriously?" Allison said. "Did you not just tell Norman that he needed to stay away from me?"

This caused Sam Erschler to fly into a rage. "I never said anything bad about you!" he screamed. As Allison walked away, he followed her out the door, shouting insults at the top of his lungs. "You fucking bitch!" Erschler yelled. "I never said anything bad about you!"

Then Brady Donaldson started harassing the Huguet sisters, as well. "You may think everything's fine right now," he shouted at them, "but you guys just wait! In September, when this goes to trial, the gloves are gonna come off!"

"Yeah," Kathleen Huguet spat back. "In September. When your brother goes to prison and gets fucked in the ass and learns what it feels like to get raped himself!" By this time a large crowd had gathered on the sidewalk around the bachelorettes and Brady Donaldson's friends.

Donaldson started making threatening gestures, and he bellowed at Allison and Kathleen Huguet, "You need to get the fuck out of Missoula!" Someone else in Brady Donaldson's group threatened to kill the Huguets.

* pseudonym

Erschler screeched at Allison, "Good luck on the fucking stand, bitch!" As the Huguets and their friends walked away, Allison recalled, "We could hear them screaming at us for blocks. I felt really bad that it ruined my sister's bachelorette party."

LITTLE PROGRESS WAS made on the plea negotiations between the Missoula County Attorney's Office and Milt Datsopoulos, Beau Donaldson's attorney, through mid-July 2012. On July 20, deputy prosecutor Shaun Donovan met with Kevin Huguet to give him an update. Three days earlier, during a conference with head Missoula County prosecutor Fred Van Valkenburg and Datsopoulos, Donovan had floated the idea of recommending a sentence of five years and allowing Beau Donaldson to serve it at a minimum-security Department of Corrections facility rather than the state prison. Donovan insinuated to Kevin that both Van Valkenburg and Datsopoulos thought it was a fair sentence.

Anticipating that Kevin Huguet might not be thrilled with such a light sentence, Donovan explained that although it was a more lenient sentence than the Huguets wanted, he thought it might be the stiffest punishment Beau Donaldson would accept in return for pleading guilty. Furthermore, if they failed to achieve a plea deal and the case went to trial, a sentence of five years at the DOC, or even less, might well be the outcome, because Milt Datsopoulos was a skilled criminal attorney with a long history of winning rape cases.

Shaun Donovan pointed out to the Huguets that Datsopoulos would tell the judge and jury that Beau Donaldson had no prior criminal record; he didn't use a weapon or act violently during the commission of the crime; he was a young man with a promising future; he had a supportive family; he accepted responsibility for his actions; and he would seek treatment for his substance abuse problems and his aberrant sexual behavior. It was understood that if the case went to trial, Datsopoulos was likely to do everything possible to impugn Allison Huguet's character, because smearing the victim is one of the most effective tactics lawyers have at their disposal when defending rapists.

Donovan also reminded Kevin Huguet that they needed to consider "the environment in Missoula." What he meant by this needed no elaboration: Beau had been a celebrated and beloved hometown high school football star who now played for the Grizzlies; the Griz were heading into the 2012 season as the reigning co-champions of the Big Sky Conference; and any jury empaneled in Missoula County would almost certainly include a significant number of loyal Griz supporters.

Shaun Donovan's rationale for recommending a lenient punishment didn't sit well with Kevin Huguet. He was furious that Donovan would even consider agreeing to a sentence of five years at a DOC facility. "We had been fighting Shaun for months about this very point. We wanted Beau to serve his time at Deer Lodge, not the DOC, where things would be easy for him, his family could visit whenever they wanted, and where all his buddies could come out and hang with him," Kevin explained. "We knew that if he was sentenced to the DOC, he'd get probation and be out on the street in no time, because that's how it usually works. So we were really adamant that we weren't going to accept anything less than hard time at the penitentiary, and we weren't going to back down from that."

When Kevin Huguet told Allison that Shaun Donovan had argued for a light sentence at their meeting, she was demoralized. Given the ongoing investigation of the Missoula County Attorney's Office by the DOJ and all the criticism from both local and national news media that Fred Van Valkenburg's office had allowed numerous rapists to avoid prosecution, she couldn't understand why Donovan and Van Valkenburg seemed so determined to go easy on Beau Donaldson. Detective Guy Baker had told her that the case he'd assembled against Donaldson was backed up with some of the strongest evidence he'd ever submitted for a rape case. With Hillary McLaughlin's testimony about Donaldson's attempt to rape her, the case had grown even stronger. So why was the prosecution so reluctant to seek an appropriately harsh sentence?

Allison was shocked that Donovan seemed to be on the verge of reneging on his pledge to settle for nothing less than significant time in the state penitentiary. "It felt like I'd been lied to," she told me, "and pushed in the direction they wanted to go. I felt like I continually had to push back to try to get the prosecutor's office to do the right thing. They made it pretty clear that they didn't like it when I spoke up or questioned what they were doing, or asked them to do more than they wanted to. It was really hard for me. I see now why most girls who've been raped don't go forward with pressing charges."

Recent sexual-assault cases in fanatical football towns such as Tallahassee, Florida; South Bend, Indiana; Seattle, Washington; and Columbia, Missouri, give credence to the notion that if the defendants are star players, it can be difficult to hold them accountable. But to the Huguet family, Shaun Donovan's suggestion that it was unrealistic to expect much, if any, prison time for Beau Donaldson because Missoulians were in thrall to Griz football seemed like a self-fulfilling prophecy.

"Shaun is a likable guy," Kevin noted. "But he's part of the local good old boys club, and he has two sons who played football for Carroll College [a private school in Helena, Montana, that won the National Association of Intercollegiate Athletics football title in 2002, 2003, 2004, 2005, 2007, and 2010]. I was highly concerned right away that his kids played on teams that won national championships. I wondered where his loyalty was going to lie. How hard is he going to fight for my kid against an accused football player? Shaun seemed way too concerned about the effect of the legal proceedings on Beau and his family. Even in our first meeting he was talking about 'Beau's poor family. Remember that they're victims as well. Beau's actions have caused them significant financial harm and emotional harm.' Like, he thinks I care about that? After what Beau did to Allison? He raped my daughter while she was sleeping. I care about only one thing, and that's justice. I want him to go to prison."

During their July 20 meeting, deputy prosecutor Shaun Donovan had given Kevin Huguet a four-page document that outlined potential sentences for Beau Donaldson and listed the pros and cons of recommending each sentence. Shortly after the meeting concluded, he e-mailed the same document to Allison, and he also invited her to meet with him to discuss potential sentences. When she read it, her mistrust of Donovan grew.

Allison Huguet arranged to meet Donovan on July 26, and she asked her sister Kathleen and Detective Guy Baker to accompany her. The discussion quickly turned to whether Allison would agree to a five-year sentence at a minimum-security Department of Corrections facility, which Donovan seemed to favor. When Allison told him she would go to trial before she accepted such a lenient punishment for Beau Donaldson, Shaun Donovan countered that getting a conviction for rape was, throughout the country, among the most difficult challenges prosecutors faced.

Donovan also warned Allison that she might believe she was strong, but being on the witness stand and getting ripped to shreds by a veteran defense attorney like Milt Datsopoulos "is a lot harder than you think."

Prior to this meeting, however, Detective Baker had assured Allison, "You have the fortitude to go to trial. I know you can do this. I will be there in the courtroom when you are testifying, and you can look over at me for support. Standing up to Beau and telling the truth for everyone to hear will give you back control. It will empower you."

Emboldened by Baker's confidence in her, Allison demanded to know why Shaun Donovan would even discuss the possibility of a short sentence at the DOC if he was sincerely committed to a longer sentence at the Deer Lodge penitentiary. Growing angry and defensive, Donovan snapped, "I've been doing this job for a long time, and you are not going to change how I do my job, Allison."

Detective Baker broke into the discussion at this point to try to dial down the tension. He politely asked Donovan if he would be willing to explain to Milt Datsopoulos that Allison was unwilling to accept anything less than a sentence in the state penitentiary.

According to Allison, Donovan replied, "I would never do that. I will not recommend a sentence simply because it's what the victim wants." This infuriated Allison, but according to the laws of Montana (and almost every other state), although prosecutors are required to consult with victims of rape about plea negotiations, they are completely free to ignore a victim's entreaties at their discretion. A rape victim has absolutely no right to veto a plea deal if he or she finds it objectionable. It came as a surprise to Allison Huguet, but deputy prosecutor Shaun Donovan was not acting as her attorney in the way that Milt Datsopoulos was acting as Beau Donaldson's attorney. Donovan's title was deputy Missoula County attorney, and his legal responsibility was to represent the interests of the state of Montana, not Allison Huguet's interests. Whenever he believed those interests diverged, Huguet was out of luck.

As this became clear to Huguet, her anger was exacerbated by the fact that earlier, when she'd asked Donovan if it would be a good idea for her to retain a lawyer to represent her personal interests, he'd repeatedly discouraged her from doing so, assuring her that it was unnecessary and might make her case harder to prosecute.

CHAPTER FIFTEEN

For the first sixteen months after she was raped, Allison Huguet found it surprisingly easy to keep her emotions under control, at least most of the time, by stuffing the trauma into some deep recess of her subconscious. That changed after Beau Donaldson's arrest. Suddenly her rape was all over the news, and it stayed in the news for months. Missoula can feel like a very small town in which everyone seems to know everyone else's business. Although she was never named by the mainstream news media, hundreds of people, perhaps thousands, learned from the gossip mill that Huguet was Donaldson's accuser, the woman responsible for his arrest. "I was surprised how quickly people found out," said Huguet's friend Keely Williams. "Because the day after Beau got arrested, people started texting me things like 'What the fuck is wrong with you and Allison? Why is she lying about being raped?' "

Donaldson told his friends and family that he and Huguet had had sex multiple times before, "so he couldn't have raped her." In turn, his friends and family spread the word throughout Missoula, and beyond, that she had falsely accused him. A great many people were led to believe that she was enjoying the attention she was getting for maliciously destroying his life.

The rumors were utterly false. In the summer of 2012, Huguet grew increasingly anxious, even paranoid—an aftereffect of the rape. If she entered a bathroom and the shower curtain wasn't pulled all the way open, she became fearful that someone was hiding behind it, and she'd panic. Before going to sleep she would check under the bed to make sure nobody was hiding beneath it. And then she would check again, and again. She had great difficulty sleeping. When a doctor recommended that she take medications to reduce her anxiety or help her sleep, she refused. "I didn't want to take something that made me fall asleep," Huguet explained, "because I was afraid I would be unable to wake up if something bad happened."

When she did fall asleep, moreover, she had recurring nightmares. "They started after Beau was arrested," Huguet told me, "when I was constantly having to fight the prosecutors about getting him sent to prison. I remember some of the nightmares really clearly."

In one of them, Huguet dreamed that she, Beau Donaldson, and her friend Keely Williams were standing on the Maclay Bridge—a decrepit one-lane bridge across the Bitterroot River, in the neighborhood where they grew up. During the summer, the bridge is a popular hangout for local teenagers, who jump from it into the chilly river below. In Huguet's nightmare, she recalled, "It was late fall or maybe winter. Beau and Keely and me were down by the bridge, and I think Beau was trying to tell me he was sorry for raping me. And then he jumped off the bridge to kill himself. I jumped in to save him, even though Keely was yelling, 'No! No! No! Let him go! Don't go after him!'

"I swam over to him, and was trying to pull him to shore, when suddenly he woke up with this look on his face," Huguet said, trying not to sob. "It was that same look he had when I saw him at the Mo Club at Thanksgiving and he was laughing at me. I realized that he wasn't drowning, and that he hadn't jumped off the bridge to kill himself. Then Beau grabbed me, held me underwater, and tried to drown me." At this point Huguet woke up, terrified. "Looking at the nightmare now," she continued, "I think it says a lot about what I was going through. I think I was struggling with the fact that I still wanted to trust Beau, my childhood friend, but he obviously was not trustworthy."

She had many such nightmares. "When I'd have a dream like that," Huguet said, "I'd wake up emotionally drained. The images from the dream would be really vivid, and they would stay in my head throughout the day. I couldn't get them out of my mind. People don't understand how exhausting that was—the nightmares, and not sleeping, and constantly worrying about who might be hiding behind the shower curtain. They just don't get what you go through, day after day, when you've been raped."

ALLISON HUGUET'S ONGOING stalemate with deputy prosecutor Shaun Donovan and the Missoula County Attorney's Office (MCAO) exacerbated her post-traumatic stress, but she refused to agree to a plea deal that didn't require Beau Donaldson to serve time in the state penitentiary. By late August, Donovan felt he'd negotiated a deal with Donaldson's attorney, Milt Datsopoulos, that the Huguet family would be able to live with. On August 20, Donovan held a meeting with Allison, her parents, Fred Van Valkenburg, and Assistant Deputy Chief County Attorney Suzy Boylan, one of the most skilled prosecutors at the MCAO, to discuss the plea agreement Donovan had drafted, hoping the Huguets would agree to it.

The meeting was quarrelsome. According to the terms of the deal, in return for a guilty plea by Donaldson, "the State agrees to recommend that the Defendant be sentenced to a term of 30 years at the Montana State Prison with 20 years of that sentence suspended." When the prosecutors asked Allison if she would agree to it, she told them she was "not willing to agree to that, at all."

Boylan tried to change Allison's mind by arguing that ten years in the state prison was "quite harsh." The Huguets responded by pointing out that a ten-year sentence meant Donaldson would in fact be eligible for parole after just two and a half years. Boylan countered that although Allison appeared to be a very strong woman, she had no idea what it was like to get up on the witness stand and be cross-examined by a ruthless defense attorney.

Boylan had seen it many times, she said, and it was almost always an unimaginably horrible experience for the victim. She also stated, quite accurately, that if the case went to trial there was a good chance that Beau Donaldson would receive a sentence that included no prison time whatsoever.

After Boylan spoke, Van Valkenburg told the Huguets that this was almost certainly the harshest deal Milt Datsopoulos and Beau Donaldson would accept and, furthermore, that he was going to present the deal to Datsopoulos regardless of whether the Huguets were on board. And if they didn't agree with the terms of the deal, Van Valkenburg added, he hoped they would at least agree not to let it become "a public spat in the media." The next day, August 21, Shaun Donovan sent the plea agreement to Donaldson and Datsopoulos to be signed.

On September 11, 2012, they signed it. That afternoon, television reporter Irina Cates posted a story on the KPAX website in which she wrote,

> Prosecutors say the victim is not completely satisfied with the plea bargain, but she understands why it had to be done.
>
> "It's beneficial to the victim and the community in the sense that there's a guarantee of a conviction. There is always a possibility when a person does not plead guilty that something else could happen, that results in them not being convicted," says Deputy Missoula County Attorney Shaun Donovan.
>
> "The reason we pled guilty is that it's a reduced recommendation substantially from the original proposal by the county attorney's office," says Donaldson's defense attorney Milt Datsopoulos. . . .
>
> During the investigation, Missoula Police detectives monitored a phone call between the victim and Donaldson, where Donaldson admitted taking advantage of her. He apologized to the woman and attributed the act to a drinking problem and pain medication.
>
> "He made a mistake, he acknowledged that mistake early

on and based on his conduct—based on his former life—we believe strongly this young man shouldn't have a big chunk of his life taken away from him," Datsopoulos said. . . .

Datsopoulos is concerned the federal investigations into the Missoula community and the sexual assault allegations involving UM athletes could affect Donaldson's case.

Four hours later, Gwen Florio announced the plea agreement on the *Missoulian* website:

"The victim has suffered an injury that no amount of punishing the defendant is going to fix," said Donovan.

Donaldson's attorney, Milt Datsopoulos, said he doesn't believe prison is the place for his client. "Hopefully, the life he's led will be the most persuasive" argument in favor of a less severe sentence, Datsopoulos said. . . .

"He made a mistake and he acknowledged that mistake early on," Datsopoulos said. According to charging documents in the case, Donaldson apologized to the woman the next day.

"This took place at a house party and both individuals had been drinking," Datsopoulos said. Everyone there "was drinking more than they should, but that's a rite of passage," he said.

Donovan said he doesn't know if the victim or her family will testify at the sentencing. But if the victim chooses, she can ask the judge to impose a longer prison sentence. "She's conflicted," he said of the plea agreement.

Datsopoulos said a more appropriate sentence would involve his client being placed in a prerelease center run by the Department of Corrections.

And he said he's concerned that publicity over the issue of sexual assault—especially "the premise that [UM athletes] have been given special consideration"—has "polluted" the environment surrounding sentencing.

"I don't think that's completely far-fetched, but we don't

want that to happen," Donovan said, adding that the County Attorney's Office seeks "an appropriate" sentence.

The articles upset Allison Huguet. She felt that Milt Datsopoulos had skillfully spun his comments to portray Beau Donaldson in a very sympathetic light, while Shaun Donovan's statements had failed to present a strong case for a harsh sentence. Even after the media announced that Donaldson had confessed to raping Huguet and had pleaded guilty, many Missoulians continued to believe that she was lying and he was innocent. A close friend of Huguet's named Valerie* told Huguet that her father had come home from a poker game and started to rant about "how messed up it was that Beau Donaldson was going to have to go to jail."

"Why?" Valerie asked her father. "Would you think the same thing if it was me who'd been raped by Beau?"

Her dad replied that the friends he was playing cards with—men who knew both Huguet and Donaldson quite well—had assured him that "Allison made up a story about being raped, and it's all a lie."

In a September 12 e-mail to prosecutors Shaun Donovan and Fred Van Valkenburg, Huguet requested a meeting to "discuss a few things." She explained that she was "a little frustrated with some of the comments" Donovan had made to reporters Irina Cates and Gwen Florio. Although she "appreciated" that he'd mentioned she "didn't necessarily agree with the plea deal," Huguet wrote, she was confused by what Donovan meant when he said she was "conflicted":

> I have remained consistent through the entire process that [Donaldson] needs to go to prison for a long amount of time and that I fully intend on testifying/making a verbal statement [to that effect] at the sentencing. . . .
>
> Milt continues to try and play this off as a "mistake"

* pseudonym

> and make Beau look like someone teachers, coaches, and principals will stand up for. [Milt also] tries to pass off some of [Beau's] responsibility . . . by saying "This took place at a house party and both individuals had been drinking. . . . Everyone there 'was drinking more than they should, but that's a rite of passage.' " . . .
>
> From the beginning I have been trying really hard to have faith and find the positives in each court hearing, but I am struggling to feel like I am being fully supported and defended by your office. I know Milt has the right to say whatever he wants to the media and I am not at all shocked by what he is saying, it would just be nice if your office could be a little more aggressive in responding to some of his claims and make your own statements reminding the public of what Beau is, which is someone who admitted [to] raping someone he describes as "a little sister." I truly do appreciate your guys time with the case and hope that you can understand my frustrations.

FRED VAN VALKENBURG was born in Billings, the most populous city in Montana. He was class president of his small Catholic high school and quarterback of its football team. In 1970, he moved to Missoula to attend the University of Montana School of Law, after which he stayed in town and worked for two years as assistant city attorney before going into private practice, working frequently as a public defender. A Democrat, he ran for the Montana Senate in 1978, won the election, and represented Missoula's district for the next twenty years, including a three-year stint as senate president. In 1985, while continuing to serve in the state legislature, Van Valkenburg began working as a deputy Missoula County attorney, and he was elected county attorney in 1998. He was reelected to the position in 2002, 2006, and, most recently, 2010—when he ran unopposed.

The prosecutors who worked for Fred Van Valkenburg liked

and respected him. He trusted the judgment of his deputy county attorneys and gave them plenty of latitude to prosecute their cases as they saw fit.

Surprisingly, given the success Van Valkenburg has had in the political arena, he's a resolutely independent thinker, and he has not been afraid to take unpopular positions and make controversial decisions. During his years in the state senate, he was a champion of women's rights and spearheaded important legislation to prevent gender-based discrimination. His self-confidence (some call it arrogance) is renowned, as is his obstinacy. He has a well-deserved reputation for fighting stubbornly for what he believes is right, public opinion be damned.

On September 19, 2012, when Allison Huguet met with Van Valkenburg to discuss her dissatisfaction with the way his office was handling her case, she was accompanied by her father, Kevin Huguet; her mother, Beth Huguet; her stepmother, Margie Huguet; and Detective Guy Baker. "Allison really wanted Detective Baker to be there," Margie told me. "I think his presence had a big effect on the meeting."

"Guy made Allison feel comfortable and safe," Kevin Huguet agreed. "He was always swinging for her." Joining Van Valkenburg on his side of the table were his lieutenant, prosecutor Suzy Boylan, and victim advocate Tanya Campbell. Notably absent was the lead prosecutor for Allison's case, Shaun Donovan.

Soon after the meeting got under way, the Huguets told Van Valkenburg that they weren't happy with the way Donovan was handling things. They said they were glad he was able to deliver a plea deal, but they were concerned that the judge might give Donaldson a lighter sentence than the plea deal recommended if Donovan didn't go to the mat for Allison at the sentencing hearing, which was scheduled to be held on October 13. "We wanted someone to argue aggressively for the stiffest possible sentence," Kevin told me, "and we didn't think Shaun would do that."

Kevin Huguet started pushing Van Valkenburg's buttons. "I asked him, 'Are you guys afraid of Milt or something? Is that what's going on here?' All of a sudden Fred's blood pressure went up, he got red in the face, and he came flying back at me. I hadn't gone into the meeting consciously intending to get him going, but it worked. By the middle of the meeting he said, 'You know what? I'll take over from here. I'll handle the sentencing hearing.'"

"Fred told me I could have anyone in the office I wanted," Allison said, "but he felt he was the most qualified."

"Allison didn't love Fred at all," Kevin mused. "But he was the biggest stick in the office. Of all the attorneys there, he was clearly the one to choose."

"In the end," Allison said, "Fred did a good job for me. But I think that had a lot to do with the *Missoulian* paying so much attention to the case, and the DOJ looking into things. It gave me a lot of leverage. That's why he was willing to listen to my frustrations with Shaun. If there had been no media coverage, no outside investigations, I don't think Fred would have even met with me."

CHAPTER SIXTEEN

In February 2012, when University of Montana dean of students Charles Couture initiated a disciplinary investigation of quarterback Jordan Johnson for allegedly raping Cecilia Washburn, the case quickly became contentious, because of Johnson's celebrity status and the scorched-earth tactics that his attorney employed to defend him.

Upon learning that Johnson had been accused of rape, the UM athletic department had arranged for him to be represented by David Paoli, a local lawyer who served on the National Advisory Board for Grizzly Athletics and had attended UM on a football scholarship in the early 1980s. Playing noseguard, Paoli anchored the defensive line for the Griz, earning accolades for his ferocious tackling. But Paoli was no dumb jock. After graduating with honors from the UM School of Law in 1986, he clerked for a federal judge, launched his own law firm in 1992, and eventually developed into a preeminent Montana attorney. In 2011, the Montana Trial Lawyers Association designated Paoli "Trial Lawyer of the Year."

For many years, Milt Datsopoulos, the attorney who defended Beau Donaldson, had provided expert assistance to numerous Griz athletes who found themselves on the wrong side of the law. But Datsopoulos was seventy-one years old. Jordan Johnson was the most celebrated athlete in the state. Influential people affiliated with the University of Montana apparently believed that fifty-one-year-old David Paoli, who was notoriously pugnacious, would be a better choice to defend Johnson, given the gravity of the allegation against him.

As soon as he was retained by Jordan Johnson, Paoli adopted extremely aggressive tactics to defend his client, sparing no expense. In the letter from Dean Couture notifying Johnson that he was being investigated by the university, Couture had warned,

> you are to have absolutely no contact of any kind, including third party, with Ms. Washburn. Also, this is a highly confidential matter, and you are prohibited from discussing your alleged misconduct with other people. Failure to comply with these directives would result in your immediate dismissal from the University.

On February 15, three days after Johnson received this warning, Paoli phoned UM legal counsel David Aronofsky to raise objections about the no-contact prohibition, arguing that as Johnson's attorney, he had a legal right to question witnesses. In a follow-up e-mail to Paoli, Aronofsky agreed but urged him to exercise restraint:

> You would be meeting your professional obligations to conduct an investigation for your client and the University will allow you to do this with the caveat that contacting the alleged victim directly or through intermediaries would not be appropriate at this time because of the no-contact instructions. I would suggest you consider going a bit cautiously on your investigation until after next Tuesday's meeting because we may all learn information there which would be useful in whatever future steps are taken.

On February 17, ignoring Aronofsky's recommendation to wait until after the opposing parties had a chance to discuss the best way to proceed, Paoli hired a private investigator, Mark Fullerton, to observe Cecilia Washburn's house, make sure she wasn't on the premises, and then interview her two housemates in order to gather evidence that could be used to cast doubt on her claim that Jordan Johnson raped her. Although hiring private investigators to do this sort of thing is common in criminal rape cases, it had seldom, if ever, been done during a UM adjudication of a Student Conduct Code violation. When Washburn returned home and learned that Fullerton had been there grilling her housemates about what they recalled about the night of February 4, she became quite upset. It was "frightening," she later testified, and she felt "violated."

Later, Cecilia Washburn discovered that David Paoli had also sent investigator Mark Fullerton to the tiny community where she had gone to high school (the population of the entire town was 171) to gather derogatory information about her. There was no mistaking that Paoli intended to mount an extremely aggressive defense of Johnson.

When Washburn realized that a private investigator was snooping into her personal life, she called Dean Couture to express her shock and revulsion. Couture phoned Fullerton and left a message ordering him to "cease and desist" invading Washburn's privacy. Paoli responded immediately to Couture with a phone message of his own, reminding Couture that he had a right to question witnesses and had, in fact, obtained permission from UM counsel David Aronofsky to contact Washburn's housemates.

ON FEBRUARY 24, Dean Couture summoned Jordan Johnson to his office for their first investigatory meeting. Paoli and Aronofsky were also in attendance. According to a legal brief filed by Paoli,

> Couture began the meeting and was immediately abrasive and antagonistic. Although the Student Conduct Code indicated that he was required to present the evidence against Mr. [Johnson] and then allow Mr. [Johnson] to respond, [Dean of Students] Couture, to intimidate, commenced the meeting by looking at Mr. [Johnson] and blurted: "did you rape Ms. [Washburn]?"

Paoli would repeat his assertion that Couture was "abrasive and antagonistic" and tried to "intimidate" Johnson throughout the adjudication process. According to Couture's associates, the dean could indeed be brusque. But attorneys and other individuals who have tangled with Paoli in court, including some who were cross-examined by him on the witness stand, find Paoli's self-righteous indignation over Couture's abrasive tone to be more than a little ironic. Almost all of Paoli's antagonists, as well as many of his admirers, are in agreement that he has an uncommonly combative disposition and will go to almost any length to win a case. "Overbearing" is a word not infrequently used to describe him. "Bully" is another.

As one lawyer who has sparred with Paoli put it, "Dave was a noseguard for the Griz, and he practices law the same way he played football: He tries to run over whoever is in front of him." Those familiar with both Paoli and Couture suggest that Couture had no choice but to be aggressive when interacting with Paoli if he hoped to hold his own and be an effective advocate for Cecilia Washburn.

Following the strictures decreed by the U.S. Department of Education in its 2011 Dear Colleague Letter, UM, like every other American college and university, was required to use "the preponderance of evidence" standard as its burden of proof when adjudicating sexual-assault complaints, rather than the "clear and convincing evidence" standard that most universities were using at the time, or the "beyond a reasonable doubt" standard used in the criminal justice system. To expel a student, in other words, the university had to determine that just 51 percent of the credible evidence indicated that the accused had committed the offense. The purpose of the lower burden of proof was to make it harder for students to get away with rape—a crime the U.S. Department of Education had determined was occurring far too frequently on American campuses.

Two months before Jordan Johnson allegedly raped Cecilia Washburn, the University Court had relied on the "preponderance of evidence" standard to find Calvin Smith guilty of rape and expel him. But the Dear Colleague Letter had been issued less than six months before Smith raped Kaitlynn Kelly, and even though UM administrators used the lower burden of proof in their case against Smith, they were tardy in revising the UM Student Conduct Code to reflect the new standard.

On February 24, 2012, during Dean Couture's first meeting with Jordan Johnson and David Paoli, Johnson's counsel, Paoli made this oversight the central thrust of Johnson's defense, noting that the burden of proof specified in the Student Conduct Code, as it appeared at the time, was still the old "clear and convincing" standard that had been in place before the Dear Colleague Letter. Therefore, Paoli argued, the older, more stringent standard must be used for the adjudication of Johnson's case.

Couture and Aronofsky countered that the university simply hadn't yet gotten around to updating the Student Conduct Code to reflect the new standard—an irrelevant technicality that should not be allowed to let Johnson get away with rape. And this assertion—that the quest for truth and justice should trump procedural nitpicking—became a pivotal issue in the determination of Johnson's case. Paoli emphatically disagreed, and he railed against the university's failure to follow the letter of the Student Conduct Code, as published. He also railed against many other aspects of the way the university handled Johnson's disciplinary proceedings.

Not surprisingly, lawyers hired to defend students in university rape cases typically despise constraints like those imposed on their profession by the University of Montana, which forbids legal counsel to speak on behalf of their clients or interrogate witnesses during the proceedings. UM's deliberate rejection of the fundamental rules of criminal law enraged Paoli, and he frequently berated Couture and other university officials for their refusal to grant Johnson basic rights guaranteed by the criminal justice system. For his part, Dean Couture reminded Paoli that the university's investigation of his client was a disciplinary proceeding, not a criminal investigation, so it was entirely proper for the university to establish its own rules.

Three months earlier, when Couture had admonished attorney Josh Van de Wetering not to speak during the university's adjudication of the Calvin Smith case, Van de Wetering had reluctantly abided. But abiding is not in Paoli's nature. It was simply impossible for him to accept that the university had a legal right to refuse to let him speak or raise objections during the proceedings. As a consequence, Paoli often disregarded the policy and indignantly demanded to be heard. Couture, in turn, responded to these outbursts by commanding Paoli to keep his mouth shut. At one point during their February 24 meeting, according to Paoli, UM counsel David Aronofsky actually ordered him "to shut up." All of which prompted Paoli to protest more forcefully than ever that Couture and Aronofsky were demonstrating a "lack of impartiality."

Couture, however, wasn't supposed to be impartial. His job was to function not as a dispassionate judge but, rather, as the university's prosecutor. When Cecilia Washburn filed her complaint with the university accusing Johnson of rape, it was Couture's responsibility as dean of students to determine if there was probable cause to pursue a university investigation, just as it was the Missoula County attorney's responsibility to determine if probable cause existed to pursue criminal charges against Beau Donaldson in the Allison Huguet case. After Couture's initial investigation led him to decide that there was ample reason to believe that Jordan Johnson had raped Cecilia Washburn, Couture was expected to assemble a case for Johnson's expulsion from UM, just as Deputy County Attorney Shaun Donovan was expected to assemble and present a case for Donaldson's criminal conviction.

A second meeting between David Paoli, Jordan Johnson, Charles Couture, and David Aronofsky was held on March 9. During this meeting, Couture told Paoli and Johnson that he "was leaning towards" a finding consistent with Washburn's allegation that Johnson had raped her.

Aronofsky agreed to provide Paoli with copies of the investigatory file Dean Couture had assembled about the case. Upon reviewing the file, Paoli found statements from witnesses supporting Washburn that, in Paoli's opinion, clearly showed Couture's "lack of impartiality and predetermination" of Jordan Johnson's guilt. For example, Paoli was irked that a "witness lauded DOS Couture on how 'extremely understanding and compassionate' he was." Paoli saw further proof of egregious bias in a statement in the file from Cecilia Washburn on February 22 in which she noted,

> I met with Charles [Couture] to discuss his previous meeting with [Johnson] and [Paoli]. From what I understand, [Johnson pleaded] not guilty to committing the crime and had a very aggressive and entitled nature with Charles. Charles also said that [Paoli] was very standoffish.

It didn't seem to have occurred to Paoli that showing compassion and understanding to an alleged victim was entirely proper behavior by Couture, or that Washburn's description of Johnson's demeanor as "very aggressive and entitled" might have been accurate.

ON MARCH 27, Charles Couture sent a letter to Jordan Johnson, informing him,

> I have found a preponderance of evidence to support the allegation that you raped a fellow student, Ms. Cecilia Washburn, at her apartment on February 4, 2012. My finding is based, in part, on the following evidence:
>
> • Contrary to your repeated assertion, text messages between you and the victim prove you and the victim were more than mere acquaintances
> • Your previous conduct in your University residence hall*
> • Your assertion that you and the victim had jointly initiated

* During his freshman year, Johnson had been disciplined by the university for becoming drunk and disorderly at a party.

getting together the night of the rape; a copy of your text message to the victim clearly proves you initiated the meeting . . .

• The complete and immediate cessation of your friendship with the victim following the night of the rape

• Your failure to attempt to retrieve your watch that you forgot at the victim's house, despite your assertion that [this] watch had been a present to you from your sister

Appropriate sanction for this type of violent physical assault are:

1. Immediate expulsion from The University of Montana
2. No further access to any University property or University-sponsored activity at any time

You have the opportunity to accept or deny the charge of having violated the Student Conduct Code and/or accept or not accept the sanctions. If you deny the charge and/or not accept the sanctions, you have the right to an administrative conference with the Vice President of Student Affairs, or her designee, and a hearing by the University Court.

Jordan Johnson responded by denying the charge and requesting an administrative conference with Teresa Branch, the vice president of student affairs. That conference was held on April 20; in addition to Branch and Johnson, Paoli, Couture, and Aronofsky were also present. At the beginning of the meeting, Paoli hand-delivered to Branch a packet of reference letters attesting to Johnson's upstanding character, accompanied by a cover letter in which Paoli reasserted that Johnson had not raped Washburn.

I respectfully request that you ask yourself why would [Jordan Johnson] risk his entire life and the lives of his family by committing such a violent act when he has never done anything even remotely close to this and well-knowing that the accuser's male roommate was only a matter of a few feet outside her bedroom door.

During the meeting, Paoli again argued that Couture's bias, his failure to adhere to the published Student Conduct Code, "the irregularity of this process," and the "unadopted burden of proof" the university was imposing on Jordan Johnson were so egregious that the charge against his client should be dismissed. But Vice President Branch was not persuaded. At the conclusion of the meeting, she denied Johnson's appeal. He immediately indicated that he would appeal to the next level: the University Court.

A hearing before the court was scheduled for May 10, but Paoli was determined to halt the case before the hearing convened. He arranged for Jordan Johnson's parents to have an audience with University of Montana President Royce Engstrom, and then, on May 4, he hand-delivered a confidential letter to Engstrom claiming that the university's adjudication of Johnson had been "undermined and tainted by serious failures of due process and fundamental fairness." Paoli asked Engstrom to remove Dean Charles Couture and counsel David Aronofsky from the case, take control of it himself, and start the process over from scratch "with a truly impartial representative."

On May 8, when David Paoli received a letter from President Engstrom denying this highly irregular request, Paoli, on behalf of Jordan Johnson, filed a motion in United States District Court for the District of Montana for a temporary restraining order to prohibit the university from holding the University Court hearing. In the event that the restraining order was rejected, on May 9 Paoli also submitted a request to the university that two members of the University Court be barred from the hearing on the grounds that they were biased against his client.

On May 10, Judge Dana Christensen denied the restraining order, and the University Court hearing took place later that same day. Although the court members blackballed by Paoli had been replaced by two different individuals, as Paoli had demanded, the court found Jordan Johnson guilty of raping Cecilia Washburn, by a vote of five to two. All seven members then voted unanimously to expel Johnson from the university.

On June 6, after reviewing this decision, President Engstrom found that the court's conclusion was "reasonable . . . based on the testimony and evidence available." Additionally, Engstrom wrote to Jordan Johnson,

> I do not find any procedural errors that served to deny a fair hearing. Both sides had the opportunity to present their respective cases and question all witnesses. The Court was constituted correctly, it conducted its business in accordance with the Student Conduct Code and it did so in a timely manner. I do not find merit in the procedural objections raised in Mr. Paoli's letters.
>
> Consequently, I am making the determination that you did violate the Student Conduct Code by committing sexual intercourse without consent. Furthermore, I uphold the Court's conclusion that you be expelled from The University of Montana. . . .
>
> The review by the President constitutes the final step at the University level. I consider the matter closed. I am sorry that your career at the University must come to an end.

Johnson still had one last opportunity to avoid expulsion, however. He could appeal his case beyond the university, by asking for an administrative review by the Montana commissioner of higher education and the Board of Regents. On June 13, Paoli requested such a review. Commissioner Clayton Christian seemingly ruled in Jordan Johnson's favor, and Johnson was not expelled. I say "seemingly" because the commissioner's office has refused to disclose the outcome of the review, or even acknowledge that such a review occurred, contending that it is barred from doing so by the federal Family Educational Rights and Privacy Act (FERPA) and Montana statute 20-25-515, both of which address issues pertaining to the privacy of student records.*

When Jordan Johnson appealed to the commissioner's office, the university's case against him vanished into the ether. It was as if the University Court proceedings never happened. Because the criminal case against him was still moving forward, Johnson wasn't allowed to train with the football team in the summer of 2012, or play for the Grizzlies that fall, but he apparently remained enrolled as a student.

Public documents released in 2013 shed some light on why Johnson was not expelled. The most revealing is a thirty-one-page letter sent to University of Montana president Royce Engstrom by the U.S. Department of Justice and the U.S. Department of Education. Dated May 9, 2013, the letter enumerated the findings of the government's year-long investigation into UM's handling of student sexual-assault allegations, and two of its paragraphs summarized Jordan Johnson's appeal to Commissioner Clayton Christian. Although neither Johnson nor Washburn was mentioned by name, there was no mistaking the case under discussion.

CLAYTON CHRISTIAN, who was appointed commissioner of higher education in December 2011 by the Montana Board of Regents, is neither an educator nor a lawyer. Christian has a bach-

* In February 2014, I filed a petition in Montana district court requesting access to public records concerning Commissioner Christian's actions, citing Article II of the Constitution of the State of Montana, which states that "no person shall be deprived of the right to examine documents . . . of all public bodies or agencies of state government and its subdivisions." In September 2014, District Court Judge Kathy Seeley ruled that "FERPA does not preclude release of the records in the circumstances presented in this case," nor does Montana statute 20-25-515. Judge Seeley ordered the commissioner's office to provide me with the records I requested, but in October 2014, Commissioner Christian filed a motion with the Montana Supreme Court appealing Seeley's decision. The court had not yet issued a decision on the appeal by the time this book was submitted for publication.

elor's degree in finance and management from the University of Montana and owns a title company. He is a successful, highly respected Missoula businessman. Prior to his appointment, a doctorate was one of the prerequisites for the job, but the regents removed that requirement just before selecting him because they believed the commissioner of higher education "should be a businessperson like Christian," according to a public statement made by the regents' vice chairman.

Despite the wall of secrecy erected by the commissioner's office around the Jordan Johnson case, public information released from other sources indicates that when Johnson appealed his expulsion to Commissioner Christian, David Paoli apparently persuaded Christian that the University Court incorrectly used "a preponderance of the evidence" as the burden of proof in finding Johnson guilty of raping Washburn, instead of holding to the more exacting "clear and convincing evidence" standard. Blatantly disregarding the Department of Education's Dear Colleague Letter, which explicitly stated that "preponderance of the evidence is the appropriate standard for investigating allegations of sexual harassment or violence," Commissioner Christian vacated the University Court's finding of guilt and sent the case back to the University of Montana to be readjudicated, this time using "clear and convincing evidence" as the burden of proof.

During its reappraisal of the Jordan Johnson case, the university hired an independent consultant to conduct an impartial reinvestigation of Cecilia Washburn's allegation. At the conclusion of the consultant's inquiry, the consultant determined that Johnson's testimony wasn't credible and that there was indeed clear and convincing evidence that Johnson raped Washburn.

University of Montana Dean of Students Rhondie Voorhees, who replaced Dean Charles Couture when he retired, in July 2012, rejected the independent consultant's determination that Johnson was guilty, however. According to the government's 2013 letter to President Engstrom, Dean Voorhees

> found both the complainant [Cecilia Washburn] and accused student [Jordan Johnson] to be credible and expressed a belief that this was "a case of differing perceptions and interpretations of the events in question." However other parts of [the dean's] analysis questioned [Washburn's] credibility. For example, some of [Washburn's] statements began with "I think" or "I don't think," and [Dean Voorhees] believed that the use of the word "think" denoted a "hesitant and equivocal response." The [dean] concluded that there was not clear and convincing evidence to find that [Johnson] committed sexual misconduct.

The upshot was that Dean Rhondie Voorhees pronounced Jordan Johnson not guilty of raping Cecilia Washburn.

In the letter to Engstrom cited above, the Departments of Justice and Education rebuked the university for using "the 'clear and convincing evidence' standard in contravention of the Dear Colleague Letter's directive to use the 'preponderance of the evidence standard.'" The feds also said that Voorhees's unilateral acquittal of Jordan Johnson "did not result in an equitable resolution" of Cecilia Washburn's complaint. But the government's findings came too late to do Washburn any good.

After Dean Charles Couture determined, in March 2012, that Jordan Johnson was guilty of raping Washburn, Johnson was given four opportunities to appeal Couture's decision. On his fourth and final try, Johnson prevailed and was declared not guilty by the new dean of students, Voorhees. Despite the letter President Engstrom wrote in June 2012 notifying Johnson that he was "to be expelled," and that Engstrom considered "the matter closed," Engstrom apparently endorsed Voorhees' ruling, because in March 2013 the University of Montana invited Johnson to return as the Grizzlies' quarterback.

When Johnson was reunited with his Griz teammates soon thereafter, most of Missoula rejoiced.

PART FOUR

Scales of Justice

It is morally impossible to remain neutral in this conflict. The bystander is forced to take sides.

It is very tempting to take the side of the perpetrator. All the perpetrator asks is that the bystander do nothing. He appeals to the universal desire to see, hear, and speak no evil. The victim, on the contrary, asks the bystander to share the burden of pain. The victim demands action, engagement, and remembering. . . .

In order to escape accountability for his crimes, the perpetrator does everything in his power to promote forgetting. Secrecy and silence are the perpetrator's first line of defense. If secrecy fails, the perpetrator attacks the credibility of his victim. If he cannot silence her absolutely, he tries to make sure that no one listens. To this end, he marshals an impressive array of arguments, from the most blatant denial to the most sophisticated and elegant rationalization. After every atrocity one can expect to hear the same predictable apologies: it never happened; the victim lies; the victim exaggerates; the victim brought it upon herself; and in any case it is time to forget the past and move on. The more powerful the perpetrator, the greater is his prerogative to name and define reality, and the more completely his arguments prevail.

JUDITH LEWIS HERMAN
Trauma and Recovery

CHAPTER SEVENTEEN

After Beau Donaldson agreed to plead guilty to the charge that he raped Allison Huguet, a hearing to determine his sentence was scheduled for October 13, 2012, but it was postponed until December 19, and then postponed again until January 11, 2013. This tried the patience of Huguet and her family. The additional delay wasn't necessarily a bad thing, however, because it gave Missoula County Attorney Fred Van Valkenburg more time to prepare, and as the scheduled day approached, it became disconcertingly clear that he was going to need every hour he could get.

Late in the afternoon on January 9, when Van Valkenburg met with Allison and Kevin Huguet to tell them what to expect at the hearing, which was then less than two days away, he confessed that he was just starting to focus on what he actually intended to say. When Allison asked him if Hillary McLaughlin was all set to testify, Van Valkenburg said McLaughlin had gotten cold feet and wasn't sure she could go through with it. This was especially discouraging news. McLaughlin's account of being attacked by Donaldson in 2008 was a crucial component of the prosecution's argument that he was a sexual predator who posed a genuine threat to the community and, therefore, needed to be incarcerated for a long time.

McLaughlin had first described the attack to Detective Guy Baker in January 2012. Then she didn't hear anything more from the Missoula police or prosecutors until the beginning of December, when Baker called to ask if McLaughlin would testify at the sentencing hearing, which at the time was expected to be held on December 19. "He told me how much it would mean to Allison if I testified," McLaughlin remembers. "But I didn't know if I wanted to step back into it, so I asked, 'Can I have a week to think about it?' Looking back, I know that was very selfish of me, but I was worried about stirring up all the anxiety I felt from Beau trying to rape me."

A week later, when Detective Baker called her back, Hillary McLaughlin says, "I told him, 'I'm sorry, but I can't do it. I just can't put myself in that situation right now.' He was like, 'Okay, if that's what you want, I will respect your decision.' I got off the phone and instantly start crying. I told my husband, 'I did the wrong thing!' So I call back Detective Baker probably five minutes later, and he doesn't answer. I leave him a voice mail asking, 'Can I have three more days to think about it? Please, just give me the weekend.' " After exhaustively considering the matter over the next few days, McLaughlin told Baker that she would testify.

"But then the hearing got switched to January 11," McLaughlin says, "and I had more time to think about how hard it was going to be to say everything in court in front of all those people." A few days before the hearing, McLaughlin changed her mind yet again and told Detective Baker she was simply too frightened to go through with it.

THE MISSOULA COUNTY Courthouse and its grounds occupy an entire downtown block. A handsome, stately building constructed in 1910 from quarried sandstone blocks, it's crowned by a domed clock tower visible from miles away. As Allison Huguet and her family walked from their car to the courthouse doors shortly before 9:00 on the morning of January 11, 2013, an overnight blizzard had abated, but the storm had left five inches of fresh snow on the ground and the temperature was seventeen degrees Fahrenheit. Up on the third floor, when Judge Karen Townsend said, "Please be seated everybody," the large courtroom was overflowing with Missoulians who'd come to learn Beau Donaldson's fate. His supporters, including family members and Griz teammates, filled the seats in the eastern half of the room; most of Allison Huguet's supporters sat on the other side. Everyone was in uncomfortably close proximity. The air was stale, and the tension in the courtroom was palpable.

Donaldson, wearing a tie and black slacks, but no jacket, sat with his lawyers, Milt Datsopoulos and Peter Lacny, at the defending counsel's table. Donaldson's broad back and shoulders strained the seams of a freshly pressed shirt. Fred Van Valkenburg and Shaun Donovan sat at the prosecuting counsel's table, representing the state, which would present its witnesses before any witnesses for the defense were called.

Van Valkenburg asked Kevin Huguet to take the stand, and Kevin got the hearing off to a dramatic start. Unable to contain his rage, Kevin began by saying, "I'm obviously pissed off." Then he pointed at Donaldson and declared, "That kid right there is a no-good rapist piece of shit that raped my daughter, and I hope he rots in hell, frankly." Almost everyone in the packed courtroom was taken aback by the vehemence of the outburst. "I know he's got a bunch of friends and family here," Kevin continued, "but I don't really care. What you did to my daughter was wrong."

Milt Datsopoulos jumped to his feet and interrupted Kevin Huguet to object, "Your Honor, this is a courtroom. Certain remarks are—"

"I think I have some latitude on the plaintiff's part of this," Kevin said, cutting Datsopoulos off.

"So, Mr. Huguet," Judge Townsend interjected, "I am going to ask you—"

"Those are the only cuss words," Kevin promised.

"All right. No more," Townsend warned.

Resuming his testimony, Kevin said, "The rapist has no idea the pain and hurt he has caused our family. . . . This rapist decided to attack and rape my daughter while she was sleeping. How long did this perverted monster look at my defenseless daughter before he decided to act out the rape of a longtime friend? After he raped her, she had to sneak out of the house, running down the street calling for help. . . . Then she turned around and realized the rapist was chasing her."

Kevin Huguet asked Judge Townsend if she, as a parent, could imagine "anything more scary" than having the man who has just "raped your daughter chasing her down a street." Furthermore, Kevin said, even after Beau Donaldson confessed to the police on tape that he raped Allison, he told his friends and family that he'd been falsely accused, and he encouraged them to slander Allison: "They've made it impossible for my daughter, who was born and raised here, to go out like a normal twenty-three-year-old and enjoy herself. Instead, it's verbal aggression and intimidation. Does this sound like the rapist has told the truth or really taken responsibility?" Kevin pointed out that Donaldson not only lied to his friends and family about what he did to Allison, he also told both of the psychologists who performed presentencing psychosexual evaluations of him that the sex they had was consensual, not an act of rape.

When Allison Huguet had a chance encounter with Beau Donaldson at the Mo Club, fourteen months after he assaulted her while she slept, Kevin said, "This rapist laughed in my daughter's face. . . . Does this sound like someone who regrets what he did? . . . He felt entitled to do anything he wanted to any woman. . . . My daughter trusted him. She knew him since first grade. They were friends, yet he could still rape her. For some reason, some people feel sorry for this rapist. . . . For the people testifying about what a good guy he is, . . . you have no idea of the tears and the pain and the hurt that was caused by this rapist, and the potential years of counseling and healing my daughter has in front of her. . . .

"I'm so proud of my daughter for standing up and not letting him get away with this," Kevin continued. "She's amazing, smart, incredible, and beautiful on the inside and out, and didn't deserve to have this happen to her. Judge, please do the right thing and send him to Deer Lodge, where he belongs."

KEELY WILLIAMS TESTIFIED after Kevin Huguet. She told the court that Allison Huguet was her "best friend" and that she had known Beau Donaldson since kindergarten. When prosecutor Fred Van Valkenburg asked her to describe the party at Donaldson's house in September 2010, Williams said there were about thirty people in attendance. She and Allison arrived around 10:00 p.m., Williams recalled, and went to bed between 2:00 and 3:00 a.m. She testified that Donaldson and Huguet did not kiss or fondle each other at all. "That would not happen. Beau had a girlfriend at the time," said Williams. The relationship between Donaldson and Huguet had never been romantic or sexual, Williams emphasized.

At the conclusion of the party, when Allison went to sleep on a couch, alone, Keely Williams recalled, "I went to wake her to have her come sleep with me, and she said, 'I'm fine. I'll just sleep here.' And so I left her on the couch." The next thing she remembers, she said, was "a phone call from Allison, crying, saying, 'Beau raped me. You need to get out of the house right now! My mom and I are outside to get you.' So I got my stuff together, and I ran outside, where Mrs. Huguet was waiting with Allison in the car."

As Beth Huguet drove Allison to the hospital, Van Valkenburg asked Williams, "What was Allison doing? How did she react during that period of time?"

"She just kept crying," Williams answered. "She couldn't even talk. She just cried the whole way. . . . The next morning, I called to see how she was."

"And what was happening then?" Van Valkenburg asked.

"She was still crying," Williams said. She then described going to the Griz game with Allison: "She tried to act like she was fine, but didn't make it hardly through the game."

Van Valkenburg asked Keely Williams if Allison ever talked about "reporting this matter to the police."

"She didn't want to go to the police," Williams replied.

"Why not?"

"She told me that she didn't want to ruin his life. . . . And she wanted to give him a chance to make it better."

Van Valkenburg asked Williams why Allison eventually decided to report the rape to Detective Baker. "I remember her saying that if she had just gone to the police right away," Williams answered, "that maybe the other girls that had been raped wouldn't feel like they wouldn't be believed, and that they could stand up for themselves, too."

"It's been nearly a year now since Beau was charged with raping Allison," Van Valkenburg said. "How has this last year been on her?"

"It's been extremely difficult."

"Why is that?"

"She felt like she couldn't come home, and couldn't be in Missoula because people were so horrible to her. And when she went back to school [in Oregon], she couldn't focus. And she had a hard time finishing college at the end, because she had so much to deal with here, and couldn't be present in school."

"Do you feel like Beau has accepted responsibility for what he did to Allison?" Van Valkenburg asked.

"No."

"Why not?"

If Beau Donaldson had accepted responsibility, Keely Williams replied, "he would have stopped his family and friends from saying horrible things about Allison and her family" during the fifteen months after he raped Allison, before she reported him to the police.

Van Valkenburg asked Williams, "What do you think the judge should do to Beau Donaldson?"

"I think the judge should sentence Beau to the thirty years he agreed to," she replied, "so that he has time to deal with the issues that he so clearly has."

Turning to Judge Townsend, Van Valkenburg said, "I have no other questions, Your Honor."

"Cross-examination, Mr. Datsopoulos?" Townsend asked.

Keely Williams had been a very sympathetic witness: sincere, utterly convincing, and likable. Because this was a sentencing hearing, and not a trial, there was no jury Datsopoulos could pander to. Calculating that he stood to gain nothing with Judge Townsend by challenging Williams's testimony, he replied, "We have no cross-examination."

The prosecution's next witness was Hillary McLaughlin. When the hearing had been postponed until January, McLaughlin lost her nerve and said she couldn't testify. Less than two days before the hearing, however, Detective Baker persuaded her to change her mind. But because she had a ten-month-old baby and the roads were icy, the state had arranged for her to testify via video to avoid having to make the treacherous two-hundred-mile drive from Great Falls to Missoula.

McLaughlin, a slight woman with long blond hair, appeared on a large video screen on the west side of the courtroom. She began by describing the party at Joanna Sutherlin's house in 2008. "I had never met Beau before," McLaughlin said, "but throughout the night he was all over me and wouldn't leave me alone." McLaughlin explained that shortly after she went to bed, "Beau walked in the door, shut and locked the door behind him, pulled down his khaki shorts and underwear," climbed onto the bed, and began to grind his naked genitals into her pelvis.

Even as McLaughlin screamed for help, and her friends were trying to break down the bedroom door, she recalled, "Beau continued to grind on top of me." After the attack, she said, "I told very few people and tried to block it from my mind. Ever since that night it has affected . . . the way I live my life. I live in constant fear of being attacked walking to and from my house, to and from work, and while in my own home. I have a very hard time trusting anybody around me.

"I have struggled with extreme anxiety," McLaughlin continued, "and I have recently been put on medication to help deal with it. This has changed the way . . . I carry myself as a person." She said she had finally decided to tell her story in public because Beau Donaldson clearly had not taken responsibility for attacking her or raping Allison Huguet, and McLaughlin hoped her statement would "help prevent it from happening to someone else. No one should have to live their life in fear because of someone else."

WHEN BETH HUGUET, Allison's mother, took the witness stand, prosecutor Fred Van Valkenburg began by asking her to tell the court about Allison's birth and the kind of relationship they had. Allison, Beth said, was "a very large baby," and her birth had been difficult: "Twenty-six hours. They had to break both of her collarbones for her to be delivered. And yet, four hours after she was delivered, she was smiling. She had curls in her hair. . . . Allison has always been happy-go-lucky, smiling. My parents have always described her as almost angelical and cherub-like . . . , wanting the best in the world for everyone, and nonjudgmental. A very loving, very caring individual who has been a spark in my life, a love in my life."

Beth Huguet testified that Allison "has always been very open and honest with me and has confided in me about a lot of things. I've always believed we've had maybe a stronger mother-daughter relationship than . . . a lot of other mothers do. I think part of this is from me being a high school teacher: I'm able to have an honest rapport with the kids. And I have a pretty good BS detector, so I can figure out when my children are telling me things."

Asked by Van Valkenburg to describe Beau Donaldson when he was growing up, Beth explained that the Target Range neighborhood where Beau and Allison were raised and attended school together is a tight community. "That group of kids," she said, "were always very close, took care of each other, looked out for each other. I know Allison always looked at Beau as the big brother that she didn't have."

When Van Valkenburg asked Beth Huguet about the night Donaldson raped Allison, she told the court about being awakened in the middle of the night by a phone call from Allison pleading, "Save me, Mom! Help me. . . . He's chasing me down an alley."

As Allison ran for her life, Beth told the court, she could hear a male voice in the background, commanding Allison to stop and warning her not to say anything. "I thought, 'God, I know that voice,'" Beth said. After driving across town to Donaldson's neighborhood, she saw Allison running along South Avenue with one hand clutching her phone and the other hand holding up her pants. "She got in the car and she just kept rocking back and forth and just crying, frantically. . . . And then she said, 'Beau raped me.'"

Beth Huguet testified that Allison asked her not to share that information with anybody. "You didn't share it with Allison's father?" Van Valkenburg asked.

"I shared it with no one," Beth said. "It wasn't my right. It was my child's right. She was an adult. . . . I needed to protect her wishes." During the months that followed, Beth said her home "became almost like a tomb" from Allison's "crying and walking in the middle of the night, and sobbing. . . . It was five months of complete, sheer hell, to say the least, to watch her go so far within herself. The raw pain, the internal raw pain that was there every day—and I could see it in her eyes—was horrific, to the point where I could barely function, to get up every day and go to school and teach and keep a smile on my face when I had a child that was suffering so horrifically."

Allison "wasn't the same person anymore," Beth continued. "There was no smiles. There was no laughs. . . . She went back to school [in Oregon] in January. But I would frequently get calls from her, about every other day, where she was having trouble focusing on school. . . . At least she was out of Missoula and the people there didn't know. But internally, she was being eaten alive. . . . She had a lot of fear and anxiety."

Beth Huguet told the court about Allison's visit to Missoula during Eastern Oregon University's Thanksgiving break in November 2011. It was an especially awkward visit, Beth said, because she and Allison were trying to keep the rape secret from her sisters and father so they wouldn't have to endure the anguish Beth and Allison were feeling. To that end, Beth explained, every day she and Allison had to "put a brave face on." Then Allison went downtown with her friends one night and ran into Beau Donaldson at the Mo Club. "I think that's when it hit her full force . . . how deep-seated her pain and fear was," Beth testified, "and that she really wasn't living. She was just managing day to day, getting up and putting one foot in front of the other."

Van Valkenburg asked Beth if she thought Donaldson had "done a good job . . . of telling his family and his friends exactly what he did to Allison."

"No," she replied, pointing out that even after confessing twice to the police that he raped Allison, "he chose to let his family and friends believe that he didn't do it. And that's not a person standing up for what's right.

"Beau has been put on a pedestal most of his life," Beth continued, suggesting that his many admirers "wanted to believe he didn't do it, and he chose to allow them to believe he didn't do it."

When defense counsel Milt Datsopoulos was given the opportunity to cross-examine Beth Huguet, he tried to elicit testimony from her that Beau Donaldson had been an exemplary friend to Allison as they grew up together. At one point Datsopoulos asked Beth if there was anything she'd observed in Donaldson over the many years she had known him to suggest "he might have some kind of violent or mean streak."

"He didn't do anything to me or my child," Beth conceded. But, she said a moment later, "I guess that's what makes this even more horrific, is that this is such an extreme betrayal between friends."

Datsopoulos kept pushing Beth to take Beau Donaldson's entire life into consideration, rather than just a single, inexplicable act. "When you measure people's lives, who they are," Datsopoulos pointed out, "you have to look at the entire spectrum of that life, not a narrow piece of it—wouldn't you say that's an accurate premise?"

"Yes," Beth Huguet replied. But then she pointed out that there are sides to people that are impossible for even family members and close friends to know. "I think Beau's sexual deviancy is a side that many of us were not aware of."

CHAPTER EIGHTEEN

When Beth Huguet finished her testimony, prosecutor Fred Van Valkenburg called Allison Huguet to the witness stand. As one of his first questions, he asked if she had ever had a romantic or sexual relationship with Beau Donaldson. "No," Allison replied. "But Beau and I were closer than I was to any other guy growing up . . . and had a lot of respect for each other, I thought."

Referring to the night Huguet was raped, Van Valkenburg asked, "Do you know where Beau Donaldson was at the time you decided to go to sleep?"

"No," she said.

"What's the next thing you remember happening, Allison?"

"I remember waking up to Beau moaning and a lot of pressure and pain," she answered. She was facedown on the couch, with her pants pulled down, and Beau was penetrating her from behind.

"Were you scared?" Van Valkenburg asked.

"Yeah," she replied. "I mean, he's got at least a hundred pounds on me. If he's willing to do that while I'm sleeping, I definitely thought he would have done a lot more to keep me from resisting, or telling somebody. . . . So I pretended like I didn't wake up." Allison described waiting until Donaldson had finished raping her and left the room, then grabbing her phone, bolting from the house, and being chased barefoot down the alley by Donaldson until she saw her mother's car. She told the court about driving back to Donaldson's house to rescue her friend Keely Williams, and being examined at the hospital. Because Donaldson hadn't used a condom, she testified, she worried that she might become pregnant with his child or have contracted "multiple STDs, including HIV."

Van Valkenburg asked Huguet how she was affected by encountering Beau Donaldson at the Mo Club in November 2011.

"At that moment," Huguet said, "it hit me that . . . as hard as I tried to separate the person who raped me and the person I grew up with, I had to realize that they were the same person, and . . . he was not sorry. He was not sorry in any way. . . . When Beau stood there and laughed in my face, I think I was forced to realize that by not going to the police, I was allowing him to think that this was okay, and I was giving him the opportunity to do this to other females. And I can be honest with you in saying that if I had found out that some girl was going through this hell because I didn't say anything, I probably would have killed myself. There is no way I could have lived with that, at all."

"What's this last year been like for you?" Van Valkenburg asked.

"It has been hell," Huguet said. "It was very obvious that Beau had not told his family or friends [the truth], as they went around this town saying horrible things about me, saying that I had made this all up."

"What do you think should happen to Beau?" Van Valkenburg asked.

She had been struggling to answer that question, Huguet replied, explaining that he was "someone that I cared about, I truly loved, and he's the person that raped me. I believe that if I didn't know Beau, if Beau was a complete stranger, I would ask for you to have him sent to prison for the rest of his life. But, unfortunately, I can't take away the fact that I care about him. I want him to get help. I want him to be the person that I grew up with."

Beau Donaldson had received many accolades when he was younger, Huguet acknowledged, and deserved the love he'd received from all the people who admired him. "I loved that person, too," she lamented. "But I don't think that person is sitting right there." Huguet gestured toward Donaldson, who hunched impassively at the defense counsel's table. "I don't think that's the same person at all," she said. "I don't think he's taken responsibility, and I think the only way he's going to get it is if he has to sit in prison."

Looking at Donaldson with a conflicted expression that conveyed both sincere concern and utter revulsion, Huguet said to him, "And honestly, I think . . . you deserve to be raped every day until you understand the pain you have caused me, until you understand what this does to you emotionally—until you get it, Beau. Until you are actually sorry. Until you can take responsibility and get help. . . . And I truly hope that you can come out of this a person of quality, a person of substance. I hope after you are punished, and after you get it, that you have a great life. . . . Until then, I don't care what happens to you."

TAKING THE WITNESS stand was difficult for Allison Huguet. She knew most of the people in the gallery, and many of them were attending the hearing to offer her moral support. But at least as many people were openly supporting Beau Donaldson, including several individuals she'd previously considered friends of her family. Seeing them sitting on Donaldson's side of the courtroom was exceedingly hurtful, and she had trouble controlling her emotions as she testified. Several times Huguet had to fight back tears, and it looked like she might not be able to proceed. On each occasion, however, she willed herself to regain her composure, and continued to speak her piece. It was a remarkable display of courage.

Huguet is a warm, cheerful woman. She doesn't look fierce, but her upbeat demeanor that day hid an abundance of tenacity. When defense counsel Milt Datsopoulos began his cross-examination of Huguet, he had no idea what was in store for him.

Datsopoulos began not by asking Huguet a question but by lecturing her. "I just want to explain to you," he pronounced, "why certain things happened. Beau admitted on at least three different occasions . . . that he took advantage of you—that he had sex with you without consent. . . . He said he was guilty of doing things to you without your consent that were horrible. . . . I think it's important for you to know that he has consistently told various people—but most importantly, law enforcement—'I made a horrible mistake. I committed a crime. I had sex with my friend. She did not give consent.' Charges were then filed. . . . And we came to court and pled 'not guilty' [at Donaldson's arraignment]. That outrages a lot of people. It's hard to understand how that occurs when you've already admitted your guilt, like Beau did." Datsopoulos explained to Allison that when Donaldson made the "not guilty" plea at his arraignment, he wasn't actually claiming that he wasn't guilty. It was merely a procedural formality.

"I understand that," Huguet replied.

"I just hope that makes you feel a little better," Datsopoulos offered.

"No, it doesn't make me feel better," she said. "What would make me feel better is if he told his family and friends the truth, so that they don't go around bashing on me and attacking me. . . . You know, that would make me feel better."

Trying a different tack, Datsopoulos said, "The thing that I was pleased to hear was that you're not here to destroy Beau." Datsopoulos pointed out that Huguet said that she wanted Beau Donaldson to acknowledge the harm he did to her and her family and that "he needs professional help; and that you want him to get that professional help."

"In Deer Lodge," Huguet interjected, referring to the state prison.

"And you also want him to be able to recover and become somebody," Datsopoulos suggested hopefully. "He's got a good mind, doesn't he?"

"He's got a sick mind," Huguet countered. "I don't know what happened to Beau, to be honest to you. Like I said, I don't know that person sitting there." She gestured again at Donaldson. "I knew the person I was growing up with. I loved that person. But

I am not willing to speak . . . about his character now or in the future, because I don't know this person."

Milt Datsopoulos tried to get Huguet to acknowledge that Beau Donaldson would benefit from psychiatric counseling. She concurred, then added, "I'm requesting that he be sent to prison, too. I definitely think he needs to be punished, as well."

"I agree that he needs to be punished," Datsopoulos said. "But there are various forms of punishment." Donaldson, he insisted, "is remorseful. He's going through a lot of pain. Yeah, he's scared. He's sad that he's in this situation. But he's also agonizing over the damage he's done to you."

"We have differing opinions on that," Allison Huguet declared.

THE FINAL witness to appear for the prosecution was Katie Burton, the probation and parole officer who'd written the presentence investigation report about Beau Donaldson, which urged Judge Townsend to follow the state's recommendation and sentence him to thirty years at Deer Lodge, with twenty years suspended. Prosecutor Fred Van Valkenburg began by asking why Burton thought her recommendation was "the appropriate sentence that should be imposed," given the wide range of potential sentences Townsend was free to choose, from no incarceration at all to one hundred years of hard time.

"I think there needs to be some punishment," Burton answered. "To take advantage of someone when they are sleeping, to take away their feeling of safety around other people, it's heinous. I mean, it's a horrible thing to have that person ever feel that they can't feel safe around other people. I think that the Montana State Prison is appropriate, given that this was an adult taking advantage of an adult [who] had been friends with him for years and years and years." Katie Burton added that Donaldson needed treatment for his substance abuse and sexual deviancy. "I think rehabilitation is very important," she said, "but I think that he needs to do some of it at the Montana State Prison and recognize how horrible his actions really are."

Van Valkenburg asked, "You understand, Katie, that if he were to get a ten-year prison sentence, that he would be eligible for parole after serving . . . two and a half years of that sentence?"

"That's correct," she said. "Yes."

"So basically, if he does what he's required to do while he's in prison, he's likely to get paroled?"

"That would be my guess," Burton replied, "as long as he completes treatment." She recommended to Judge Townsend that Donaldson be required to complete both chemical-dependency treatment and sex-offender treatment while incarcerated at the Montana State Prison before he was deemed eligible for parole.

Because this was a sentencing hearing, rather than a trial, Judge Townsend was free to question witnesses, and she wasn't shy about doing so. "One of the matters that has been discussed in this case," she said, "or at least bandied about, is whether or not Mr. Donaldson should be considered for the Boot Camp Program." She was referring to a 120-day, military-style boot camp at the Treasure State Correctional Training Center; this had been suggested by Milt Datsopoulos as an alternative to incarceration in the state prison. "Do you have any opinion about that as a potential proposal?" Townsend asked Katie Burton.

"I think the Boot Camp is a great program," Burton replied. "It's probably one of my favorites. . . . The only problem I find with the Boot Camp . . . is they don't do sex-offender treatment in there."

"So he could not, in fact, get the sex-offender treatment that you're recommending . . . if he were a Boot Camp inmate?"

"No," Burton answered, "he would not."

CHAPTER NINETEEN

After Katie Burton was excused, Milt Datsopoulos called the first witness for the defense, Bob Eustace, a teacher at Big Sky High School who had coached football and basketball and taught health when Beau Donaldson and Allison Huguet were students there. Datsopoulos asked him, "Why are you here? Why do you think it's important?"

"I think it's gut-wrenching," Coach Eustace answered, looking ill at ease, "that, you know, obviously, somebody has been violated and harmed. . . . The things that I have seen from Beau, you know, he's been trustworthy. He's been respectful. . . . He had empathy for others. So it seems very out of character that he would perform this type of act."

Datsopoulos asked Eustace, "What are some of the characteristics that you've observed, some of the persona of this guy, that you think is important for the judge to consider?"

"I think what I saw, especially in the classroom or as a coach, [was] that he treated other people extremely well," Eustace replied. "Obviously, we try to prevent bullying and stuff like that, but there's kids who were younger and very small, and were bullied by kids who were older than they were. And, you know, Beau came in, stepped up, and protected those kids and made sure that they weren't harmed. . . . So, you know, I had a lot of respect for that."

Datsopoulos said, "You and I spoke just once before today. . . . And one of the comments you made during that conversation was that you really do not believe that Beau Donaldson should go to prison, even though he admitted to a very serious criminal act here. Why do you say that?"

"I think that the Beau Donaldson I knew . . . ," Eustace said, "I wouldn't think that he would reoffend. I think, you know, granted, you know, obviously this has escalated . . . and created huge amounts of problems and grief for . . . the victim's family, and just a terrible situation. . . . That's why I say I think he has empathy, and that I would feel secure that he wouldn't reoffend. So that would be my personal opinion on that."

A few minutes later, Datsopoulos asked Coach Eustace if he believed "this type of crime" required some punishment.

"It's one of the worst crimes I think a person can commit," Eustace replied, "to be honest with you."

This didn't seem to be the response Milt Datsopoulos had been hoping for. Appearing flummoxed, he inquired, "Is there anything else you want to say, Mr. Eustace?"

Eustace launched into a rambling, largely incoherent riff. "You know, from the time that I've known Beau and known him well, I just thought that, you know, when I judge kids—and I try not to judge them. I try to lead them on and help them as far as school. But, you know, there's some kids I'm really concerned with as far as what their course is, and where they're going to end up. . . . You know, Beau really never was in that category. And, you know, I would think that he would definitely be able to change his life around."

"Are you concerned if he spends any significant time in prison that it could damage his prospects and who he is?" Datsopoulos asked.

"Well, my thoughts on prison is," Eustace answered, "the fact is, you put a person in there because that person could harm somebody else in society. . . . If I thought that he was going to harm somebody in society again, I would never testify for him."

"Thank you," Datsopoulos said. "I have no further questions."

Prosecutor Fred Van Valkenburg began his cross-examination by asking, "Mr. Eustace, you think that this is one of the worst crimes that anyone can commit, but you don't think Beau Donaldson should go to prison, even though he committed one of the worst crimes there is?"

"I think it's a terrible crime," Coach Eustace agreed. But he suggested that one of the worst punishments a person could suffer was harm to his reputation, and Donaldson's "reputation has been destroyed. You know, he's got a felony. There's no use for him to go back to school. . . . What professional job can he get? You know, look what's happened to his family. . . . And I would definitely concur with the fact that he should get treatment . . . for chemical and sex offender."

"Does Big Sky High School have rules?" Van Valkenburg asked.

"They do," Eustace answered.

"And when people violate those rules, do they get punished?"

"We like to think so, yes."

"Why do they get punished?"

"To keep order and to make sure that things run correctly."

"And does that help other students who don't violate the rules know that, if they do violate the rules, they might get punished, too?" Van Valkenburg asked.

Eustace tried to dodge the question by suggesting that because of the school's confidentiality policy, most students would be unaware of any disciplinary action against other students. But Van Valkenburg kept pressing. "So if a football player gets kicked off the team or is not allowed to play, nobody knows that?" he asked.

Eustace continued to dodge: "I'm not saying that. I'm just saying we have teacher-student confidentiality, and that I can't talk to students in my class."

Van Valkenburg tried a different angle: "Did you learn anything about Beau Donaldson this morning?"

"I was heartbroken for Allison," Eustace replied. "I'll be honest with you: It was so hard to listen to that testimony. It was terrible, yes."

"I have no further questions, Your Honor," Van Valkenburg said.

"Anything further?" Judge Townsend asked Datsopoulos.

"Nothing more, Your Honor," he replied, and then he asked if his witness could be excused from the courtroom.

"I'd like to ask him a question," Townsend pronounced, to the surprise and visible dismay of both Milt Datsopoulos and Coach Eustace. "I didn't hear an answer to either of the attorneys' questions about 'Do you think Beau Donaldson should be punished?' "

"Punished in what way, Judge?" Eustace inquired.

"I'm asking you whether he deserves any kind of punishment. And then if your answer is yes, I want to know what kind you think he ought to have."

"I think that Beau can be a productive member of society," Eustace said. "I think he can help society, and I think he could be a positive member of society. I think definitely I believe he should go through alcohol treatment, sex-offender treatment, and successfully complete those two treatments. For me, . . . prisons didn't really [benefit] the person being incarcerated. Were they rehabilitated? I didn't think so. So how many people have to go back, and go back? That worries me. I think Beau can be productive."

"So," Judge Townsend declared, looking peeved, "I still don't think I have an answer to my question. You seem to be avoiding it."

"Well," Eustace said, "my thought is, if he was put on, whatever, suspension, or is sentenced—"

Cutting him off, Townsend interjected, "So he gets a free pass, is what you're saying."

"I don't think it's a free pass," Eustace protested. "I think he should be made to come in and, you know, go through those treatments. . . . Don't we have a system that can monitor him and do that?"

"So he checks in once a month," Townsend said. "He has to tell his probation officer where he's living, and he has to go to treatment. You think that's enough in this case?"

"If he violates that," Eustace offered, "we can always send him to jail, can't we?"

"You think that's enough for what he did in this case?" Townsend demanded.

Eustace replied with a non sequitur: "The Beau I had previously known, to be honest with you, was a decent kid."

"And so what you heard today doesn't change your mind about who this person is?" Townsend asked.

Eustace started to answer with yet another dodge: "I am devastated with what happened with Allison. I can't—"

Impatient with his refusal to answer her questions, Townsend interrupted to ask, "Was she your student, too?"

"I did not have Allison in class," he said. But he told Townsend that he taught sex education, "So I understand the implications of, you know, having sex without consent."

Judge Townsend had begun to suspect that when Eustace had agreed to testify on Donaldson's behalf, he'd been led to believe that the sex between Donaldson and Allison was consensual, and had no idea that Donaldson had raped Allison while she was asleep and then chased her down an alley. To confirm her suspicion, Townsend asked Eustace, "But you did not know, really, all the details before you showed up today—am I correct in assuming that?"

"I would say it's a terrible crime," Eustace prattled on, ignoring the question yet again. "I'm glad I'm not in your shoes. But it's a terrible crime, and I think there's no way Allison couldn't have negative effects from that. You know, do our schools give kids second chances? We try to give them second chances. I don't know, you know, what kind of second chance you give a person, you know, in this system. You know, do you put them in jail and he becomes a criminal? I don't know. That seems, from my perspective, to be what happens in our criminal justice system."

Realizing that Coach Eustace was never going to provide a direct answer to her original question—should Beau Donaldson be sent to prison for raping Allison Huguet?—Judge Townsend gave up. She allowed Milt Datsopoulos to ask Eustace a few softball questions, and then she told the coach, "Thank you, sir. You may step down. You're excused."

Allison Huguet was seated in the gallery with her family and her friend Keely Williams, trying to suppress the pain and bilious rage she felt as Eustace testified in support of Beau Donaldson. "It was incredibly unnerving that Mr. Eustace and other male staff from our high school came to the trial to support Beau," Williams recalled. "It was like a kick in the gut to Allison."

"It was extremely hurtful," Allison agreed, her emotions boiling to the surface as she remembered the moment. "Eustace teaches sex education to high school kids. And he refused to say that Beau needed to be punished, even after confessing to raping me? I couldn't believe what I was hearing. What kind of message does that send to his students?"

ALTHOUGH KAREN TOWNSEND had been a judge for only three years, she'd earned wide respect from the Missoula bar for her fairness and legal acumen. Before being elected district court judge in Montana's Fourth Judicial District, she'd served for eight years as chief deputy Missoula County attorney, under Fred Van Valkenburg, and had spent eighteen years prior to that working as a deputy Missoula County attorney. The challenge she faced at Beau Donaldson's sentencing hearing—as her questioning of Bob Eustace suggested—was to arrive at a punishment that was proportional to the seriousness of Donaldson's crime while at the same time providing an opportunity for his rehabilitation. The difficulty of reconciling these aims became increasingly apparent as the hearing continued.

The next witness for the defense was John Peterson, a Missoula drywall contractor who was a childhood friend of Beau's father, Larry Donaldson. Peterson's kids had grown up with Beau Donaldson and Allison Huguet in the Target Range neighborhood. Donaldson "didn't seem to be a typical jock," Peterson testified. "He didn't act privileged." From an early age, Peterson had made a point of having his son and daughter work for him. "I want them to understand what it's like to actually have to earn a living," he explained. For that reason, he'd hired their friends as well, including Donaldson: "Beau was always one of the first ones I'd call. . . . My trade is a physical trade. He seemed to excel at it."

Over the previous year, following Donaldson's arrest, Peterson said he'd employed him on dozens of construction sites. "You couldn't ask for a better employee. He's very respectful to the other people that work with me, all the other tradesmen on the jobs. . . . It's hard to go somewhere where somebody doesn't know Beau. And he's always been greeted with handshakes and hugs. You know, it doesn't seem to me that he's a threat to society."

"You've certainly heard this morning some frankly heart-wrenching testimony," Milt Datsopoulos observed. "What do you make of that? Like Mr. Eustace, do you believe Beau should be punished for this?"

"Certainly," Peterson answered, "I believe Beau should be punished for this. . . . All those nice things I've just said about Beau, I can say about Allison. . . . I've been to her birthday parties. I've coached her in softball. . . . This is an awful, terrible place to be right now. If I was Superman, I'd spin the earth around backwards, and I'd make all of this go away. . . . Beau is a friend. I don't want him to go to prison."

"No matter what the court does today," Datsopoulos said, "Beau will be leaving here in handcuffs. And at some point, he'll be back in the community. When he's out, would you rehire him as an employee?"

"Yes, I would," Peterson replied. "We all know where Beau was headed, what he had in front of him. All those doors are closed. The only one that's remotely cracked open is the one I have, you know, a tradesman. . . . He's a hard worker, and I could train him to do it. I don't know what else to do."

John Peterson was articulate and genuine on the stand—a very effective witness for Beau Donaldson. But Fred Van Valkenburg is a skilled litigator, and after Milt Datsopoulos sat down, Van Valkenburg began his cross-examination with a perfectly aimed strike. "Mr. Peterson," he said, "at the very beginning of the testimony here, you told us you have a daughter?"

"Yes, sir," Peterson replied.

"How old is she?"

"She's twenty-six years old."

"So, if Beau Donaldson had chosen to rape your daughter instead of Allison," Van Valkenburg asked, "how would that affect your testimony today?"

"Well," Peterson answered, "I'd be testifying as Mr. Huguet did, not as an impartial person. That's apples and oranges. Allison Huguet and Kristen Peterson are two separate people."

"I guess they are," Van Valkenburg mused, "because Kristen didn't get raped, did she? . . . But basically what you're telling us is you'd have the same reaction Mr. Huguet did?"

"I'm sure I would."

If Donaldson had raped Kristen Peterson instead of Allison Huguet, Van Valkenburg demanded, "that would tell you [something] a hell of a lot different about Beau Donaldson, wouldn't it?"

"Hypothetically. . . . I don't know," Peterson stammered. A moment later he conceded, "I guess, yes."

CHAPTER TWENTY

Before his sentencing hearing, Beau Donaldson was ordered to undergo psychosexual evaluations from two different psychologists—one hired by the defense, the other hired by the prosecution—to determine how likely he was to rape again and to assess his potential for responding favorably to sex-offender therapy. When the psychologist who performed the first evaluation, Dr. Robert Page, appeared at the hearing as a witness for Donaldson, Milt Datsopoulos asked him to explain the purpose of evaluating his client.

The purpose, Dr. Page answered, was to obtain information about his personality traits and the risk he posed to the community, in order "to provide the most responsible recommendations for not only the rehabilitation of the individual, but rehabilitation in the least restrictive environment while maintaining safety to society." Page added that all the data he'd analyzed suggested that Donaldson was "within the low-to-moderate-risk range." According to Page, his evaluation also showed that Donaldson would respond well to sex-offender therapy while living in the community, as long as he was "monitored for abstinence from drugs and alcohol, one hundred percent."

Datsopoulos asked Dr. Page if Beau Donaldson was "remorseful—sincerely remorseful—and contrite for his actions."

"At this point," Page said, "I believe he's got some remorse. I just can't put my finger on exactly whether or not that's absolutely genuine, in terms of the effect of his actions on the victim, or whether it's, you know, more related to a fear" of the punishment he might receive. "So," Page explained, "I would be irresponsible telling you that I know there's genuine remorse going on in Beau Donaldson right now."

When it was his turn to cross-examine Dr. Page, prosecutor Fred Van Valkenburg asked him about the importance of punishing Donaldson, not only in terms of his rehabilitation but also for Allison Huguet's recovery from being raped. Van Valkenburg pointed out to Page, "I think you said, based on your work with victims, one of the things that victims really need is a sense of retribution. Is that what you meant?"

Dr. Page answered, "One of the things that victims respond to therapeutically is the retribution of the perpetrator, that's true."

Retribution, Van Valkenburg continued, "primarily involves the punishment of the perpetrator, in the sense that if the victim feels that there has been some retribution or punishment," it's easier for her to heal than "if the victim thinks that the perpetrator essentially got away with what he did."

"Well stated," Page said. "Yes."

A couple of minutes later, Van Valkenburg asked Dr. Page about a clinical interview of Beau Donaldson he'd done. "Would it be fair to say that Mr. Donaldson's account of what happened, what he told you in that clinical interview, differed very significantly from what was set out in the police reports?"

"Yes," Dr. Page replied.

"And would it be fair to say that he essentially tried to tell you in that interview that he really didn't commit the offense of sexual intercourse without consent, because he thought this woman was consenting to what he was doing?"

"I would interpret it that way at the time," Page agreed. Denial was not uncommon in perpetrators undergoing this kind of evaluation, he said: "It's an indication of the necessity [for aggressive] sex-offender treatment."

"And it's also, I guess, an indication that if he's not being truthful with you in the clinical interview, you're not getting the whole picture," Van Valkenburg parried.

"Yeah," the psychologist reluctantly conceded. But Dr. Page insisted that he was nevertheless able to discern enough about Donaldson to recognize "a lack of accountability that needs to be addressed in treatment." The more pertinent question, Page said, was whether such sex-offender treatment needed "to be done in a residential setting or not" to be effective.

After Dr. Page was excused from the courtroom, the defense called its next witness, Dr. Jim Myers, the psychologist who'd been hired in advance of the hearing by the prosecution to conduct the second psychosexual evaluation of Beau Donaldson. Like Dr. Page, Dr. Myers testified that his assessment indicated that Donaldson was "a low risk to reoffend," and therefore he recommended that Donaldson "be allowed to enter an outpatient treatment program," rather than being required to receive treatment while incarcerated.

During his cross-examination, Van Valkenburg noted that a big part of what Myers relied on to make a risk assessment was the personal history of the perpetrator. "And to a large extent," Van Valkenburg argued, "that means [the perpetrator's] criminal history. . . . So if someone has done bad things but has never gotten caught before, they come up as a low risk even if they've done a whole bunch of bad things that haven't gotten caught."

"That's true," Dr. Myers concurred. "They could have ten offenses and only been charged with one right now. That's a problem with risk assessment."

Van Valkenburg reminded the court that two years before Beau Donaldson raped Allison Huguet, he'd attempted to rape Hillary McLaughlin. "And were it not for the fact that [the assault of McLaughlin was discovered] in the course of this sentencing process, that would not be factored in at all."

Myers agreed. Furthermore, he acknowledged, when he'd asked Donaldson about what had happened with McLaughlin, Donaldson had lied about it and insisted that he hadn't tried to rape her.

This prompted Van Valkenburg to remind Dr. Myers that during his evaluation of Beau Donaldson, Donaldson had also lied about what he'd done to Huguet. "So wasn't it pretty odd," Van

Valkenburg demanded, "after he had already entered a guilty plea, that he was essentially telling you he had consensual sex with Allison Huguet?"

"Yes, and I asked him about that," Myers replied. "I said . . . , 'How can you go and say you're guilty [in the plea agreement], and here you are, telling me you're not guilty?' " Donaldson tried to explain away the lie by telling another lie: He claimed he didn't know that Huguet was asleep when he had sex with her and learned that she was unconscious only "after the fact."

As Van Valkenburg was wrapping up his questioning, he asked Dr. Myers about an entry-level treatment program for drug and alcohol dependency that Donaldson, after he'd been arrested, had completed with a clinical social worker named Paul Sells. Van Valkenburg wondered if Myers knew what the treatment provided by Sells "consisted of."

"Not really," Dr. Myers answered. "I know it's more of an education thing, and also trying to get people to express and talk about their feelings. And that's where Beau ran into some trouble. . . . He has a hard time talking about his feelings, expressing his emotions, which kind of goes along with the mold a lot of us guys are cut from, I guess. Anyhow, that was a problem for him within therapy."

"He certainly never got involved in any community sex-offender treatment, did he?" Van Valkenburg asked.

"No," Myers answered, "he never did."

"I have no other questions," Van Valkenburg told the court.

But before Judge Townsend excused Dr. Myers from the witness stand, she wanted to ask him some questions of her own. Myers, it turned out, had talked to both Paul Sells and Beau Donaldson about the efficacy of Donaldson's treatment for chemical dependency. Townsend asked Myers if Sells had given him "sort of a different picture" of how successful the therapy had been, compared to the picture Donaldson had provided.

"He did, Your Honor," Myers said.

"In fact, he said it didn't go as well as Beau told you, right?" Judge Townsend inquired.

"That's right."

Townsend asked if Sells had told Dr. Myers "that Donaldson was 'not adept at processing feelings and engaging in any real therapy.'"

"He did say that, Your Honor," Myers confirmed.

"So how is he going to take advantage of any kind of therapy if . . . he won't do it?" Townsend asked.

According to Paul Sells, Myers answered, "It wasn't so much that Beau didn't see a need for treatment. It's just that, yes, he does have a hard time processing things. There's a lot of shame, and guilt, embarrassment, humiliation where he is. He's having a hard time talking about that." Dr. Myers pointed out, however, that Beau Donaldson's willingness to actively engage in therapy, including sex-offender therapy, would probably be different if it were required as part of his sentence. "When somebody is court-ordered to complete treatment," Myers said, they learn to talk "pretty quickly, and express feelings, and start dealing with things."

"Because there is a hammer over their head?" Townsend asked.

"Yeah," Myers answered.

THE FINAL TWO witnesses for the defense were Beau Donaldson and his father, Larry Donaldson. Larry appeared on the stand first, with his wife standing silently beside him. Looking exhausted, he said of his son, "He is a young man. He's remorseful. That doesn't, you know, make it right. Let him make it right; he will. . . . And there's no reason to hate. I can't hate anyone, because I can't heal if I hate you. And we have to heal."

Addressing the Huguets, Larry Donaldson said, "The Huguet family and the Donaldson family have to heal, or we'll fail. And I want to heal. And I want Beau to be responsible to help your daughter heal. And he will, as she asked. . . . I know that's a big thing to ask, but he will help her heal. . . . And, Allison, I've known you forever. It made me cry. It makes me cry when I look at my boy. But I can forgive my son, because I know the love in his heart. . . .

"You know, alcohol won again. It's a very destructive deal. I don't drink. I haven't drank since my kids were born. I didn't teach them to drink, and I don't condone drinking. And give him a chance. Let him understand what it does. . . .

"Whatever has went on in this community over the past year [regarding the slandering of Allison] has nothing to do with Beau, or instigated by Beau, or instigated by me or my wife or my family. I mean, when it happens, what's involved again? Alcohol. That's when we hate each other, is when we drink.

"And I love my boy. . . . I'll see you soon. I hope sooner than later. I'll be your rock now, because you've been my rock all your life."

Finally, it was Beau Donaldson's turn to address the court. "I just want to start off by apologizing to everyone involved," he said in a faltering voice, "most first to Allison and her family and her close friends; and secondly my family and friends and everyone that this has affected. . . . And I hope that me being here and apologizing helps Allison heal, helps her with what she has lost by me breaking our friendship that night by taking advantage of her."

When Donaldson returned to the defense counsel's table, Fred Van Valkenburg stood to make his closing statement. "Your Honor, this case is an extremely good example of what rape often really looks like," he began. Most rapes, he explained, involve people "who know each other. . . . And there is a huge violation of trust when that occurs. . . .

"When you read the letters that have been submitted on behalf of Beau Donaldson, you'd think we were talking about whether he should get the most valuable player award or he should . . . just be excused for having made a mistake. . . . And I think that comes about, by and large, because I don't think Beau Donaldson has been honest. He hasn't been honest with his own family. He hasn't been honest with the people that he knows best. He hasn't been honest with the community of Missoula as to what he actually did. He's having to finally face up to what he did, and it's very difficult for him to do that.

"It's very moving when he's on the witness stand telling people how sorry he is. But if you go back to the very first witness in this sentencing hearing, Mr. Huguet, it's also very moving to see what Beau Donaldson did to the Huguet family. . . .

"The state has agreed to make a recommendation of thirty years in the Montana State Prison, with twenty years suspended. That's what I recommend the court do. . . . Mr. Donaldson will become eligible for parole within two and a half years of the time that he starts serving that sentence. I think that will give him the time and the opportunity to complete, without a doubt, sex-offender treatment."

According to Montana's sentencing policy, Van Valkenburg noted, "the very first thing the court should consider is to punish each offender commensurate with the nature and degree of harm caused by the offense, and to hold the offender accountable. We've had cases where the court has had to sentence people to as much as one hundred years in prison for a rape, and to deny parole eligibility. The state is not asking for anything like that in this case. But what we're asking for is a very reasonable sentence, one that I think reflects the seriousness of the offense Mr. Donaldson committed. . . . It's not just Allison Huguet that he's offended. We know that he's done this to at least one other person. . . .

"People in Missoula need to know that if you rape an acquaintance, it is a serious crime, and that there needs to be a punishment that fits the crime."

MILT DATSOPOULOS, as Beau Donaldson's lawyer, was given the opportunity to have the final word. As he delivered his closing statement, he brought to mind a quarterback scrambling to throw one last Hail Mary pass. "This is one of those cases that's unusually difficult because a good person committed a tragic and very serious criminal activity that wounded a young lady," Datsopoulos offered. "And she's . . . going to continue to need assistance and time to try to heal and get on with her life. I'm not trying to diminish that. . . .

"The fact of the matter is, the punishment that has occurred already is massive here. The shame, the humiliation, the destruction of a reputation. . . . All I'm asking the court to do is look at the broad, available forms of punishment and tailor that punishment, not only to the crime but to the defendant. . . .

"This system of criminal justice in the United States is insane. We've got a country that sentences more people, particularly young people, to prison, per capita, than any country in the world. And they get sentenced for a longer period than any other country in the world. I'm talking about countries like Uganda and Venezuela. And this is part of what happens when you take young people and you use a meat cleaver like Mr. Van Valkenburg wants to be used here.

"What I'm recommending is five years [at the] Department of Corrections. The Department of Corrections is part of the Montana State Prison system. If you sentence him to the Department of Corrections, he doesn't walk out of here with a slap on the wrist. He's taken out of here in handcuffs. He's taken to an incarceration facility that in many ways is much tougher than a prison, because you're in very tight quarters with extraordinary rules, and you're there for six months to a year."

When Datsopoulos finished, Judge Townsend thanked him, then addressed the perpetrator. "So, Mr. Donaldson," she asked, "is there anything additional you want to say before I impose sentencing?"

"No," Beau Donaldson replied meekly.

"Would you stand, please," she ordered. When Donaldson was on his feet, she said, "The court finds this an incredibly troubling case . . . because I think what has happened here is that a young woman's trust has been violently taken away from her, and in a way that has caused substantial damage to her, and that the impact of the act has had substantial impact on her family.

"My recollection is that one of the witnesses who testified today wished that he were Superman, where he could turn the world backwards and prevent this night from ever happening at all. . . . I've often wished that I had a magic wand, that I could wipe away the kind of hurt that has happened to somebody, and even for folks accused of crimes . . . so that they don't have to face these kinds of consequences. But, Beau, there are consequences for your behavior. Even though you have lived a pretty good life up until this point, there is absolutely no excuse for what you did this night. . . . It's hard for this court to accept that it was just a mistake, like making a wrong turn someplace, or adding up something incorrectly. . . . The court will sentence you to the Montana State Prison for the period of thirty years, with twenty of those years suspended. . . . You're remanded to the custody of the sheriff for imposition of sentence."

As Judge Townsend pronounced his fate, Beau Donaldson's body went slack and he began to weep. His girlfriend screamed hysterically from the gallery. A detention officer cuffed Donaldson's hands behind his back, then escorted him from the courtroom through a side door. Upon exiting the courthouse, he was taken to jail to await transport to Deer Lodge, an eighty-five-mile drive down the frozen interstate.

That evening, Hillary McLaughlin found herself in an unfamiliar state of mind: She wasn't anxious. She decided to share this wonderful development with Allison Huguet, with whom she had never previously communicated. "I texted Allison," she said. "I told her it was the first time in four years I had felt at peace. Until that moment, I hadn't realized how much my life had been affected by Beau attacking me." Testifying against Donaldson had been incredibly stressful for McLaughlin, she acknowledged: "I think the worst part was having to appear in front of everybody and say, 'My name is Hillary McLaughlin,' and then start telling my story. But now I'm so glad I did it." McLaughlin was silent for a moment. She glanced down at her hands, then looked up with a pained expression and told me, "I think back—and Allison tells me not to do this—but I wonder if I had reported what Beau did to me right after he did it, maybe I could have prevented her from being raped."

PART FIVE

Trial by Jury

The U.S. legal system is organized as an adversarial contest: in civil cases, between two citizens; in criminal cases, between a citizen and the state. Physical violence and intimidation are not allowed in court, whereas aggressive argument, selective presentation of the facts, and psychological attack are permitted, with the presumption that this ritualized, hostile encounter offers the best method of arriving at the truth.

Constitutional limits on this kind of conflict are designed to protect criminal defendants from the superior power of the state, but not to protect individual citizens from one another. . . . All citizens are presumed to enter the legal arena on an equal footing, regardless of the real advantages that one of the parties may enjoy. The Constitution, therefore, offers strong guarantees for the rights of the accused, but no corresponding protection for the rights of crime victims. As a result, victims who choose to seek justice may face serious obstacles and risks to their health, safety, and mental health.

JUDITH LEWIS HERMAN
"The Mental Health of Crime Victims"
Journal of Traumatic Stress, April 2003

CHAPTER TWENTY-ONE

On March 16, 2012, ten months before Beau Donaldson was sent to prison for raping Allison Huguet, Cecilia Washburn reported to the Missoula police that she had been raped by Donaldson's teammate Jordan Johnson. At the time, Johnson was already being investigated by the University of Montana for allegedly raping Washburn.

On May 23, 2012, the University Court issued a ruling that Johnson was guilty of rape. On June 6, after reviewing the court's decision, President Royce Engstrom ordered him expelled.

On July 31, 2012, while Jordan Johnson's expulsion from the university was under confidential appeal, Missoula County prosecutors filed court documents charging him with sexual intercourse without consent, a criminal charge that potentially had far more serious consequences than expulsion. If found guilty, Johnson could be sent to prison for life.

On August 7, 2012, a week after the criminal rape charge against Jordan Johnson was filed, Johnson's lawyers filed a motion in Montana district court to dismiss the case. It caught more than a few Missoulians by surprise when they noticed that the motion had been written by Kirsten Pabst.

AS CHIEF DEPUTY Missoula County attorney, Pabst had been Fred Van Valkenburg's second-in-command, in charge of prosecuting sexual assaults. In March 2012, the same month Cecilia Washburn went to the police to report that she was raped by Johnson, Kirsten Pabst unexpectedly resigned from the Missoula County Attorney's Office after fifteen years on the job to start her own law firm. In a *Missoulian* article announcing her decision to leave, she explained that a solo practice would allow her more flexibility and more free time. "I want to focus on my family and horses and dogs," she told reporter Gwen Florio.

So it came as a shock when, scarcely a month later, Pabst quietly joined forces with lawyer David Paoli as defense counsel for Jordan Johnson in a case that was expected to culminate in one of the most viciously contested and highly publicized trials in the history of Missoula. When the trial got under way, Pabst would be using her considerable expertise against her former colleagues in the prosecutor's office to keep Johnson from joining Beau Donaldson in prison.

Had she remained in office, Kirsten Pabst probably would have been the lead prosecutor in the Johnson rape case. Her motion on August 7 to dismiss the criminal charge against him was the first public indication that, instead, she intended to do everything in her power to help Jordan Johnson beat the rap.

Pabst's motion was the opening salvo in this battle. In asking the court to throw out the case, Pabst argued that there was a lack of "probable cause to sustain the charge of sexual intercourse without consent." This, of course, was the same reason Pabst gave for refusing to charge Calvin Smith with raping Kaitlynn Kelly back in November 2011, when Pabst was still a prosecutor.

According to the Department of Justice's investigation of the Missoula County Attorney's Office, from January 2008 through April 2012 the Missoula Police Department referred 114 reports of sexual assault of adult women to the MCAO for prosecution. A "referral" indicated that the police department had completed its investigation of the case in question, determined that there was probable cause to charge the individual accused of sexual assault, and recommended that the case be prosecuted. Of the 114 sexual assaults referred for prosecution, however, the MCAO filed charges in only 14 of those cases. The reasons most often given for declining to prosecute were "insufficient evidence" or "insufficient corroboration"—that is, lack of probable cause. Kirsten Pabst was in charge of sexual-assault cases for all but the final two months of the fifty-two-month period investigated by the DOJ.

Throughout the United States, decisions about whether or not to file charges in sexual-assault cases are generally left up to the discretion of prosecutors, who enjoy nearly complete immunity from both criminal and civil liability for their decisions—especially when they decline to prosecute. If a prosecutor doesn't want to pursue a case, she can simply state that there is "insufficient probable cause," and the case will not be prosecuted. Although this leaves victims with no recourse when their cases are disqualified, prosecutors will argue that such wide latitude is necessary to keep the wheels of the criminal justice system turning.

But it isn't so easy to dismiss a case for lack of probable cause when you are no longer a prosecutor, as Kirsten Pabst discovered after she went to work as a defense lawyer for Jordan Johnson. As counsel for the accused, she needed the sanction of a judge to make the charges against her client disappear. In the motion Pabst submitted to the court seeking dismissal of the Johnson case, she argued that the charging documents filed by Van Valkenburg's office ("the State") presented

> a materially incomplete and misleading version of the facts. . . . The State then sent the incomplete, misleading and prejudicial document to multiple members of the media. Such conduct . . . violates Johnson's right to Due Process. Based upon [this] conduct . . . and considering the omitted and corrected facts that should have been contained in the charging documents, dismissal is the only appropriate remedy.
>
> This case has arisen in the unfortunate context and under the cloud of a federal Department of Justice investigation into complaints about how the University of Montana, the Missoula City Police Department and the Missoula County

> Prosecutor's Office handle cases involving alleged sexual assault. . . .
>
> Understandably, the State would like to demonstrate its reflexive and compassionate response to victims of sexual crimes. . . . Unfortunately, while multitudes of competent and noble exercises of prosecutorial discretion* go unnoticed, the State has chosen to use Jordan's case—one which lacks probable cause—as a means to try to send a message. The collateral damage to Jordan and his family is immeasurable. . . .
>
> Because the State's grounds for charging Jordan are based entirely upon the alleged victim's statements, the contradictions of her story would have completely undercut the alleged probable cause for the crime.

Two weeks after Pabst filed her motion to dismiss, chief prosecutor Fred Van Valkenburg responded with a brief protesting that she had

> filed a thinly veiled press release under the guise of a legal proceeding. [Her] motion is rife with irrelevant, unnecessary, prejudicial, and objectively inadmissible evidence. . . . [A pre-trial motion is] not the place to dispute the State's evidence, offer alternative interpretations of the evidence, or make determinations of witness credibility. Determinations of witness credibility lie squarely with the province of the jury. . . . Nor is a pre-trial motion an appropriate way to make a claim that a rape victim did not act like a rape victim should.

* Kirsten Pabst is congratulating herself here for the many cases she declined to prosecute when she ran the sexual-assault division at the Missoula County Attorney's Office.

Judge Karen Townsend, whose job it was to rule on Pabst's motion to dismiss, found Van Valkenburg's argument more cogent than Pabst's. In a court order dated September 5, 2012, Townsend decreed,

> [T]he Court does not believe that the State omitted material facts. . . . Looking at everything, using common sense and drawing permissible inferences, . . . the Court . . . concludes that there is a "fair probability" that the defendant committed the offense of sexual intercourse without consent. . . .
>
> For the reasons outlined above, Defendant's Motion to Dismiss is **DENIED.**

ON FEBRUARY 6, 2013, two days before the trial of Jordan Johnson was scheduled to begin, reporter Jim Robbins observed in a piece published in the *New York Times,*

> Mr. Johnson's trial comes on the heels of the sentencing of a former Grizzlies running back, Beau Donaldson, who pleaded guilty to raping a childhood friend in 2010 as she slept in his apartment. . . .
>
> Questions have been raised about whether Mr. Johnson can get a fair trial amid such controversy. Court officials have assembled an extra-large pool of 400 for the jury selection that begins Friday.
>
> "You have to believe that the presumption of innocence is somehow affected," said Milt Datsopoulos, who represented Mr. Donaldson and is also on the National Advisory Board for Grizzly Athletics, a booster organization. He believes that his client's sentence was more severe than it would have been had there not been what he called "a toxic atmosphere" in Missoula.
>
> "They made him a poster child for a supposed major

problem," Mr. Datsopoulos said of Mr. Donaldson. "I don't think a problem exists."

Datsopoulos expanded on this theme in an article by Lester Munson posted on ESPN.com on February 8:

> "The mess that has developed is an unfortunate thing," said Datsopoulos. . . . "The accusation that the county attorney has not pursued cases against football players is totally not true. It is now hard to get a fair trial. The presumption of innocence has been flip-flopped, and football players are now presumed to be guilty."
>
> Instead of preferential treatment for football players, Datsopoulos asserts, the prosecutors are "very aggressive in their cases against football players and in their demands for stiff sentences. The deputies in the office of the county attorney are female and activist, and they make every case a matter of women's rights and a gender issue." . . .
>
> "It is certain," Datsopoulos said, "that the environment created in Missoula is responsible for the 10-year sentence. [Donaldson] did the right thing; he is a quality guy; he told the police what he did; he wanted to clear it up, and it has cost him dearly."

Contrary to the spin provided by Milt Datsopoulos in advance of Jordan Johnson's trial, however, the combination of Johnson's status as such a cherished member of the Griz and the fact that the trial was being held in Missoula almost certainly worked to Johnson's advantage. The town is known as Grizzlyville for good reason, a point driven home by the public outcry ignited by a statement made by Pat Williams—a University of Montana alumnus and a member of the Montana Board of Regents of Higher Education, the body that oversees the state university system. Williams, who represented Montana in the U.S. Congress from 1979 to 1997, told Lester Munson,

> The football team was recruiting too many thugs. Rape was not the only problem. There was vandalism, there were personal assaults, and there was destruction of property. The players were pampered and adored. Too many of them had the feeling they were bulletproof and immune to the rules that all of us must follow. They acted like arrogant marauders.

Williams's comments to Munson about thuggery—and similar comments Williams made to the *New York Times* and a Montana radio station—angered Griz fans, who circulated a petition demanding that he be kicked off the Board of Regents.

JURY SELECTION FOR *State of Montana v. Jordan Todd Johnson* commenced on Friday morning, February 8, 2013, and was completed on midday the following Monday, February 11, with seven women and five men being seated in the jury box. After a break for lunch, the trial got under way with opening statements from each side. The prosecution went first. "This case is about a young woman who is horribly betrayed by someone that she trusted," Special Deputy Missoula County Attorney Adam Duerk began. "There is one person on trial in this matter. Not Grizzly football, not that young woman who accused Mr. Johnson of the crime."

The only person who was on trial, Duerk made clear, was Jordan Johnson, and he had been charged with sexual intercourse without consent. Duerk emphasized to the jury that according to Montana law, "resistance by the victim is not required to show lack of consent. Force, fear, or threat is sufficient alone to show lack of consent." And then he provided a detailed account of what happened in Cecilia Washburn's bedroom on the night of February 4, 2012.

Duerk, a slender man in his early forties with curly black hair, was an expert litigator at a Missoula law firm. He'd been appointed as a special prosecutor to assist the Missoula County Attorney's Office during the Jordan Johnson trial and was working pro bono.

In his opening statement, his task was to tell a brief story to the jury, based on the evidence to be presented in the days ahead, that would be more compelling than the story defense counsel Kirsten Pabst would be telling immediately after he finished. Everyone knew that the main thrust of Adam Duerk's opening statement would be that Washburn explicitly and repeatedly told Johnson that she didn't want to have sex with him that night. Everyone knew that the main thrust of Pabst's opening statement would be that Washburn consented to have sex with Johnson.

Cecilia Washburn was lying, or Jordan Johnson was lying. Or perhaps both of them were misrepresenting key details of their respective accounts. There wasn't enough incontrovertible evidence to prove whose version came closest to the truth, however. The outcome of the trial would thus hinge on bits of tangential substantiation and the testimony of individuals who weren't in Washburn's bedroom when the alleged rape occurred. Most of the evidence was subject to conflicting interpretations. Whoever assembled the most persuasive narrative from these disjointed shards of information—whoever told the best story, in other words—was most likely to sway the jury. The opening statements would be bare-bones summaries of the full-length narratives each side intended to flesh out as the trial ran its course.

Many of the details of what transpired between Washburn and Johnson were undisputed. Johnson texted Washburn at 2:00 in the afternoon on February 4, and they formulated a plan to watch a movie at Washburn's residence that night. Around 10:45, Johnson phoned Washburn and asked her to give him a ride to her house. She drove over, picked him up, and then drove back to her place. Around 11:00 they went into her bedroom, closed the door, and inserted a movie into her DVD player. Washburn's housemate Stephen Green was slumped on a couch just outside the door, engrossed in a video game.

Soon after the movie started, Jordan Johnson and Cecilia Washburn began making out, they took each other's shirts off, and had sex without a condom. The intercourse lasted only a few minutes.

While Johnson was penetrating Washburn from behind, he realized he was about to climax, withdrew his penis from Washburn's vagina, and ejaculated into his hand. Immediately after ejaculating, Johnson wiped the semen off his hand and his penis, gathered his clothing, and went into an adjacent bathroom. While he was in the bathroom, Washburn pulled on her own clothes and then sent a text to Green that said, "Omg, I think I might have just gotten raped. he kept pushing and pushing and I said no but he wouldn't listen . . . I just wanna cry . . . omg what do I do!" A few minutes later, Washburn drove Johnson home.

"On many of these points," prosecutor Duerk told the jury, "there is very little difference in the account between Cecilia's version and the defendant's version." Duerk emphasized, however, that when it came to a handful of crucial details, their accounts of what happened diverged in ways that couldn't be reconciled. "She'll tell you that before anyone's pants came off," Duerk said, "before the defendant was on top of her, before there was any penetration at all, she told him no, multiple times, in multiple ways. She said, 'No, not tonight.' Playfully at first. . . . But then as things got more heated, she made it clear through words and actions that she did not want to have sex.

"She'll take the stand," Duerk continued, "and tell you that she was very clear with the defendant. . . . But the defendant kept going. He positioned himself on top of her. . . . His demeanor changed. He became more aggressive. And, in her words, 'It got real scary, real fast.' Again she said no. . . . The defendant put his forearm across her chest and held her down. He stripped her leggings and underwear off; her underwear was still hooked on her ankle. She began to push him away. . . . The defendant said, 'Turn over, or I'll make you.' At that point, Cecilia continued to resist. She was scared. She was in shock. She was starting to shut down, but even then she said no. And then he did flip her over, he penetrated her, and he ejaculated."

Afterward, Cecilia Washburn was "shaking, scared, and in shock," Duerk told the jury. She got up and sent the text to Stephen Green, her housemate, saying she thought she'd just been raped. "Green texted her back and said, 'What are you doing? Get out of there.' . . . She gets dressed and she does get out of there, which brings us to the point of the story when Stephen Green saw her face." The jury, Duerk said, would hear Green testify that Washburn was distraught and didn't want to talk. And when she returned from driving Johnson home, she was hysterical.

Adam Duerk hastily ran through some of the other witnesses the prosecution would be putting on the stand, and what they would be saying. Nurses who examined Washburn the day after the rape would testify that they found erythema (slight bruising) on her chest and lacerations inside her vagina. Friends and psychologists would testify that Washburn was suffering from post-traumatic stress. Dr. David Lisak, characterized by Duerk as "a nationally known expert and professor of psychology from the University of Massachusetts," would testify "that there is no way to tell who is a rapist. There's also no normal way to respond to rape. That victims often deny or minimize what they've been through. That victims try to make everything appear normal after a rape. That self-blame is common, and while the event is occurring, in the presence of the perceived threat, that victims often freeze."

As Duerk's allotted time to speak ran out, he told the jury that what they were being asked to do was difficult, but "ultimately it is up to you to weigh all of the evidence in this matter. It's up to you to determine the credibility of those witnesses that you hear from."

CHAPTER TWENTY-TWO

Kirsten Pabst's talents come to the fore in a courtroom. She has a knack for charming a jury with her candor and her sly sense of humor, even as she is eviscerating a witness on cross-examination. It was obvious why defense attorney David Paoli had asked her to help him represent Jordan Johnson. Paoli is a force to reckon with, but charm is not one of his attributes.

During the seventeen years Pabst worked as a prosecutor in Missoula and Great Falls, she'd tried and won a lot of cases. She boasts on her website of having "a 99 percent success rate at trial." But the reason her winning percentage is so high is that she didn't accept cases for prosecution during those seventeen years unless she was almost certain she would win in court or strong-arm the defendant into copping a plea. According to the investigation of the Missoula County Attorney's Office by the U.S. Department of Justice, during the final four-plus years of Kirsten Pabst's tenure running the criminal division of the MCAO, the MCAO prosecuted only 12 percent of the sexual-assault cases involving adult women referred to it by the Missoula Police Department.

Pabst's phenomenal success rate should therefore be cause for concern, rather than congratulation. As an experienced prosecutor told me, "If you're winning 99 percent of the time you go to trial, you're not prosecuting nearly enough of the cases that land on your desk."

What Pabst's record actually shows is that she was adept at

recognizing what made some rape cases problematic to prosecute. And in the spring of 2012, when she started working as defense counsel for Jordan Johnson, she made good use of that aptitude. Pabst quickly identified Cecilia Washburn's greatest vulnerabilities, and then exploited them ruthlessly.

It's not enough to simply disparage the accuser, though. Veteran defense lawyers say that to win a trial, you also need to make the defendant seem likable. Jurors have to have sympathy for a defendant before they will acquit him. Early in her opening statement, therefore, Pabst started singing Jordan Johnson's praises. "People who know Jordan," she said, "will tell you he's different. He's different than your typical teenager.* He's different than your stereotypical football player. . . . He's described as shy, quiet, reserved, polite, respectful, and has actually never been to downtown Missoula at night. He's never been to a tailgate [party]."

In fact, Jordan Johnson, like most college students, had done plenty of partying and excessive drinking, and Pabst knew it. During jury selection the previous day, when Judge Townsend asked prospective jurors if any of them had a professional relationship with Johnson, a man who worked nights as a DJ at a downtown drinking establishment replied that he didn't think he could be an unbiased juror because Johnson sometimes drank there. During his freshman year at UM, moreover, Johnson had been disciplined by the university for getting drunk and running amok in his dormitory.

But none of Johnson's previous bad behavior was revealed in the courtroom. Before the trial began, Judge Townsend had ruled that in accordance with the Family Educational Rights and Privacy Act, a law enacted by Congress in 1974 to protect the privacy of students, the prosecution was forbidden to mention anything about Johnson's campus improprieties, including the University of Montana's adjudication of the charge that he raped Cecilia Washburn. Pabst was therefore confident that she wouldn't be challenged

* Although Johnson was twenty years old when the trial was held, he was nineteen when he allegedly raped Cecilia Washburn.

about Johnson's peccadillos, and she continued her characterization of him as a paragon of virtue. "Jordan, by all accounts, including Miss Washburn's," Pabst told the jury, "is the opposite of the ignorant and generalized football thug. He's never been in any kind of trouble with the law."

Having established that Johnson was an upstanding young man, Pabst devoted the rest of her opening statement to vilifying his accuser. Pabst, who had been a fine arts major before she became a lawyer, painted a misleading portrait of Washburn as a dishonest, insecure, emotionally unstable young woman who desperately craved the status that would be hers if she could ensnare the star quarterback of the Griz as her boyfriend.

Cecilia Washburn was "pretty and articulate, and seemingly self-assured," Kirsten Pabst told the jury. "However, according to Miss Washburn, she had a rough childhood and described being extensively bullied as a child at her day care, in junior high, and some in high school, to the point where she said she was diagnosed with an anxiety disorder in seventh grade and had to see a counselor to address panic attacks and thoughts of suicide. She started school in Great Falls but had to transfer to [a high school in a very small town] where her father was a teacher, to get away from the bullying."

Although Washburn first met Jordan Johnson in February 2011, when he was a freshman and she was a sophomore, she didn't want to have sex with him at the time, Pabst asserted, because Johnson hadn't become the star of the Grizzly football team yet and "nobody really knew who he was. . . . Jordan and Miss Washburn started texting each other on a friendly basis. . . . They went out on a few dates, as us older people call them. They watched TV, they watched some movies, they went and shared some ice cream, had a couple of make-out sessions as well. . . . One time, while kissing, Jordan attempted to take the relationship to the next level and tried to unbutton her pants. She told him no, and he respected the instruction, [and] stopped. . . . Washburn was not particularly interested in him at this point."

In Kirsten Pabst's version of events, however, Cecilia Washburn changed her mind about having sex with Jordan Johnson when he became famous. During the 2011 football season, according to Pabst, Washburn began to regard Johnson as a potential boyfriend, because he'd become the first-string quarterback and "was really taking off and really seeing some success. . . . After a couple of games that fall, Miss Washburn texted Jordan, congratulating him on his good playing." By the end of December, when the Griz were crowned co-champions of the Big Sky Conference—thanks largely to Johnson's brilliant performance on the field—he was likely the most popular person in all of Missoula.

THE NIGHT BEFORE the rape allegedly occurred, Kirsten Pabst told the jury, "Jordan and some of his friends went to the Foresters' Ball. . . . Miss Washburn was also there. She saw Jordan from across the room and approached him and hugged him. He was with his friends Bo [Tully] and Alex [Bienemann]." According to pretrial statements made by Johnson and Bienemann, Cecilia Washburn wrapped her arm around Johnson, put her mouth to his ear, and said, "Jordy, I would do you anytime." Pabst didn't share this infelicitous proposition with the jury, though, because in advance of the trial, Judge Townsend had ordered Jordan Johnson's defense counsel, David Paoli and Kirsten Pabst, to say nothing about it, citing Montana's "rape shield law," which decrees that an accuser's previous sexual conduct is inadmissible as evidence. Skipping over the incident, Pabst said that Washburn and Johnson drifted apart soon thereafter, and Johnson "didn't see Miss Washburn again that night except for a hug good-bye."

Pabst described the exchange of texts the following afternoon that culminated in Jordan Johnson phoning Washburn at 10:45 p.m. and asking her to pick him up at his house. "Jordan will tell you that he considered that he might have sex with her that night," Pabst said. "He didn't expect it, but it certainly wasn't out of the realm of possibilities. . . . He was just going to play it by ear and go with the flow." Kirsten Pabst's account of what happened before Johnson and Washburn went into her bedroom wasn't substantially different from the account provided by prosecutor Adam Duerk in his opening statement. But Pabst's version of what occurred next was completely at odds with Duerk's version.

The way Pabst told it, Cecilia Washburn was just as eager to have sex as Jordan Johnson: "She got on top of him, topless, and then they continued to make out. They rolled over so that she was on her back. . . . She had on black stretch pants, and Jordan took them off of her and she lifted her hips a little bit so he could get the waistband down around her waist. Jordan asked her about a condom, because at that point, to him, it became pretty clear what was going to happen. He didn't have one with him. And she told him, 'That's okay.' They continued to kiss.

"Jordan took off his pants and they had sex in the missionary position for a few minutes," Pabst continued. "Jordan, extremely excited, thought that he was going to ejaculate, so he pulled out for a second. They changed positions, with him guiding her onto her stomach. She lifted up a little bit again so that he could reenter her from the back. She turned her head back towards him and said in a flirty tone, 'Oh, you're bad.' Her message to Jordan at every turn was that she was willing and she was interested.

"Jordan didn't last long in this position. He pulled out and ejaculated in his hand, not inside of her. He then asked for a towel so he could clean up the mess. There was no discussion about whether she was satisfied. There was no snuggling. It was a little bit awkward. Not what she had been expecting. Jordan was a little clueless that she had wanted something more. At that point, Miss Washburn started to realize that [this] was not exactly what she had been expecting to happen, either. Suddenly, to her, it seemed like her feelings didn't matter. And maybe, sadly, they didn't."

Making the same assertion she had made to the University of Montana court to explain why she'd refused to prosecute Calvin Smith for raping Kaitlynn Kelly, Pabst declared, "Ladies and gentlemen of the jury, this is a case that's not about rape, but about a girl's regret." Pabst argued that Cecilia Washburn's disappointment over a sexual encounter that hadn't lived up to her high expectations was transformed into an accusation of rape by the "brewing storm" of the Missoula rape scandal.

Furthermore, Pabst insisted, the entire scandal, the investigations that accompanied it, and the prosecution of Jordan Johnson all resulted "because of a vocal, disgruntled woman* who had claimed to be the victim of a sexual assault, and was extremely unhappy with the way she says she was treated by a police detective. . . . She complained to the chief of police. Her outrage prompted a series of news stories that appeared throughout the first six months of [2012] intimating that the Missoula Police Department and Missoula County Attorney's Office were mishandling sexual-assault cases.

"The repetitive news stories prompted a federal investigation by the Department of Justice," Pabst continued, "into whether the police and prosecutor's office were taking sexual assaults seriously. Meanwhile, the Missoula Police Department, in response to the criticism, announced a new policy on its treatment of victims. It specifically mandated that investigators believe everybody who comes through their doors complaining of a sexual assault, and assured the public that from here on out, it would make every effort to be more sympathetic towards women who have alleged abuse.

"Suddenly, [Cecilia Washburn] was getting a lot of attention from her friends," Pabst explained to the jury. "Attention from the dean of the pharmacy school. . . . Attention by Dean Charles Couture, the then dean of students; by the Crime Victim Advocate office; by the nurse, [Claire] Francoeur. . . . Miss Washburn got

* Pabst was referring to Kerry Barrett, yet again. The screed Pabst posted on her personal blog on June 19, 2012, blamed Barrett, Kaitlynn Kelly, and reporter Gwen Florio (without naming them) for manufacturing the rape scandal. Now Pabst was blaming Barrett and Florio for unfairly bringing about the prosecution of Jordan Johnson, too.

attention by the investigator and by the prosecutor. Her regret was replaced by sympathy, attention, and support, and a little bit of drama, and a little bit of celebrity. . . . Her regret, fueled by drama, became purpose. She received a new public—and important—identity: victim."

Having provided the jury with Cecilia Washburn's purported motive for falsely claiming that she was raped by Jordan Johnson, Kirsten Pabst moved on to a new theme. "When the state charges a man with rape," she said, "it must focus on what [the accused and his accuser] are thinking. Because it's required to prove beyond a reasonable doubt that, one: The woman didn't want to have sex; and, two: The man knew that she didn't want to have sex. . . . We will ask you to keep those two critical questions in mind throughout the entirety of the case. Jordan fully admits that they had sex that night. But Miss Washburn gave him every indication that she was into it. She encouraged him. She participated. . . . If she changed her mind at some point, she did not communicate that to him."

Pabst repeatedly urged jurors not to believe Washburn: "Her story, at face value, appears sincere. But, ladies and gentlemen . . . , pay close attention to the layers beneath the surface. . . . When two stories conflict, and someone is charged with a crime, the jury's task is to drill down into credibility. . . . Do you believe this girl beyond a reasonable doubt? Are you convinced? . . . Miss Washburn wanted a relationship with the star quarterback. That's why she gave him sex. She is, perhaps rightfully, angry about that. But the fact that he didn't give her a relationship does not make what happened that night a crime. It does not make him guilty of rape. . . . We trust that you'll be able to withstand the political storm, stay steady regardless of any hysteria, and just be fair. . . . 'No' definitely means no. But, in all fairness, 'yes' also means yes."

CHAPTER TWENTY-THREE

As defense counsel for Jordan Johnson, Kirsten Pabst and David Paoli had a professional responsibility to sow doubt about Cecilia Washburn's credibility at every opportunity. Throughout the trial, to fulfill this duty, Pabst and Paoli made misleading statements about Washburn without compunction.

Montana lawyers are required to adhere to the Montana Rules of Professional Conduct, which are based on the American Bar Association Model Rules of Professional Conduct. According to both the Montana Rules and the ABA Model Rules, "In the course of representing a client a lawyer shall not knowingly make a false statement of material fact or law to a third person." It's nevertheless common for lawyers to deliberately make untrue statements in court, and they usually get away with it, especially defense counsel.

"There's a double standard," Rebecca Roe told me. According to Roe, who supervised the sexual-assault unit in the King County Prosecuting Attorney's Office for eleven years, "Judges tend to hold prosecutors to a higher level of truthfulness than defense counsel." Furthermore, she said, "If prosecutors make statements in court that aren't true, and the defendant is convicted, the defense can appeal and get the conviction overturned. But there is no corresponding deterrent when defense lawyers make untrue statements, because if a defendant is acquitted, the prosecution can't appeal."

Seemingly by design, the American legal system encourages defense counsel to be as mendacious as possible. As Monroe Freedman, a legal ethicist and former dean of Hofstra Law School, has written, "The attorney is obligated to attack, if he can, the reliability or credibility of an opposing witness whom he knows to be truthful." It's an essential component of our adversarial system of justice, based on the theory that justice is best achieved not through a third-party investigation directed by an impartial judge but, instead, through vigorous disputation by the interested parties: trial by verbal combat.

The preamble to the ABA Model Rules states, "As advocate, a lawyer zealously asserts the client's position under the rules of the adversary system" and the lawyer has an "obligation zealously to protect and pursue a client's legitimate interests, within the bounds of the law."* Lawyers for each side are expected to fight as hard as they can, with the judge doing little more than acting as a referee to ensure that rules and procedure are followed. Because antagonistic counsel are motivated to present the strongest evidence and advance the most persuasive arguments in support of their respective clients, a fair trial is ensured, the truth will come to light, and the jury will be given a sound basis for rendering a just verdict. That's the theory.

In reality, the system promotes chicanery, outright deceit, and other egregious misconduct by trial lawyers. As the legal scholar Franklin Strier points out,

> [A]lthough we expect attorneys to adhere to the rules of evidence and confine their strategies to the ethical boundaries of the rules, they often bend the rules and stretch the strategies. . . . As a result, trial lawyers ostensibly enjoy a unique privilege in plying their trade: They are largely

* In an effort to encourage lawyers to act more honorably, in 2004 the Montana Supreme Court removed every mention of "zealously" from the preamble to the Montana Rules of Professional Conduct. The revised preamble states, "As advocate, a lawyer asserts the client's position under the rules of the adversary system." It's not clear that this revision has had any effect on the conduct of Montana lawyers.

> unanswerable to society for behavior that would be morally questionable elsewhere.

In the adversarial system, it's more important to follow legal procedure than to speak the truth. Due process trumps honesty and ordinary justice. Trials degenerate into clashes that bring to mind cage fights, characterized by wildly exaggerated claims, highly selective presentation of the facts, and brutal interrogation of witnesses.

The excessive partisanship of the adversarial system becomes especially problematic when the offense being adjudicated is rape, which all but guarantees that lawyers for the accused party will attempt to turn the tables and put the victim on trial. As Judith Lewis Herman, professor of psychiatry at Harvard Medical School, explains in "The Mental Health of Crime Victims,"

> Involvement in legal proceedings constitutes a significant emotional stress for even the most robust citizen. For victims of violent crime, who may suffer from psychological trauma as a result of their victimization, involvement in the justice system may compound the original injury. . . . Indeed, if one set out intentionally to design a system for provoking symptoms of posttraumatic stress disorder, it might look very much like a court of law.
>
> The mental health needs of crime victims are often diametrically opposed to the requirements of legal proceedings. Victims need social acknowledgement and support; the court requires them to endure a public challenge to their credibility. Victims need to establish a sense of power and control over their lives; the court requires them to submit to a complex set of rules and procedures that they may not understand, and over which they have no control. Victims need an opportunity to tell their stories in their own way, in a setting of their choice; the court requires them to respond to a set of yes-or-no questions that break down any personal

> attempt to construct a coherent and meaningful narrative. Victims often need to control or limit their exposure to specific reminders of the trauma; the court requires them to relive the experience by directly confronting the perpetrator.

The trial of Jordan began on Friday, February 8, 2013, and ended three weeks later on Friday, March 1. The first of the thirty-five witnesses called to testify was Cecilia Washburn, the victim. Under friendly questioning by Montana Assistant Attorney General Joel Thompson (who was collaborating with the prosecutors in the Missoula County Attorney's Office because it was such a high-profile case), Washburn spent more than a day on the stand providing a detailed account of the events described by prosecutor Adam Duerk in his opening statement. When Thompson was finished, the defense was given the opportunity to cross-examine Washburn, and David Paoli's questions weren't as genial.

Right away, Paoli attempted to establish that Washburn was vindictive, and her statements unreliable. His first question was "It's true, is it not, that when I talked to you previously [during a pretrial deposition], you told me that you wanted Jordan to suffer?"

"No," Washburn replied, prompting Paoli to produce a transcript of the deposition and present it to her on the witness stand.

"You said and believed," Paoli recited, "that you wanted him to suffer like you believed you have suffered; isn't that right?"

After reading the transcript, Washburn admitted she'd said that.

A few minutes later, Paoli grilled Washburn about her childhood, trying to establish that she was emotionally unstable. "You have said and you have written that you were bullied in day care; is that right?" he asked.

"Yes," she replied.

"And you were bullied in junior high school?" he continued.

"Correct." . . .

"And you got bullied so bad that you had to go get counseling; is that fair?"

"Yes."

"And you had anxiety attacks then?"

"Yes."

"Panic attacks?"

"Yes."

"Suicidal ideations, then?"

"Yes."

"And the bullying continued in high school, didn't it?"

"It fizzled. I mean, . . . it wasn't as common as it was in junior high."

"And in high school there were two girls that bullied you; isn't that what you told me?"

"Yes."

"And of course your father would have known about it; isn't that right?"

"No."

"Well, your father worked in the school?"

"Yes."

"Did you tell your father about the bullying?"

"No."

"Would it surprise you that neither of your parents recall that you were bullied in that period of time?"

"No."

"It would not surprise you?" Paoli demanded again.

"No," Washburn answered.

Earlier, under friendly questioning from prosecutor Joel Thompson, Cecilia Washburn had said that she "had never thought in a million years" that she would ever be raped. After reminding her of this statement, Paoli demanded, "But you, in fact, had a very specific dream—a nightmare, frankly—on Christmas 2011, about being raped; isn't that right?"

"If that's what the record shows," Washburn answered, "then yes."

Paoli showed her a text message she'd sent on December 26, 2011, and then asked, "So this dream you had was about a Grizzly player raping you; isn't that right? . . . And it's not just any football player."

Cecilia Washburn's nightmare had been about Trumaine Johnson (no relation to Jordan Johnson), who had played cornerback for the University of Montana, extremely well, and in 2012 was drafted by the St. Louis Rams, and went on to become a star in the National Football League. But in December 2011, a week before Washburn had the dream, Trumaine Johnson was tased and arrested by the Missoula police after brutally beating a man at a party in his apartment following a Griz football game, an incident prominently reported in the Montana news media.

In Washburn's nightmare, Trumaine hit her over the head and raped her in a van. At the time she had this dream, Trumaine was in fact the roommate of the man who was Washburn's boyfriend.

THROUGHOUT HIS CROSS-EXAMINATION of Cecilia Washburn, defense counsel David Paoli aggressively challenged every conceivable inconsistency in her prior testimony. Some of these alleged inconsistencies were potentially damaging. For example, Jordan Johnson claimed that shortly before they had sex, Washburn asked him if he had a condom, and when he said no, according to Johnson, she replied, "It's okay." Washburn claimed this conversation never happened. But four months before the trial, when UM Dean Rhondie Voorhees grilled Washburn during Johnson's appeal of his expulsion from the University of Montana, and Voorhees asked Washburn whether she and Johnson had talked about a condom, Washburn seemed to waffle and didn't answer the question.

Paoli zeroed in on this. "You and Jordan had a discussion about a condom, didn't you?" he asked Washburn.

"We did not," she answered without hesitation.

"You will admit that you have been equivocal in the past about whether you had a discussion about a condom, correct? . . . And you were equivocal with Dean Rhondie Voorhees . . . and didn't have a response, correct?"

"Correct."

"So now the issue has become important, and you're clear about whether you had that discussion?"

"Correct."

Paoli also jumped all over Washburn about inconsistencies that seemed of no consequence. For instance, he tried to make hay out of conflicting accounts about whether Washburn ate anything during the five or ten minutes that elapsed between the alleged rape and driving Johnson home. "You grabbed a snack, didn't you?" Paoli demanded.

"No," Washburn said.

"You're aware that Stephen [Green, Washburn's housemate] has said you went in and grabbed a snack?"

"Yes."

"And what do you make of . . . what Stephen's testimony is versus your testimony?"

"I can't make comments on Stephen's testimony. That's his testimony. But I didn't grab a snack." . . .

"He doesn't have any reason to make that up, does he?" Paoli continued.

"No."

"He's just telling what he thought he saw you doing in the kitchen, right?"

"Right."

Referring to a diagram, Paoli asked, "And it's true, is it not, that in this kitchen, you keep your food down here towards the dining room?"

"Yes," Washburn replied. "Right next to the sink."

Paoli spent even more time haranguing Washburn about whether she had contacted a lawyer to discuss filing a civil claim against Johnson. After confirming that she had indeed contacted a lawyer, Paoli asked, "This is a lawyer in Atlanta who files lawsuits for money; isn't that right?"

"I don't know what she does," Washburn replied.

"Did you look at her website? . . . Did you look at her many victories and the money that she's earned for clients? . . . Did it include jury verdicts for money?"*

"No, it did not." . . .

"Have you engaged the services or retained this Atlanta law firm?"

"No, I have not."

"Have they told you to get back to them after this is all over?"

"No, they have not." . . .

"Are you planning on filing a lawsuit against Jordan Johnson?"

"No."

"Are you planning on filing a lawsuit against the University of Montana?"

"No."

"Are you planning on filing a lawsuit against the Grizzly football team?"

"No," Washburn answered.

EVENTUALLY PAOLI GOT around to challenging Washburn's claim that she'd made it explicitly clear to Jordan Johnson that she did not want to have sex on the night he allegedly raped her. Brandishing a document titled "Cecilia Washburn Reflection," which she'd written three or four days after the incident, Paoli asked, "You gave a lot of thought to this, didn't you?"

"I did," Washburn answered.

Paoli handed Washburn a copy of the document and asked, "So in your reflections, you wrote that you thought this whole situation was your fault, right? . . . So what were the mixed signals that you gave that made you think this was all your fault?"

* Trial lawyers almost always advertise the large monetary sums they've won for clients. On his own website, Paoli boasts of several six-figure jury verdicts and settlements he's won.

"Maybe it was the clothes I was wearing, us making out, or me taking off my shirt that made Jordan think I wanted to have sex," Washburn answered.

"And then you regret not having called to Stephen [Green, her friend and housemate] or done more to resist Jordan?" Paoli continued.

"I should have screamed out to my roommate in the living room," she answered, "or used more force to resist him, yes."

Paoli handed Washburn a copy of a Facebook message she sent to a friend in Great Falls named Bryan Court, eighteen days after the alleged rape. "And you express again in this document that all you can think about is how you could have prevented it, right?" Paoli asked.

"Yes," Washburn answered.

"And how you should have tried harder, right?"

"Yes." . . .

"And then your thoughts lead you to say, 'And now I keep thinking, well, maybe I did want it, and that's why I didn't punch him or kick him or bite him'?"

"That's the first part, yes," Washburn replied, but then she reminded Paoli (and the jury) that there was a second part to the Facebook message he'd neglected to mention.

Paoli conceded that there was a subsequent statement, in which Washburn said, "It's all ridiculous because I know I didn't ask for this." But Paoli immediately resumed asking questions intended to show that she was lying about being raped: "And then you say, 'It just seems like the more and more this drags on, the more and more I feel guilty about it.' Isn't that right?"

"Yes."

"And you express concern in here, in your own words, that the whole situation makes you feel like you just lied?"

Washburn acknowledged, "It makes me feel like I lied, yes."

"And then you say, 'Maybe my other friends will think I lied about it, or what if it really is my fault. . . . It's so frustrating.'" . . .

"I wrote that, yes," Washburn confirmed.

In her Facebook message to Bryan Court, Washburn also mentioned her childhood anxiety disorder. "That's the anxiety disorder you had prior to this, right?" Paoli asked.

"In the seventh grade," Washburn answered.

"And that's the anxiety disorder and suicidal ideations that you have told us that you went and got counseling for; isn't that right? . . . And those are the things that I asked you whether your parents obviously should know about, and you said, 'Yes, they do.' Isn't that right?"

"Yes," Washburn answered.

A little later, Paoli asked yet again, "So, Miss Washburn, you gave Jordan Johnson mixed signals; isn't that right?"

"It could be seen that way," she answered.

"And you have told us you could have been clearer? . . ."

"Yes."

"And you have told and expressed on several different occasions that you considered yourself responsible and you felt guilty for what happened; isn't that right?"

"Right." . . .

"So you understand that when you say things to people or when you write them down, . . . individuals rely on what you say. . . . And we should be able to rely on them; isn't that right?" Paoli scolded.

"Yes," Washburn replied.

WHEN PROSECUTOR JOEL THOMPSON was given the opportunity to question Cecilia Washburn again ("redirect examination," in lawyers' parlance), he began by saying that he wanted to "clarify" a few of the statements defense counsel David Paoli had elicited from Washburn. He handed her a copy of the Facebook message she'd sent to her friend Bryan Court, and asked Washburn to read a portion of it that Paoli had deliberately passed over.

"'I have been thinking about this whole messed-up situation,'" Washburn read aloud to the jury, "'and it's driving me crazy, and making me think crazy thoughts.'"

Thompson asked her if the intent of the message was to let her friend know that she was having "crazy thoughts."

"Exactly," Washburn answered. "My crazy thoughts."

"Mr. Paoli didn't ask you about that part of it, did he?"

"No."

During Paoli's cross-examination, he'd repeatedly posed questions to Washburn requiring her to acknowledge that, during the period when she claimed she was being raped, her housemate Stephen Green was playing a video game in the living room, a few feet outside her bedroom door. Prosecutor Thompson pointedly asked Washburn, "Have you ever claimed that you made any kind of sound that Stephen should have heard?"

"No, I have not," she answered.

"You readily admit that you did not scream?" he asked.

"I did not scream."

"Mr. Paoli asked you about your statement about how you could have been more clear with Jordan; can you explain what you meant by that?"

"I could have done more things to prevent him from raping me. I could have screamed, but I didn't. I could have rolled off the bed, but I didn't."

"Could have scratched his eyes out, couldn't you?"

"I could have done that, too."

"So when you are referring to the fact that you could have been more clear, does that mean that you didn't give sufficient signals to him that you were not consenting?" Thompson asked.

"No, I gave him sufficient signals," Washburn replied.

"Mr. Paoli also asked you about things that could have happened differently that night. You could have screamed. He asked you that also, correct?"

"Correct."

"Were you prepared to have a confrontation with the defendant in your home that night?"

"No."

"Would screaming have caused a confrontation?"

"Yes."

"Would fighting with him have caused a confrontation?"

"Yes."

"Why weren't you willing to have a confrontation?"

"Because I just wanted him out of my house. I wasn't prepared for that, . . . and I'm not that type of person, either. I just wanted him gone." . . .

Thompson asked Washburn, "Did you have any plans to sue anybody over this or make any money off this allegation?"

"No," she answered.

"Are you here because Jordan Johnson didn't snuggle with you after sex on that night?"

"No."

"Are we here because the quarterback refused to be your boyfriend?"

"No." . . .

"Have you prospered in any way from this process?"

"No."

"Have you at times regretted coming forward at all?"

"Yes," Washburn replied, specifying that she'd felt this way as recently as the previous week.

"When you made that comment about wanting Jordan to suffer, that Mr. Paoli talked to you about, why did you say that?" . . .

"Because it seemed like he wasn't being held accountable for his actions. I'm the one suffering through the trauma, and he was walking around campus like nothing happened. . . . I want him to feel the pain that he inflicted on me."

CHAPTER TWENTY-FOUR

The second witness called by the prosecution was Dr. David Lisak, the clinical psychologist considered to be one of the nation's foremost experts on acquaintance rape. He was asked to provide "educational testimony": information about what the best research reveals about rapists and their victims. Defense lawyers David Paoli and Kirsten Pabst were so worried about the potential impact of Lisak's testimony on the jury that they filed a pretrial motion to prevent him from testifying, but Judge Karen Townsend denied it, and Lisak was allowed to appear.

Prosecutor Joel Thompson began by asking Dr. Lisak about "misconceptions about rape"—rape myths. When people hear the term "rapist," Lisak said, many of them "think of a guy in a ski mask, wielding a knife, hiding in the bushes, breaking into a home. And it's a scary image, and it does happen, but . . . the vast majority of rapes, well over eighty percent, are actually non-stranger rapes." One of the other myths, he added, was the widely held belief that "a non-stranger assault is less serious and has less serious harm, but the research shows that victims of non-stranger assault are equally affected as victims of stranger assault."

Wondering about other misconceptions, Thompson asked Lisak if rapists can be identified by personality or a psychological profile. "There's no profile of a rapist that you can use to say either somebody is or that somebody isn't," Lisak said.

"But surely rapists are creepier than the average population?" Thompson asked.

"Actually, no," Lisak answered. We all like to think that we would be able to recognize the sort of person who might be a rapist, he said, "but the truth is, we can't."

"So rapists can be likable?" Thompson asked.

"Absolutely," Lisak answered.

"Sociable?"

"Absolutely." . . .

"Can they be thought of outwardly as kind?" Thompson inquired.

"Yes," Lisak answered.

"Gentle?"

"Yes."

"Even timid?"

"Yes, even timid, some of them," Lisak said.

Thompson encouraged Dr. Lisak to tell the jury what scientific research has revealed about the psychological impact of rape. Lisak explained that being raped is often profoundly traumatic to the victim. In the last ten or fifteen years, he said, there has been a great deal of research about how traumatic experiences affect the brain "at a neurobiological level" and why people sometimes react to being sexually assaulted in ways that are very different "from what we would expect intuitively."

"So when we talk about how victims react to trauma," Thompson asked, "is there any one way that they react?"

"No," Lisak answered. "There is an enormous variability in how victims react in sexual assault."

Prosecutor Joel Thompson wondered why, if a woman realized a man was trying to rape her, she wouldn't "fight to the death" instead of letting herself be subjected to such a traumatic experience.

It is a common assumption that any woman threatened with being raped would do everything in her power to physically resist, Dr. Lisak said, "but it's not what we find. . . . In fact, most women who are sexually assaulted do not resist. The fear is overwhelming. They often feel helpless. Sometimes they make a conscious choice not to resist because they are afraid if they resist, they will be hurt even worse." Many victims report afterward to the police that they actually tried "to placate the assailant as a strategy to avoid further harm."

Asked to elaborate, Lisak explained, "One of the things that is difficult for most of us, frankly, to understand about a rape, is that there doesn't have to be a gun to the head, there doesn't have to be a knife present, there doesn't have to be a verbalized threat for the act itself to be enormously terrifying and threatening. . . . There is a difference between sexual violence and other forms of assault. Sexual violence is so intimate." When your body is penetrated by another person against your will, Lisak said, it often induces a uniquely powerful kind of terror. According to many peer-reviewed studies, a large percentage of the victims of non-stranger rapes "actually feared they were going to be killed," even when "there was no weapon and no overt violence."

Thompson asked how rape victims typically reacted immediately afterward, according to the research.

"There are many different kinds of responses," Lisak said. "Victims of non-stranger rape are often very confused about what happened. They may be very upset. Distressed. But they don't automatically label what's happened to them as rape. In fact, there's a lot of research about this." It's not uncommon, he explained, for victims to "go back and forth between feeling like something really bad happened to them, and being very confused, and even trying to deny that something bad happened to them . . . as a way of trying to essentially tell themselves that, no, something bad didn't happen to me."

Dr. Lisak noted that a great amount of research had been conducted into the effects of trauma on the brain. "And what we now understand," he said, is that traumatic experiences impact the brain so profoundly that memories associated with trauma "are categorically different from what we think of as normal memory. . . . We have even identified the brain structures that are primarily responsible for this difference."

If a victim made an equivocal statement such as " 'I think I was just raped,' would that strike you as unusual?" Thompson asked.

"No," Lisak answered. "It's quite common. . . . If somebody is experiencing something very traumatic, it's scary but it's enormously confusing. It's overwhelming. And one of the first reactions for many people is to try to undo it, to try to pretend like it didn't happen." In a related phenomenon, Lisak explained, it's common in the aftermath of a rape to see the victim have "quite extensive interaction with the person who's alleged to have committed the assault" as an "attempt to try to undo it. . . . You know, if I interact with this person normally, then I can tell myself that . . . what I feared just happened to me didn't really happen."

"But in the immediate aftermath," Thompson suggested, "couldn't we at least say that no rape victim in her right mind would give her perpetrator a ride home afterwards?"

"No," Lisak answered. "I personally have encountered that on many occasions. . . . That is not that uncommon."

"That's certainly hard to understand, isn't it, for the layperson?" Thompson asked.

"Well," Lisak answered, "it's hard to understand from outside of the experience. I think that's the challenge here. . . . These kinds of assaults are not a normal part of most people's experience."

Thompson asked, "Is there an element of self-blame that is important in non-stranger rapes?"

"Yes," Lisak answered. "It's extremely common for victims, actually, of both stranger and non-stranger rape, although you see it, oftentimes, more intensely in non-stranger victims. They blame themselves almost in any way imaginable." When you are sexually assaulted by someone you know and trust, Lisak explained, "the world is all of a sudden a very, very terrifying and unpredictable place." Self-blame becomes an irrational strategy for regaining a sense of control, because to accept that what happened was beyond one's control is "far scarier" than blaming oneself. Psychologically, he observed, self-blame is "much easier" and "feels better" than living in fear.

Moreover, Lisak said, self-blame seems "to be more accentuated" when victims are raped by an acquaintance. He said that non-stranger rape is "oftentimes more difficult to recover from," as well, because "if you have been assaulted by somebody you thought you could trust, how do you restore your sense of trust in the world or in people? And how do you trust yourself?" After being betrayed and violated by a person you were sure would never harm you, "how do you then trust your own judgment thereafter? . . . That's a hard thing to resolve. And it seems to feed self-blame. . . . You say, 'Well, it was my fault it happened, so I'll fix the things that I did wrong, and that will prevent this from happening to me again.'"

"GOOD MORNING!" defense counsel Kirsten Pabst said with an icy smile as she greeted David Lisak to begin her cross-examination. "How was your stay?"

"Very nice," Lisak replied. "Thank you."

"You're from Massachusetts?" she inquired.

"That's right," he answered.

"You are a professor from Massachusetts?" she asked.

"I retired from teaching in May," he said, "so I'm no longer a professor."

"You're an erstwhile professor from Massachusetts," Pabst noted with disdain.

Lisak's testimony—skillfully elicited by prosecutor Joel Thompson and buttressed by an abundance of peer-reviewed research—had been powerful, and it undermined some of the key arguments Pabst and David Paoli were relying on to keep Jordan Johnson from being convicted. Lacking effective counterarguments to refute Lisak, Pabst resorted to ad hominem attacks. For the remainder of the trial, she and her co-counsel, David Paoli, would repeatedly refer to Lisak as "the professor from Massachusetts," "the Boston professor," or some variation thereof, to remind the good Montana folk sitting in the jury box that he was an East Coast intellectual who probably drove a Prius, lived in an ivory tower, and was out of touch with the real world.

Kirsten Pabst also portrayed Dr. Lisak as a highly paid anti-rape crusader who reflexively endorsed the claims of anyone purporting to be a victim of sexual assault. "So you testify on behalf of people who allege that they have experienced trauma at the hands of another? . . . And you get paid for that?" she asked him.

"Yes," Lisak answered.

"You said it's about three hundred and twenty-five dollars an hour?" she asked.

"Yes." . . .

"Dr. Lisak," Pabst demanded, "with all due respect, this is a very personal area for you, is it not?"

"If you're referring to the fact that I was abused when I was a kid," Lisak answered, "certainly then. But now I'm fifty-eight years old."

"But isn't it true that it was your experience when you were a little boy that led you into the area and gave you this passion for this work that you do?" she asked.

"If you're trying to imply that . . . I'm biased toward victims," he answered, "I think I've managed over the course of my professional life and my development as an individual to understand that life is more complicated than that."

Moving along, Kirsten Pabst interjected a bit of humor as she jumped to a new avenue of interrogation. "I don't know you very well," she quipped in a coy voice, "but I want to talk about sex. . . . Would you agree that not all sex is bad sex?"

"Yes," Lisak answered.

"And would you agree that not all bad sex is nonconsensual? . . . Just because it's bad sex doesn't mean it's rape."

"Correct."

"And awkward sex is not necessarily rape."

"Correct." . . .

"Disappointing sex is not necessarily rape; you'd agree?"

"Yes." . . .

"Would you also agree that there is more than one way to communicate consent," Pabst asked, "ranging from a look," to written consent with a notary public present, "and a lot of things in between?"

"Yes," Dr. Lisak agreed, but then he added, "Sometimes the person on the receiving end thinks they are perceiving consent when in fact it hasn't been communicated."

Not wanting the jury to go down this path, Pabst steered the discussion back to the "continuum of consent." Sometimes, she argued, "a smile, depending on the relationship, can constitute consent. Or a kiss."

"I would disagree with that," Lisak said.

"What about a French kiss?" Pabst inquired.

Giving no ground, Lisak pointed out that it was easy to misunderstand the meaning of a smile or any kind of kiss.

"Okay," Pabst said. "So two married people having sex, you're saying that there needs to be a discussion about it first—'Do you want to have sex?' 'Yes, I do'—before it's consensual?"

"No," Lisak answered. "I think when there is obviously a more intimate relationship between two people, then the methods of communication are much more fluid and . . . have much more history to them. So I think there are a lot more ways in which two married people can communicate to each other and understand each other. And that would be much less so with people who don't know each other as well." . . .

Pabst asked, "You stated there's a great variability in the response to sexual assault, correct?"

"Yes," Lisak answered.

"But you would also agree there's a great variability in the response to good consensual sex?"

"Sure."

"And a great variability in response to bad consensual sex?"

"Yes." . . .

"You testified that victims, generally speaking, often deny and minimize their assault during and after the event," which, Pabst noted, leads to the victims blaming themselves for being raped. But what if the event in question actually wasn't rape? Pabst wondered. What if it was simply bad consensual sex? And if the alleged victim wasn't raped, she argued, what Lisak interpreted as self-blame might in fact be a woman who'd made a bad decision "acknowledging responsibility."

"That's right," Lisak conceded.

Dr. Lisak had made it clear to the jury from the outset that, at the request of the prosecution, he had not examined the facts of the Jordan Johnson case. His testimony was intended to be strictly "educational," to share his expert knowledge of non-stranger rape as a societal phenomenon. But, Kirsten Pabst wondered, if he *had* looked at the facts of this particular case, was it possible that "you may have come to the conclusion that the alleged complainant made a false report?"

Lisak acknowledged that anything was possible.

"But that would have been inconsistent with the objectives for which you were hired," Pabst sneered, implying that Lisak's statements should not be trusted because he'd been paid by the prosecution to testify.

"The objective for which I was hired," Lisak reminded both Pabst and the jury, "was simply to . . . provide educational testimony."

"About nothing in particular?" Pabst inquired sarcastically.

"Objection!" Joel Thompson protested from the prosecutors' table.

"Sustained," declared Judge Townsend. "Are you finished, Ms. Pabst?"

"I am," Pabst replied, unchastened. "Thank you."

CHAPTER TWENTY-FIVE

Cecilia Washburn's housemate Stephen Green was the next witness called by the prosecution. A twenty-two-year-old premed student, Green testified that he and Washburn were "best friends. . . . We shared everything about each other's life." When questioned by prosecutor Joel Thompson whether Washburn seemed "preoccupied" with Jordan Johnson or had ever talked about wanting him for a boyfriend, Green said no.

Thompson asked Green how Washburn seemed on the afternoon before she was allegedly raped—did she make a big deal of the fact that Johnson was coming over to see her that night?

Washburn "seemed sort of nonchalant about it," Green said. "She just mentioned that her friend was going to come over and watch a movie, and that was about it."

At 11:41 p.m., as Stephen Green sat on the living room couch, absorbed in a video game called *Forza Motorsport,* he received the text from Cecilia Washburn that said, "I think I might have just gotten raped. he kept pushing and pushing and I said no but he wouldn't listen . . . I just wanna cry . . . omg what do I do!"

"I didn't really know what to do," Green admitted. Shocked by Washburn's text, he remained on the couch and replied two minutes later with a text of his own that said, "What are you doing? Get out of there."

A few minutes after that, Washburn came out of her room by herself and headed toward the kitchen, whereupon Green jumped up to intercept her and ask what had happened. "She looked like she had been crying or was about to cry," Green recalled. "Like her eyes were watering up and she looked really distressed." Washburn told Green that she didn't want to talk about it, kept walking into the kitchen, and "got, like, a snack or something from the cupboard," Green testified.

Prosecutor Joel Thompson asked Green if he knew Washburn was about to leave the house.

"Yeah," Green answered. "I think she told me that she was going to give [Jordan Johnson] a ride home." Soon thereafter, Johnson came out of Washburn's bedroom, walked past Green without saying anything, and exited the house through the kitchen door. "I stayed on the couch and waited for her to come back," Green said. "I was really anxious the entire time."

When Cecilia Washburn returned, Green testified, "She came in through the back door into the kitchen, and I heard her, so I ran in there, and she leaned up against the refrigerator and was crying really heavily, so bad that she couldn't really talk. . . . [She was] gasping for air. . . . I ran up to her and hugged her and asked her what happened. . . . She told me that . . . he kept pushing and pushing and she tried to say no, but he wouldn't listen." Green said he "hugged her for a while, and she just cried on my shoulder." . . .

"Were you able to get her calmed down?" Thompson asked.

"Yeah, a little bit," Green answered. "And then we went and sat on the couch in the living room, and she was still pretty upset. . . . She was telling me that she didn't want anybody to find out. And that she didn't, like, want to report it to the police or anything." When Green disagreed and urged her to report that she'd been raped, Washburn repeated that "she didn't want anybody to find out about what had happened," Green testified.

In her opening statement, Kirsten Pabst had asserted that Cecilia Washburn falsely accused Jordan Johnson of raping her to gain attention and become a celebrity. Thompson asked Stephen Green, "Did it seem like she wanted to be a celebrity?"

"No," Green replied.

"Did it appear as though she enjoyed her new identity as a victim?"

"No." . . .

"But she liked the attention, didn't she?"

"No." . . .

"From your observations of her on a daily basis, have you been able to see the patterns in which she copes and deals with the stress?" Thompson asked.

"She distances herself from everybody," Green testified. "She will just kind of disappear into her room or something like that, and not want to talk to anybody, not want to say anything. She just kind of internalizes it."

CLAIRE FRANCOEUR, the nurse-practitioner and forensic medical examiner at the First Step sexual-assault resource center who'd examined Allison Huguet and Kelsey Belnap, was called as a witness by the prosecution at the end of the trial's first week. She showed the jury photographs and a video of Cecilia Washburn's genitals while describing the forensic exam she performed the day after Washburn was allegedly raped. Prompted by questions from prosecutor Adam Duerk, Francoeur pointed out abrasions and a small laceration inside Washburn's vagina, as well as minor bruises on her collarbone. She also testified that she found tenderness throughout the vaginal wall and tenderness on the side of Washburn's head. All of which, she said, were "consistent with sexual trauma, though nonspecific."

After the video of Washburn's genitals finished playing and the public was readmitted to the courtroom, defense counsel David Paoli, bent on impugning Francoeur's credibility, began an especially contentious cross-examination. "Nurse Francoeur . . . ," he began, "your job is not to determine, and you can't determine, nonconsensual versus consensual [sex]; isn't that right?"

"Correct," she answered.

Paoli then lambasted Francoeur for failing to read some medical literature he'd asked her to review. "I gave you some of that literature on May 10," he thundered, "and you hadn't even reviewed it by December, when I took your statement; isn't that right?"

"That's correct," she replied.

"The literature I gave to you on May 10," Paoli continued, "have you read it to date?"

"I have not read the article in its entirety, no," Francoeur answered.

"There were three articles. You haven't read any of them, have you?" he demanded. When Francoeur said she didn't recall, Paoli became even angrier. "What does it mean when you say you don't recall?" he raged. "Because you've done that with me a lot!"

"Objection!" prosecutor Adam Duerk barked, but Paoli ignored him and continued berating Francoeur.

"Objection!" Duerk shouted again, protesting that Paoli was being argumentative.

"Sustained," Judge Townsend agreed.

"You became friends with Cecilia Washburn, didn't you?" Paoli spat.

"I would not describe her as a friend," Nurse Francoeur replied.

"How would you describe her?"

"As a patient." . . .

"You said that part of your responsibilities as a medical professional was to refer her to a lawyer? . . . You referred her to an Atlanta law firm, did you not?"

"I gave her a name," Francoeur explained.

"And you made contact with that law firm on her behalf, didn't you?"

"I did not."

"You had made contact with that law firm to tell them that Ms. Washburn was going to be calling them?"

"It was not me who made that contact." . . .

"And this was about the time that Ms. Washburn was going to go to the police department; isn't that right?"

"I believe it was before then. I don't recall the exact date." . . .

"Let me remind you when she went to the police: March 16. And you know that because you went with her; isn't that right?"

"That's correct."

Paoli professed that he was shocked that Francoeur, a nurse, would accompany a patient to the police station or refer a patient to a lawyer. In a voice edged with scorn, he inquired, "That's part of your medical professionalism?"

Francoeur replied that such consultation was part of providing "patient-centered" care, in accordance with the standard protocols of her profession.

"Patient-centered and litigation-fueled? Is that part of what it is?"

"Objection!" shouted Duerk.

"Sustained," Judge Townsend concurred.

Paoli nevertheless continued hectoring Francoeur about referring Washburn to a lawyer for several more minutes. "And it is part of your professional practice to refer [your patients] to lawyers in Atlanta," he fulminated. "Is that right?"

"It's part of my job to refer them to whatever resources they need," she wearily replied, "including attorneys."

Finally realizing that he had perhaps dwelled overly long on this point, Paoli stopped badgering Francoeur about the propriety of referring an alleged victim to a lawyer and started badgering her about the way she performed Cecilia Washburn's forensic exam. Paoli even suggested that it was not Jordan Johnson who caused the injuries to Washburn's genitalia but Francoeur, when she conducted the examination. As evidence of her ineptitude, he pointed out that the finger of one of the surgical gloves she wore had a minuscule rip. "The torn glove is really outside the standard of care, isn't it?" he asked.

"It's outside of the standard, yes," Francoeur agreed.

Paoli brought up the laceration inside Washburn's vagina that Francoeur had identified in the video. "This small laceration, it's approximately a millimeter, isn't it?" he asked.

"I'd have to look at the tape again," she answered, "but that sounds about right: one to two millimeters." . . .

"I mean, it's tiny, correct?" Paoli continued.

"Yes." . . .

When he inquired if the laceration could have been made prior to the alleged assault, she said yes. "Even up to a week before; isn't that right?" he asked.

"It would be rare to see injuries up to a week before, but it could be."

Paoli asked if the tenderness and abrasions Francoeur had found on the wall of Cecilia Washburn's vagina and the red marks she'd identified on Washburn's collarbone could have been caused by consensual sex. "It's possible," Francoeur conceded.

When David Paoli finally completed his cross-examination, prosecutor Adam Duerk was given an opportunity to interrogate Nurse Francoeur again. "In terms of your care and treatment with Ms. Washburn, did you maintain your objectivity?" he asked.

"I did," she replied.

"Did your examination of Ms. Washburn cause any of the injuries, either the genital or the nongenital injuries?"

"No."

"Did the way that you conducted this First Step acute sexual trauma examination violate any guidelines that you're aware of?"

"No." . . .

"Do these guidelines, the 2004 national protocols, talk about your duty to provide information about civil attorneys to a victim?"

"They do."

"Do these national guidelines tell you that you are supposed to help victims communicate with law enforcement officers?"

"They do." . . .

"Was there anything in Cecilia Washburn's history that indicated to you that these injuries were caused prior to February 4, 2012?" prosecutor Adam Duerk asked.

"No," Nurse Francoeur replied.

"Objection, Your Honor!" defense counsel David Paoli protested.

Judge Townsend asked Paoli and Duerk to approach the bench for an off-the-record conference to discuss Paoli's objection. As the lawyers were leaving the bench after huddling with Townsend, Paoli muttered something under his breath to Duerk—a threat or imprecation, apparently, because Duerk turned toward Paoli and angrily demanded, "Excuse me? What was that?"

Paoli said nothing, but he stood chest to chest with Duerk, glaring down at him. For a long beat, Paoli—who probably weighed at least a hundred pounds more than Duerk—looked like he was about to deliver a head butt to the bridge of Duerk's nose. Townsend defused the standoff by pointedly declaring, "You may continue, Mr. Duerk," after which Duerk resumed his redirect examination of Francoeur, and Paoli retreated to the defense counsel's table.

"Did the torn glove affect the ultimate findings of your examination in this case?" Duerk asked.

"No," Francoeur replied. Cecilia Washburn's genital injuries, she assured the jury, were "consistent with sexual trauma."

CONNIE BRUECKNER, the Missoula police detective assigned to be the lead investigator for the Jordan Johnson case, was called by the prosecution to testify in support of Cecilia Washburn. Under direct examination by prosecutor Adam Duerk, Brueckner testified that Cecilia Washburn had cooperated fully with her investigation, including voluntarily turning over her cell phone and allowing the police to download all of the twenty-nine thousand text messages it contained, many of which defense counsel David Paoli used in court to try to smear Washburn's reputation. To some degree Johnson also cooperated with Brueckner's investigation, but, suspiciously, he deleted all the texts about Washburn he'd sent in the aftermath of the alleged rape, before Detective Brueckner had an opportunity to ask for them. And because Washburn didn't go to the police until six weeks after the alleged rape, Johnson's cell-phone carrier had deleted his texts from its system by the time Brueckner began her investigation.

Three months after the night in question, Brueckner and another detective, named Dean Chrestenson, interviewed Jordan Johnson at the police station in the presence of defense counsel Kirsten Pabst. As an adjunct to Detective Brueckner's testimony during the trial, Duerk played a videotape of this interview. As they watched the video in the courtroom, the members of the jury heard Detective Chrestenson admonish Johnson, "There's two people in that room together, and one of you is lying. Your behavior after the incident—that, to me, is the most alarming part." What's more, Chrestenson said, Johnson had plenty of reason to lie, because if he were convicted it would end his dream of playing professional football after college or becoming a football coach.

Upon hearing this, Johnson began to sob. "I don't care about all that," he told Chrestenson. "I just want to be a kid again. I don't care about football."

At one point in the video, Johnson told Detective Brueckner that he said almost nothing to Cecilia Washburn from the time they started making out on Washburn's bed until she dropped him off at his house after the alleged rape, and she spoke to him only once: Washburn playfully uttered, "'Oh, you're bad,'" Johnson recalled, "when I turned her over." As soon as he uttered these words, however, Johnson seemed to regret admitting that he'd turned her over, and he quickly added, "Well, we changed positions."

After the video ended, prosecutor Adam Duerk asked Detective Brueckner if she'd found this bit of testimony "significant in any way."

"I did," she said, explaining that Johnson's statement corroborated Washburn's testimony that "she was turned over by Mr. Johnson."

When defense counsel David Paoli cross-examined Detective Brueckner, he asserted that when Cecilia Washburn was on the witness stand nine days earlier, Washburn had testified that "she assisted [Jordan Johnson] in changing positions."

Brueckner countered that Paoli was misrepresenting Washburn's words. Washburn had in fact testified that Johnson said, "Turn over, or I'll make you," and then she'd said, "And then at that point he grabbed my hips and flipped me over. . . . I just knew I was going to get raped. . . . I did assist him, but it was because I gave up."

As Detective Brueckner shared Washburn's testimony with the jury, however, Paoli abruptly cut her off, because he didn't want the jurors to be reminded of what Washburn actually said. Instead, Paoli wanted to elicit testimony from Brueckner that would support an argument he'd been making for much of that afternoon: that Detective Brueckner had been negligent in her sworn duty to seek exculpatory evidence—that is, evidence that might show Johnson's innocence—during her investigation of the alleged rape.

Earlier in his cross-examination, Paoli had said, "Detective Brueckner, I know that you take your job seriously. And tell me what the main goal of your job is."

"To find the truth," she said.

"And justice?" he asked.

"Yes."

"How do you do that?"

"I do interviews," Brueckner answered. "Gather evidence. Try to corroborate the person's statement or refute it."

"Try to find exculpatory evidence?"

"Yes."

"You're required to be impartial, are you not?"

"Yes." . . .

"It would be improper to develop a relationship with the complaining witness, isn't that correct?" Paoli asked.

"I would need you to define 'relationship.' . . ."

"Well, at any time did you know that Miss Washburn was talking to this Atlanta litigation law firm prior to coming in and making her report? . . . Did you have any idea, or did Claire Francoeur indicate to you in any way, that she was thinking about not reporting to the police until she talked to the Atlanta law firm? . . . Has Miss Washburn ever told you that she had obtained the services of a law firm out of Atlanta?"

"No," Brueckner answered.

"Detective Brueckner," Paoli demanded, "you have been involved in . . . the Department of Justice investigation of the Missoula Police Department, isn't that correct? . . . You have given a statement or been interviewed? . . . And when did you give that?"

"I don't know—June, maybe? It was shortly after the [DOJ] announcement to the media," Brueckner answered.

"So that was . . . in the midst of your investigation in this case, correct? . . . Did that [DOJ] interview make an impression on you?"

"Yeah," Brueckner affirmed. "I thought it was a really positive conversation."

"And did it cause you to redouble your efforts on this case?"

"No. . . . I had done plenty of work on the case prior to that interview, and it didn't affect me at all."

David Paoli interrogated Detective Brueckner in this fashion for an especially long time, intending to demonstrate to the jury that she had developed an improper personal relationship with Washburn, causing Brueckner to shirk her responsibility to dig for evidence that might prove that Johnson had been falsely accused. Quoting Article 10 of the Canons of Police Ethics, Paoli asked, "As a law enforcement officer and a lead detective, you shall be concerned equally in the prosecution of the wrongdoer and the defense of the innocent; isn't that right?"

"Yes," she answered.

He wondered how she squared this ethical duty with a police department policy enacted the previous March. The new protocol required Missoula cops, when initiating a sexual-assault investigation, to believe the victim's claims until the evidence demonstrated otherwise. "You would agree with me," Paoli demanded, cloaking his assertion as a question, "that this policy . . . destroys the objectivity and impartiality [of police investigations], doesn't it?"

"No," Brueckner answered, "not at all."

Riled by her response, Paoli protested, "You can maintain your objectivity and impartiality, even though you're required . . . to believe the accusation until it's proved otherwise?"

"That's part of the investigatory process: to gather evidence to corroborate or refute somebody's statement," Brueckner calmly replied. Missoula Chief of Police Mark Muir drafted the new policy, she explained, "as a result of some issues in the community." . . .

"So community pressure caused the new policy to be instituted?" Paoli asked.

"I don't know about that," Detective Brueckner answered. "I think it . . . brought awareness to potential problems." The new policy was intended to help patrol officers respond better, she explained, by providing them with guidelines for investigating sexual assaults more effectively.

DEFENSE COUNSEL DAVID PAOLI'S fixation on the new police policy came with a backstory. As his co-counsel, Kirsten Pabst, had mentioned in her opening statement on behalf of Jordan Johnson, eleven days earlier, the new policy had been formulated in response to a pair of *Missoulian* articles Gwen Florio wrote in January 2012 about sexual-assault victims Kerry Barrett and Kaitlynn Kelly and the way the Missoula police handled their cases. Florio's reporting prompted city councilwoman Cynthia Wolken to invite Chief of Police Mark Muir to participate in an open forum that would give the public an opportunity to ask questions about his department's response to Missoula's rape crisis.

When the forum was convened, Muir admitted that the department would benefit from "more definitive sexual-assault procedures" and that "the victim needs to be our priority." Cops, he said, should treat victims the way the cops themselves "would want to be treated under the exact same circumstances—to give every victim that same compassion." And then he pledged that within six weeks he would enact a "better policy with respect to sexual assault."

After Chief Muir spoke, Kerry Barrett took the microphone to slam both the police and the Missoula County Attorney's Office for their mishandling of her case and Kaitlynn Kelly's case, reserving her harshest words for Kirsten Pabst, who was in charge of prosecuting rape cases for the Missoula County Attorney's Office at the time.

True to his word, Muir put the new police policy into place soon thereafter, on March 19, 2012, which happened to be three days after Cecilia Washburn went to the Missoula police to report that she had been raped by Jordan Johnson. It also happened to be eighteen days after Pabst quit working as a prosecutor to start her own law firm.

After Kirsten Pabst resigned from the Missoula County Attorney's Office, she joined David Paoli as defense counsel for Jordan Johnson. When Pabst and Paoli blamed Kerry Barrett and Kaitlynn Kelly for the new police policy during Johnson's trial, and used the new policy as a cudgel to batter Detective Brueckner and her investigation of the alleged rape, it was perhaps a sensible tactic—a potentially effective application of lawyerly artifice. But Pabst and Paoli reacted to the new police policy with a degree of outrage that suggested that Kerry Barrett had gotten under their skin and they considered it a personal affront.

Actually, the question of whether the new police protocol trampled Jordan Johnson's constitutional rights had already been argued by both sides, and the matter had been resolved by Judge Townsend two weeks before the trial even began. After their initial motion to dismiss the Johnson case had been rejected by Townsend in September 2012, David Paoli and Kirsten Pabst had filed a second motion to dismiss in early January 2013, arguing, "The Missoula Police Department's policy requiring officers to initiate investigations into sex crimes with the belief that they are true violates the presumption of innocence and due process" and "led to a completely biased investigation" of Jordan Johnson. "The rule in criminal cases is clear," Pabst asserted, citing a 1957 Montana case,

State v. McLeod: "Every presumption in favor of the defendant's innocence shall be indulged until the evidence establishes his guilt beyond a reasonable doubt."

In a response brief filed by the prosecution, however, Deputy Chief Missoula County Attorney Suzy Boylan exposed glaring flaws in Pabst's claim, pointing out that Pabst had neglected to mention other important aspects of the new policy,

> which require police officers to "obtain the information necessary to determine a crime is being alleged" and "establish whether a crime occurred."
>
> There is nothing unusual about assuming an initial report of a crime is true and conducting an investigation to determine whether sufficient evidence of a crime exists . . . for possible prosecution. That is standard procedure whether the crime is a sexual offense, an embezzlement, a robbery, or any other case. The reason for specifically institutionalizing this is the historically skeptical treatment of victims of sexual offenses that has not existed for victims of other types of offenses. . . . Every victim of a crime should be heard and a thorough investigation conducted. The policy merely reflects that notion.
>
> More importantly, the Defendant is asserting . . . a right he did not have at the investigative stage. The presumption of innocence is not a specifically enumerated constitutional right; it is a doctrine embodied in the right to a fair trial. In other words, it is a *trial right*.

To buttress the prosecution's argument, Boylan cited a 1979 U.S. Supreme Court case, *Bell v. Wolfish,* and a 1994 military case, *U.S. v. Dickey:*

> The role of presumption of innocence is often confused by laypersons and courts. . . . The presumption of innocence

> is a rule of evidence for the courtroom that defines a part of the accused's due process rights. . . . It does not control the pretrial functioning of law enforcement officials, commanders, or magistrates.

After considering Kirsten Pabst's motion to dismiss and Suzy Boylan's response, Judge Karen Townsend wrote,

> The Court finds that the Missoula Police Department's policy . . . is not in violation of the presumption of innocence. It is not improper for the police to have this policy because, as Dr. David Lisak noted in his expert witness disclosure, the percentage of false [rape] reports is very low. The purpose of an investigation is to look for evidence of a crime as well as evidence of innocence. . . . [I]t is not until the time of trial that the defendant is . . . entitled to the presumption of innocence. . . .
>
> IT IS HEREBY ORDERED that the Defendant's Second Motion to Dismiss is DENIED.

So Pabst and David Paoli lost this skirmish. But now that the trial was under way, Judge Townsend's rejection of Pabst's motion to dismiss the case was irrelevant. Here in the courtroom, with Detective Connie Brueckner on the witness stand, Paoli was free to argue all over again that the new police policy was unfair. And in order for the prosecution to win the current battle, it wasn't an erudite judge whom prosecutor Adam Duerk needed to persuade. He had to convince the twelve laypersons seated in the jury box, none of whom had gone to law school, that the new policy did not infringe on Jordan Johnson's constitutional rights or taint Brueckner's investigation.

To accomplish this, when Paoli finished his cross-examination for the defense, Duerk handed Detective Brueckner the portion of the new Missoula police policy that had gotten Paoli's knickers in such a twist and asked her to read it aloud to the court. "A victim's distress," she began,

> may create an unwillingness or psychological inability to assist in the investigation. Officers and investigators play a significant role in both the victim's willingness to cooperate in the investigation and ability to cope with the emotional and psychological aftereffects of the crime. Therefore, it is especially important that these cases be handled from a nonjudgmental perspective, so as not to communicate in any way to a victim that the victim is to blame for the crime. Every sex crime investigation is to be initiated with the belief it is true until evidence demonstrates otherwise.

Duerk pointed out to the jury that the language Paoli found so outrageous was based on guidelines published by the International Association of Chiefs of Police, which recommended that all sexual-assault reports "should be taken as valid unless evidence proves otherwise."

When Duerk asked Detective Brueckner why the new policy was important, Brueckner answered that it "acknowledges what a sensitive topic this is, and how difficult it is for victims to come forward." She explained that the policy helped prevent police officers, during their initial contact with rape victims, from derailing the cases by inadvertently alienating the victims and scaring them away. The policy, she declared, "gives the victims a voice in the process."

Police routinely presume that victims of other crimes, such as burglaries, are telling the truth, Duerk noted. "If you refuse to believe a victim in the beginning of a case," he asked Brueckner, "would any crime ever get investigated in the first place?"

"No," she answered.

CHAPTER TWENTY-SIX

Before the trial began, defense lawyers David Paoli and Kirsten Pabst submitted a list of twenty-five individuals they intended to call as character witnesses for Jordan Johnson, but Judge Townsend declared that having so many people present evidence of his good character would be a "waste of time" and ruled that only five character witnesses would be allowed to testify. Michael McGowan, who ran a Missoula private equity firm and was the team chaplain for the University of Montana football team, was the first of the five to appear on the witness stand.

McGowan testified that Johnson "participated in all of the services that I offered." Although McGowan had never attended seminary and did not have a divinity degree, on game days he provided a voluntary chapel thirty minutes before the kickoff. "Many of the players participate," he explained, but "not all." He would perform blessings, pray for their injuries to heal, lead the team in prayer before they ran onto the field, and then lead another prayer after the game. In addition, he said, "during the week, I make myself available if someone has an injury or they have some issues they want to discuss.

"My interactions with Jordan Johnson have been always in a group setting," McGowan acknowledged. "He's very respectful, unassuming, and a young man of integrity. . . . He's not a very boisterous or vocal person. . . . He's very, very cool under pressure." Johnson, McGowan added, "does not use expletives—I have never heard Jordy actually swear, which is, frankly, unusual." McGowan marveled over the fact that "Jordan can handle his emotions probably better than I can, which is unique for someone of that age." In very stressful settings, McGowan explained, "he's able to basically rein those in and keep himself contained, which I think is self-control."

When David Paoli asked if McGowan had ever observed Jordan Johnson acting entitled, McGowan replied, "I have not seen that."

"How about antisocial?" Paoli asked.

"I have not seen that."

"Self-absorbed?"

"No."

"Hypermasculine?"

"No. . . . That's the antithesis of his character. . . . He doesn't draw attention to himself, in a group or individual setting, from my observation," McGowan testified.

"Is he narcissistic?" Paoli asked.

"No," McGowan answered.

A moment later, prosecutor Suzy Boylan began her cross-examination by asking Mike McGowan if he knew the scientific definition of the terms " 'antisocial,' 'hypermasculine,' and 'narcissistic,' . . . or are you testifying just based on sort of your common understanding of those words?"

"Common understanding," he admitted.

Referring to McGowan's role as a volunteer chaplain for the Griz football team, Boylan asked, "You don't spend any time alone with the players; is that right?"

"I have really no need to," McGowan answered.

"And you therefore haven't spent any time alone with the defendant, right?"

"I have spent time in a group setting with him—for instance, sitting on an airplane or at a meal—but never a one-on-one setting."

"And you never talk to him about his love life, correct?"

"No."

"And . . . he hasn't confided anything to you?"

"No he hasn't." . . .

"You gave us some pretty nice attributes of the defendant. But you would agree that someone with those attributes could still do something bad or wrong, right?" Boylan asked.

"Well, I gave you my observations," McGowan answered.

"Right," Boylan said. "But when we spoke to you on the phone in your pretrial interview, . . . did you tell us that you're not saying that someone with those attributes—meaning the positive attributes you just described—can't do something bad?"

"That is what I said."

Boylan's cross-examination was unexpectedly effective. It served as a provocative reminder that even individuals we admire can have skeletons in their closets.

AT 4:10 IN the afternoon, after twenty-seven minutes of testimony, Mike McGowan was excused, and the most highly anticipated witness of the entire trial took the witness stand: the defendant, Jordan Johnson, wearing a pale blue, button-down shirt with an open collar. Defense counsel Kirsten Pabst began by asking him about his family. Johnson described growing up with his parents and an older sister in Coburg, Oregon, a tiny community beside the Willamette River, just outside of Eugene. He spoke about his relationship with his father, Marty—a math teacher and coach—as "special. . . . I was lucky enough to have him as my football coach in high school football. I think we are a lot closer than most fathers and sons." When Pabst asked Johnson what activities he did with his mother, he replied that mostly they "just spend time together. She helps me when I have to find presents for people. She goes shopping for me."

"Is it fair to say you're very close?" Pabst asked.

"Yes," Johnson answered.

"Your whole family is pretty close?"

"Very," he said in an emotional voice, momentarily losing his composure.

As Jordan Johnson testified, he revealed himself to be taciturn and self-possessed, confirming what Mike McGowan had said about him. In answering Pabst's questions, Johnson seldom said more than yes or no, and he almost never uttered more than a few words at a time. His reticence left space for others to imagine whatever traits they wished to see in him. At times he seemed cold and somewhat aloof, but it was easy to like Johnson, and hard not to feel sorry that he was in this predicament.

"Do you get easily embarrassed?" Pabst asked Johnson.

"Yeah," he answered.

"Have you always been like this since you were a kid?"

"Yes."

"Are you more talkative now than you were when you were little?"

"No."

Just before 5:00, after Johnson had spent just forty-five minutes on the stand, the court was adjourned for the evening, and Judge Townsend reminded everyone that there would be no proceedings the next day, because the trial was in recess every Tuesday in order to allow Townsend to take care of other court business.

When the trial reconvened on Wednesday morning, February 27, 2013, Townsend announced that Jordan Johnson's testimony would be interrupted briefly so that a character witness—Rudy Herr, a pastor who'd flown from Oregon to testify on Johnson's behalf—could finish his testimony in time to catch a plane home. Herr had been Johnson's youth pastor and the coach of his ninth-grade football team; he had known Johnson since Johnson was five years old. Herr stated that he'd "studied the Bible with Johnson" and that his son was one of Johnson's childhood friends.

Rudy Herr told the jury that despite Johnson's impressive accomplishments as a football player, "he doesn't carry himself like he's the greatest thing to ever walk the earth." Johnson was honest, truthful, "and has incredible self-control," Herr testified, echoing what almost everyone else had said about Johnson's ability to remain calm and perform well when the stakes were high.

Under cross-examination by prosecutor Joel Thompson, Herr acknowledged that Jordan Johnson had told him about the rape accusation during a short conversation the previous summer, and had said the sex was consensual. Thompson asked Pastor Herr if consensual sex without a condom was morally acceptable to him. "I was disappointed," Herr admitted.

SIXTEEN MINUTES AFTER taking the stand, Rudy Herr was excused, and Jordan Johnson resumed his testimony. Defense counsel Kirsten Pabst began by asking him, "What was your impression of Miss Washburn?"

Johnson answered, "That she was a really nice, a smart girl."

"Did you like her?" Pabst asked.

"I liked her as a person. I didn't like her as, like, a girlfriend type like," he replied.

"Do you think she liked you?"

"Yes."

Pabst asked Johnson to describe what happened on February 4, 2012, starting from the time he woke up, and he gave an account of what transpired over the fourteen hours that followed. Most of the details were in accord with the account Cecilia Washburn had provided to the jury two weeks earlier, and Johnson answered Pabst's questions in the assured, practiced manner of someone who had already told this story numerous times during the University of Montana disciplinary investigation and the criminal investigation leading up to this trial. Washburn's testimony had seemed equally well rehearsed, for the same reason.

But if their stories were much the same, they couldn't have been more at odds in describing what happened between approximately 11:20 and 11:30 on the night of February 4, when Johnson and Washburn were fooling around in her bedroom. Johnson's account began to diverge sharply from Washburn's at the point just after he'd pulled her shirt off, with her permission, as they were lying on their sides, face-to-face. According to Johnson, "We were still kissing, and then I take her pants off."

"How did you do that?" Pabst asked.

"She arched up a little bit to help me get them off," he explained.

"Did she show any reluctance at that point?"

"No."

"Did you touch her anywhere?"

"Yeah, in her genital area."

"Over the clothes or under the clothes?"

"It was when she had underwear, just underwear, on. [I touched her] on top and underneath." . . .

"How did she react to that?"

"She liked it."

"And how do you know?"

"Because she wasn't resisting in any way and she was still kissing me." . . .

"At any point, did you take off her bra?"

"Yes." . . .

"Did she seem interested in that?"

"Yes."

"After you took off her bra, did you touch her . . . breasts at all?"

"No."

"Was there a point where she touched you?"

"I don't remember."

"You don't remember her touching your crotch?"

"No."

"At some point did you have a discussion with her?" . . .

"She asked if I brought a condom," Johnson replied, "but that was after we were both naked." . . .

"So then what happened?" Pabst asked.

"Then I got on top of her and she asked me if I had a condom and I said no. And she said 'It's okay.' "

"So then what did you do?"

"We had sex."

"In what position?"

"Missionary." . . .

"And did she show any reluctance when you were having sex in this position?"

"No. If she would have, I would have stopped."

"Did she seem upset during any of this?"

"No."

"How long were you having sex with her in that position?"

"Probably two or three minutes."

"And then what happened?"

"Then I pulled out."

"Why did you pull out?"

"Because I thought I was going to ejaculate."

"What did you do after that?"

"I didn't ejaculate, and we changed positions," Jordan testified. "I started to turn her over, and she knew what I was doing, and then she said, 'Oh, you're bad,' in a kind of giggling tone." . . .

"So did she turn around and look at you?" Pabst asked.

"Yes."

"And what did she say?"

" 'Oh, you're bad.' "

"In a kind of teasing voice?"

"Yes."

"And what did you take that to mean?"

"That she liked it. . . . Then we had sex in that position for about the same amount of time."

"And did you think she was into it?"

"Yes. . . . She was moaning." . . .

"Was she lubricated?"

"Yes." . . .

"And what did you do?"

"I pulled out and ejaculated into my hand and on the bed."

"So how long did the total sex part of it last?"

"Five minutes."

"And at what point did she say no?"

"She never said no."

"How do you know that?"

"Because she didn't. I would have heard her, and I would have listened to her, and I would have stopped," Johnson said.

"Do you know what she was thinking?" Pabst asked.

"No." . . .

"Did she ever fight you off?"

"No."

"Did she ever push at you?"

"No."

"Did you tear her pants off?"

"No."

"Did you grab her hips?"

"No."

"Do you think she had an orgasm?"

"I don't think so."

"Why not?"

"I honestly have no idea, but that's just my guess."

"After you pulled out and you said you ejaculated in your hand, what did you do after that?"

"I asked her if she had something to clean it up with. . . . She grabbed the hand towel." . . .

"And why did you want to clean it up?"

"Because I didn't want it on the bed or on my hand." According to Johnson, Washburn got out of bed "pretty much right after" he asked her for the towel.

"Did you ask her then to come back onto the bed to snuggle with you?" Pabst inquired.

"No," Johnson answered.

"Cuddle?"

"No."

"Did you kiss afterwards?"

"No."

"Did you say anything to her like 'That was great'?"

"No."

"Why not, Jordan?"

"I don't know. I just didn't."

"What was going on in your head at that point, after you ejaculated?"

"Well, I asked her for something to clean it up with, and as I was cleaning it up, she started to put on her clothes, and so I put on my clothes, and then I went into the bathroom, because I had to go pee."

While he was in the bathroom, at 11:41 p.m., Cecilia Washburn sent the much-discussed text to her housemate Stephen Green indicating that she'd just been raped. Kirsten Pabst, not surprisingly, made no mention of this text as she questioned Jordan Johnson. She did, however, ask Johnson to describe what happened after Washburn left the bedroom. He said, "I put on the rest of my clothes, my shoes, and walked out past Stephen Green and got in the car with Cecilia."

"Did Cecilia seem upset at all?" Pabst asked.

Johnson answered, "No." . . .

"So what's going on in your head?"

"I was kind of starting to think about Kelli [Froland], in that I didn't want her to know that I had sex with another girl. . . . Because I really liked Kelli." . . .

"At the point where you got into the car for Cecilia to give you a ride home," Pabst asked, "did you anticipate a continued friendship with [Cecilia]?"

"I didn't, really," Johnson confessed, but he thought it was possible that "they would talk again." . . .

"How were you feeling about the evening?"

"That we had sex, and that afterwards I wish we wouldn't have, because of Kelli."

"So did you talk at all on the ride home, the two-minute ride home?" Pabst inquired.

"No," Johnson said. When Pabst asked what happened after

they arrived at his house, he answered, "I said, 'Thanks for having me,' and got out of the car." Then he "went in the house and went into my room."

AFTER PABST FINISHED her direct testimony, prosecutor Adam Duerk strode to the dais to cross-examine the witness. He asked if Johnson thought Washburn was smart, and Johnson said yes. "You thought she was a nice girl, correct?" Duerk inquired.

"Yes," Johnson answered.

"And you never really thought of Cecilia Washburn as a good friend. . . . You didn't know Cecilia Washburn very well through any of this; is that fair?"

"Yes."

"But you liked her. . . . You went out on a few dates together?" . . .

"Yes." . . .

"You didn't see anything in Cecilia Washburn that indicated to you that she was mean?" . . .

"No."

"You didn't see anything on those dates . . . that made you think that she was crazy, correct?"

"Correct."

Adam Duerk pointed out to Jordan Johnson that he never really had a "boyfriend-girlfriend relationship" with Washburn "and the relationship that you did have, to the extent one existed, you didn't really think it was going anywhere. . . . In fact, you thought it was going nowhere, correct?"

"Yeah." . . .

"Now, in terms of your relationship with Kelli Froland, there was a relationship there; fair?"

"Yes." . . .

"You went on dates with Kelli?"

"Yes."

"You brought her over to your house?" . . .

"Yes." . . .

"So she met your family?" . . .

"Yes."

"Nothing like that ever happened with Cecilia Washburn, correct?"

"Correct."

Duerk paused for a moment, then asked Johnson about the sex that took place when Washburn was kneeling on the bed, facedown with her buttocks raised, as he penetrated her from the rear. "While you're having sex with her from behind," Duerk inquired, "your hands are on Cecilia's forearms, correct?"

"Yes," Johnson answered.

"Her arms are above her head, correct?"

"Yes."

"All your weight was in your hands, correct?"

"Most," Johnson hedged.

Duerk asked Johnson to look at page 42 of the statement he gave to Detective Brueckner on May 2, 2012. "I'm looking at your third answer down," Duerk said. "I'd like to read your statement . . . , and please tell me if I've read it correctly. Okay?"

"Okay," Johnson said.

Duerk recited, " 'But all my weight is in my hands.' " Duerk looked up at Johnson and asked, "Did I read that correctly?"

"Yes," Johnson acknowledged.

Launching into a series of brief, piercing questions, Duerk asked, "So her hands are above her head, correct?"

"Yes," Johnson calmly answered.

"Your hands are on her forearms?" . . .

"Yes."

"You're penetrating her from behind . . . and all your weight is on your hands?" . . .

"Yes."

"So she was pinned to the bed, correct?"

"I don't know."

"You had your hands on her forearms and you were holding [her] forearms down, correct?"

"Yes."

"And you're behind her, correct?"

"Yes."

"All your weight is on those forearms, correct?"

"Yes."

According to his official Griz publicity profile, Jordan Johnson's height was six feet, one inch, and he weighed two hundred pounds. As he sat on the raised witness stand at the front of the courtroom, Johnson's heft and muscular physique were unmistakable. Appraising Johnson with an accusing gaze, Duerk asked, "You're a big person, correct?"

"I don't know," Johnson answered.

"All your weight was in your hands?" . . .

"Yes."

"So you were pinning her down; is that fair?"

"Fair."

"So she was pinned to the bed, correct?"

"I guess."

"And you said nothing at this point?" Duerk asked.

"Right."

Before the trial, Cecilia Washburn had testified that at this particular moment during the alleged rape, Johnson had angrily declaimed, "You said you wanted it! You said you wanted it!" But Duerk couldn't share this information with the jury because the prosecution had asked for, and been granted, a judicial order prohibiting the defense from mentioning that twenty-four hours before the alleged rape at the Foresters' Ball, according to Johnson and his friend Alex Bienemann, Washburn told Johnson, "I would do you anytime." If the prosecution asked Johnson about telling Washburn, "You said you wanted it!," the defense would have been allowed to bring up the fact that Washburn had allegedly offered to have sex with Johnson "anytime."

So Duerk simply asked Johnson, "You didn't talk to her at all during this, right?"

"Correct," Johnson answered.

"Then you pulled out and ejaculated?" . . .

"Yes." . . .

"Now, during sex, everything seemed normal to you?"

"Yes."

"You didn't have any sign that she was reluctant in any way. . . . And if she had said anything like 'No, not tonight,' . . . or indicated in any way that she wasn't completely into it, you would have stopped and asked her what was going on, right?"

"I would have just stopped." . . .

"But nothing seemed weird to you at all?" Duerk inquired.

"Correct," Johnson answered.

"Nothing seemed weird to you during the sex?" . . .

"Correct."

"Nothing seemed weird to you after the sex?" . . .

"Correct." . . .

"She seemed fine to you. . . . According to your testimony, she wasn't upset at all this entire time, correct?"

"She wasn't."

"Okay. And you would have known if something was wrong?" . . .

"Yes."

"Mr. Johnson," Duerk asked, "Cecilia sent a text message within minutes after you penetrated her, correct?"

"Yes," Johnson answered.

"She sent this text right after the intercourse was over?" . . .

"I believe so." . . .

"You've seen that text message?" . . .

"Yes." . . .

"And that text message had a time-and-date stamp on it, correct?"

"Correct." . . .

"This text message said, 'I think I might have just got raped, he kept pushing and pushing. I said, no, but he wouldn't listen. I just want to cry. Oh my God, what do I do?' Correct?"

"Yes." . . .

"Now, this was the first time that you'd had sex with Cecilia, correct?"

"Yes."

"And let me just make sure I've got this straight," Duerk said. "You really had no conversation the entire time?" . . .

"Correct," Johnson replied.

"This is your first time with Cecilia?" . . .

"Yes."

"And your first time, you pinned her forearms to the bed, correct?"

"My hands were on her forearms." . . .

"Okay. You admitted that before. So you pinned her to the bed, right?"

"Yes."

"After the intercourse, you left?" . . .

"She drove me home."

"And on that ride home, you claim nothing was wrong with Cecilia, right?"

"Correct." . . .

"And you said that you would have known if something was wrong?" . . .

"Yes." . . .

Having methodically led Jordan Johnson to the edge of the cliff, Adam Duerk asked the question intended to nudge him into the abyss: "You would agree that something is clearly wrong when someone sends a text message indicating they've just been raped, right?"

"I don't know," Johnson said.

"You don't know?" Duerk scoffed.

"Correct," Johnson answered.

Incredulous, Duerk demanded, "That seems normal to you? If someone sends a text indicating they've just been raped?"

"That's not normal," Johnson admitted.

"That is not normal," Duerk affirmed. Then he asked, "You would agree that if . . . the events of that night had happened as Cecilia described it, this text would make sense, correct?"

"If it happened," Johnson agreed. "But it didn't."

"If it did not happen as Cecilia described it," Duerk countered, "this text would be completely crazy to send, correct? . . . And you said that you had never seen any indication that Cecilia was crazy before this night happened, correct?"

"Correct." . . .

"You would agree that if a woman says no, and a man does not stop his sexual advances and penetrates her, that is rape, correct?"

"That's true." . . .

"You would agree that a woman can change her mind in the middle of sexual activity and still say no?" . . .

"Yes."

"You would agree that if she physically resisted, you did not have consent, correct?"

"Correct."

"You would agree that if she put her knees up to stop you, you didn't have consent, correct?"

"Correct." . . .

"You would agree that if you held her down with your forearm, you did not have consent?" . . .

"Correct."

"And you have no explanation for the bruising on her chest or shoulders?" . . .

"Objection, Your Honor!" Kirsten Pabst protested. "That misstates the evidence. There is no bruising."

"I don't think that misstates the evidence," Judge Townsend pronounced. "Overruled."

Resuming his interrogation without missing a beat, Adam Duerk again asked Jordan Johnson if he could explain the bruises on Cecilia Washburn's chest and shoulders. Johnson acknowledged that he couldn't. "You'd agree that if you held Cecilia's head down while you penetrated her from behind, that would indicate you did not have consent, correct?" Duerk asked.

"Correct," Johnson replied.

"You'd agree that if you . . . bruised her genitals or injured her genitals, that may indicate you did not have consent, correct?"

"I don't know."

"You'd agree that if you had said, 'Turn over, or I'll make you,' you did not have consent?" . . .

"Correct."

"Thank you. I have nothing further at this time."

JORDAN JOHNSON WAS excused from the witness stand at 11:15 Wednesday morning, after testifying for 157 minutes, including his appearance on Monday. His father, Marty Johnson, was called to testify a little after 2:00 on Wednesday afternoon. Under gentle questioning from defense counsel Kirsten Pabst, Marty said he was midway through his thirtieth year coaching football and teaching math to high school students in Eugene, Oregon. "How close is your family?" Pabst asked.

"I can't imagine there being very many families that do as many things together as we do," Marty answered. "So I would say we are extremely close." As his father spoke these words, Jordan wept openly in his chair at the defense counsel's table. He cried intermittently for the remainder of his father's testimony, at times putting his head in his hands or resting it on the table.

"How often do you talk to Jordan?" Pabst asked.

"Probably more than he would like me to," Marty answered. "I communicate with him multiple times every day." . . .

"How would you describe his personality?"

"He's quiet. He's an extremely humble kid. Very, very respectful." A few minutes later, Marty added, "I'm like any parent. I'm proud of my kids. But my . . . livelihood is being around adolescents, young adults, high school–age kids. And I can say, with my right hand to God, I haven't been around a more honest young man than Jordan. I just feel lucky to have him as my son."

"Have you noticed changes in your son since this allegation was lodged?" Pabst asked.

"Jordy is an extremely strong and resilient young man, but it's had a huge effect on him. Huge effect."

"What effect on your family?"

"It's— Short of losing a child, I couldn't imagine a worse situation [than] to have this kind of accusation [about] a kid of his background. I don't know, maybe there are stories of things that are more devastating. But I wake up every day feeling suffocated. And it's been that way for thirteen months now."

Prosecutor Adam Duerk realized that cross-examining such a sincere and immensely appealing witness would only be counterproductive for the prosecution. So after fifteen minutes on the stand, Marty Johnson was excused. At least three or four members of the jury looked like they were on the verge of breaking into tears as he walked back to the gallery, where he sat beside his wife for the remainder of the trial.

CHAPTER TWENTY-SEVEN

The final two witnesses—one called by the defense, the other by the prosecution—testified on Thursday, February 28, 2013. The defense witness, a psychiatrist and neurologist named William Stratford, had never examined Cecilia Washburn, but he'd reviewed her counseling and medical records at the University of Montana's Curry Health Center at the request of David Paoli and Kirsten Pabst. Stratford argued that although the records indicated that Washburn suffered from anxiety and depression in the aftermath of her sexual encounter with Jordan Johnson, the symptoms she exhibited did not rise to the level of post-traumatic stress disorder.

The prosecution witness, David Bell, was a physician at the Curry Health Center who treated Washburn after she was allegedly raped. He testified that the symptoms she displayed matched all the criteria for PTSD.

Friday, the first day of March, was the trial's final day. More people were jammed into the gallery than on any previous day. Five television cameras bristled from tripods next to the jury box. Most of the Griz football team and many of the coaches were present. Jordan Johnson's family sat on the east side of the gallery. Cecilia Washburn and her family were seated on the west side.

Prosecutor Suzy Boylan began the state's closing argument by saying the case "was about the differences between being raped by a stranger and being raped by someone you know and trust. It's a case about the difference between science and myths. . . . It's not about football, or the university, or misunderstanding, or miscommunication, or mixed signals. And it's not about an insensitive lover that didn't cuddle enough. It's about a defendant who didn't take no for an answer."

No one with a heart, Boylan continued, could fail to "be moved by some of the testimony in this case, from the defendant's father, for example. It's okay to have that sympathy. It's okay to find the defendant, or his dad, or their supporters likable. But you can't acquit him because of feelings. You can't acquit because you feel for the defendant and his family, any more than you can convict because you feel for Cecilia and her family. . . .

"The state has to prove the elements of the offense beyond a reasonable doubt. . . . This is not beyond a shadow of a doubt or beyond all doubt. To prove something beyond all doubt or beyond a shadow of a doubt would require a camera, or all of us being there as the situation unfolds. . . . Conflicting accounts are not automatically reasonable doubt. It is not fair to a victim—or to a defendant, for that matter—to be judged based on myths, misconceptions, or stereotypes. But that's exactly what the defense is hoping that you'll do. So [Dr. David Lisak was] here to dispel some of those myths and misconceptions. That's what experts do."

Lisak had pointed out that "rapists can be men who are good-looking, who are likable, charming, gentle, and even timid," Boylan reminded the jury. He made it clear that "there is no profile" of a rapist. Nobody can be ruled out. "Good people can do bad things."

Washburn had stated that when she was being raped, it felt "like a dream where you want to scream but you can't," Boylan said. "She described being in complete shock." When she texted Stephen Green, "I think I might have just gotten raped," Washburn "wasn't confused about whether she had been raped or not," Boylan asserted. "She told us, 'I was sure I got raped, but I didn't want to believe it'—one of the classic responses described by Lisak."

A person who commits rape, Boylan said, "especially one like this, is the person who's in control. He's in control of the time, the place, the victim." But the rapist can't control everything,

Boylan told the jury, "and those things he can't control are what you should be looking at." Although most rape victims don't report what happened to the police, Jordan Johnson couldn't control whether Washburn would be "in that small fraction of women who do choose to report. He couldn't control that she sent that text. He couldn't control how her body would show signs."

Johnson, Boylan continued, "left two kinds of marks on Cecilia Washburn that night, the physical marks and the psychological marks. And those marks . . . tell you a story of what happened in that room as surely as if a camera had been in there. The first is the mark he left on her chest. He had no explanation for it, but it was there. . . . The genital injuries, as you have seen, can be explained away in many ways." Boylan conceded that these wounds were not a smoking gun. But the trauma Washburn experienced left an unmistakable psychological mark. "Call it PTSD," Boylan said, "call it long-term anxiety, call it whatever you want—the defense can deny the diagnosis, but they cannot dispute the symptoms, the symptoms that everybody in her life has seen."

Before February 4, 2012, Boylan noted, Cecilia Washburn "was vibrant, she was social, she was outgoing. She didn't take medications. She didn't see a counselor. She was a normal young woman who earned a place in a highly competitive and very demanding academic program. After February 4, she struggled. . . . And it has been absolutely established that Cecilia Washburn changed drastically after February 4."

Washburn, Boylan said, is not the "hysterical drama queen the defense would have you believe she was prior to February 4." Jordan Johnson's attorneys, Boylan explained, "need you to believe" that Washburn conforms to "a very obvious stereotype of a woman that's hysterical, vengeful, and deceptive. The crazy woman they warn you about. But that's not who you met in this trial."

Rape, Boylan pointed out, is the only crime in which the victim is presumed to be lying. "If a person was mugged in an alley," she asked the jury, "would we be skeptical of the victim's testimony . . . because there weren't any eyewitnesses?" Would we doubt the victim of a burglary, Boylan wondered, "because they left the door unlocked?" The victim is the wrong person to blame, she argued, whatever the crime. It's the offender who needs to be held accountable.

There was reason to believe that Jordan Johnson was "a decent young man," Boylan acknowledged. "But he committed a crime." The jury had been presented with all the evidence they needed "to give Cecilia the accountability she deserves," she said. "We humbly ask that you convict this defendant of sexual intercourse without consent."

DEFENSE COUNSEL DAVID PAOLI'S truculence in the courtroom could be grating. But even his harshest critics would probably concede that the unflagging intensity of his advocacy for his client was an extraordinary feat. When Paoli stood at the dais and began his closing argument, his defense of Jordan Johnson had consumed his life for the previous thirteen months. His complexion was ashen. He needed a haircut. Puffy folds of skin drooped beneath his eyes, and his jowls sagged heavily over his starched collar and the knot of his yellow tie. He looked like he hadn't slept for a year.

Despite his exhaustion, or perhaps because of it, Paoli's summation was delivered with manic energy. Words flew out of his mouth like panicked bats hurtling from a cave. "Justice needs to be fought for," Paoli declared. "The truth needs to be fought for. The truth does not require an explanation. The truth does not require an expert from Boston." Jordan Johnson "has completely denied" Cecilia Washburn's account, Paoli asserted. The prosecutors "stand here and take a big chunk of their opening to talk to you about the expert from Boston who's here to be educational, . . . and how he's more smarter [*sic*] than all of us. And then, on the other hand, they even encouraged you to use your common sense, except when it comes to the Boston expert. He knows better. I thought it was condescending and presumptuous for them to say to you, 'He knows so much more about this, so you need to listen to him.' I don't buy that. The judge instructed you to use your common sense, and I hope you will, because common sense is what's needed in this case."

Paoli's assault on Dr. David Lisak was relentless: "The Boston expert was needed because there's so much to explain here. They want to call it counterintuitive." Ridiculing Lisak's explanation for why rape victims often failed to flee, or scream, or fight back when they were assaulted, Paoli warned the jury not to be fooled. When people are afraid, he asserted, they run. "That's common sense. That's not expert stuff from Boston."

A few minutes later, Paoli said, "I want to talk to you real quickly about the environment in which we're trying this case. . . . It's intense. These people are under intense pressure. And the police are under intense pressure. The Department of Justice is talking to [Missoula County Attorney Fred] Van Valkenburg and his staff. . . . And we know about the police department policy—a special policy that was instituted as a result of political social pressure." It was the only police policy, Paoli asserted, that deprives people of their constitutional right to due process. "And we all know from civics that that just isn't right. That's not what this country is."

Paoli asked the jury a rhetorical question: "Do you believe Miss Washburn beyond a reasonable doubt? Even the people who know her best doubt her. I'm not being mean," he said. "I'm just being factual." Citing the text message in which Cecilia Washburn said, "I think I might have just gotten raped," Paoli pronounced, "She didn't know! She did not know!" If Washburn didn't know whether she'd granted consent, Paoli demanded, how could Jordan Johnson have known whether she'd granted consent? Paoli also brought up Washburn's passivity during the alleged rape and pointed out, "It's common sense to talk about the fact that she didn't scream, she didn't roll off the bed, she didn't move in any way."

To discredit Washburn's account of how Johnson pinned her on the bed with his forearm across her chest, pulled off her pants, flipped her over, unzipped his own pants, and then penetrated her from behind while holding her forearms down, Paoli produced a life-size cardboard facsimile of Washburn. "This is sixty-eight inches tall," he told the jury. "That's her height." Then he laid the replica of Washburn on the courtroom floor, placed himself on top of it, and demonstrated how it would have been impossible for Johnson to do what she said he'd done—ignoring the fact that the cardboard cutout was flat, whereas both Washburn and Johnson had testified that she was kneeling, with her buttocks raised, when Johnson penetrated her. As Paoli performed this crude reenactment of the alleged rape, Cecilia Washburn and her family watched from the gallery with horror and disgust.

In marked contrast to Washburn, Paoli told the jury, "Jordan Johnson testified to you directly, consistently. . . . She wants to say that he's some kind of animal that flips a switch and then does some terrible things. And that's not the truth. . . . You all saw Jordan. . . . He's as everyone describes him. He's quiet. He's contemplative. He does not seek the spotlight. He does not jump up on the pedestal. He played football. And we gave him the status. He didn't take it. He played football well, and we gave him the status, all of us. And that's part of the reason he's here. High profile. Celebrity. DOJ. That's why he's here."

Paoli asked the jury, once again, to ponder Washburn's seemingly inexplicable behavior immediately after she was allegedly raped: eating a snack, responding to the text from Brian O'Day with a smiley-face emoticon, and then driving Johnson home without giving any indication that she had just been raped. "This is all the stuff that they need the Boston expert to explain," Paoli said derisively, "because it doesn't show this violent encounter at all. Not at all. . . . The truth does not require an explanation. I'm sure my dad told me this one. My dad was a tire salesman."

"Objection!" prosecutor Suzy Boylan declared. "Your Honor, counsel is testifying again."

"Sustained," Judge Townsend agreed.

"I have heard that if you're explaining, you're losing," Paoli continued, unfazed by the interruption. "If you're constantly having to explain, you don't have the evidence. . . . And the chief explainer, of course, is the Boston expert."

As Paoli was concluding his two-hour summation, he asked the jury a rhetorical question: Why would Jordan Johnson rape Cecilia Washburn when he knew her housemate was sitting just outside her bedroom door? Why would he even think of committing such a reckless act, given his high profile in the community, his sterling reputation, and everything he stood to lose? "It doesn't add up," Paoli insisted.

AFTER DAVID PAOLI sat down, prosecutor Joel Thompson took the dais to present the state's rebuttal statement. "A long time ago," he told the jury, "people figured out that if you repeat something that isn't true enough times, then people will start to believe that. . . . Mr. Paoli comes up here, and he gave you, I submit, an extraordinarily deceptive closing argument, and misrepresented many facts."

Gesturing toward Cecilia Washburn's family in the gallery, Thompson noted that Paoli "continues to claim that those people sitting over there with Cecilia, as they sit here today, doubt her story. Absolutely false." Cecilia's family, Thompson explained, reacted the same way most other families of rape victims react: with shock, and disbelief, and self-criticism. "That's exactly what Dr. Lisak explained to you was the science," Thompson said. "And what's interesting is, Dr. Lisak becomes 'the Boston expert,'" in Paoli's derogatory characterization: "He's other than us. . . . He's not from here. So we can't believe him."

No expert in the world, Thompson testified, would have been credentialed enough to satisfy David Paoli and Kirsten Pabst. "So we got an expert from Boston to come in here. The best. The best to explain to you the truth about the science, because it is counterintuitive and it is paradoxical. And what he told you in this courtroom, ladies and gentlemen, was not his opinion. He was telling you what decades of research have shown." Lisak provided the jury with the scientific background they needed to understand the evidence, Thompson said, while Paoli and Pabst "firmly staked out territory on the opposite side of scientific research. . . . They have said, 'Disregard what [Dr. Lisak] told you, because we desperately need to play on your possible ignorance and your possible misunderstanding of rape myths.' That is not a way we get to the truth, ladies and gentlemen. Manipulating the evidence, misrepresenting the evidence, is not a way we get to the truth."

Joel Thompson pointed out that he sometimes prosecutes homicide cases. "A body speaks of how it was killed," he said. "A drop of blood speaks of who left it." In similar fashion, he said, the bruises and red marks on Cecilia Washburn's body "speak to whose account is true." The defense was trying to pressure the jury into believing otherwise, he argued, because "the defendant's life hangs in the balance."

Thompson cautioned the jury members against acquitting Jordan Johnson because they might be inclined to think, "The damage is done. I don't want to ruin two lives—one is already ruined, let's not ruin another." Such reasoning would be wrong, Thompson said, because "considerations of sentencing or consequences outside of your decision [about guilt or innocence] are not in any way relevant to what is true. And we don't look to you as much for justice . . . as we look to you for truth. . . . Your only responsibility is rendering a true verdict. The harm done in this case was not done in this trial. It was done in the rape of Cecilia Washburn."

To determine the truth, Thompson observed, "We have to rely on the evidence. . . . And the best evidence is that Cecilia Washburn went in that room one person [on the night of February 4, 2012] and came out a very different person. . . . It's been suggested that maybe this was just a lie [by Washburn] that got out of control. Well, if that's true, it would have to have been a lie concocted within . . . three to five minutes," because she sent that troubling text ("Omg, I think I might have just gotten raped. he kept pushing and pushing and I said no but he wouldn't listen") less than five minutes after the rape allegedly occurred.

"So what you're finally left with, ladies and gentlemen, is two stories of what happened in that room," Thompson told the jury. According to one of these competing narratives, a young man in a relationship with another woman texts Cecilia Washburn because he wants to get laid and he thinks she is eager to have sex with him. "It's Saturday night," Thompson explains. "He's had a few beers and his buddy says to him, 'Get 'er done.' "

Cecilia Washburn, "on the other hand, is tired, unshowered, sleeping, takes no time to clean herself up, dress nice, or put on makeup." Although she hoped to have sex with Johnson at some point in the future, she did not want to have intercourse with him that particular evening. "He thought he was having sex that night," Thompson pronounced, but "she did not." When Washburn made this explicitly clear to Johnson, he ignored her and raped her. "To the defendant, it was normal. No words, no talking afterwards. He goes into the bathroom, leaves the house, and the next words he utters to her are 'Well, thanks,' when she drops him off. He admits . . . her text message to Stephen Green doesn't make sense. And he's right: It doesn't make sense." Nor does the emotional distress witnessed afterward by Green, Thompson added, because Washburn's reaction is inexplicable if she wasn't raped.

Cecilia Washburn's version of what happened, Joel Thompson continued, "involves the defendant changing, going from gentle and trusted to forceful and scary in a heartbeat. She's in a secure, safe place, with a trusted person who would never harm her." But then the defendant starts using force to get what he came for. "She says no," Johnson continued. "She resists. She puts her knees up. She pushes him away."

But Johnson was determined to have sex that night, so he raped her. And the trauma of that rape, Thompson said, "was written all over her the minute she left the room."

The defense attorneys, Thompson said, "would have you believe that this unrebutted emotional reaction was either caused by a lack of snuggling or a realization that the man . . . wasn't going to be her boyfriend." But Cecilia Washburn was not in fact a woman scorned, "or hiding a pregnancy, or trying to get advantage in a child custody case, or any of the other reasons we might think someone would make a false allegation. She has no motive to endure what she and her family have endured in this last year. And what they continue to endure. She will not leave this courtroom all better. You saw it on her. You saw it on her friends and her family.

"Don't let yourself be confused," Thompson implored. "Attorneys know that confusion is the next of kin to doubt, because it feels the same way." But the confusion the defense worked so hard to create "is not doubt," he said. Cecilia Washburn's only motive for reporting that Jordan Johnson raped her was to hold him accountable for what he did and to prevent him from doing it to anyone else. "That," Thompson told the jury, "is your motive."

CHAPTER TWENTY-EIGHT

Prosecutor Joel Thompson finished his rebuttal at 1:08 p.m. Friday afternoon, prompting Judge Karen Townsend to tell the twelve jurors to gather up their notebooks, head for the jury room, and start deliberating. As the courtroom emptied, Jordan Johnson's father leaned over the gallery railing and embraced his son.

Just after 3:30, an announcement was made that a verdict had been reached, and the people milling around the courthouse hurried back to the courtroom. For a jury to arrive at a verdict in less than two and a half hours after such a long, complex trial was highly unusual, and it took almost everyone by surprise. Because few had anticipated that the jury would finish deliberating so quickly, and most of the spectators had left the courthouse to have lunch, when Judge Townsend called the court back to order, the audience in the gallery was only about a third as large as the audience for the closing arguments. Johnson sat down at the defense counsel's table, between David Paoli and Kirsten Pabst, betraying no emotion. Neither Cecilia Washburn nor any of her family were present to hear the jury's decision.

A little before 4:00, the jury forewoman handed the verdict to the bailiff, who read it to the court: "We the jury, duly empanelled and sworn to try the issues in the above-entitled cause, enter the following unanimous verdict: To the charge of sexual intercourse without consent: We the jury, all of our number, find the defendant, Jordan Todd Johnson, not guilty."

Raucous cheering filled the courtroom. Johnson, Paoli, and Pabst burst into tears and embraced. The *Missoulian* Twitter feed erupted with commentary, almost all of it expressing support for Johnson, Paoli, and Pabst and/or berating Cecilia Washburn:

> INNOCENT! I would love for the accusers name to be released and plastered everywhere like Jordan's was
>
> Justice was done today on a case that never should have gone to trial.
>
> Paoli is a damn good lawyer, justice has been served
>
> Hopefully UM will stop getting such a bad rep now.
>
> @egrizfans: Jordan Johnson found Not Guilty . . . In related news, Gwen [Florio] now taking applications for a new scapegoat.
>
> Missoula loves you Jordy!!!! We have been behind you the entire time!
>
> Now sue her for every last dollar . . . #Civil retribution
>
> Women who falsely accuse men of rape should be thrown in prison.
>
> Glad it's over, happy he was found not guilty. Hope he comes back to play Griz football again. A big speed bump in his life.
>
> So glad Johnson was found not guilty! That girl seemed like nothing but an attention seeker
>
> Even if the UM apologized and offered to re-instate JJ, I don't see how he could possibly continue at the UM . . . #freeagent

---

JOHNSON HAD BEEN suspended from the University of Montana football team on July 31, 2012, and did not practice or play for the Grizzlies for the entire 2012 season. Immediately after the trial, he appealed his suspension, and on Tuesday, March 5, 2013, the university announced that he had been reinstated to the team, "effective immediately." Most of Missoula was jubilant that he would be back on the field when the 2013 season commenced, in September. In 2011, before he was suspended, Johnson threw for 2,400 yards and 21 touchdowns; ran for 506 yards and another 4 touchdowns; and led the Griz to an 11–3 record.* In 2012, without Johnson, the team's record was 5–6. It was UM's first losing season since 1985.

ALTHOUGH MISSOULA COUNTY ATTORNEY Fred Van Valkenburg didn't participate in the trial itself, he was in charge of the office responsible for prosecuting the case, and he observed the proceedings from the gallery on the final day. As the courtroom emptied on Friday afternoon, and David Paoli and Kirsten Pabst headed outside to take a victory lap in front of the television cameras that had been set up on the courthouse lawn, Gwen Florio, with notebook in hand, approached Van Valkenburg near the courtroom rail to ask what he thought of the verdict. "The outcome here is a 'not guilty' verdict," Van Valkenburg grumbled. "It is *not* an 'innocent' verdict."

* After an eighteen-month investigation, the NCAA forced the football team to vacate their final five wins of the 2011 season; as a consequence, the Grizzlies' official record has been revised from 11–3 to 6–3. But the sanction had nothing to do with the rape scandal. It was imposed for numerous violations of NCAA rules, the most serious of which was allowing two Griz players, Trumaine Johnson and Gerald Kemp, to receive free legal representation when they were charged with obstructing a peace officer, disorderly conduct, and resisting arrest after police were called to break up a party at Johnson's apartment. A melee ensued, during which Johnson and Kemp were tased by the cops and thrown in jail. The lawyer who provided the free representation was Darla Keck, a shareholder in Milt Datsopoulos's law firm.

Florio included Van Valkenburg's comment in an article posted on the *Missoulian* website that evening. Three weeks later, Pabst fired back at her former boss on her personal blog. Van Valkenburg and his prosecutors, she wrote in a 2,400-word jeremiad posted on *Pabstblawg,*

> are bitter and have no respect for the jury's verdict. They will probably never admit that Jordan is innocent, that their decision to charge the case was premature and wrong.

Pabst claimed in this blog post that the Missoula County Attorney's Office decided to prosecute a case that lacked legal merit because of the intense pressure Van Valkenburg was under from Department of Justice investigators; he wanted to send a message that Missoula prosecutors had compassion for rape victims:

> I would venture a guess that the next time the Missoula County Attorney's Office is called upon to decide whether questionable charges should be filed, the name Jordan Johnson will ring in their ears. I hope that prior to sending a message to the world, they will, at the very least, review the available evidence; that they will consider the permanent ramifications . . . on all involved; that they will be cognizant of the personal and financial costs associated with the decision; and that they will remember that, on occasion, people are untruthful about abuse.

As it turns out, insights about the verdict offered by Joanne Fargo,* one of the seven women on the jury, suggest that Cecilia Washburn might indeed have been telling the truth about what Jordan Johnson did to her. "Ms. Washburn could have been raped," Fargo told me nineteen months after the trial. "The evidence presented by the prosecution from the rape center Ms. Washburn went

* pseudonym

to for evaluation was convincing to me." Fargo said she found "Ms. Washburn completely credible. She seemed invested in her studies and focused on a career. I did not believe she manufactured her story of vengeance or malice of any kind. She seemed far too intelligent to have attempted to profit by false claims" against Johnson.

"From the testimony presented," Fargo reflected, "I got the impression [Jordan Johnson] pursued [Cecilia Washburn]. He had called her several times before she agreed for him to come to her residence. She hadn't prepared for the date. Seems like if she were going to snag the quarterback she would have showered." If Johnson were anything other "than a cad," Fargo added, instead of forcing himself on Washburn, he would have "saved" himself for Kelli Froland, the woman he professed wanting to have a serious relationship with.

Even though Fargo believed that Johnson might have raped Washburn, however, she also believed that the jury arrived at the correct verdict. The defense raised reasonable doubts, she said, "about whether Mr. Johnson was aware . . . the sex was nonconsensual," and the verdict was "based wholly on the letter of the law as instructed by the judge. . . . No one can really be sure Ms. Washburn made her intent clear to him." According to Fargo, it was hard for the jury "to say in the moment" whether Johnson "took 'no' as no. He made a noticeable impression on all in the courtroom when he stated 'she moaned'" while they were having intercourse, which the jury interpreted as a sign that Washburn was enjoying the sexual encounter.*

* Asserting that an alleged rape victim was moaning seems to be an effective means of persuading police, prosecutors, judges, and/or jurors that the sex was consensual, rather than an act of rape, even though people moan in fear and pain, as well as pleasure. But the "moaning" defense worked for Jordan Johnson, it worked for the four Griz football players accused of raping Kelsey Belnap in 2010, and it worked for Jameis Winston, the Heisman Trophy–winning quarterback for Florida State University, when he was accused of raping a female student in December 2012. Two years later, when Winston was asked during a student conduct hearing "in what manner,

Fargo said that testimony about the condom was also "a key point in the decision-making process." Most of the jurors believed Johnson when he testified that Cecilia Washburn asked if he had a condom, Fargo explained: Washburn's "testimony was ambiguous. The defense made a clear point of that fact. Johnson said he didn't have a condom. Her response was that was okay," which jurors understood to be an expression of consent on her part.

There wasn't unanimous agreement about the verdict, initially. "When the first paper vote was taken" in the jury room, Fargo told me, "there were only three or four people who voted 'guilty.'" But after "additional discussion and a second paper vote," eleven of the twelve jurors were convinced that Johnson should be acquitted. When the lone holdout for a guilty verdict was eventually swayed, according to Fargo, "the handful of [jurors] questioning her were very respectful of her opinions. I was convinced she was comfortable with changing her vote through the thoughtful exchange of ideas."

Even though Paoli and Pabst persuaded the jury to acquit Johnson, Fargo said, "In no shape, way, manner, or form was I comfortable with Mr. Paoli's or Ms. Pabst's brand of practicing the law. I would characterize it as bullying. . . . I found it beyond annoying, and I was frequently frustrated it was allowed, ad nauseam. The thing is, they occasionally made a point. It would have been better received without the theatrics."

Joanne Fargo believed that Johnson probably benefited from the fact that several members of the jury were of a sufficiently advanced age to be mystified by the behavior of modern college students, for whom text messages are the default mode of communicating with one another. "Texting was a foreign concept" to

---

verbally or physically," the female gave consent, he claimed she provided consent by "moaning." Winston was cleared of misconduct.

The moaning defense isn't always successful, however. When Kaitlynn Kelly accused UM student Calvin Smith of raping her in October 2011, Smith said part of the reason he believed Kelly consented to having sex was that "she was moaning," but the University Court found him guilty of rape, regardless.

some of her fellow jurors, Fargo observed, so the significance of the text Washburn sent to Stephen Green saying, "Omg, I think I might have just gotten raped" might well have been lost on them. They were baffled about why "she didn't scream out or run to her friend outside the bedroom," instead of taking the time to type a message on her phone. Fargo, on the other hand, understood that "texting was Ms. Washburn's usual form of communication. Texting what had happened to her made sense."

Serving on the jury was an ordeal, Fargo emphasized. It was "a very long, tedious, and emotion-driven trial" that "taught me a good deal about myself and others. More data received than I could ever envision. I would characterize the bulk of my experience as a nightmare I would not care to repeat. . . . I had prepared myself for the long haul, but wasn't prepared for the toll it would take on me emotionally and, eventually, physically." Media coverage of "the trial went nationwide," she said, "and people I didn't know suddenly knew me. . . . The courtroom was filled every single day. It was a suffocating crush, at times, and certainly toward the end.

"I felt like I had a target painted on me," Fargo told me. "People would constantly come up to me and start a conversation—'I know you are unable to discuss the trial, but'—and then give their opinions. Without exception, everyone leaned toward [Jordan Johnson's] innocence. Ms. Washburn was always spoken of in the negative. In fact, I was astounded by the ignorance of acquaintance rape. . . . A very old concept of rape prevails. According to this mind-set, there can only be two precursors to rape: (1) A stranger jumps out from the bushes; (2) There is no rape unless the woman puts up a fight, to the death if necessary."

PART SIX

Aftershocks

On the playing field, every single mistake a player makes is pointed out and criticized until corrected. By design, on the field of real life, the athlete rarely faces similar accountability. . . . Sadly, and too often with tragic repercussions, athletes don't distinguish right from wrong because they actually have no idea of what is right and what is wrong. Rules don't apply. Acceptable standards of behavior don't apply. Little infractions become bigger ones, and adults turn a blind eye. If someone gets into trouble, the first move is for an authority figure, usually in the form of a coach, to get them out of it.

When that doesn't work, whether they're high school quarterbacks or pro-ball pitchers, one of two things happens. Sometimes, especially at the high school level, the community rallies around the accused, wanting to believe that "boys will be boys." . . . We don't want to admit that in all these stories, it's not about the individual, or the individual sport, but about the culture we have allowed to grow around them. . . .

It is in vogue now to blame and condemn athletes. They should be held accountable for their behavior. . . . But we are just as culpable, allowing them to exist in a realm all their own and not caring a bit about what we have turned them into—as long as they bring us victory.

Buzz Bissinger
"The Boys in the Clubhouse"
New York Times, October 18, 2014

CHAPTER TWENTY-NINE

Just before the Jordan Johnson trial began, the *New York Times* published an article in which Montana Regent Pat Williams said, "We've had sex assaults, vandalism, beatings by football players. . . . The university has recruited thugs for its football team, and this thuggery has got to stop." Williams was widely denounced for these remarks by Griz fans, who circulated a petition demanding that he be removed from the Board of Regents.

On March 10, 2013, nine days after Johnson was acquitted, Williams published a guest column in the *Missoulian* to address the ongoing criticism, and to try to save his job. He wrote,

> We Montanans have always preferred straight talk from those who represent us. My choice of words with the reporter was candid; chosen to illuminate my concern with the actions of outlier, convicted student-athletes whose behavior have [*sic*] damaged public and personal safety as well as scarred our university. . . .
>
> For 50 years I have worked to improve and enhance educational opportunities for young people across our state and throughout the nation. As a teacher and a member of the Board of Regents, I will continue to defend our efforts to educate the next generation and form leaders of conscience. If I turned a blind eye to violence in our university communities it would impede these goals.

A week later, David Paoli responded to Williams with a *Missoulian* guest column of his own. It made Paoli look like a sore winner:

> Pat Williams is a friend of mine. So, he will understand my advice. . . .
>
> Williams abused his position as a regent to ignorantly blast University of Montana student-athletes. . . .
>
> When he was roundly criticized for his bombastic statements, he wrote a guest opinion to explain himself. Pat, when you are explaining, you're losing. . . .
>
> More than his offensive language, the timing of Williams' ambush is more concerning. His quotes ran on Feb. 6 in a *New York Times* story regarding a highly publicized trial set to begin two days later. His "thugs" and "thuggery" quotes were printed two paragraphs above a discussion of whether the falsely accused could receive a "fair trial amid such controversy." . . .
>
> Montanans expect honest, reasoned judgment and respect from their representatives. Montanans do not expect cheap quotes to the *New York Times* to develop more frenzy and throw kerosene on an already blazing situation. . . .
>
> Williams is not a racist. However, his use of the racial epitaphs [*sic*] "thugs" and "thuggery" are racist. Anyone who has lived in D.C. or Seattle or Berkeley or anywhere else knows very clearly that the use of these words have [*sic*] serious and hurtful racial overtones. The use of these racial slurs requires an apology.

Five days after Paoli's piece ran, the *Missoulian* published a rejoinder from former Montana Supreme Court justice Terry Trieweiler, one of the most esteemed lawyers in the state:

> Missoula lawyer David Paoli is a friend of mine. So I'm certain he won't be offended by my opinion of what he characterized as "advice" to Pat Williams. . . .

Let me preface my remarks by pointing out that I've been a college football fan all of my life. Football paid for my college education. And, I've been a season-ticket holder to Grizzlies football for many years.

Still, I've been mystified by the reaction of many Grizzlies football fans to Williams' remarks describing too many of the team's players as "thugs" and his commitment as a regent to end the "thuggery."

Paoli lambasted Williams' remarks as "ignorant," "abusive of his position as a regent" and unfair to Paoli's client. He threw in a little race-baiting for good measure, even though the term used by Williams is racially neutral and the offenders he referred to were both black and white.

It seems to me, on the other hand, that anyone who doesn't recognize the problems Williams described wouldn't be fit to serve as a regent and that the real "ignorance" is demonstrated by attacking the messenger for his unpleasant message.

It might be helpful to review the conduct over the past five years that he accurately characterized as "thuggery."

It includes a fatal shooting by Jimmy Wilson and his teammate Qwenton Freeman's refusal to participate in the investigation, even though he witnessed it, following which Wilson was found not guilty and they were welcomed back to the team; Freeman's numerous convictions for acts of violence and ultimate dismissal from the team; Freeman's armed burglary with the assistance of several other players; the brutal assaults on another student on campus by two other players; Trumaine Johnson's and Andrew Swink's violent assault on another student; Johnson's and Gerald Kemp's obstruction of a peace officer; Beau Donaldson's rape of a female companion; several players' alleged involvement in a gang rape; the University of Montana president's admission, following an independent investigation, that a number of players had been involved in sexual assaults; and the recent brutal beating and robbery of a convenience store clerk by a former player with a history of other violent and illegal conduct. Throw in several other violent assaults on women by some of these same players.

During the same period of time, seven players have been arrested for driving under the influence of alcohol or drugs—a couple of them repeat offenders.

As a result of this history, the university is being investigated by the NCAA, the Justice Department, and the U.S. Department of Education's Office of Civil Rights.

If people who kill others, rape others, beat others, and burglarize and rob others aren't thugs, then what are they? And, how much thuggery does it take before a member of the Board of Regents is free to say we need to do something about it?

While it is true that Paoli's client was recently acquitted of the charges against him, Paoli takes himself and the acquittal too seriously when he infers that the acquittal of one player vindicates the entire program, or makes Williams' comments any less true. . . .

As alarming as this five-year pattern of conduct should be, the greater long-term problem will come from the culture of entitlement that causes players here, and elsewhere, to think they are unaccountable for their conduct because of their athletic ability and the knee-jerk reaction of program supporters, including Paoli, to anyone who questions where and how things might have gone wrong.

There's no one in the state more qualified to serve on the Board of Regents than Pat Williams. He has spent a lifetime in service to public education and was defending the Constitution, including the rights of the accused, at some political cost, long before most of his detractors took any interest in the criminal justice system. To think his appointment could be derailed over comments that were both honest and long overdue, though, would suggest one miscalculation on Pat Williams' part—his belief that most Montanans appreciate "straight talk."

In 2012, Governor Brian Schweitzer nominated Williams to the Montana Board of Regents of Higher Education, to a term due to expire in 2019, but the nomination required confirmation by the state senate. On March 20, 2013, the Montana Senate Education Committee held a confirmation hearing on Williams's nomination, and most of the hearing was spent debating Williams's comments to the *Times.* Jim Foley, who had been forced to resign as UM's vice president for external relations after playing a controversial role in the university's rape scandal, and had served as Williams's staff director when Williams was a U.S. congressman, argued against Williams's confirmation. His former boss's published statements, Foley fulminated, "were callous and injurious, both to the citizens of this state and to the thousands of UM student-athletes and UM alumni around this country. . . . Enough is enough with this name-calling against young men who in most cases can't defend themselves against words."

On April 4, the Montana Senate voted on Pat Williams's confirmation. The tally was 26–23 to reject his nomination, and he was ousted from the Board of Regents.

TEN DAYS AFTER the Jordan Johnson trial ended, Allison Huguet was at her father's house in Missoula, watching the five o'clock news, when she learned from a report broadcast by the local NBC affiliate that Beau Donaldson had asked the Sentence Review Division of the Montana Supreme Court to reconsider the sentence he'd received for raping her.

Huguet was astounded. To avoid a jury trial, and a possible sentence of up to one hundred years in prison, in September 2012 Donaldson had signed a plea deal with the state of Montana in which he agreed to plead guilty to raping Huguet in return for a guarantee that he would be sentenced to no more than ten years at the state prison. The deal also included a condition that unambiguously stated, "By signing below and accepting the benefit of this agreement the Defendant expressly waives any right to appeal. . . . Defendant further waives any right . . . to make application for sentence review."

The state had held up its end of the bargain on January 11, 2013, when Judge Karen Townsend sentenced Beau Donaldson to ten years at the state prison. Yet Donaldson was now trying to rescind his promise not to appeal his sentence to the supreme court.

The Sentence Review Division, consisting of three judges, nevertheless agreed to hold a hearing to reconsider Donaldson's sentence. These judges could decide to reduce his sentence. But they could also decide to increase it, so requesting the review was not without risk. Milt Datsopoulos, Donaldson's lawyer, said Donaldson was willing to take that risk because "we felt so strongly" that the sentence was "clearly excessive."

The hearing to review the sentence was held on May 2, 2013, in a small room inside the Montana State Prison at Deer Lodge, where Beau Donaldson was incarcerated. Milt Datsopoulos addressed the court first. He felt the sentence was excessive because of Judge Townsend's "failure to provide the option of a sentence to the Department of Corrections rather than a sentence directly to the Montana State Prison."

Datsopoulos argued that the sentence imposed hadn't been balanced with the need to rehabilitate Donaldson, to help prevent him from becoming a recidivist. "Unlike a lot of star athletes," Datsopoulos told the court, Donaldson "was a good student. . . . He was a person of value, substance, ability, and was no threat to the community." Were it not for alcohol, he insisted, "this young man wouldn't be in prison. His whole life is, almost, pristine. . . . Incarcerating Donaldson in the state prison wasn't necessary," Datsopoulos maintained, saying that it was "avoidable" by letting him serve his time at the Department of Corrections instead.

Following Datsopoulos, Beau Donaldson told the court, "I do take responsibility for the actions that I've done . . . and the hurt that I've caused. And, I just feel that if I can get the opportunity to be sentenced to the Department of Corrections, I can not only rehabilitate myself, but make myself a better person."

Donaldson's mother, Cathy, testified that Beau "has always been a good person. . . . He was raised that way. . . . Yes, he does need to be punished. But he also needs a chance. He was just shy of twenty-one years old when he made a very, very bad decision. . . . When my son puts his mind to something, he will do it. His goal is to have a life. My goal for him is finish his college education, find happiness, get married, have children, be a wonderful father. I am not as young as I would like to be. But I would like to be able to be alive to see that. I plead and pray that you have read and looked at everything, and you have open eyes and an open heart. Because there's a plate missing at my dinner table, and I want it back."

Cathy Donaldson told the three judges that Beau's "sentence is our sentence. I'm selfish. I want to see him in a program where he can get the help that he needs. I don't want to see him sitting in a cell and not getting the opportunity that he deserves."

Larry Donaldson, Beau's father, asserted to the court that Beau "is the only person that's been totally honest from day one. . . . He's never varied from the truth." When Beau called Larry from jail to say he'd been arrested, Larry said, "He told me, 'If I did something wrong, Dad, I need to take responsibility.' . . . He's a big part of a lot of people's lives. Just give him a chance. . . . I love you, Beau."

WHEN IT WAS her turn to testify, Allison Huguet began by explaining that she "came today not because I want to be here, at all." Then she turned toward Beau Donaldson and, choking up with emotion, said, "Listening to your mom breaks my heart." Immediately thereafter, her voice hardened, however, and she told the judges that Larry Donaldson's claim that Beau "is the only one that's been honest" was not only untrue but "a complete slap in the face." After Beau Donaldson's arrest, Huguet pointed out, he lied to numerous people, saying that she had consented to have sex with him on the night he'd raped her and falsely claiming that she'd had consensual sex with him on other occasions before the night he raped her.

Huguet was infuriated by Milt Datsopoulos's statement that requiring Beau to serve his sentence in the state prison was "avoidable." She said, "Well, raping me was also avoidable. And it's a choice he made." She observed that Donaldson could have requested a trial but chose to make a plea deal instead. "I cannot understand why Beau even has the right to ask for a review of his sentence," she said, after he'd explicitly agreed to waive that right in the plea deal.

Datsopoulos, Huguet reminded the court, claimed Beau's "life had been pristine," because his criminal record listed no serious prior offenses. "However," she said, "if you looked at all the facts in this case, you will see that Beau absolutely has a lot of past criminal behavior." She noted that Donaldson had admitted to underage drinking; lying to the police; illegally obtaining and using Adderall, painkillers, and cocaine; and disorderly conduct charges that had landed him in jail the weekend before he was arrested for raping her. Moreover, Donaldson had sexually assaulted Hillary McLaughlin.

"While Beau may not have been charged for . . . these acts, some of which are felonies," Huguet continued, "it does not take away from the fact that these crimes had very serious effects on others. It is clear that Beau has gotten away with a lot during his short twenty-three years of life. And it worries me that if this sentence is reduced, he will once again be sent the message that his actions are acceptable." Milt Datsopoulos, she said, brought up Donaldson's "age and potential" as a reason why sentencing him to the state prison was excessive. The only potential Huguet saw in Beau Donaldson, she noted, "was a potential for hurting a lot of females. Being a young and charming football player, Beau had—and I'm sure still would have—a very large victim pool."

Allison Huguet said, "As we grow up, we are taught to stay away from strangers and creepy people in the alleyways, . . . and not to go anywhere without someone you trust. [But] what happens when it's the person you trust who rapes you? . . . I'm tired of living in this hell."

Her family had been forced to suffer the hell of the rape's aftermath, too, she explained: "My mother, specifically, is not here today because she, emotionally, can't handle any more of it. She can't even look at me without having flashbacks of picking me up in the middle of the road that night. Or hear my voice without being reminded of my screams for help, or telling her that Beau had just raped me and was chasing me down an alleyway."

If Beau Donaldson "was truly remorseful, and understood the pain and damage he has caused," Allison Huguet said, "he would know he deserves the sentence he has been given, and then some. He would take responsibility for his actions all of the time" and not just while trying to get his sentence reduced. "He would not allow his friends and family to blame me or slander my character for what he has done," she continued. "I'm deeply frustrated by the fact that he thinks he deserves this [sentence] review. . . . I don't get to go to a review board and ask them to reduce the pain I feel daily; or take away the flashbacks, nightmares, or anxiety; or restore my sense of safety and security, or my trust in people. I don't get to ask them to give me back my innocence or joy, or the life that he has sucked right out of me. And, somehow, he thinks he's the one that's been punished too harshly?"

Weeping, Huguet told the judges, "The night that Beau chose to wait until I was alone, asleep and defenseless, walk over to me, pull down my pants, pull down my underwear, pull down his pants, pull out his dick, and shove it into me, he gave me a life sentence—a life in which I have to work every day to get through the pain. Some days I have to convince myself it is even worth it. I don't get to go to a review board and ask them to reduce the life sentence he has forced on me. There is a reason why people say that rape is the worst crime a person can survive."

Allison Huguet said she wanted Beau Donaldson "to get help and treatment. But at the end of the day, he has to be punished.

And the only thing that is excessive in this case is the amount of suffering that Beau has caused."

When Huguet finished, Hillary McLaughlin addressed the Sentence Review Division via a video feed from Great Falls. "To hear that Beau Donaldson wants a lighter sentence for sexually assaulting a stranger and raping a lifelong friend is extremely hard for me to understand," she told the judges, and then she described Donaldson's attempt to rape her in 2008. Afterward, McLaughlin explained, instead of reporting it to the police, she tried to put the incident "in the back of my mind and just forget about it," without success.

"Due to Beau Donaldson," she said, "I have lost my sense of comfort with nearly every person I meet. I have lost who I was before I met him. I live in constant fear of being attacked at any moment. . . . I am constantly looking over my shoulder. I had never experienced anxiety, but now I am treated daily for it. I get nervous, anxious, and scared at any given moment. . . . I struggle with being alone in my own home. And as a twenty-three-year-old woman, I am afraid of the dark. I wake up with nightmares of being attacked, and I'm up for hours on end because I can't get these visions out of my head. Even while I was screaming and telling him to get off me, he continued to try and sexually assault me. . . . I am stuck living and remembering this feeling for the rest of my life. I am stuck with fear, anger, hurt, nervousness, and anxiety."

Like Allison Huguet, Hillary McLaughlin was appalled that Donaldson was claiming that his sentence was unfairly harsh. "I think he got off easy," McLaughlin declared to the court, "and I hope by telling my story, you realize that his maximum sentence of ten years is temporary, but mine is forever."

MISSOULA COUNTY ATTORNEY Fred Van Valkenburg had accompanied Huguet to Deer Lodge, and after McLaughlin completed her testimony, he addressed the panel of judges. "I'd like to begin," he said, "by telling you a couple of things about the two witnesses you've just heard from." When Missoula police and prosecutors first learned that Donaldson had assaulted Hillary McLaughlin, Van Valkenburg explained, she was "initially very reluctant to get involved in the prosecution." But she came to understand "that silence was essentially acting as approval for Beau Donaldson's actions," and although it was difficult and unpleasant to testify at his sentencing hearing, she felt it was "a duty on her part to try and protect future victims."

As for Allison Huguet, Van Valkenburg said, the morning after Donaldson raped Huguet, she told him she would not report him to the police if he would seek counseling, treatment for his drug and alcohol abuse, and sex-offender treatment. During the fourteen months following the rape, however, "it became increasingly clear to Allison that Beau had no real intention of keeping those promises to her." Instead, Donaldson continued "to drink, to take drugs, to party, to laugh in her face when he saw her."

Around this same time, Van Valkenburg told the court, the *Missoulian* published several articles quoting anonymous women who said they had been raped by football players from the University of Montana. "Allison began to think, 'My God, Beau Donaldson is out there raping other women because I failed to report the case involving him,'" Van Valkenburg explained. So she went to the police and reported that he'd raped her, resulting in his arrest. Subsequently, Donaldson entered into a formal plea agreement with the state, and the agreement had a provision that said, "The Defendant expressly waives any right to appeal" or ask to have his sentence reviewed. "Yet," Van Valkenburg lamented, "here he is at sentence review. . . . The court should take that into consideration." The sentence Donaldson received is "reasonable under the circumstances," Van Valkenburg observed, and "Judge Townsend thought long and hard" before imposing it.

The state, Van Valkenburg pointed out, "had a strong case against Beau Donaldson because of his tape-recorded confession. There wasn't really much reason for us to negotiate with the defense, at all. But we did, because, to some degree, . . . any time you go to a jury trial, it's a roll of the dice." It took a long time for Van Valkenburg's office to convince Allison Huguet to support the plea deal proposed by the state, because she thought thirty years in prison with twenty suspended was too light a sentence, he said. "But one of the things we told her was" that if this sentence is imposed, "it won't get set aside later on, on an appeal or by a sentence review panel."

Beau Donaldson "has, essentially, put himself in the situation that he's in right now," Fred Van Valkenburg said. "But he's done more than that. He's given a horrible black eye to something that is a source of tremendous pride to the people of Montana: the University of Montana football program . . . and the University of Montana, in general. . . . Enrollment is way down. The university has a budget shortfall of $16 million this year. That's going to affect every student at the University of Montana." And Donaldson, he asserted, "is one of the people principally responsible for that.

"Judge Townsend is a thoughtful, reasoned jurist," Van Valkenburg continued. "She imposed a reasonable sentence on this defendant. And I would respectfully ask you to uphold this sentence." Van Valkenburg paused for a moment, then added, "And I will tell you, it's a little tempting to ask for a [slightly stiffer sentence], but I won't. I will just ask that you uphold the sentence that Judge Townsend imposed. Thank you."

At this point, one of the three judges scolded Milt Datsopoulos for promising that if the sentence imposed by Judge Townsend fell within the parameters of the plea agreement—as it in fact did—he would "not put the victim through any further proceedings, appeals, sentence review, or otherwise." So, this judge demanded, how did Datsopoulos explain his request for a sentence review?

Datsopoulos answered that he felt Beau Donaldson deserved a new sentence because the plea agreement was "coercive."

This was a preposterous assertion. Nobody had forced Beau Donaldson to take a plea deal. Nothing had prevented him from going to trial and having his future decided by a jury of his peers.

In Missoula, Grizzly football exists in a realm apart, where there is a pervasive sense of entitlement. University of Montana fans, coaches, players, and their lawyers expect, and often receive, special dispensation. Datsopoulos had built a thriving law practice in this environment, and he appeared to believe that his client's pledge not to appeal his sentence wasn't meant to be taken seriously. Because Beau Donaldson was on the football team, the promise shouldn't apply.

None of the three judges appointed to the Sentence Review Division by the Montana Supreme Court was from Missoula, however. When it became clear to Datsopoulos that they weren't impressed by his claim that Donaldson had been coerced into making a plea deal, he tried a final, desperate maneuver. He attempted to convince the judges that Donaldson deserved a lighter sentence because when he'd confessed to raping Huguet at the time of his arrest, he'd knowingly done so without a lawyer present, thereby "eliminating the potential" for Datsopoulos to mount an effective defense. This voluntary confession, Datsopoulos argued, proved that Beau Donaldson accepted responsibility for his crime and wanted to make things right.

Maybe. But on the day Donaldson was arrested, when he went to the police station and gave his statement to Detective Guy Baker, Baker had just informed Donaldson that he'd secretly recorded Donaldson's phone confession to Huguet, so Donaldson was already aware that the police knew the truth.

The judges weren't swayed by any of Datsopoulos's arguments, and they upheld the sentence imposed by Judge Townsend: thirty years in the Montana State Prison, with twenty years suspended. Donaldson would be eligible for parole in July 2015.

It's both instructive and disturbing to think about how Huguet's case might have turned out differently if Detective Guy Baker hadn't obtained a confession from Donaldson. Without a recorded admission of guilt, Chief Deputy Missoula County Attorney Kirsten Pabst might have determined that there was insufficient probable cause to charge Donaldson with rape and declined to prosecute him—just as she declined to prosecute Calvin Smith for raping Kaitlynn Kelly, and as Fred Van Valkenburg himself had declined to prosecute the football players accused of raping Kelsey Belnap.

And even if Beau Donaldson had been charged, it would have been a much more challenging case to prosecute without a confession. Milt Datsopoulos might have refused to accept a plea deal, sending the case to trial. Whereupon Donaldson would have testified that the sex was consensual, and Datsopoulos would have elicited testimony from Donaldson's friends corroborating this claim. At which point Datsopoulos would have launched a ferocious attack on Huguet's character. It's not hard to imagine a jury being persuaded that there was reasonable doubt about whether Huguet had consented to have sex that night. In that eventuality, Donaldson would have been found not guilty, just as Jordan Johnson was found not guilty; and Donaldson would now be a free man, unrehabilitated and unregistered as a sex offender, able to rape again.

Huguet received plenty of reminders that many people continued to believe that she'd falsely accused Donaldson of rape and that he was innocent—even people she had thought were her friends. Two days after Donaldson's sentence review hearing, one such person, a young woman who had grown up with Donaldson and Huguet in Missoula's Target Range neighborhood, posted a hateful message to Huguet on Facebook:

> Do you not understand you are messing with someone else's life, not just for a short moment, but for the rest of their lives. . . . Suck it up and own up to your own damn mistakes, act your age! We are not in middle school any more where things are brushed off, this is real life. Karma is a nasty bitch and I cannot wait until she comes back to bite you in the ass.

CHAPTER THIRTY

Back in May 2012, when the U.S. Department of Justice had announced that it was investigating the Missoula County Attorney's Office, the Missoula Police Department, and the University of Montana for their unsatisfactory response to sexual-assault complaints over the previous three years, the police and the university agreed to cooperate fully with the investigations. Missoula County Attorney Fred Van Valkenburg, however, declared that the MCAO would not cooperate with the DOJ, and he defiantly refused to give federal investigators access to prosecutors in his office or their case files.

A year later, shortly after the Jordan Johnson trial, the DOJ completed its investigations of the Missoula police and the University of Montana and announced that it had reached formal agreements with both institutions to overhaul the way they handled sexual-assault cases. The DOJ reported that its agreement with UM was "a blueprint that can serve as a model for campuses across the nation," and some months thereafter, an independent auditor reported that the Missoula Police Department was making "steady progress" in complying with the changes decreed by the DOJ, as well.

Fred Van Valkenburg, meanwhile, remained adamant in his refusal to work in concert with the DOJ, claiming it had no legal authority to investigate the MCAO. Permitting the feds to interview Missoula prosecutors and examine their case files would set a dangerous precedent, he claimed, which would allow "the heavy hand of government" to meddle in the affairs of thousands of district attorneys nationwide.

In an attempt to persuade Van Valkenburg to abandon his obstinacy and start cooperating with the Justice Department, in December 2013, Michael Cotter, U.S. attorney for the District of Montana, sent Van Valkenburg a proposed agreement between the DOJ and the MCAO that would improve "the safety and security" of sexual-assault victims in Missoula. It would compel the MCAO to hire in-house investigators (instead of relying solely on the police department to investigate sexual-assault cases); hire in-house victim advocates; and establish a designated sexual-assault unit. It would also oblige MCAO prosecutors to meet face-to-face with every victim who reported a sexual assault, and it would require supervisors to review every case declined for prosecution to ensure that the decision hadn't been "inappropriately influenced" by a failure to understand "the dynamics of non-stranger sexual assault."

Michael Cotter's effort to end the DOJ's twenty-month standoff with the MCAO had the opposite of its intended effect, however. Van Valkenburg interpreted Cotter's proposal as a thinly veiled threat to sue the MCAO if Van Valkenburg didn't agree to the DOJ's demands, and Van Valkenburg took umbrage. He responded by essentially telling the DOJ to kiss his ass.

Fred Van Valkenburg asked the Missoula Board of County Commissioners for $50,000 to fund a lawsuit challenging the DOJ's right to tell his office what to do. In making his pitch to the commissioners, Van Valkenburg argued that by suing the DOJ, he could make an important statement about barring the federal government from intruding into local legal matters, while simultaneously saving Missoula taxpayers as much as $400,000 over two years—his estimate of how much it would cost the county to pay the salaries of the new personnel the MCAO would be forced to hire if it acquiesced to the DOJ's demands.

On January 9, 2014, after the commissioners pledged to fund a lawsuit, Van Valkenburg sent U.S. Attorney Michael Cotter a six-page letter reiterating his refusal to comply with the dictates of the

Department of Justice—which, he said, would force the Missoula County Attorney's Office to "unnecessarily spend hundreds of thousands of tax payer dollars to do what it already does." Instead, Van Valkenburg offered an alternative proposal: If the DOJ would get off his back, the MCAO would make a commitment "to assist" the Missoula Police Department and the University of Montana Office of Public Safety as they fulfilled their respective agreements with the DOJ.

Fred Van Valkenburg was happy to help city and university cops submit to the lash of the DOJ, in other words, but it would be a cold day in hell before the Missoula County Attorney's Office would let itself be tyrannized by the federal government. Furthermore, Van Valkenburg threatened, if the DOJ failed to "affirmatively indicate in the next two weeks" that it was willing to accept his alternative proposal, he was "prepared to take any action necessary" to prevent the DOJ from imposing its will on his office.

Given Van Valkenburg's famously stubborn disposition, few Missoulians were surprised by his desire to kick sand in the face of the DOJ, but some prominent citizens thought suing the federal government was a horrible idea. On January 15, 2014, the *Missoulian* published an open letter to the county commissioners from a respected clinical psychologist, Frances Marks Buck, who'd provided therapy to numerous local crime victims. Under the headline "Van Valkenburg's Ego-Based Fight Affects Community's Well-Being," Buck wrote,

> In Montana, unlike some states, the state attorney general has no jurisdiction or oversight of county district attorneys. The only "oversight" is the electorate. . . .
>
> There are clear problems in the functioning of the Missoula District Attorney office, both with the district attorney himself and a number of assistant district attorneys.
>
> In my opinion, Fred Van Valkenburg's stance of non-cooperation with the DOJ is ego-based, not principle-based. . . . He has focused on the "right" of the DOJ to

investigate, not how he, his assistant district attorneys, and the community could benefit from the recommended changes.

Van Valkenburg was unmoved by Buck's letter. On February 11, when the feds hadn't budged from their position, Van Valkenburg filed a lawsuit against the Department of Justice, U.S. Attorney General Eric Holder, and U.S. Attorney Michael Cotter, seeking "a judgment declaring that the defendants do not have the authority to investigate or sue the Missoula County Attorney or his office." Van Valkenburg based his legal claim on the federal common-law doctrine of "absolute prosecutorial immunity," which serves "the same purpose that underlies the immunity of judges and grand jurors," namely, "to protect the judicial process."

The DOJ responded to the lawsuit seventy-two hours later, on Valentine's Day, by releasing a twenty-page report, personally addressed to Fred Van Valkenburg, that documented the failings of the Missoula County Attorney's Office in blistering detail, based on a far-reaching investigation that included interviews with former MCAO prosecutor Kirsten Pabst, former Missoula police chief Mark Muir, nine Missoula detectives and police officers, and more than thirty female victims of sexual assault. When the DOJ had announced its investigation in May 2012, it had noted that at least eighty alleged rapes had been reported in Missoula over the preceding three years. But the findings sent to Van Valkenburg in February 2014 revealed that there were actually 350 sexual assaults reported to the Missoula police between January 2008 and May 2012, a span of fifty-two months. As part of its investigation, the DOJ asked an eminent supervisor of a police sexual-assault unit and an eminent sex-crimes prosecutor to review these cases.

According to the DOJ Valentine's Day report,

> Women consistently told us that Deputy County Attorneys treated them with indifference or disrespect, and frequently made statements to women victims, advocates, and the public diminishing the seriousness of sexual violence and minimizing

> the culpability of those who commit it. We learned that prosecutors did not communicate with female victims about their cases, did not inform them of the charges to be filed and did not seek their input about the type of relief to seek against the accused if convicted. In many cases, prosecutors failed even to return victims' phone calls.

Even though Montana law requires prosecutors to consult with victims of all felony and misdemeanor crimes, the DOJ investigation revealed that "the County Attorney's Office often neglects to hold these consultations with sexual assault victims" and that "the interactions that the County Attorney's Office *does* have with victims of sexual assault often leave them feeling offended, disregarded, and disbelieved by prosecutors." In one instance cited in the report,

> a Deputy County Attorney quoted religious passages to a woman who had reported a sexual assault, in a way that the victim interpreted to mean that the Deputy County Attorney was judging her negatively for having made the report. Advocates told us that Deputy County Attorneys "said terrible things to victims," including saying to one woman, "All you want is revenge."
>
> One woman described her interaction with a Deputy County Attorney as "traumatic." Another woman stated that, by the time the prosecution was over, she was so frustrated by the Deputy County Attorney's treatment and the MCAO's failure to keep her informed about key developments in the case that she "would never suggest" that another woman pursue a sexual assault prosecution in Missoula. She said further that it "broke her heart" that other women had to go through a similar process to have their cases prosecuted. . . .
>
> [A] young woman who had suffered a gang rape as a student at the University of Montana . . . described feeling re-traumatized by the experience of seeking to have the assault

> prosecuted by the County Attorney's Office. As a result of hearing about that experience, a friend of the woman declined to report her own rape to either the police or prosecutors. In another example, a clinical psychologist told us that she had counseled numerous sexual assault survivors in Missoula who had pursued criminal charges against their assailants and described their experiences with the County Attorney's Office as being so horrendous that, when the psychologist herself was sexually assaulted, she was reluctant to have her case prosecuted.

The report warned, "Since the majority of sexual assaults are committed by repeat offenders," the effect of the MCAO's failure to file charges was compromising "the safety of women in the Missoula community as a whole," because "perpetrators who escape prosecution remain in the community to reoffend." In an observation directed specifically at Fred Van Valkenburg, the DOJ report noted,

> Public comments you have made further suggest that, at the very least, sexual assault is not a high priority for MCAO. . . . For example, in responding to questions about delays in charging decisions, you reportedly said that your attorneys review charging decisions in sexual assault cases "when they have spare time." While you subsequently attempted to explain that by "spare time" you were referring to the "additional time" after other courtroom and litigation functions have been completed, the statement seems inconsistent with the diligent investigation and prosecution of sexual abuse. . . .
>
> Of equal concern, we found that the County Attorney's Office declined to prosecute nearly every case of non-stranger assault involving an adult woman victim who was, at the time of the assault, subject to some type of heightened vulnerability—for example, in cases where the assault was

> facilitated by drugs or alcohol, . . . even when the assailant had confessed or made incriminating statements. . . .
>
> For instance, a woman reported that she had been drugged and raped by an acquaintance the previous day. Missoula Police officers developed evidence that included video footage of the alleged assailant slipping something into the woman's drink. The Missoula Police also obtained admissions by the assailant that although he did not remember putting something in the woman's drink, it was possible he had and, as he stated, "If I were trying to make her relax it would be Xanax." When confronted with the video footage, the assailant also stated, "My memory tells me no, but I can't argue with surveillance." The Missoula Police obtained a search warrant for the suspect's home and learned that the suspect had recently refilled prescriptions for two drugs common in drug-facilitated sexual assaults, including Xanax. Nonetheless, MCAO declined to charge the case, citing insufficient evidence, but with no documented further explanation. Moreover we found no indication that the County Attorney's Office had given any guidance to Missoula Police detectives about how to develop evidence that it believed *would* be sufficient to support bringing charges in this case.

ON FEBRUARY 21, 2014, one week after the DOJ's damning report was released, Van Valkenburg responded with a five-page broadside that vehemently denied the DOJ's allegations. His reaction to the report was "frustration, disbelief and outrage," he wrote:

> It is no coincidence that the DOJ released this letter to the press only after I filed a federal court action seeking clarification of the DOJ's authority. The letter provided to the press is clearly retaliatory. The DOJ is trying to use the media to improperly influence public opinion about the issue

> of sexual assault cases. This is a politically-calculated and irresponsible move on their part. . . .
>
> There are 11 attorneys within the criminal division of the County Attorney's Office, 7 of whom are women. Each attorney is personally responsible for upwards of 125 criminal cases at any given time. It is safe to say the workload for our attorneys is high, especially in light of limited time and resources. Despite these obstacles, all criminal victims are given priority whether women, children or men. It is a flat out lie for the DOJ to claim sexual assault cases are given the lowest priority.

Plenty of Missoulians applauded their embattled county attorney for standing up to the DOJ. One of these admirers was former Missoula police chief Mark Muir, who'd retired two months earlier. In a guest column published in the *Missoulian,* Muir referred to the DOJ as "Attorney General Eric Holder's team of ultra-liberal, Washington, D.C., legal staff" and contended that Fred Van Valkenburg had "courageously chosen a bold and wise strategy in suing the United States Department of Justice for its abuse of power."

Support for Van Valkenburg's lawsuit was far from universal, however. On the same day that Van Valkenburg released his angry response to the DOJ report, the *Missoulian* published an article written by Mike Brady, the city's new police chief, and John Engen, who'd been mayor since 2005; they made a convincing argument that the DOJ's investigation of the Missoula Police Department, and the resulting agreement between the city and the DOJ to change the way rape investigations were handled, had made Missoula a safer place for women. "It's close to a year since the city of Missoula entered into an agreement with the United States Department of Justice Civil Rights Division," Brady and Engen wrote, "and we're the better for it." They pointed out that police officers were now better trained to handle the unique challenges of acquaintance rape, making them more sensitive to the needs of rape victims, and that the department had adopted better policies and procedures that vastly improved police cooperation with the county attorney's office and victim advocates. The police department had also commissioned an external review of its performance "to ensure that we're always improving and that we're accountable to the citizens we serve."

Although Brady and Engen didn't come right out and say it in their *Missoulian* article, they clearly believed it would benefit Missoula if Fred Van Valkenburg swallowed his pride, abandoned his lawsuit, and started working with the DOJ.

CHAPTER THIRTY-ONE

Fred Van Valkenburg's pissing match with the Department of Justice took place during the run-up to the election for Missoula County attorney, after he'd already indicated that he would not seek reelection when his term expired, at the end of 2014. In November 2013, as the contretemps between Van Valkenburg and the DOJ escalated, the saga took a strange turn when Kirsten Pabst announced that she would be entering the race to replace her former boss as county attorney. In declaring her candidacy, Pabst told KECI television reporter Emily Adamson that the county attorney's office needed "more cooperation and less fighting," and then added, "I think most importantly we need more compassion."

Twenty months earlier, when Pabst had resigned as chief deputy Missoula County attorney, she'd said she quit in order to spend more time with her "family and horses and dogs." But a month after leaving the prosecutor's office, she seemed to contradict this explanation by joining David Paoli as defense counsel for Grizzly quarterback Jordan Johnson. Then, during the long lead-up to the trial and throughout the debilitating trial itself, she and Paoli relentlessly vilified Johnson's alleged victim, Cecilia Washburn, as part of their successful effort to persuade the jury that Johnson wasn't guilty.

During the final six years of her fifteen-year tenure at the Missoula County Attorney's Office, Kirsten Pabst had been responsible for overseeing the prosecution of sexual-assault cases. Most of the problematic cases mentioned in the DOJ report were either cases Pabst had handled directly or cases managed by other prosecutors under her supervision.

While campaigning to run the county attorney's office, Pabst disputed the veracity of the DOJ allegations. And if some cases had been mishandled by MCAO prosecutors while she was working there, she suggested, Fred Van Valkenburg was to blame. "I was in a place where I was really trying to effectuate positive change and I was running into barriers and it was difficult to do," Pabst told *Missoulian* reporter Kathryn Haake. "As county attorney, I will be in a better place to make that happen."

But if Pabst were to win the election and become county attorney, Haake pointed out, returning to the MCAO as *la patrona* was likely to be awkward, in light of criticisms some of her former workmates had made about Pabst's tactics during the Johnson trial. Haake noted,

> Deputy County Attorney Jen Clark said Pabst employed rape stereotypes and rape myths in her defense of Johnson. Clark admits that defense attorneys use such tactics, but it was shocking to witness that coming from a former colleague and prosecutor, she said. . . .
>
> "In the last couple of years, [Pabst] wasn't very engaged as a supervisor and a mentor," Clark said.
>
> Clark also offered that her former boss "burned bridges" with other agencies, like First Step, Just Response and the Crime Victim Advocates Office.
>
> "I am concerned about the future working relationships and communication with those agencies, particularly when dealing with sexual assault cases," Clark said.

In an article posted on the website BuzzFeed, Katie J. M. Baker reported that Fred Van Valkenburg dismissed Kirsten Pabst's attempts to deny responsibility for the MCAO's problems and throw him under the bus instead. "I don't take her statements about 'it's time to move the County Attorney's Office in a new direction,'" Van Valkenburg told Katie Baker, "as anything more than political rhetoric calculated to help her get elected." According to Baker, Van Valkenburg said that when Pabst was chief criminal deputy attorney, she had free rein to establish any policy she thought was appropriate: "She was an integral part of the management of this office for over five years."

Kirsten Pabst was running against two opponents in a primary election scheduled for June 3, 2014. Her rivals were Jason Marks, an assistant chief criminal deputy attorney at the MCAO who had worked under Pabst from 2007 until she quit in 2012, and Josh Van de Wetering, who'd served as Cecilia Washburn's personal attorney, pro bono, throughout both the University of Montana's adjudication of her case against Jordan Johnson and the criminal prosecution of Johnson by the MCAO. Because all three candidates were Democrats, and no Republican had registered to run, whoever won the primary would be the next Missoula county attorney.

Jason Marks had declared his candidacy in November 2013, a week before Pabst announced that she was entering the race. Marks pledged to cooperate with the DOJ, institute new policies for prosecuting cases, and improve communication with victims. But the MCAO's reputation took such a savage hit from the DOJ investigation that in March 2014, a number of Marks's supporters, including Missoula Mayor John Engen, urged him to suspend his campaign. Two months before the election, Marks dropped out of the running, explaining in a press release,

> It has been difficult separating my work, and that of my colleagues, from the controversial issues surrounding this office and the DOJ investigation. I have heard loud and clear that voters feel it's important to have someone outside the office become the next county attorney.

If Missoula voters wanted their next county attorney to be someone untainted by the failings of the MCAO under Van Valkenburg and Pabst, Josh Van de Wetering appeared to be in a perfect position to win the election. Although he'd worked as a deputy Missoula County attorney for two years early in his career, he'd left in 1998, just before Fred Van Valkenburg started running the MCAO, to work for the DOJ as an assistant United States attorney. Van de Wetering was a well-regarded federal prosecutor when he quit in 2008 to go into private practice. In his campaign to become the new Missoula county attorney, he pledged to make sexual assault and violence against women "a top priority" and said he was eager to take "difficult cases" to trial and allow juries to determine the outcome.

Kirsten Pabst, however, wasn't about to concede the election to Van de Wetering. Partnering with David Paoli to keep Jordan Johnson out of jail had made Pabst wildly popular with legions of Griz fans who were eager to see her defeat the lawyer who'd represented Johnson's accuser—"the little woman who lied about rape," as a female fan described Cecilia Washburn on an Internet forum.

During the 2012 football season, when Jordan Johnson was forbidden to play because he'd been charged with raping Washburn, the Griz won only five games and lost six. After he was found not guilty, during the 2013 season—which was under way when Pabst announced her candidacy—Johnson led the team to ten wins, three losses, and the FCS play-offs. This dramatic turnaround did not escape the attention of Pabst or anyone else in Missoula. She often boasted of her role in Johnson's acquittal on the campaign trail, and she featured the verdict prominently on her website.

Although Pabst worked shoulder to shoulder with Paoli to defend Johnson, she did not join Paoli's law firm. While practicing law as her own, one-woman firm, though, Pabst leased office space from Paoli's firm, and when she decided to run for Missoula County attorney, Paoli volunteered to run her campaign. To raise funds for her, he created a political action committee, which he christened Montanans for Veracity, Diversity and Work, or MVDW—a cheeky reference to Van de Wetering's initials. With Paoli's support, Pabst conducted an extremely negative campaign, attacking Van de Wetering without letup.

In a breathtaking display of chutzpah, given her attacks on Cecilia Washburn in the Jordan Johnson trial and her reluctance to prosecute rape cases when she was chief deputy county attorney, Pabst used her resignation from the county attorney's office in March 2012, just before the DOJ investigation got rolling, to portray herself as a reformer and a longtime victim's advocate. On a candidate questionnaire, she explained that she was running for the head prosecutor's job because

> [t]he next Missoula County Attorney needs the leadership, experience and vision to bring the office in a new direction. We need to restore the public trust through accountability, education and transparency. It is time for this divided community to begin healing. . . . I am committed to better delivery of services to victims of crime . . . through cooperation, communication and compassion.

Compassion, Pabst emphasized, would be one of her primary objectives if elected:

> Victims of crime are thrust into the court process through no fault of their own. Compassion means that we need to treat victims the way we would treat our own family, being conscientious of their trauma and fear while helping them navigate the criminal justice system, without forfeiting objectivity.

With the help of the MVDW PAC that Paoli established for her, Pabst received $29,000 in campaign contributions, more than three times as much money as Van de Wetering, who was not supported by a PAC. Among the most generous contributors to Pabst's campaign was Paoli's fellow defense lawyer and Griz booster Milt Datsopoulos. Four days before the election, MVDW mailed out thousands of flyers asking, "Can we trust Josh Van de Wetering to be our County Attorney?" The answer, according to MVDW, was no.

On June 3, 2014, after Missoulians went to the polls and the votes were tallied, Pabst received 7,762 votes, Van de Wetering received 4,559 votes, and Jason Marks received 1,018 votes. Kirsten Pabst was declared the presumptive Missoula County attorney, and was slated to begin her four-year term on January 1, 2015.

Six weeks after the election, the Montana commissioner of political practices, Jonathan Motl, ruled that MVDW had knowingly violated Montana law by failing to disclose campaign expenditures during the final days of Pabst's campaign. Motl declared that both Van de Wetering and the public had been denied their right to know, prior to the election, exactly how much Pabst had spent for such things as the mailing that smeared Van de Wetering. Motl determined that the violation of Montana's campaign practices laws by Paoli and MVDW's treasurer, J. Michael Barrett, "was by choice and deliberate."

Paoli and Barrett were required to pay a fine, but the amount was still being negotiated more than eight months after the election. Even though Pabst shared an office with Paoli and they'd worked together closely on her campaign, Motl uncovered no documents or other hard evidence indicating that Pabst and Paoli had "coordinated" on the expenditure of campaign contributions. The results of the elections were allowed to stand without challenge, and Pabst was not penalized in any way.

On June 10, 2014, a week after Kirsten Pabst was elected county attorney, Fred Van Valkenburg, now a lame duck, ceded to the inevitable, reluctantly abandoned his lawsuit against the Department of Justice, and agreed to comply with its directives for improving the prosecution of sexual assaults. Nevertheless, at a public event memorializing the agreement, Van Valkenburg stood at the podium and let it be known that he hadn't given up the fight willingly.

Continuing to insist that the DOJ had no jurisdiction over his office, Van Valkenburg groused that the unsparing report issued four months earlier by Acting Assistant U.S. Attorney General Jocelyn Samuels "was the single most unprofessional thing I have seen in my practice of law in forty-one years. It hurts hugely to see my staff defamed. . . . I can't tell the number of sleepless nights I've had thinking about how this happened. Why did the United States Department of Justice do what they did here?"

As Van Valkenburg uttered these words, Jocelyn Samuels was standing a few feet away. After he finished speaking, she made it clear that she disagreed with his assessment of the DOJ's investigation. If the lawsuit hadn't been dropped, and the DOJ had been forced to go to trial, Samuels stated, "I am confident we would have prevailed.* That said, today is a day for looking forward."

* Samuels is probably right. A tightly reasoned paper titled "Improving Prosecution of Sexual Assault Cases," by Amy Knight Burns (published in the *Stanford Law Review Online* in July 2014), makes a powerful argument that the DOJ did in fact have legal authority to both investigate and sue the MCAO. While acknowledging that "prosecutors generally receive significant immunity for their choices and are subject to little supervision," Burns states, "[t]he Missoula County Attorney . . . is an elected official. If he is not required to answer to any investigation concerning his failure to protect constitutional rights of a large group of constituents, a slim majority, or even a plurality, of voters could continue to support an unconstitutional regime that deprives a large number of citizens of rights to which they are entitled."

CHAPTER THIRTY-TWO

By the time Fred Van Valkenburg abandoned his suit against the Department of Justice and started preparing for his retirement, the underlying causes of the Missoula rape scandal were clear. The University of Montana, the Missoula Police Department, and the Missoula County Attorney's Office all shared responsibility.

Until media attention forced the university to take action, its policies for handling sexual-assault allegations were confusing and, occasionally, contradictory. Sometimes university officials didn't report sexual assaults to the Missoula police. Sometimes campus safety officers didn't report sexual assaults to the Missoula police. These mistakes were corrected quickly once they were recognized, however. A much thornier and more vexing problem was the popularity of the university's football program, along with the millions of dollars it contributed to the local economy. The adoration of the Griz football team created a pernicious atmosphere of entitlement. Coaches reinforced the team's sense of prerogative by failing to report athletes accused of sexual assault or other crimes to university officials.

For its part, the Missoula Police Department enabled rapists to escape accountability by neglecting to provide up-to-date training for detectives and patrol officers, which allowed hidebound stereotypes and invidious misconceptions about rape victims to undermine the effectiveness of sexual-assault investigations. To the police department's credit, soon after it was made aware of its shortcomings, it took significant steps to rectify them, even before the DOJ launched its investigation. In March 2012, for example, the police department enacted a new policy requiring cops to begin sexual-assault investigations by believing the claims of victims—the policy that Kirsten Pabst and David Paoli so vehemently maligned at the Jordan Johnson trial. Additionally, as soon as the DOJ announced its investigation of the police department, it immediately agreed to cooperate with the feds, demonstrating a genuine desire to fix what was broken.

Which brings us to the Missoula County Attorney's Office. When apportioning blame for Missoula's rape crisis, it's fair to say that the MCAO deserves the lion's share. But its failings did not result, by and large, from incompetent deputy county attorneys. Most of the MCAO prosecutors are in fact talented, highly dedicated public servants. The fundamental cause of the breakdown, rather, was an office culture that neither encouraged prosecutors to aggressively pursue challenging cases nor provided them with the specialized training necessary to do so effectively. The many bungled cases, that is to say, resulted from the failure of Kirsten Pabst and Fred Van Valkenburg to give their staff the guidance, training, and support they needed to be effective.

As the DOJ report pointed out, the successful prosecution of rape cases—particularly cases involving non-stranger rape—requires a sophisticated grasp of the latest legal and scientific knowledge. "It is imperative," the report admonished, "for state and local prosecutors to be aware of rape myths and how juries may be influenced by these myths." Prosecutors needed to understand the neurochemical basis for the counterintuitive behavior that victims often display during sexual assaults, and in their aftermath. They had to be able to explain to juries why rape victims don't always respond in a manner that conforms to jurors' expectations, as well as why victims may not be able to recall the details of being raped. Prior to the initiation of the DOJ investigation, the report noted, "the County Attorney's Office provided little, if any, such training."

The prosecutors' inadequate training not only impeded the effectiveness of the MCAO, it also impeded the ability of the police department to carry out its duties. Police detectives, according to the DOJ report, were "frustrated" by the refusal of the MCAO to prosecute seemingly strong cases:

> The work of Missoula Police detectives is compromised by the fact that, even if they expend the resources to conduct a comprehensive investigation, the Missoula County Attorney's Office often will not charge the case. One woman reported that the Missoula Police detective in her case informed her that because "no one had a limb cut off and there was no video of the incident," prosecutors "wouldn't see this [the rape] as anything more than a girl getting drunk at a party." . . . [I]n one case from early 2013, a detective told both the victim and the offender . . . that the County Attorney's office would never file charges in the case—despite the fact that the detective acknowledged to the victim that she had been raped by the offender.

After reviewing police files for more than three hundred sexual-assault cases, a prosecutorial expert brought in to assist the DOJ investigators concluded that in some instances, "Missoula Police officers had developed substantial evidence to support prosecution, but MCAO, without documented explanation, declined to charge the case." This expert noted that the county attorney's office refused to prosecute some sexual-assault cases even when detectives provided prosecutors with a confession or an eyewitness.

Between 2008 and 2010, every time the Missoula police referred a case to the MCAO for prosecution, detectives included a form that prosecutors were supposed to fill out if they rejected the case, explaining their reasons for doing so. But prosecutors "rarely documented their decision to decline prosecution in a meaningful way," according to the DOJ report. The most common explanation written on the referral forms was simply "insufficient evidence" or "insufficient corroboration." In cases submitted after 2010, DOJ investigators discovered that prosecutors didn't bother returning the forms at all. This was extremely frustrating to the police detectives, because they were the ones who had to inform victims that their cases had been closed, but they weren't given any specific information they could offer to these victims about why the MCAO had declined to prosecute.

In one case described in the DOJ report, the Missoula police obtained a confession from a man who admitted raping a woman while she was unconscious. The Missoula police referred the case to the county attorney's office with a recommendation that the prosecutor charge the suspect with rape, but the county attorney's office declined to file any charges, citing "insufficient evidence." In another case, the report continues,

> the Missoula Police obtained incriminating statements from a suspect who admitted to having intercourse with a mentally ill woman, including statements that he couldn't "determine" how soon he had stopped having sex with the woman after she asked him to stop and told him he was causing her "vagina" to "hurt." The Missoula Police referred the case to the County Attorney's Office, recommending that the prosecutor charge the suspect with sexual intercourse without consent. Despite the incriminating statements, the County Attorney's Office declined to bring any charges in the case.

THE MISSOULA RAPE crisis aired a lot of unpleasant truths and generated no small amount of anguish. More than a few of those tainted by the scandal remain in denial, like Fred Van Valkenburg. But the reforms prompted by the *Missoulian*'s reporting and the subsequent DOJ investigation were significant, nevertheless. The revamped practices have already increased the likelihood that any given sexual assault in Missoula will be successfully prosecuted, even with Kirsten Pabst now running the Missoula County Attorney's Office. The agreement between Van Valkenburg, the Montana attorney general, and the U.S. Department of Justice requires the MCAO to submit to two years of oversight by an independent "Technical Advisor," who will be paid $150,000 to keep close tabs on the effectiveness of the MCAO under Pabst's leadership.

It should be reiterated, moreover, that the deficiencies at the heart of the Missoula imbroglio were not unique to western Montana. The DOJ investigation identified 350 sexual assaults of women that were reported to the Missoula police during the fifty-two months from January 2008 to May 2012. The Bureau of Justice Statistics estimated that in 2010, the annual rate of sexual assaults of women in cities with populations under 100,000 was 0.27 percent, which for Missoula* equates to 90 female victims per year, or 390 over a period of fifty-two months. This suggests that, rather than being the nation's rape capital, Missoula had an incidence of sexual assault that was in fact slightly less than the national average. That's the real scandal.

Part of the reason so many rapists are able to offend with impunity is that our adversarial system of justice "has erected formidable procedural obstacles to conviction,"† as Richard A. Posner explains in his book *The Problems of Jurisprudence:*

> These have succeeded in reducing the probability of convicting innocent persons to an extremely low level, but the price is that many guilty persons are acquitted (especially those who can afford to hire top-quality lawyers), or are allowed to plead guilty to crimes much less serious than those they actually committed.

Posner, the most cited legal scholar in the country, is a Republican who was nominated by President Ronald Reagan to a seat on

* According to 2010 census data, the female population of Missoula was 33,456.

† Unless the defendant can't afford a good lawyer, of course. But that's a topic for another day.

the U.S. Court of Appeals for the Seventh Circuit. And here's what a liberal Democrat, Harvard Law School professor Alan Dershowitz, has to say about our adversarial justice system in his provocative book *The Best Defense:*

> I have learned that despite the constitutional presumption of innocence, the vast majority of criminal defendants are in fact guilty of the crimes with which they are charged. Almost all of my own clients have been guilty. . . .
>
> I am not unique in representing guilty defendants. That is what most defense attorneys do most of the time. The Perry Mason image of the heroic defender of innocent victims of frame-ups or mistaken identification is television fiction. . . .
>
> Once I decide to take a case, I have only one agenda: I want to win. I will try, by every fair and legal means, to get my client off—without regard to the consequences. . . .
>
> There's an old story about the lawyer who has just won a big case for his client and cables him: "Justice has prevailed." The client fires off a return telegram: "Appeal immediately." The story underlines an important point about the realities of our legal system: nobody really wants justice. Winning is "the only thing" to most participants in the criminal justice system—just as it is to professional athletes. Criminal defendants, and their lawyers, certainly do not want justice; they want acquittals, or at least short sentences. . . .
>
> The courtroom oath—"to tell the truth, the whole truth and nothing but the truth"—is applicable only to witnesses. Defense attorneys, prosecutors, and judges don't take this oath—they couldn't! Indeed, it is fair to say the American justice system is built on a foundation of not telling the whole truth. It is the job of the defense attorney—especially when representing the guilty—to prevent, by all lawful means, the "whole truth" from coming out.

Because the legal system stacks the deck more heavily against sexual-assault victims than victims of other crimes, it's easier to keep the whole truth from coming out when the defendant in question has been charged with rape. It's part of the cost of the constitutional right to due process.

Nevertheless, a small but influential cadre of cops, prosecutors, and academics has developed a set of "best practices" that can help prosecutors win more rape trials, even while scrupulously respecting the rights of the accused. These practices have been systematized by the National District Attorneys Association and End Violence Against Women International, and they are now being taught to cops and prosecutors nationwide. Seminars are offered in such subjects as the science of trauma, in order to improve techniques for interviewing rape victims and help prosecutors debunk rape myths when they face skeptical jurors.

Similar skills are being taught to university adjudicators of sexual-assault cases. But holding campus rapists accountable presents a set of unique challenges, because the university adjudication process hasn't been standardized and, thus, varies tremendously from one institution to another. A handful of colleges and universities have established effective systems for investigating and resolving rape allegations, but at too many institutions of higher learning, the procedures for adjudicating sexual-assault cases bring to mind a goat rodeo and are fair neither to victims nor those accused of assaulting them. Some of the country's most esteemed universities (Harvard being a prime example) have the most dysfunctional, poorly conceived sexual-assault policies.

In April 2014, to encourage universities to come to grips with the problem, President Barack Obama released a report titled "Not Alone," which announced a detailed plan to provide schools with protocols for improving their response to sexual assaults. A few days later, to turn up the heat, the U.S. Department of Education's Office for Civil Rights publicized a list of fifty-five colleges and universities under investigation for violating federal laws concerning the handling of sexual-violence complaints. The list, which has since grown to more than ninety schools, includes many high-profile institutions, among them Harvard; Princeton; Dartmouth; Amherst; the University of California, Berkeley; the University of Colorado; the University of Denver; the University of Connecticut; Florida State; Emory; the University of Chicago; Boston University; the University of Massachusetts, Amherst; Michigan State; Sarah Lawrence; Ohio State; Swarthmore; Temple; Vanderbilt; and Southern Methodist University.

Critics have attacked the Obama administration's plan, insisting that universities have no business adjudicating sexual assaults. The American Council of Trustees and Alumni (ACTA), a conservative organization founded by Lynne Cheney, the wife of former vice president Dick Cheney, has been one of the most vocal critics. In a statement released to the media in June 2014, ACTA president Anne D. Neal wrote,

> Sexual assault is a serious matter.
>
> That is why Congress should vigorously oppose efforts by the Obama Administration and the Department of Education's Office of Civil Rights (OCR) to reduce criminal matters to sensitivity brigades on our college campuses.
>
> Rape and sexual assault are felonies and they are matters for the police and criminal justice system—not universities. The higher education community simply is not equipped to play judge, jury and executioner in matters that require the careful eye of police and jurists. Both accusers and the accused are given short shrift when due process and the Constitutional safeguards of the criminal justice system are swapped for amateur investigators and ad hoc college tribunals. . . .
>
> Title IX—which initially focused on gender equity in college sports—has now become a catch-all provision to justify massive federal intrusion. Congress should take steps immediately to roll back this unintended expansion, first, by defunding the OCR until there is public notice and rulemaking

> on these issues. OCR should not be allowed, for example, to lower evidentiary standards in disregard of Constitutional principles and Americans' deep respect for due process—by bureaucratic fiat. . . .
>
> It should come as no surprise that, when students admit to spending a majority of their time sleeping and socializing, as they do today, they fill the void created by a lack of academic rigor and substance with drinking and extreme behaviors.

In a *Washington Post* column published in June 2014, George Will, the Pulitzer Prize–winning author and Fox News pundit, disparaged Obama's efforts to address what Will dismissed as "the supposed campus epidemic of rape, a.k.a. 'sexual assault.'" After accusing the White House of making "victimhood a coveted status that confers privileges" and, thus, encourages victims to "proliferate," Will further complained,

> Now the Obama administration is riding to the rescue of "sexual assault" victims. It vows to excavate equities from the ambiguities of the hookup culture, this cocktail of hormones, alcohol and the faux sophistication of today's prolonged adolescence of especially privileged young adults. . . . Academia is learning that its attempts to create victim-free campuses—by making everyone hypersensitive, even delusional, about victimizations—brings increasing supervision by the regulatory state that progressivism celebrates.

The reaction to Will's remarks was caustic and swift. "The last word I ever expected to hear to describe a rape victim is 'privileged,'" wrote Jessica Valenti in the *Guardian*. "It takes a particular kind of ignorance to argue that people who come forward to report being raped in college are afforded benefits of any kind."

United States Senators Richard Blumenthal of Connecticut, Dianne Feinstein of California, Tammy Baldwin of Wisconsin, and Robert Casey of Pennsylvania posted a letter to Will online, blaming him for fostering a culture that enables rape:

> [Y]ou trivialize the scourge of sexual assault, putting the phrase in scare quotes and treating this crime as a socially acceptable phenomenon. It is in fact a spreading epidemic, and you legitimize the myths that victims and victim advocates have worked tirelessly for decades to combat.
>
> Your column reiterates ancient beliefs about sexual assault that are inconsistent with the reality of victims' experiences, based on what we have heard directly from survivors.

Despite the deeply flawed ways that many universities investigate and adjudicate rape allegations, it's important that they not be allowed to abdicate their institutional responsibility and simply turn over sexual-assault cases to law enforcement agencies, as ACTA president Anne Neal, and others, have argued they should. Criminal investigations of students accused of rape should be undertaken *in addition* to universities' disciplinary proceedings, not in lieu of them. The criminal justice system simply moves too slowly and is constrained by too many "formidable procedural obstacles," as Judge Posner put it, to reliably punish campus rapists and remove them from the academic community. Expelling a rapist isn't an ideal outcome, because the offender remains on the loose, free to rape elsewhere. Expulsion is far better than no punishment at all, however. At least it spares the victim from having to live and study in close proximity to her assailant.

The oft-repeated claim that university adjudications categorically deny the constitutional right of due process to perpetrators is specious. Campus disciplinary proceedings cannot, and should not, be held to the same restrictive standards as criminal proceedings, because they don't result in incarceration or require the rapist to register as a sex offender. University officials, like high school officials, must be allowed to expel students who pose a threat to other students, without waiting many months, or even years, for the criminal justice system to run its course—a course that all too often fails to convict individuals who are guilty of rape, or even charge them with a crime.

There is nothing inherently wrong with universities relying on a lower evidentiary standard—"a preponderance of evidence"—for the burden of proof. A preponderance of evidence is all that's required of plaintiffs to prevail in most civil litigation, even when the defendant has been accused of a wrongful act that violates criminal law. O. J. Simpson was infamously acquitted of the murders of Nicole Brown Simpson and Ron Goldman, because the government failed to convince a jury that Simpson was guilty of the criminal charges beyond a reasonable doubt. Nevertheless, when Simpson was found liable for the wrongful death of Goldman in a civil lawsuit by Goldman's father, based on a preponderance of the evidence, few Americans believed the verdict was unjust.

All colleges and universities require students to follow the rules of the institution they attend. If a student violates school policy by failing classes, or cheating on exams, or dealing drugs, or sexually assaulting another student, school officials not only have the right to sanction the offending student, they have an obligation to do so.

When a student is accused of sexual assault, a university needs to render its judgment with great care, because to be labeled a rapist carries an indelible stigma, and to incorrectly find the student guilty could cause him lasting harm. But a university needs to take just as much care not to incorrectly find the student innocent, because doing so would send the message that he was falsely accused, unjustly stigmatizing the victim and compounding the trauma of being raped. It's easy to forget that the harm done to a rape victim who is disbelieved can be at least as devastating as the harm done to an innocent man who is unjustly accused of rape. And without question, the former happens much more frequently than the latter.

Females between sixteen and twenty-four years old face a higher risk of being sexually assaulted than any other age group. Most victims of campus rape are preyed upon when they are in their first or second year of college, usually by someone they know. And it's during the initial days and weeks of a student's freshman year, when she is in the midst of negotiating the fraught transition from girlhood to womanhood, that she is probably in the greatest danger.

Instead of shirking their legal and moral obligations by leaving it up to law enforcement agencies to protect female students, universities need to formulate procedures for adjudicating sexual-assault complaints that are uniform, streamlined, and fair to all parties. The process should swiftly identify student offenders and prevent them from reoffending, while simultaneously safeguarding the rights of the accused. Establishing such a process will be difficult, but it's not rocket science. The challenge can be met, and must be met, because failing to do so would be unconscionable.

IN 2012 I LEARNED that Laura Summers,* a woman in her late twenties with whom my wife and I have a close relationship, had been raped when she was in her mid-teens by a male peer. A few years later she was sexually assaulted by a different acquaintance; this time the perpetrator was a trusted family friend. The men who assaulted her didn't just steal her innocence; they poisoned her understanding of who she was. They transformed her into a kind of ghost, trapped forever in the act of being violated.

In the wake of these betrayals, Laura sought relief by focusing obsessively on her career, sometimes working forty-eight hours or more without a break. She gobbled Adderall to stay awake and guzzled alcohol to fall asleep, following this regimen for years with grim perseverance. It was an unconscious attempt to annihilate herself, she now recognizes, in order to escape the despair that hounded her without respite.

I wasn't aware that Laura had been assaulted, or was so disconsolate, until she ended up at The Meadows, a facility in Arizona that treats trauma and addiction. During the period that preceded her arrival there, Laura repeatedly found herself engaging in one-

* pseudonym

night stands with uncaring men. She told me that while she was at The Meadows, "I learned about the concept of 'trauma repetition,'* and my therapists identified for me that my sexual acting-out was a reaction to the trauma of being sexually assaulted—self-destructive behavior that happened almost entirely when I was highly inebriated, the same conditions of the original assaults." She was trying to take back control of her life from the men who had raped her. It was a heartbreaking effort to make the world safe again.

Laura suffered intensely for many years from being sexually assaulted. And her misery, she said, was magnified by the stigma attached to the unhealthy compulsions that tyrannized her existence after the assaults. In this regard she was like many other rape victims. Their self-destructive behaviors are often held up as "proof" that they are unreliable and morally compromised, or that they deserved to be raped.

AFTER LAURA TOLD me about what she'd endured, I was angry with myself for being so uninformed—not only about her ordeal but about non-stranger rape in general. So I resolved to learn what I could about it. I did a lot of reading, and I sought out rape survivors who were willing to share their stories. Writing this book was an outgrowth of that quest.

As the scope of my research expanded, I was stunned to discover that many of my acquaintances, and even several women in my own family, had been sexually assaulted by men they trusted. The more I listened to these women's accounts, the more disturbed I became. I'd had no idea that rape was so prevalent, or could cause such deep and intractable pain. My ignorance was inexcusable, and it made me ashamed.

For five months in 2006 and 2007, while doing research for an earlier book, I was embedded with combat troops in Afghanistan. After that book was published, some veterans I'd come to respect

* Another term for what Sigmund Freud called the "repetition compulsion."

urged me to join their weekly group therapy sessions. Over the years that followed, several vets in the group—soldiers and Marines who had served in Vietnam, Iraq, and Afghanistan—talked movingly about their struggles with post-traumatic stress. And some of what they described sounded a lot like what Laura was grappling with.

When I mentioned this to Trisha Dittrick, the therapist who supervised our group, she told me she wasn't surprised. Rape and war, she explained, are among the most common causes of post-traumatic stress disorder, and survivors of sexual assault frequently exhibit many of the same symptoms and behaviors as survivors of combat: flashbacks, insomnia, nightmares, hypervigilance, depression, isolation, suicidal thoughts, outbursts of anger, unrelenting anxiety, and an inability to shake the feeling that the world is spinning out of control.

There is no "cure" for PTSD. The repercussions of severe emotional trauma, whether from war or rape, are typically felt for decades. But there are ways to transcend the trauma and recapture the ordinary pleasures of existence. Counseling from a skilled therapist can certainly help. And so can speaking the truth about the unspeakable nature of the harm. By such means, Laura Summers managed to regain her equilibrium and find a measure of peace. A significant part of her healing, she said, came from sharing the excruciating facts of her ordeal with her family and friends after suffering in secret for so long.

Rapists rely on the silence of their victims to elude accountability. Simply by recounting their stories and breaking that silence, survivors of sexual assault strike a powerful blow against their assailants. Inevitably, many victims who come forward will be disbelieved, and will fail to find justice in the courts, in the halls of academia, or anywhere else. But by speaking out, they are likely to encourage other victims to tell their stories, too, and may find that they've advanced their own recovery in the bargain. As more and more survivors emerge from the shadows and reveal the pervasiveness of sexual assault, they draw strength from their numbers. This collective fortitude touches all victims, even those too fearful to speak for themselves, by eradicating the undeserved sense of shame that is so often borne in isolation.

DRAMATIS PERSONAE

Note: An asterisk following a name denotes a pseudonym.

Adams, Zeke*: University of Montana student accused of sexually assaulting Kerry Barrett in September 2011.

Aronofsky, David: University of Montana's chief legal counsel; he participated in the university's adjudications of Calvin Smith for the 2011 rape of Kaitlynn Kelly and of Grizzly quarterback Jordan Johnson for the alleged 2012 rape of Cecilia Washburn.

Baker, Guy: Veteran Missoula police detective who investigated the 2010 rape of Allison Huguet by Beau Donaldson and the alleged 2010 gang rape of Kelsey Belnap.

Banks, Brian: Student falsely accused of raping Wanetta Gibson in Long Beach, California, in 2002. Banks served more than five years in prison before Gibson admitted that Banks had not raped her.

Barrett, Kerry: University of Montana student who accused Zeke Adams of sexually assaulting her in September 2011.

Barz, Diane: Former Montana Supreme Court justice who conducted an investigation into the apparent eruption of rapes at the University of Montana in 2010 and 2011.

Belnap, Kelsey: University of Montana student who was allegedly gang-raped by four members of the Grizzly football team in December 2010.

Bienemann, Alex: University of Montana football player who was a housemate of Grizzly quarterback Jordan Johnson when Johnson allegedly raped Cecilia Washburn in February 2012.

Bierer, Ali: Friend of Cecilia Washburn who urged her to have a forensic medical examination at the First Step Resource Center after Washburn told Bierer she had been raped by Grizzly quarterback Jordan Johnson in February 2012.

Blood, Mark: Missoula police detective who partnered with Detective Guy Baker to investigate the rape of Allison Huguet in September 2010 and the rape of Kelsey Belnap in December 2010.

Boylan, Suzy: Missoula County prosecutor who participated in the prosecution of Beau Donaldson for raping Allison Huguet in 2010 and the prosecution of Jordan Johnson in 2012.

Brady, Mike: Missoula police chief who succeeded Chief Mark Muir after Muir retired, in December 2013.

Brueckner, Connie: Missoula police detective who investigated the October 2011 rape of Kaitlynn Kelly by Calvin Smith and the alleged February 2012 rape of Cecilia Washburn by Grizzly quarterback Jordan Johnson.

Burton, Katie: Missoula probation and parole officer assigned to the Beau Donaldson case.

Campbell, Tanya: Missoula crime-victim advocate.

Cates, Irina: Reporter for the Missoula television station KPAX who broke the news that University of Montana quarterback Jordan Johnson had allegedly raped Cecilia Washburn in February 2012.

Clark, Jennifer: A Missoula County prosecutor.

Cotter, Michael: U.S. attorney for the District of Montana, married to Montana Supreme Court Justice Patricia O'Brien Cotter.

Couture, Charles: University of Montana dean of students who conducted investigations of the alleged 2010 gang rape of Kelsey Belnap by four Griz football players, the 2011 rape of Kaitlynn Kelly by Calvin Smith, and the alleged 2012 rape of Cecilia Washburn by Grizzly quarterback Jordan Johnson.

Datsopoulos, Milton: Defense lawyer who represented Beau Donaldson when he was charged with the 2010 rape of Allison Huguet.

Donaldson, Beau: Grizzly football player convicted of raping Allison Huguet in September 2010.

Donaldson, Brady: Older brother of Beau Donaldson, the Grizzly football player convicted of raping Allison Huguet in September 2010.

Donaldson, Cathy: Mother of Beau Donaldson, the Grizzly football player convicted of raping Allison Huguet in September 2010.

Donaldson, Larry: Father of Beau Donaldson, the Grizzly football player convicted of raping Allison Huguet in September 2010.

Donovan, Shaun: Missoula County prosecutor who participated in the prosecution of Beau Donaldson, the Grizzly football player convicted of raping Allison Huguet in September 2010.

Duerk, Adam: Missoula lawyer, deputized as a special prosecutor, who participated in the prosecution of Grizzly quarterback Jordan Johnson for allegedly raping Cecilia Washburn in February 2012.

Engen, John: Mayor of Missoula.

Engstrom, Royce: President of the University of Montana.

Erschler, Sam*: Friend of Allison Huguet and Beau Donaldson.

Eustace, Bob: Teacher and football coach at Missoula's Big Sky High School who coached Beau Donaldson.

Fairmont, Betsy*: Friend of Kelsey Belnap who was present when Belnap was allegedly gang-raped in December 2010.

Fargo, Joanne*: Jury member at the trial of Jordan Johnson for allegedly raping Cecilia Washburn.

Florio, Gwen: Senior reporter for the *Missoulian* whose numerous articles exposed the Missoula rape scandal.

Foley, Jim: Vice president for external relations at the University of Montana who resigned after playing a controversial role in the university's rape scandal. Prior to serving as UM vice president, Foley had been chief of staff for Pat Williams, a member of the U.S. House of Representatives from Montana.

Francoeur, Claire: Nurse-practitioner at the First Step Resource Center who performed forensic examinations of Allison Huguet after she was raped by Beau Donaldson in September 2010, Kelsey Belnap after she was allegedly gang-raped by four Grizzly football players in December 2010, and Cecilia

Washburn after she was allegedly raped by Griz quarterback Jordan Johnson in February 2012.

Froland, Kelli: University of Montana student with whom Griz quarterback Jordan Johnson wanted to have a romantic relationship at the time he allegedly raped Cecilia Washburn in February 2012.

Green, Stephen: Friend and housemate of Cecilia Washburn; Green was playing a video game just outside the door of her bedroom when Washburn was allegedly raped by Griz quarterback Jordan Johnson in February 2012.

Haake, Kathryn: Reporter for the *Missoulian*.

Herr, Rudy: Youth pastor and childhood football coach to University of Montana quarterback Jordan Johnson who testified as a character witness for Johnson at his trial for allegedly raping Cecilia Washburn.

Huguet, Allison: Longtime friend of University of Montana football player Beau Donaldson who was raped by Donaldson in September 2010.

Huguet, Beth: Mother of Allison Huguet and first wife of Kevin Huguet.

Huguet, Kathleen: Younger sister of Allison Huguet.

Huguet, Kevin: Father of Allison Huguet.

Huguet, Margie: Second wife of Kevin Huguet and stepmother of Allison Huguet.

Huguet, Sarah: Older sister of Allison Huguet.

Johnson, Jordan: University of Montana quarterback accused of raping Cecilia Washburn in February 2012.

Johnson, Marty: Father of Jordan Johnson.

Johnson, Trumaine: University of Montana football player (unrelated to Jordan Johnson) arrested in December 2011 for assaulting another student at a party. Johnson became a star cornerback for the St. Louis Rams after leaving UM.

Jones, Nancy*: University of Montana roommate of Kaitlynn Kelly who was present when Kelly was raped by Calvin Smith in October 2011.

Kato, Dillon: Reporter for the *Montana Kaimin* who wrote about the sexual assaults of two University of Montana students by a Saudi exchange student in February 2012.

Keck, Darla: Lawyer in Milt Datsopoulos's law firm who provided free legal representation to Griz cornerback Trumaine Johnson in December 2011 when he was charged with disorderly conduct and resisting arrest.

Kelly, Kaitlynn: University of Montana student who was raped by Calvin Smith in October 2011.

Lacny, Peter: One of two lawyers representing Beau Donaldson at the January 2013 hearing to determine Beau Donaldson's sentence for raping Allison Huguet in September 2010.

Lang, Mitchell: Missoula police officer who interviewed Kelsey Belnap at the hospital after she was allegedly gang-raped in December 2010.

Lisak, David: Clinical psychologist who is one of the nation's foremost experts on rape and its associated trauma.

Marks, Jason: Prosecutor in the Missoula County Attorney's Office.

McGowan, Michael: Chaplain for the University of Montana football team who testified as a character witness for Jordan Johnson at his trial for allegedly raping Cecilia Washburn.

McLaughlin, Hillary: Resident of Great Falls, Montana, who was sexually assaulted by Beau Donaldson in Missoula in 2008.

Merifield, Jamie: Missoula police detective who investigated Zeke Adams's alleged sexual assault of Kerry Barrett.

Moore, Michael: *Missoulian* reporter who wrote an article about the gang rape of Kelsey Belnap.

Morin, Lori: Assistant dean for student affairs at the University of Montana School of Pharmacy when Cecilia Washburn, who was one of her students, was allegedly raped by Griz quarterback Jordan Johnson in February 2012.

Mortimer, Sharon*: Friend of Beau Donaldson and second cousin of Hillary McLaughlin, Mortimer was present at the 2008 party at which Donaldson attempted to rape McLaughlin.

Motl, Jonathan: Montana commissioner of political practices.

Muir, Mark: Missoula police chief.

Myers, Jim: One of two psychologists who evaluated Beau Donaldson after he was arrested in January 2012 for raping Allison Huguet.

O'Day, Jim: University of Montana athletic director who was fired in March 2012 as the Missoula rape scandal escalated.

Pabst, Kirsten: Missoula County prosecutor who declined to charge Calvin Smith with rape after he sexually assaulted Kaitlynn Kelly; shortly thereafter, Pabst resigned from the Missoula County Attorney's Office and became defense counsel for Griz quarterback Jordan Johnson when he was charged with raping Cecilia Washburn.

Page, Robert: One of two psychologists who evaluated Beau Donaldson after he was arrested in January 2012 for raping Allison Huguet.

Paoli, David: Defense counsel for University of Montana quarterback Jordan Johnson when he was accused of raping Cecilia Washburn in February 2012.

Perez, Thomas: Assistant attorney general for the Civil Rights Division of the U.S. Department of Justice who announced in May 2012 that the DOJ was investigating the way eighty sexual-assault cases had been handled by the Missoula County Attorney's Office, the Missoula Police Department, and the University of Montana.

Peterson, John: Missoula drywall contractor who employed Beau Donaldson.

Pflugrad, Robin: Head football coach at the University of Montana who was fired in March 2012 as the Missoula rape scandal escalated.

Richards, Ralph*: Friend of Calvin Smith who testified at the University Court hearing at which Smith was found guilty of raping Kaitlynn Kelly in 2011.

Roe, Rebecca: Seattle lawyer in the King County Prosecuting Attorney's Office from 1977 through 1994, where she supervised the Special Assault Unit for eleven years.

Ronan, Lewis*: Portland State University student who allegedly raped Keely Williams in September 2008.

Samuels, Jocelyn: Acting assistant U.S. attorney general in 2014, when the federal government settled its lawsuit with Missoula County Attorney Fred Van Valkenburg.

Sells, Paul: Clinical social worker who treated Beau Donaldson for drug and alcohol dependency after he was arrested in January 2012 for raping Allison Huguet.

Smith, Calvin*: University of Montana student who raped Kaitlynn Kelly in October 2011.

Smith, Mary*: Mother of Calvin Smith, who raped Kaitlynn Kelly in October 2011.

Styron, Benjamin*: University of Montana football player who was the boyfriend of Betsy Fairmont. Kelsey Belnap was allegedly gang-raped during a party at Styron's apartment in December 2010.

Sutherlin, Joanna*: Friend of Hillary McLaughlin who invited McLaughlin to a party at her home in 2008; there, Beau Donaldson tried to rape McLaughlin.

Thompson, Joel: Montana assistant attorney general who served as a prosecutor at the trial of University of Montana quarterback Jordan Johnson, who was accused of raping Cecilia Washburn in February 2012.

Townsend, Karen: Judge for Montana's Fourth District Court who sentenced Beau Donaldson for raping Allison Huguet; she also presided over the trial of University of Montana quarterback Jordan Johnson, who was accused of raping Cecilia Washburn in February 2012.

Trieweiler, Terry: Former justice on the Montana Supreme Court who wrote a 2013 opinion piece in the *Missoulian* in support of Pat Williams after Williams was widely criticized for remarking that the University of Montana football team "was recruiting too many thugs."

Tully, Bo: University of Montana football player who was a housemate of Grizzly quarterback Jordan Johnson when Johnson allegedly raped Cecilia Washburn in February 2012.

Van de Wetering, Josh: Missoula lawyer who represented Calvin Smith at the 2011 UM University Court hearing that found Smith guilty of raping Kaitlynn Kelly. Van de Wetering also served as Cecilia Washburn's personal attorney after she accused Griz quarterback Jordan Johnson of raping her in February 2012.

Van Valkenburg, Fred: Prosecutor in charge of the Missoula County Attorney's Office during the Missoula rape scandal.

Voorhees, Rhondie: University of Montana dean of students who replaced Charles Couture when he retired in July 2012.

Vreeland, Brian: Missoula police officer who interviewed Kerry Barrett on the night she was allegedly sexually assaulted by Zeke Adams in September 2011.

Washburn, Cecilia*: University of Montana student who was allegedly raped by Griz quarterback Jordan Johnson in February 2012.

Williams, Keely: Allison Huguet's close friend who was allegedly raped by Lewis Ronan in Portland, Oregon, in 2008. Williams was sleeping in a nearby bedroom when Huguet was raped by Beau Donaldson in September 2010.

Williams, Pat: Former U.S. congressman representing Montana from 1979 to 1997 was appointed to the Montana Board of Regents of Higher Education in 2012.

Witt, Greg*: Friend of Kaitlynn Kelly who urged her to invite Calvin Smith up to her dorm room on the night that Smith raped Kelly in 2011.

Wolken, Cynthia: Missoula city councilwoman who held a public forum in January 2012 to discuss the rash of unprosecuted rapes in Missoula.

ACKNOWLEDGMENTS

I am immensely grateful to Allison Huguet, Keely Williams, Hillary McLaughlin, Kerry Barrett, Kaitlynn Kelly, Kelsey Belnap, and Laura Summers for talking to me and trusting me to tell their stories. They are strong, courageous women.

For their important contributions to this book, I owe special thanks to Kevin Huguet, Beth Huguet, Margie Huguet, Joanne Fargo, Guy Baker, David Lisak, Josh Van de Wetering, Terry Trieweiler, Becky Hall, Sarah Sand, Rebecca Roe, Mike Meloy, Kimberly Hult, Bill Meyer, Michelle D'Arcy, Trisha Dittrick, Martin Shapiro, Catherine Rebish, Stephanie Morrow, Janet Foss, Bill Briggs, Pat Joseph, David Roberts, and Sharon Roberts.

At Penguin Random House, I am deeply indebted to Bill Thomas, Alison Rich, Kathy Trager, Rose Courteau, Bette Alexander, Andy Hughes, Kathy Hourigan, Maria Carella, John Fontana, Lorraine Hyland, John Pitts, Suzanne Herz, Beth Meister, Janet Cooke, Sonny Mehta, Carol Janeway, LuAnn Walther, Kate Runde, Catherine Tung, Amy Metsch, Anne Messitte, Russell Perreault, John Siciliano, Dan Zitt, Anke Steinecke, Laura Golden, Bill Shannon, Nancy Rich, Joelle Dieu, Serena Lehman, Deborah Foley, and Pauline James. Thanks to Bonnie Thompson for copyediting the manuscript.

For providing counsel, support, and inspiration over the years, thanks to Steve Rottler, Dave Jones, Roger Briggs, Roman Dial, Peggy Dial, Neal Beidleman, Amy Beidleman, Ron Harris, Mary Harris, Sally La Venture, Mike Pilling, Kerry Kirkpatrick, John Winsor, Bridget Winsor, David Trione, Michael Moore, Laura Brown, Helen Apthorp, Pamela Brown,

Ed Ward, Matt Hale, Chris Gulick, Deborah Shaw, Nick Miller, Mark Fagan, Sheila Cooley, Sam Brower, Tom Sam Steed, Carine McCandless, Mark Bryant, Tom Hornbein, Harry Kent, Owen Kent, Ruth Fecych, David Rosenthal, Charlie Conrad, Jonathan Southard, Masood Ahmad, Chip Lee, Erica Stone, Richard Blum, Greg Child, Chris Reveley, Annie Finley, Chris Wejchert, Monty McCutcheon, Martin Shapiro, Ray Meyers, Judy Nogg, Craig Brown, Denny Sedlack, Dan Janosko, Eric Ackerman, Christian Somoza, Scott Van Dyke, Lori Smith, Eric Zacharias, Coco Dughi, Jenny Feiger, Jeremy Rodgers, Ania Mohelicki, Marie Tillman, Sean Penn, Eddie Vedder, Amy Berg, Erica Huggins, Lance Black, Dan Stone, Charley Mace, Rick Accomazzo, Gerry Accomazzo, Dave Turner, Geoff Friefeld, Conrad Anker, Jenni Lowe-Anker, Steve Swenson, Pamela Hainsworth, David Quammen, Jimmy Chin, Renan Ozturk, Chai Vasarhelyi, Doug Chabot, Genevieve Chabot, Mike Alkaitis, Josh Jespersen, Jeremy Jones, Cecilia Perucci, Roberto Santachiara, Brian Nuttall, Christine Durnan, Drew Simon, Alexandra Martella, Eric Love, Josie Heath, Margaret Katz, Carol Krakauer, Karin Krakauer, Wendy Krakauer, Sarah Krakauer, Andrew Krakauer, Bill Costello, Tim Stewart, Robin Krakauer, Rosie Lingo, Ali Stewart, Shannon Costello, Maureen Costello, Ari Kohn, Miriam Kohn, Kelsi Krakauer, A. J. Krakauer, Devin Lingo, Zay Lingo, and Abilene Rose Lingo.

SELECTED BIBLIOGRAPHY

Armstrong, Ken, and Nick Perry. *Scoreboard, Baby: A Story of Football, Crime, and Complicity.* Lincoln: Bison Books, 2010.

Aronofsky, David. "Legal Issues & Recommendations." Memorandum to University of Montana President Royce Engstrom, February 28, 2012.

Atkinson, Matt. "Rape and False Reports." *Oklahoma Coalition Against Domestic Violence & Sexual Assaults.* www.ncdsv.org/images/OCADVSA_RapeAndFalseReports_2010.pdf.

Baker, Katie J. M. "Former Prosecutor Set to Take Over Missoula Office That Mistreated Rape Victims on Her Watch." BuzzFeed, April 15, 2014. http://www.buzzfeed.com/katiejmbaker/missoula-county-prosecutor-kirsten-pabst#.mv828lZ88X.

———. "My Weekend in America's So-Called 'Rape Capital.'" *Jezebel,* May 10, 2012. http://jezebel.com/5908472/my-weekend-in-americas-so-called-rape-capital.

———. "University of Montana Quarterback Charged with Rape." *Jezebel,* August 1, 2012. http://jezebel.com/5930780/university-of-montana-quarterback-charged-with-rape.

Barz, Diane. "Status Report." Letter to University of Montana President Royce Engstrom, December 31, 2011.

Bhargava, Anurima, and Gary Jackson. "RE DOJ Case No. DJ 169-44-9, OCR Case No. 10126001." U.S. Department of Justice and U.S. Department of Education Letter to University of Montana President Royce Engstrom and University Counsel Lucy France, May 9, 2013.

Bissinger, Buzz. "The Boys in the Clubhouse." *New York Times,* October 18, 2014.

Bloomekatz, Ari. "Brian Banks, Exonerated in Rape Case, Cut from Atlanta Falcons." *Los Angeles Times,* August 30, 2013.

Blumenthal, Richard, Dianne Feinstein, Tammy Baldwin, and Robert P. Casey, Jr. "Dear Mr. Will." Letter from United States Senators to George Will, *Politico,*

June 12, 2014. http://images.politico.com/global/2014/06/12/2014_06_12_george_will_letter.html.

Brady, Mike, and John Engen. "DOJ Decision Has Made Missoula Better." *Missoulian,* February 21, 2014.

Breiding, Matthew J., Sharon G. Smith, Kathleen C. Basile, Mikel L. Walters, Jieru Chen, and Melissa T. Merrick. "Prevalence and Characteristics of Sexual Violence, Stalking, and Intimate Partner Violence Victimization—National Intimate Partner and Sexual Violence Survey, United States, 2011." Report, Centers for Disease Control and Prevention, September 5, 2014.

Brownmiller, Susan. *Against Our Will: Men, Women, and Rape.* New York: Ballantine, 1993.

Bucks, Frances Marks. "Van Valkenburg's Ego-Based Fight Affects Community's Well-Being." *Missoulian,* January 15, 2014.

Burns, Amy Knight. "Improving Prosecution of Sexual Assault Cases." *Stanford Law Review Online,* 67, no. 17, July 5, 2014.

Cates, Irina. "Ex-Griz Donaldson Pleads Guilty to Rape." KPAX.com, September 11, 2012. http://www.kpax.com/news/ex-griz-donaldson-pleads-guilty-to-rape/.

———. "Griz QB Served with Restraining Order After Alleged Sexual Assault." KPAX.com, March 15, 2012. http://www.kpax.com/news/griz-qb-served-with-restraining-order-after-alleged-sexual-assault/.

Cohan, William D. *The Price of Silence: The Duke Lacrosse Scandal, the Power of the Elite, and the Corruption of Our Great Universities.* New York: Scribner, 2014.

Colb, Sherry F. "'Yes Means Yes' and Preponderance of Evidence." *Dorf on Law Blog,* October 29, 2014. http://www.dorfonlaw.org/2014/10/yes-means-yes-and-preponderance-of.html.

Culp-Ressler, Tara. "This Is Why One Study Showed 19% of College Women Experience Sexual Assault and Another Said 0.6%." *thinkprogress.org,* December 11, 2014. http://thinkprogress.org/health/2014/12/11/3602344/estimate-college-sexual-assault/.

Dederer, Claire. "Why Is It So Hard for Women to Write About Sex?" *Atlantic,* March 2014.

Dershowitz, Alan M. *The Best Defense.* New York: Vintage, 1983.

Doe, John, Plaintiff, vs. The University of Montana, Defendant. United States District Court for the District of Montana, Missoula. CV 12-77-M-DLC. Order, June 26, 2012.

Dougherty, Michael Brendan. "The Rape Culture That Everyone Ignores." *The Week,* December 9, 2014. https://theweek.com/articles/441689/rape-culture-that-everyone-ignores.

Engstrom, Royce. "Sexual Assault Report." Memorandum to UM Campus Community and Missoula Community, March 22, 2012.

Fletcher v. Montanans for Veracity, Diversity and Work. Commissioner of Political Practices of the State of Montana. No. COPP 2014-CFP-028. Dismissal of Complaint Against Kirsten Pabst, Summary of Facts and Findings of Sufficient Evidence to Show a Violation of Montana's Campaign Practices Act as to Montanans for Veracity, Diversity and Work, July 16, 2014.

Florio, Gwen. "Attorney: Ex-Griz Donaldson Will Plead Guilty to Rape Charge." *Missoulian,* September 5, 2012.

———. "Donaldson Pleads Guilty to Rape; Prosecution Wants 30-Year Sentence." *Missoulian,* September 11, 2012.

———. "Griz Football Player Jailed on Rape Charge." *Missoulian,* January 7, 2012.

———. "Griz QB Allowed Back at Practice by Legal Misunderstanding, Says Woman's Attorney." *Missoulian,* March 28, 2012.

———. "Justice Department Investigating 80 Missoula Rapes; County Attorney Blasts Feds." *Missoulian,* May 1, 2012.

———. "Lead Detective in Johnson Case: City Revised Policy on Sexual Assaults." *Missoulian,* February 22, 2013.

———. "Missoula County Attorney's Heir Apparent Leaving for Solo Practice." *Missoulian,* February 26, 2012.

———. "Missoula Police: 2nd Attack May Be Linked to Alleged Sex Assault Involving UM Football Players." *Missoulian,* December 20, 2011.

———. "Officials: Evidence Threshold Is High for Rape Charges." *Missoulian,* January 8, 2012.

———. "Research Varies on Frequency of False Rape Reports." *Missoulian,* January 7, 2012.

———. "Saudi Student Accused of UM Rape Has Fled the U.S." *Missoulian,* February 24, 2012.

———. "Student Says She Was Sexually Assaulted by UM Football Players; County Filed No Charges." *Missoulian,* December 21, 2011.

———. "3 UM Football Players Allegedly Involved in Sexual Assault on Campus." *Missoulian,* December 16, 2011.

———. "TRO Dismissed Against Griz QB; New Civil Agreement Forbids Contact with Accuser." *Missoulian,* March 24, 2012.

———. "UM Dean Implicated 4 Football Players in Gang Rape, Emails Reveal." *Missoulian,* May 19, 2012.

———. "UM Hires Outside Investigation of Alleged Sex Assault Involving Multiple Students, Victims." *Missoulian,* December 15, 2011.

———. "UM Keeps Mum on Reasons for O'Day, Pflugrad Firings." *Missoulian,* April 1, 2012.

———. "UM Student Accuses Grizzlies Quarterback of Rape." *Missoulian,* March 20, 2012.

———. "UM Vice President Sought to Punish Alleged Rape Victim, Emails Reveal." *Missoulian,* May 20, 2012.

———. "University of Montana Helps High-Profile Athletes Find Top Lawyers." *Missoulian,* November 6, 2011.

———. "Woman Claims Sexual Assault by Griz QB; Court Issues TRO." *Missoulian,* March 17, 2012.

Florio, Gwen, and Keila Szpaller. "Jordan Johnson Found Not Guilty of Rape." *Missoulian,* March 1, 2013.

Freedman, Monroe H. *Lawyers' Ethics in an Adversary System.* Indianapolis: Bobbs-Merrill, 1975.

Freud, Sigmund. *Beyond the Pleasure Principle.* New York: W. W. Norton, 1961.

Gerson, Allan, ed. *Lawyers' Ethics.* New Brunswick, NJ: Transaction, 1980.

Goldstein, Dana. "The Dueling Data on Campus Rape." Marshall Project, December 11, 2014. https://www.themarshallproject.org/2014/12/11/the-dueling-data-on-campus-rape.

Grether, Nicole. "Men's Rights Activist: Feminists Have Used Rape 'as a Scam.'" Al Jazeera America, June 6, 2014.

Gross, Bruce. "False Rape Allegations: An Assault on Justice." *Forensic Examiner,* Spring 2009.

Haake, Kathryn. "Former Deputy to Run for Missoula County Attorney." *Missoulian,* November 22, 2013.

———. "Jason Marks Ends Campaign for Missoula County Attorney." *Missoulian,* March 29, 2014.

———. "Missoula County Attorney Election: Pabst Has 'Clear Ideas' for Improvements." *Missoulian,* April 15, 2014.

———. "Missoula County, State, DOJ Sign Agreements to Improve Handling of Sexual Assault Cases." *Missoulian,* June 10, 2014.

———. "PAC That Backed Pabst Violated Law, State Official Finds." *Missoulian,* July 18, 2014.

Harwell, M. Claire, and David Lisak. "Why Rapists Run Free." *Sexual Assault Report,* 14, no. 2, November–December 2010.

Heller, Zoë. "Rape on the Campus." *New York Review of Books,* February 5, 2015.

Herman, Judith Lewis. "The Mental Health of Crime Victims." *Journal of Traumatic Stress,* 16, no. 2, April 2003.

———. *Trauma and Recovery.* New York: Basic Books, 1997.

Kanin, Eugene J. "False Rape Allegations." *Archives of Sexual Behavior,* 23, no. 1, February 1994.

Kato, Dillon. "Rape Suspect Said to Have Fled U.S." *Montana Kaimin,* February 23, 2012.

Kidston, Martin. "Petition Seeks Regent Williams' Ouster for 'Thugs' Comment." *Missoulian,* February 13, 2013.

———. "State Appeals Order to Release Records of UM Quarterback's Disciplinary Hearing." *Missoulian,* October 16, 2014.

Kingkade, Tyler. "Fewer Than One-Third of Campus Sexual Assault Cases Result in Expulsion." Huffington Post, September 29, 2014. http://www.huffingtonpost.com/2014/09/29/campus-sexual-assault_n_5888742.html.

Kittredge, William. *The Next Rodeo: New and Selected Essays.* Saint Paul: Graywolf, 2007.

Krakauer, Jon, Petitioner, v. State of Montana, by and Through Its Commissioner of Higher Education, Clayton Christian, Respondent. Montana First Judicial District Court, Lewis and Clark County. Cause No.: CDV-2014-117. Memorandum and Order on Cross Motions for Summary Judgment, September 25, 2014.

Krebs, Christopher P., Christine H. Lindquist, Tara D. Warner, Bonnie S. Fisher, and Sandra L. Martin. "The Campus Sexual Assault (CSA) Study." Final Report, National Institute of Justice, October 2007.

Lauerman, John. "College Men Accused of Sexual Assault Say Their Rights Violated." Bloomberg News, December 17, 2013.

Lisak, David. "False Allegations of Rape: A Critique of Kanin." *Sexual Assault Report,* 11, no. 1, September–October 2007.

———. "Understanding the Predatory Nature of Sexual Violence." *Sexual Assault Report,* 14, no. 4, March–April 2011.

Lisak, David, Lori Gardinier, Sarah C. Nicksa, and Ashley M. Cole. "False Allegations of Sexual Assault: An Analysis of Ten Years of Reported Cases." *Violence Against Women,* 16, no. 12, December 2010.

Lisak, David, and Paul M. Miller. "Repeat Rape and Multiple Offending Among Undetected Rapists." *Violence and Victims,* 17, no. 1, 2002.

Lockwood, Patricia. "The Rape Joke." *The Awl*, July 25, 2013. http://www.theawl.com/2013/07/rape-joke-patricia-lockwood.

LoMonte, Frank D. "UM Cries Wolf over Johnson Privacy Issue." *Great Falls Tribune,* November 17, 2014.

Lonsway, Kimberly A., and Joanne Archambault. "The 'Justice Gap' for Sexual Assault Cases: Future Directions for Research and Reform." *Violence Against Women*, 18, no. 2, February 2012.

Lonsway, Kimberly A., Joanne Archambault, and David Lisak. "False Reports: Moving Beyond the Issue to Successfully Investigate and Prosecute Non-Stranger Sexual Assault." *The Voice,* 1, no. 1, 2009.

Maclean, Norman. *"A River Runs Through It" and Other Stories*. Chicago: University of Chicago Press, 1976.

Macur, Juliet. "Transcript of Winston Hearing Reveals Accuser's Words, and Florida State's Complicity." *New York Times,* December 23, 2014.

Mayrer, Jessica. "Still Fighting: County Attorney Fred Van Valkenburg Stands Firm in the Face of Mounting Criticism." *Missoula Independent,* September 5, 2013.

McCaskill, Claire. "Sexual Violence on Campus." Report, U.S. Senate Subcommittee on Financial and Contracting Oversight, July 9, 2014.

McWhorter, Stephanie K., Valerie A. Stander, Lex L. Merrill, Cynthia J. Thomsen, and Joel S. Milner. "Reports of Rape Reperpetration by Newly Enlisted Male Navy Personnel." *Violence and Victims,* 24, no. 2, 2009.

Mellen, Greg. "Long Beach Unified Wins Judgment Against Accuser in False Rape Case Against Brian Banks."

Mollo, Kimberly. "Profile of a Journalist: Gwen Florio." Feature Well, May 13, 2011. https://thefeaturewell.wordpress.com/2011/05/13/profile-of-a-journalist-gwen-florio/.

Moore, Michael. "UM Rape Victim Comes Forward About Attack, Response from University." *Missoulian,* January 15, 2012.

———. "University of Montana Has Problem with Sex Assaults, President Says." *Missoulian,* January 17, 2012.

Morris, David J. *The Evil Hours: A Biography of Post-Traumatic Stress Disorder.* Boston: Houghton Mifflin Harcourt, 2015.

Muir, Mark. "Van Valkenburg Is Right: Time to Muzzle Holder and DOJ." *Missoulian,* February 18, 2014.

Munson, Lester. "QB's Trial Begins Amid Larger Scandal." ESPN.com, February 8, 2013. http://espn.go.com/espn/otl/story/_/id/8921202/university-montana-qb-rape-trial-begins-amid-larger-sex-assault-scandal-plaguing-missoula.

Neal, Anne D. "Statement of the American Council of Trustees and Alumni." News release, June 25, 2014.

Nerbovig, Ashley. "Missoula Sexual Assaults Spur Controversial Media Coverage." *Montana Journalism Review,* May 17, 2013. http://dev.mjr.jour.umt.edu/?p=1794.

Pabst, Kirsten. "Which Right Would You Sacrifice?" *Pabstblawg,* March 22, 2013.

———. "Why Reporters Should Be Elected Officials." *Pabstblawg,* June 19, 2012.

Paoli, David R. "Williams' Comment Jeopardized a Fair Trial." *Missoulian,* March 17, 2013.

Perez, Thomas E., and Michael W. Cotter. "Re: The United States' Investigation of the Missoula Police Department." U.S. Department of Justice letter to Missoula Mayor John Engen, May 15, 2013.

Posner, Richard A. *The Problems of Jurisprudence.* Cambridge, MA: Harvard University Press, 1990.

Powers, Ashley. "A 10-Year Nightmare over Rape Conviction Is Over." *Los Angeles Times,* May 25, 2012.

Raphael, Jody. "The Duke Lacrosse Case: Exploiting the Issue of False Rape Accusations." *Violence Against Women,* 14, no. 3, March 2008.

Rennison, Callie Marie. "Privilege, Among Rape Victims." *New York Times,* December 21, 2014.

Robbins, Jim. "Montana Football Team at Center of Inquiry into Sexual Assaults." *New York Times,* May 22, 2012.

———. "Trial of Former College Quarterback Accused of Rape Starts Friday in Montana." *New York Times,* February 6, 2013.

Roiphe, Katie. "Date Rape Hysteria." *New York Times,* November 20, 1991.

Samuels, Jocelyn, and Michael W. Cotter. "The United States' Investigation of the Missoula County Attorney's Office." U.S. Department of Justice letter to Missoula County Attorney Fred Van Valkenburg, February 14, 2014.

Sebold, Alice. *Lucky.* New York: Scribner, 1999.

State of Montana, Plaintiff, vs. Beau A. Donaldson, Defendant. Montana Fourth Judicial District, Missoula County. Cause No. DV-12-34. Sentencing Hearing, transcript, January 11, 2013.

State of Montana, Plaintiff, vs. Beau A. Donaldson, Defendant. Montana Supreme Court, Sentence Review Division. Sentence Review Hearing, transcript, May 2, 2013.

State of Montana, Plaintiff, vs. Jordan Todd Johnson, Defendant. Montana Fourth Judicial District Court, Missoula County. Cause No. DC-12-352. Court filings and transcripts of proceedings, 2012–2013.

Strier, Franklin. "Adversarial Justice." *World & I,* July 1998.

Taylor, Stuart, Jr., and KC Johnson. *Until Proven Innocent: Political Correctness and Shameful Injustices of the Duke Lacrosse Rape Case.* New York: Thomas Dunne, 2007.

Toland, John. *The Last 100 Days.* New York: Random House, 1966.

Toobin, Jeffrey. *The Run of His Life: The People v. O. J. Simpson.* New York: Random House, 1996.

Trieweiler, Terry. "'Straight Talk' Was Long Overdue." *Missoulian,* March 22, 2013.

U.S. Department of Education. "U.S. Department of Education Releases List of Higher Education Institutions with Open Title IX Sexual Violence Investigations." News release, May 1, 2014.

U.S. Department of Justice. "Justice Department Announces Investigations of the Handling of Sexual Assault Allegations by the University of Montana, the Missoula, Mont., Police Department and the Missoula County Attorney's Office." News release, May 1, 2012.

———. "Rape and Sexual Assault Victimization Among College-Age Females, 1995–2013." Special report, December 2014.

Valenti, Jessica. "The Only 'Privilege' Afforded to Campus Rape Victims Is Actually Surviving." *Guardian,* June 10, 2014.

———. *The Purity Myth: How America's Obsession with Virginity Is Hurting Young Women*. Berkeley, CA: Seal Press, 2010.

van der Kolk, Bessel A. "The Compulsion to Repeat the Trauma." *Psychiatric Clinics of North America,* 12, no. 2, June 1989.

Van Valkenburg, Fred. "Missoula County Attorney Response to Department of Justice Letter Dated February 14, 2014." News release, February 21, 2014.

White House. "Not Alone: The First Report of the White House Task Force to Protect Students from Sexual Assault." Report, April 2014.

Will, George. "Colleges Become the Victims of Progressivism." *Washington Post,* June 6, 2014.

Williams, Pat. "Pat Williams: Deep Commitment to UM." *Missoulian,* March 10, 2013.

Woo, Stu. "Montana and Its Troubled Football Team." *Wall Street Journal,* April 12, 2012.

Yehuda, Rachel. "Post-Traumatic Stress Disorder." *New England Journal of Medicine,* 346, January 10, 2002.

Yoffe, Emily. "The College Rape Overcorrection." Slate, December 7, 2014. http://www.slate.com/articles/double_x/doublex/2014/12/college_rape_campus_sexual_assault_is_a_serious_problem_but_the_efforts.html.

Young, Cathy. "Excluded Evidence: The Dark Side of Rape Shield Laws." *Reason,* February 2002.

———. "Guilty Until Proven Innocent: The Skewed White House Crusade on Sexual Assault." *Time,* May 6, 2014.

———. "The Noble Lie, Feminist Style." *Weekly Standard,* August 1, 2011.

———. "The Rape Charge as a Weapon." *Boston Globe,* May 1, 2006.

ALSO BY

JON KRAKAUER

UNDER THE BANNER OF HEAVEN

A Story of Violent Faith

Jon Krakauer's literary reputation rests on insightful chronicles of lives conducted at the outer limits. In *Under the Banner of Heaven* he shifts his focus from extremes of physical adventure to extremes of religious belief, taking readers inside isolated American communities where some 40,000 Mormon Fundamentalists still practice polygamy. Defying both civil authorities and the Mormon establishment in Salt Lake City, the renegade leaders of these Taliban-like theocracies are zealots who answer only to God. At the core of Krakauer's book are brothers Ron and Dan Lafferty, who insist they received a commandment from God to kill a blameless woman and her baby girl. Beginning with a meticulously researched account of this appalling double murder, Krakauer constructs a multi-layered, bone-chilling narrative of messianic delusion, polygamy, savage violence, and unyielding faith. Along the way he uncovers a shadowy offshoot of America's fastest growing religion, and raises provocative questions about the nature of religious belief.

True Crime

ALSO AVAILABLE

Into the Wild

Into Thin Air

Three Cups of Deceit

Where Men Win Glory